Midday in Italian Literature

MIDDAY IN ITALIAN LITERATURE

VARIATIONS ON AN ARCHETYPAL THEME

NICOLAS J. PERELLA

PRINCETON UNIVERSITY PRESS
PRINCETON, NEW JERSEY

Copyright © 1979 by Princeton University Press
Published by Princeton University Press, Princeton, New Jersey
In the United Kingdom: Princeton University Press, Guildford, Surrey
All Rights Reserved
Library of Congress Cataloging in Publication Data will be
found on the last printed page of this book
This book has been composed in VIP Bembo
Designed by Bruce Campbell
Clothbound editions of Princeton University Press books
are printed on acid-free paper, and binding materials are
chosen for strength and durability.
Printed in the United States of America by Princeton
University Press, Princeton, New Jersey

Contents

Preface • *vii*
Introduction • *3*
I. *From Dante to Pindemonte* • *33*
II. *The Nineteenth Century* • *70*
III. *Gabriele D'Annunzio* • *114*
IV. *Some Twentieth-Century Voices* • *145*
V. *Giuseppe Ungaretti* • *201*
VI. *Eugenio Montale* • *240*
Conclusion • *263*
Notes • *267*
Bibliography • *329*
Index • *331*

Preface

> The very subtitle of Leopardi's canzone [*To Spring*]: *or concerning Antique Fables* alerts us. *Antique* [*Antico*] is *antiquus*, but it may also be *anticus*. And in fact it means remote historical times; but also the opposite of *posticus*, a cardinal point, the south and the hour of the south: *or concerning Fables of Long-ago* and *or concerning Meridian Fables*.... Thus the word will properly carry an ambivalent sense, just as the very hour [i.e., midday] evoked is itself ambiguous.
> (*Giuseppe Ungaretti*, "Second Discourse on Leopardi")

The gathering together of the specific texts to be considered in this study has as its chief raison d'être the fact that they are all concerned, in one way or another, with the response to or the implementation of a major archetypal image—the sun in its most dramatic but also its most ambiguous moment—by a highly cultivated people of the south, living in one of those areas that promoters of tourism are wont to call "the land of the sun." Given the particular nature of the encounter and the topos, certain images will of necessity recur as constant ingredients in many of the texts. Above all, of course, will be that of the overarching presence—stated or implied—of the sun at its zenith. One can expect that each age will have an emphasis or slant of its own in connection with this time of day but to be categorical or formulaically reductive in seeking to define it involves the risk of falsifying the character of the various reactions to midday. For though a given age may reveal a predominant attitude or bias (and the eighteenth century will show the greatest uniformity), individual authors' experiences, or at least their accounts of the experience, may vary significantly. It will also be evident that the same author may experience and express both the positive and the negative values of midday.

All in all, the variety and the intensity of the encounters of Italians with midday have produced a remarkable and, in some ways, unique psychological and literary record. But that the quality of their experience is not necessarily unique in an absolute sense is due precisely to the archetypal nature of the image (like that of the sea) and the encounter. Indeed, if it were not perhaps more elusive even than the ambiguity of midday itself, the title of the present book might well have been *Antiquest felt at Noon*, a curious but evocative phrase used by a semicloistered nineteenth-century New England poet in a lyric ("Further in Summer than the Birds") whose sophisticated and perhaps too cunningly wrought liturgical references clearly show that she was profoundly acquainted with the peculiarly elemental or numinous quality of noontide. An *antique* or *strange* quality, if one likes; not, however, in the sense of an untrustworthy fantastication such as the word suggests, say, in *A Midsummer Night's Dream* when, in the splendidly ironic passage (V, 1) about the equivalence that obtains among the lunatic, the lover, and the poet, Theseus declares the adventures that have befallen two pairs of lovers to be "more strange than true," so that he "never may believe these antique fables," but rather in the sense of a feeling that is primordial or uncanny in its impression of depth and absoluteness. We shall find that such words as *antique*, *ancient*, and *primary* have a way of attaching themselves to the concept of midday. The very expression "antique fables" is the subtitle of Leopardi's hymn to spring, "Alla Primavera, o delle favole antiche," a poem whose true center is an evocation of a noontide nympholepsy. From a philological point of view, Giuseppe Ungaretti's interpretation of that subtitle in the sense of southern midday fables, or, better yet, of a *midday delirium*, is wholly arbitrary, but it is poetically so and not without its pertinence to the poem and to this study.

Though I have decided against Emily Dickinson's line as a title, I would hope that even these brief comments have given the reader a hint of the kind of inquiry this book aims at. By the same token, in addition to what is set forth in the introduction by way of orientation to my subject, I have found it useful and inevitable (the more so since we are dealing with

Preface ix

literary texts), to make occasional comparative references to significant examples of the midday theme in literatures other than Italian.

While the idea of an examination of the treatment in a national literature of a theme such as noontide, with its strong religious and philosophical implications, may suggest something in the nature of a treatise in the field of cultural anthropology, I believe no one will mistake the present study for anything other than an essay in literary criticism with a concern almost equally divided between the history of ideas and the interpretation of poetic expression. Indeed, I have not hesitated to undertake a close reading and analysis of formal elements when I have thought it necessary to do so in order either to elucidate the meaning of a text or to bring out its aesthetic value. It may appear that in the more extensive attention given to certain modern authors I have sought to evaluate their fundamental poetic and philosophical visions too exclusively *sub specie meridiei*. It hardly needs to be said that there is much more to these authors (e.g., Leopardi, D'Annunzio, Ungaretti, Montale) than can be seen in their use of any one topos. If the treatment accorded them by me seems ambitious, it is only because in their work the image of midday happens to occupy a large place, critical enough to be the key to an essential part of their world. In some instances my judgment of texts will not appear to depart greatly from received critical opinion, although my particular angle of vision and the cultural context in which a given passage is considered can be expected to shed additional light on it. On the other hand, there are cases in which my divergence from the accepted interpretation is radical. Finally, there are a number of texts that, because of their difficulty or obscurity, have attracted little or no critical attention.

In connection with this last point, I owe an immense debt to my colleague Ruggero Stefanini upon whose learning and literary sensibility I have so often drawn during the writing of this essay. Those cases in which my views may be most debatable can only be those in which I either did not consult him or chose not to follow his advice. My colleagues Arnolfo Ferruolo and Catherine Feucht gave me precious assistance with much of the translating. The scrupulous reading given to my original manuscript by the readers of the Princeton University Press was both gratifying and indispensable to me. I am grateful also for the counsel and encouragement of Diane Beck, R. Miriam Brokaw, and Gretchen Oberfranc. Again, the solicitous staff of the Interlibrary Loan Department of the University of California at Berkeley made it possible for me to see much material that is difficult to come by. Research grants from my university and a sabbatical leave have been invaluable to me. Karin Gerstung has continued to amaze me by her ability to prepare typescripts from the scraps of paper on which my handwritten version is first offered to her. A very special thanks goes to Barbara Westergaard without whose painstaking copyediting much more infelicitous phrasing might yet remain to vex the reader. I have been sustained chiefly by my wife, to whom this book is dedicated.

Translations supplied for the texts discussed in the main part of this study are my own unless otherwise indicated. Shorter foreign quotations that are woven into the discourse are translated only when their meaning is not immediately apparent from the exposition. The translations are purely for the convenience of readers with little or no Italian and are meant to be as close as possible to the original texts in meaning and word order. One of the great temptations in translating poetry (in particular, modern poetry) is that of trying to gloss an obscure or strange phrase with words that one hopes will "clarify" the author's "real" meaning. It is a pitfall I have tried to avoid. Obviously, it would be rash to think that I have never betrayed any of my authors, but in the majority of cases where my translation may seem obscure, peculiar, or confused, it is because the original is so. Thus I believe it is unwise and even wrong to render, say, Ungaretti's phrase *confuso silenzio* (referring to death) as *troubled silence* or *uneasy silence*. The Italian expression is no less strange or difficult than the English equivalent *confused silence* for which I have opted even while understanding *confuso* to have the meaning of *indistinct*. At any rate, my interpretation of the texts or those parts of them that are my concern is entrusted primarily to the essay proper.

Midday in Italian Literature

Introduction

Je me souviens du redoutable océan de midi
(Paul Eluard)

References to the various seasons have been in evidence in Western literature from the time of antiquity to the present, and there have been periods—the eighteenth century in particular—when the verbal representation of nature has taken so specific a turn in this direction as to make the poetic description of the seasons a dominant mode and, one may even say, a veritable genre. In this respect, the name that will first, and quite properly, come to mind is that of James Thomson, author of *The Seasons*, a title that was to reappear in the work of many other writers and composers in the eighteenth century. In terms of archetypal (and mythical) significance, the seasonal cycle of the year is matched and, in its poetic representation, often accompanied by the solar cycle of the day. Thus descriptions of the four seasons are often given by way of depiction of the four parts of the day in connection with any one season, although ideally each part of the day corresponds to a particular season: spring = morning (or sunrise), summer = midday (or sun at the zenith), autumn = evening (or sunset), winter = night (or lunar and stellar sky).[1] Of course, the second half of the eighteenth century also saw the production of a number of independent poems or groups of poems on the diurnal solar cycle, generally though not always under the title "The Four Parts of the Day."

But both the seasonal and the diurnal solar cycles are symbolically equated with the "four" ages of man. It was easy and perhaps even natural to make sunrise, sunset, and night take on symbolic significance by referring them to the cycle of human life. For the reflective man not deprived of feeling, such moments could inspire both solemn thoughts and sweetly melancholic reveries. Although the projection of human moods and emotions onto landscapes (i.e., nature) implied by this psychological process was to reach its greatest vogue with the Romantics of the nineteenth century, the tendency (itself ancient) was already conspicuous in the preceding century. Despite the fact that Rousseau would have us believe that it is the given aspect of nature that arouses a particular mood and meditation, the truth is that the basis of the symbolic or affective value connected with nature is perhaps no less subjective in him than in Coleridge who in his "Ode on Dejection" openly avowed:

> O Lady! we receive but what we give,
> And in our life alone does Nature live.

In terms of the perception of or the attempt at "knowing" nature, poets of "thought" have been willing to speak of a participatory role of the mind by which the reality that has seized our attention is something that the mind "half perceives and half creates" (to paraphrase Wordsworth) or, in the words of Wallace Stevens,

> What
> One believes is what matters. Ecstatic identities
> Between one's self and the weather and the things
> Of the weather are the belief in one's element.[2]

In the final analysis, such pronouncements are not so radical as to deny that reality is phenomenal or to seek to replace reality entirely with the imagination, although one suspects that by these and similar pronouncements the poets do mean to suggest that the imagination, or the act of creation, is more important (or more demanding?) than the pure act of perception which by itself is poetically, or humanly, valueless. At the very least, in the choice of metaphors and images that a poet makes in expressing the human experience and awareness of nature (i.e., landscapes and the weather) there is surely a clue to the poet's temperament, and one can agree with Gaston Bachelard who says that the imagination is nothing other than the subject transported into things.[3] All this may be readily granted without subverting a conviction that more than

Introduction 5

any other moment or aspect of nature, midday seems to belie the idea of a subjectivistic projection of human moods onto nature. At the same time, however, the last thing I wish to suggest is that there is no interiorization of noonscapes along with their perception. And insofar as there is any "poetry" in the texts that are to follow, it is because, as Coleridge in his essay "On Poesy and Art" once put it succinctly, "in every work of art there is a reconcilement of the external with the internal."[4] If I may call again on Wallace Stevens—a poet in whose work summer and noon are dominant images used sometimes to symbolize the fullness of the imagination and sometimes the primacy of phenomenal reality—we can say that what he said of himself at the end of his life in "The Planet on the Table" applies in varying degrees to most of the writers whose encounters with midday are to occupy our attention:

> His self and the sun were one
> And his poems, although makings of his self,
> Were no less makings of the sun.[5]
>
> (7-9)

In symbolic terms, noontide, or the sun at its zenith, has not been wholly reducible to what it should correspond to in the traditional division of the "four" periods of human life, namely, the time of fullness of strength and vitality, whereas its archetypal equivalent, summer, is frequently and without difficulty so conceived. Here it will be instructive, in introducing our theme, to consider an exchange from Paul Claudel's play entitled, significantly enough, *Partage de midi* (*Break of Noon*). Aboard a ship that is so far out at sea that no land is in sight, the interlocutors, Almaric and Mesa, surprised by the advent of noontide, express the following reaction to it:

> *Almaric*: La pleine force du soleil, la pleine force de ma vie. C'est bon que l'on puisse voir la mort en face et j'ai force pour lui résister.
> *Mesa*: Midi au ciel, Midi au centre de notre vie. Et nous

voilà ensemble, autour de ce même âge de notre moment, au milieu de l'horizon complet, libres, déballés. Décollés de la terre, regardant derrière et devant.[a]

While the juxtaposition of the diurnal solar cycle with the human life cycle is here accompanied by the optimistic suggestion that midday (in both cycles) is the point of greatest strength, there is in the exchange a clue to the ambiguity and indecision that we shall find so frequently connected with that moment. For Almaric's words also specifically associate the midday sun with the thought of death. The ambiguity also depends on the fact that noon, as the title of the play suggests, is a point of division and *passage*, a moment of suspension or incertitude between the past and the future. In this intimation of a moment of crisis lies one of the most fundamental truths concerning midday.[6]

Even when midday is perceived as the time of fullness and maximum strength, it brings with it a sense of something so absolute that, more often than not, man has not felt himself to be a match for it. Thus it is a "spot of time" that has tended to overmaster man, menacing and bewildering him, suspending him in a state of indecision (or casting him into an inactive torpor), or filling him with panic (or numinous) dread. This is especially the case when it is a midday during the height of summer. For then the sun may appear not as beneficent Helios or Apollo but as the hostile Gorgon. Fierce or enervating heat, unshadowed, absolute light, and uncanny silence combine to make noontide, especially in the Mediterranean lands, a time of the negative demonic power of nature, though we shall find notable exceptions to this negativity in more than one writer.

If it is true that in literature midday appears less frequently than the other three main parts of the day (and especially since the preromantic sensibility of the eighteenth century, the

[a] *Almaric*: The full strength of the sun, the full strength of my life. It is good that one can look death in the face, and I have the strength to resist it.
Mesa: Midday in the sky, Midday at the center of our life. And here we are together, around this same age of our moment, in the middle of the full horizon, free, unburdened. Released from the earth, looking behind and ahead.

moon and nocturnal poetry have dominated), its presence, more so than that of the others, is almost always fraught with special meaning. When Theocritus has his rustic swain refuse the invitation to pipe at noon—

> No, shepherd, no, not I. Not at midday;
> I'm afraid of Pan. It's the time he rests,
> Weary from the hunt. His temper is quick;
> Fierce anger is always on his breath[7]

—he is reflecting a longstanding sense of sacredness and dread among the Greeks in connection with midday. Indeed, there is ample evidence to show that noontide was an hour in which the presence of divinities or semidivinities (sirens and nymphs as well as the more august goddesses and Pan) could be sensed or witnessed by mortals; but to behold them then was a dangerous and at times fatal adventure.[8] The most famous and the most important of such accounts is the story of Actaeon as handed down by Ovid (in *Metamorphoses*, III, 143 ff.). Because of the echo it was to have through the centuries, it is appropriate to recall its highlights. At midday when the sun, having paused in its course, seems to pierce the very fields with its burning rays, Diana and her nymphs rest from the chase and retire to their sacred grove. There in the clear waters of a spring they carry out their ablutions. As chance would have it, one day the young hunter Actaeon, after a successful morning hunt, stumbles into this spot at that fateful hour and beholds the goddess and her nymphs in their divine nakedness. As the frightened and shrieking nymphs smite their breasts, the youth is doomed by the outraged Diana who, without reaching toward the shore for her bow, splashes water on him, thereby transforming him into a stag which is chased through the forest and savagely slain by the hunter's own hounds.

A similar account of nympholeptic terror was given by Callimachus in his version of the blinding of Tiresias. In the hymn on Pallas Athena at her bath, Tiresias too figures as a young hunter who has chanced to espy an august goddess in her nakedness at midday. Athena blinds the youth, explaining, however, that it is not she personally who wishes to do so, but that the ancient law of Chronos calls for the punishment of any mortal who unbidden beholds a divinity. Out of regard for the youth's mother who is her cherished companion, Athena compensates Tiresias with the gift of prophecy and of insight into mysteries. That the goddess in both these cases is naked suggests that what is involved is an interdiction against a face-to-face encounter with divinity, no less so than in the case, say, of the Old Testament interdiction involving Moses and Jahweh. In both accounts, beholding the goddess is a profanation of midday precisely because that is the sacred hour of divinity alone, the hour of numinous dread and crisis. It is not without reason, then, that Ovid and Callimachus both make a point of repeating twice that the time of the encounter was midday.

It is also significant that the ill-fated youths in the accounts given by Callimachus and Ovid are hunters. Though there is no prurient element in their innocent character, the tales clearly establish a close relationship between midday and sexuality. This is perhaps more readily seen in Ovid. The sultriness of noon causes even Diana to have to bathe and drives Actaeon, however unwitting, on a quest through unfamiliar terrain toward an encounter that is inevitable: "per nemus ignotum non certis passibus errans / pervenit in lucum: sic illum fata ferebant" (175-176).[b] Midday eroticism will occupy much of our attention in the following chapters of this study. For the moment, one or two observations may be made here. The first concerns a motif of special significance that is directly connected with Ovid's tale and many like it that must have been current in the popular superstitions of antiquity. This is the tradition that developed in medieval Christian legends wherein the "midday demon" was frequently identified with Diana (Diana-Artemis) as an enchantress exercising malefic and erotic energies to the detriment of man. It is the view of Caillois that while the Ovidian account of Actaeon's tragic story had something to do with this specific

[b] Wandering with uncertain steps in those unfamiliar woods, he arrived at that [sacred] place; thus the fates led him.

Introduction 9

identification, the truly determining factor leading to the identification lies in the suggestiveness of the homophone in the name of the goddess: Diana = MeriDiana.[9] But here we ought not to forget that the Ovidian account of midday eroticism has something of a "profane" biblical counterpart in the well-known episode of Susanna and the lecherous elders. It is during the hot noontide that the chaste Susanna, too, is in the habit of bathing in her garden pool. The two elders, who know of this custom, come secretly to spy on her day after day until their lust drives them from unbecoming voyeurism to an attempt at rape. The tale, which is recorded in Daniel 13 of the Septuagint and the Catholic versions of the Old Testament was to become a popular subject in Renaissance painting. But of course it was already popular in the Middle Ages, and in the eleventh century the tale was retold by Hildebert, bishop of Tours, in a way that reveals the influence of Ovid, and with even more emphasis on the connection between the heat of midday and uncontrollable erotic energy.[10]

At least two other Ovidian references to midday sexuality should be remembered here. In the *Amores* (I, 5) when recounting his sexual adventure with Corinna, Ovid explicitly states at the beginning of the tale that the event took place in the great heat of noontide, and at the end he augurs himself many such midday encounters: "Proveniant medii sic mihi saepe dies." While it is true that this conquest takes place indoors, the suggestion of the sylvan *locus amoenus* as the ideal or imagined setting is made when the poet compares the darkness of the room to the shade one finds in a forest. More in keeping with the sense of irrepressible midday erotic energy is the story of the nymph Callisto raped by amorous Jove at the height of a fiercely hot noontide (*Metamorphoses*, II, 417 ff.). Finally, perhaps no less influential than Ovid's texts, though in a somewhat different key, is the version of the theme recorded earlier by Virgil in the unmythical context of his second eclogue where an oppressive noontide figures as the symbol or external representation of the erotic heat of a shepherd-swain. While all living creatures seek refuge in the shade, Corydon alone, to the accompaniment of the relentless shrill of cicadas, walks restlessly beneath an implacable sun in a fiery midday atmosphere that both mirrors and feeds the burning passion of the unrequited lover. The importance of Virgil's eclogue in the development of later midday eroticism is perhaps no less than that of Ovid's texts.

Contributing to and merging with the midday mythology of the Western tradition was the biblical notion hinted at two paragraphs back in the reference to the "midday demon," a concept that eventually was itself in part connected with erotic energy though originally it belonged to another order of experience. The Vulgate version of Psalm 91 (90):6 speaks of the *daemon meridianus* as being among the forces from which the Lord preserves the righteous. The concept and the expression go back at least to the Septuagint rendering of the psalm, which suggests a carry-over of the Greek notion of Pan whose connection with midday could be not only one of imposing stillness or exciting erotic passion but also that of causing sunstroke and "Panic" terror. The fact that the earliest Hebrew texts of the psalm do not speak specifically of a demonic agency but of "the destruction that wasteth at noon," as the King James version correctly has it, does not make too much difference.[11] At the very least, the Hebrew version seems to make midday synonymous with the summer sun at its cruelest, felt perhaps to be responsible for endemic diseases in hot southern lands. The connotation of noon, at any rate, is no less negative here than is the concept of the *daimon* in the Septuagint and the Vulgate, although a *daimon* as a power of nature is not always negatively perceived, and the sense of something numinous is preserved by the personification of the midsummer-midday pestilential sun into a *daemon meridianus*.[12]

A significant offshoot of this motif developed among the early Christian ascetical writers (e.g., Evagrius Ponticus and John Cassian) who identified the "midday demon" with a demonic agency said to induce acedia, the boredom or abulia that seemed to overcome cloistered or solitary monks at noontide, tempting them away from their meditations and duties.[13] Although this may seem to be an aberration from the biblical concept, it is not difficult to appreciate that the

Introduction

psychological uneasiness and spiritual crisis of ascetics should have been associated both literally and symbolically with the distressful and critical hours of midday, especially but not exclusively among anchorites of the Egyptian desert. In the early part of the fifth century, Cassian, besides commenting that some of the earlier authorities declared the noontide demon of the psalm to be the acedia of clerics, speaks of this spiritual malady as a fever that attacks the monk at the sixth hour (noon) with its burning heat—an image that suggests the vehement sun of midday.[14] It is not without interest, moreover, that Cassian hints at an element of sexual desire in connection with the noontide crisis of the monk. Be that as it may, the relationship between noontide and boredom, while a real one, is not of primary importance in the phenomenology of midday. At most, the demon of acedia is but one of the faces of the noontide devil.[15]

Concerning the deeper significance of the demonic character of midday, the modern philosopher Cornelis Verhoeven has a page that nicely elucidates the sense of the numinous and the "bewilderment" that so often seize man during noontide:

> Midday, antipole of midnight, is the zenith of day and light and thus is light in its most ambivalent form. At noon, clarity, light, and heat become something absolute, cease to be functions, are transformed into concrete substances, and replace all other concrete substances. Midday threatens to destroy the world that was built up by the morning. In this world man loses his grip on reality; he no longer recognizes it. It acquires the demonic character of that which is entirely different and in it loses its matter-of-factness. In this paradox of light which is the southern noon, things lose their contours which only a tempering of light can give them, movements cease, and sound becomes impotent while in its place the silence becomes audible. . . . The heat and light of noon are paralyzing. The noonday devil commands silence and halts the rhythm of life in order to impose his own. He is an occurrence which cannot be predicted or overwhelmed by the light of reason, the absolute master of the other. . . . The noonday devil is also the per-

sonification of absolute light. Unlike the light of early morning it does not glide past things, playfully and respectfully, leaving them unaltered in their own obscurity. It halts unashamedly, and becoming tangible, takes the place of things. This light is no longer truth but desolation.[16]

Even more than midnight, then, the "hour of Pan" (or Diana, or the noontime devil, as the case may be) has remained the haunting or demonic hour par excellence through the centuries, again particularly in the hot southern lands. The mythologizing of it has often been in the direction of neutralizing it, though we may note that even the siesta, by virtue of being a retreat from it, is an acknowledgment of midday's mastery over man. Without doubt, the retreat from a hostile element of nature such as the scorching noontide sun makes good sense. Indeed, it is perhaps first of all an instinctive reaction, deriving from an inborn behavior mechanism that exists in the biological makeup of man and other animals.[17] So too one can expect that the debilitating heat of a southern noontide would be a natural invitation to indolence. And yet, such naturalistic explanations can account for only a part of the extraordinary psychological repercussions and metaphysical implications that arise from man's encounters with midday. With the siesta, midday indolence becomes ritualized into a quasi-religious or magic formula for avoidance of real encounter, and in some cases this tendency will be made to serve as a vehicle for blessed repose in which the menacing face of the hour is avoided.

But something more needs to be said here in connection with the important element of silence to which Verhoeven has barely referred, because it is in fact an essential element in the creation of that sense of something uncanny and forbidding often experienced at noontide. First, it may be noted that the meridian silence is of a quality so peculiar that it is perceived as one with the light and the heat. Another modern philosopher, Max Picard, struck by the extraordinary character of this phenomenon, has written:

Not the darkness but the light belongs to silence. That is never so clear as in the summer noon when the silence is

Introduction 13

utterly transformed into light. . . . The silence is as it were uncovered, and light appears as the inwardness of silence. . . . In these summer noons the silence is quite uncovered, and the light within lies naked to the eye. Nothing moves, nothing dares to move. . . . The light seems so much the essence of silence that the word seems quite unnecessary. The light is all at once the fulfillment of the silence.[18]

In a poem on midday that will be touched on later in this study, A. C. Swinburne refers to "a splendour of silence," and there is a fascinating line in T. S. Eliot's *The Waste Land* that speaks of "Looking into the heart of light, the silence." The phenomenon is stunningly expressed in a case of reciprocal synesthesia that occurs in the lyric "Undulna" by Gabriele D'Annunzio:

> In ogni sostanza si tace
> La luce e il silenzio risplende.[c][19]
>
> (85-86)

Physical objects are silenced by the light that has permeated them, and the silence reverberates with luminosity.

A related kind of synesthetic impression to be noted here has to do with the fact that two of the most recurrent images of southern noontides—the wild stridulation of the cicadas and the heat and light of the hour—seem almost to be perceived as a single sensory phenomenon though they belong to different realms of sensation. The two elements of course are complementary, and together they contribute to the overall sense of physical and psychic distress or bewilderment experienced by the subject who finds himself exposed to naked midday. When we reflect that mention of the cicada is principally an auditory image, we can see that the synesthetic fusion of the two components, implicit in noonscapes (with or without erotic significance) since Virgil's second eclogue, is what the contemporary poet Andrea Zanzotto gives explicit expression to in his baroquely splendid image of the *flame of the cicadas*.[20]

[c] In every substance the light is still
And the silence shines forth.

In the passage quoted earlier from Verhoeven, the philosopher noted that at noon "sound becomes impotent while in its place the silence becomes audible." This point needs to be stressed here: there is no true midday without silence. The shrill of the cicadas that are mentioned so frequently by writers who evoke noontide impressions (and the mention of cicadas is sometimes all that is needed to indicate noontide) is not perceived as one of the sounds of life that might break or prevent the deepness of midday's silence. Certainly, we will not accuse the poets of contradicting themselves or of being poor observers when we find them referring simultaneously to the profound quiet and the shrill "song" of the cicadas in the same noonscape. If anything, the cicadas' wild chirr throws the silence into greater relief. That is, it is perceived as an aspect of the silence, the highly charged air of tension and crisis that paradoxically characterizes the noontide stasis when the midday demon is about. We can go even further and note that when no cicadas (or other insect or bird) are in fact present to be heard, then noontide creates its own acoustic impression that bespeaks the hour's tension. The fierce tension and crisis of the meridian silence is expressed vividly by a modern writer of the south, the Sicilian novelist Vitaliano Brancati, who compares it to the "deafening" effect of thunder that seems to break from all directions: "Il cosidetto silenzio meridiano è assordante come un tuono che si scarichi da tutti i punti del cielo."[21] We shall have more than one poet's word for this psycho-aural phenomenon.

But here let us pause for a moment on the idea that the taut silence of midday, capable of creating its own auditory impression, is connected with yet another major characteristic of noontide, yet another ambiguity that has already been hinted at in what we have said thus far. This is the motion-immobility paradox. Midday is as much the crisis of motion as it is of light. If midday often seems to bring a moment of total repose, there are times when it is perceived as a delirium of movement. And it is not uncommon to find the two impressions or sensations present in the same meridian spot of time. In his studies on the psychology of the imagination's use of the opposing images of dynamic movement and repose, Bachelard noted that in a large number of metaphors borrowed from the realm of nature ("material images") one can actually sense an ambivalent synthesis that dialectically unites the two extremes and clearly shows an undeniable solidarity between the opposing processes of extroversion and introversion.[22] What we may add to this thought is that both of these apparently contradictory phenomena—ceaseless movement and total quiet—have long been experienced or desired by man as a means of achieving a condition of happiness. They figure, then, as the two poles of happiness. By means of the one—ceaseless movement—man dreams of overcoming the threat of death by devouring all things and thereby avoiding the reabsorption of himself into thinghood. By means of the other—total repose—he dreams of a fullness which is perhaps the secret desire for a death that is the return to the original source that is alone eternal.[23] In the matter of analogies or correspondences between man's *état d'âme* and the landscape or state of nature that poets have always explored and exploited, it is a singular fact that either one of these opposing phenomena may be experienced in the same noontide setting. Moreover, no other moment of nature's life seems to imbue either of the two impressions with the intensity that characterizes them at midday. And perhaps only at midday are they sometimes sensed as being present together, albeit more often than not in an apparently antagonistic relationship. The highly charged light and stillness of noontide vibrates with a potential for unlimited motion.

In observing that silence as the fundamental quality of light is not without its "vibrations," the turn-of-the-century Italian aesthetician Angelo Conti noted that music and light share a common function as revealers of the mystery of the universe, both being unmediated (i.e., nonconceptual) "objectifications" of the will. (Conti was a Platonist and a Schopenhauerian.) Now it is interesting to see that in his symbolistic aesthetic of light, midday is specifically ruled out as an hour for revelation or penetration:

Like music, light expresses itself in the form of vibrations; like sonorous vibrations, luminous vibrations are the rhythm of the will. The light brings us a twofold message: it is the voice of illusion, and it is one of the most profound words of the mystery. Light illuminates and obfuscates. But primarily it has a divine quality: it is silent. In the meridian hour, when it pervades the plains, light confounds and disperses the power of thought and of the imagination. It reveals its essence only among cliffs, at the edge of caverns, in the quiet of moonlight, in the shadows within cathedrals, in the rays with which it streaks immortal marbles, or when it floods down from the sky into deserted colonnades and abandoned cloisters.[24]

Conti's predilection for the mysterious play of half-lights, chiaroscuro effects, filtered sunlight (as in temples and cathedrals), nocturnes, and the tamed light of dawn or evening is amply attested to in his book where such phenomena serve as the setting for a poetical if vaguely mystical waxing on his intuition of the "secret" in the "soul of things." That he should make a point of excluding midday is obviously a matter worth pursuing in the present study, for what is involved is much more than just a belated Romantic taste, though of course it is also that. It is true that the aesthetician (better, the aesthete) felt that the silence of the lunar and stellar sky offered man the opportunity of sounding the "mystery," provided one were not afraid to look into its "infinite space." The timorous soul, he says, runs away from the mystery as soon as its presence is felt, whereas the enchanted soul pursues it and merges into it as though into a primordial or "original element" (pp. 79-80). By this latter expression Conti apparently has in mind Schopenhauer's notion of the metaphysical unity of things underlying the realm of appearance, but also, as his subsequent exaltation of Wagner's *Tristan and Isolde* reveals, the return to the "night" where love and death merge in *oblivion* (the word is his book's subtitle). When he says that light, in one of its functions, is the voice of illusion, he is speaking of light shining on the illusory phenomenal world that Schopenhauer referred to as *māyā*, a term used often also by Conti. And it is to this concept that he applies a paraphrase of Tristan's curse of deceitful day (p. 245). Thus light in its other capacity, as a profound "word" of the mystery, is a light that will extinguish itself after it has gently led us to the darkness that is the surpassing of illusions and the extinction of desire. The solar god Apollo is therefore the divinity of a false or deceiving light (p. 247). This would seem to explain Conti's negative reference to midday's light. But there may be more ambiguity in it yet.

The light that attracts and "speaks" to him, we have seen, is in fact a mediated light, a light that loves and needs shadows. When the light is unmediated and uninterrupted as it is on the open plains at midday—the shadowless hour!—he is, by his own admission, "bewildered." Of course, as he says, "light illuminates and obfuscates." But there is obscurantism to spare in his own poeticizing mysticism, and we are, I believe, justified in wondering whether he has not in fact betrayed a timorous attitude of his own in this recoil from the naked light and silence of midday. At any rate, the questions his antipathy to midday raise have relevance to our theme in general. Is what is revealed at midday an obfuscation because, in "illuminating," the light tricks the mind by giving the appearance of reality to an illusory world, or is it that what is revealed may be an illumination of too concrete and harsh a reality, one that is not submissive to the play of shadows? In either case midday is uncompromising in its imposition of a light and a silence so intense as to be immediately perceived as a negative absolute that insists on its own terms and is anything but sweet. One is not easily "enchanted" by midday, but we shall see that it is not without its compelling attraction, its "fascination," for those who are not so daunted by it as to retreat into an attitude that seeks to rationalize a nonrational and overmastering encounter. There is no suggestion of demonic dread in any moment of Conti's half-light mysticism which, for all its nocturnalism, is pretty tame stuff, lacking anything even like the authentic *frisson* that is connected with darkness in, say, Edmund Burke's aesthetic of the sublime. It is at bottom a pseudoirrationalism. In his refusal or inability to stand in the unsubduable sun of midday, it is not the light of the "deceitfully" illuminating intellect that he has spurned. On the contrary, he has, in spite of himself, borne testimony to the presence of the noontide demon. And he has engaged in what Wallace Stevens (in "The Motive for Metaphor") calls

> The motive for metaphor, shrinking from
> The weight of primary noon,
> The ABC of being.[25]
>
> (14-16)

Or is it nonbeing? Stevens's appositive terms defining *primary noon* conclude with the line "The vital, arrogant, fatal, dominant X." For the American poet noon is the hard steel of an irreducible reality, but it is nonetheless the reality of an absolute that is itself ambiguous enough in its implications for man. Shrinking or seeking refuge from noon is, we have suggested, an instinctive reaction.[26]

Vast expanses of land or sea often have the effect of creating the emotion we know as the sublime, and this may even be the case when it is midday. But again, at that hour it is more likely that man will seek to avoid being "exposed." For it is really man who is "naked" then, and, like the animals, he feels his vulnerability all the more in open space. Thus the real physical retreat is often made to the forest where, as the poet Sidney Lanier wrote in "The Marshes of Glynn," we may find

> Beautiful glooms, soft dusks in the noon-day fire,
> Wildwood privacies, closets of lone desire.
>
> (12-13)

The special dread—for it is more than animal fear—of noon in wide spaces that Conti unwittingly reveals is perfectly expressed by Lanier in this poem. During the long summer noontide (and the apparent greater duration of noon in summer is to be noted) the poet has been calmed and nourished in the forest refuge. If, in the unmediated light of noon, the nakedness of man is revealed and he is diminished by the sun, the forest can restore or preserve his faith—"And belief overmasters doubt"—and with the advent of evening, finally, the exploration of vastness may be undertaken without fear:

> But now when the noon is no more, and riot is rest,
> And the sun is a-wait at the ponderous gate of the West,
> . . . .
> Oh, now, unafraid, I am fain to face
> The vast sweet visage of space.
> (21-22, 35-36)

The encounter with midday in such terms as we have been discussing was given expression by Paul Valéry in one of the most fascinating poems on midday, "Le cimetière marin" ("The Graveyard by the Sea"). To attempt to do anything approximating full justice to this poem is out of place here, but, as in the case of the Claudel passage touched on earlier, some mention of it will be useful to our study. It is when the sun is at its zenith, imposing a total immobility on all things and shedding a light that creates the sensation of what seems to be an undifferentiated unity—"Midi le juste"—that Valéry seems moved by a quasi-ecstatic urge to seek to penetrate the Absolute (the midday moment itself), perhaps with a hope for a view of the self in the future, perhaps with a mystical desire for merger. The effort, however, meets with failure, a frustrating *échec*, as that very light and immobility that apparently attracted the poet prove forbidding and impenetrable.[27] Significantly, it is at the midway point of the poem that we find the recognition of the absolute nature of midday, its character of "otherness" and the impossibility of communion with it. Such, it appears, is the meaning of the two lines that follow:

> Midi là-haut, Midi sans mouvement
> En soi se pense et convient à soi-même.[d]
> (75-76)

Midday is the revelation of a fullness, *of the Absolute sufficient unto itself*. Indeed, as seems to be indicated by the sun's relentless blaze upon the tombs of the cemetery, what may be in-

---

[d] Midday high above, Midday without motion
Thinks itself and suffices unto itself.

volved here is a noontide revelation of a metaphysical nothingness. For this reason, the midday stasis or pause with its cosmic silence must not be allowed to absorb us. Following rebuff or recoil, the poet's salvation, if we may call it that, is to shake off the invading noontide paralysis or torpor:

> Non, non! . . . Debout! Dans l'ère successive!
> Brisez, mon corps, cette forme pensive!
> Buvez, mon sein, la naissance du vent!
> (127-129)

With the arrival of the breeze that signals that the midday crisis has passed—and now we are at the end of the poem—the poet recovers from the temptation to strive toward or surrender to the Absolute (or to nothingness?) and is ready to plunge into the multiplicity of life: "Le vent se lève! . . . il faut tenter de vivre!" (139).[28]

Ecstasy would seem to be misplaced at noon, and Valéry's poem, no less than Lanier's or the aestheticizing mysticism of Conti, gives an account of the impossibility or the danger of sustained and full mystic surrender at that moment. Modern psychological research appears to bear this out. In her investigation of the causes that trigger out-of-doors experiences of ecstasy, Marghanita Laski notes in her subjects "the preponderant mention of sunlight as the weather most apt for ecstasy," followed closely by fine lunar and stellar nights. "In relation to nature, ecstasy seems most commonly to be induced by mountains, hills, and water, by *starlit nights, fine dawns and sunsets*, by spring and autumn days, by trees and flowers, by the flight and song of birds, by light and wind and by the sweet smells of the countryside." Speaking specifically of the parts of the day when ecstasy is experienced, she notes: "In none of the texts is noon on a sunny day given as the time of the ecstasy."[29] Significantly, it appears to be an excess of light, more than heat, that forbids the possibility of ecstasy and the experience of merger.

Despite the amount of evidence that one can muster to show that midday is experienced chiefly as a time of danger to be avoided, a time for retreat, it would be wrong to assume that it always repels, that it is always experienced as a wholly negative encounter with the *daimon*. The opening of Valéry's "Le cimetière marin" shows at least a first moment of attraction and reaching out toward the noontide immobility felt as something absolute and eternal. And I find it hard to think that the sentiment of timelessness expressed by Rimbaud in the following ecstatic cry could refer to anything other than a noontide experience:

> Elle est retrouvée!
> —Quoi?—l'Eternité.
> C'est la mer mêlée
> Au soleil.[e]
> ("Délires II: Alchimie du verbe")

At any rate, for mystics whose desire to be freed from the tyranny of time leads to a yearning for a condition of immobility or stasis, the sun standing still at the zenith may be taken not only as an image of perfection of the Absolute, even as in Valéry's verses quoted earlier, it may figure as a spatial symbol of the very act of transcending time and, in the case of Indian thought, of escaping from the cosmos itself:

> Indeed, the *Chandogya Upanishad* (III, ii) affirms that for the sage, for the enlightened one, the Sun stands still: "But after elevation into the zenith it [the Sun] will neither rise nor set any more. It will remain alone in the Centre (*ekala eva madhyhy sthata*). Hence this text: 'There [namely, in the transcendental world of the *brahman*] it has not set, nor did it ever rise. . . .' It neither rises nor sets; once for all (*sakrit*) it stands in heaven, for him who knows the doctrine of the *brahman*."[30]

The sun, which in its diurnal movement is itself an image of time, is said to remain motionless (at the zenith) for the en-

---

[e] It is recovered!
—What?—Eternity.
It is the sea joined
With the sun.
("Delirium II, Alchemy of the Word")

lightened. As Eliade notes: "The *nunc fluens* paradoxically transforms itself into the *nunc stans*. Illumination and understanding achieve the miracle of an escape from Time."[31] Here then the midday stasis is an image not only of perfection in itself, but also of the enlightened man's release from time. Now it may be objected that what the *Chandogya Upanishad* speaks of cannot be thought of as an ecstasy as generally understood in the West. That is true, of course, though it does not lessen the importance of the passage for our purposes. The direction of the Indian release from time is nirvana. But for the West we may refer to the experience and thought of no less than Friedrich Nietzsche.

In a context that differs from the Hindu experience, but still with a grounding in a profoundly lived revelation of the quality of eternity in midday that is not unlike that experience, the great noontide was to become the central myth of Nietzsche in whose works the references to this moment—physical and metaphorical—are many. With him, too, the symbolic and metaphysical value of the image depends upon a real encounter with midday in nature. During the hot August of 1881, Zarathustra and the crucial revelation of the eternal return came to Nietzsche at a moment of ecstatic suspension under an Alpine zenith by Lake Silvaplana in the Upper Engadine in Switzerland. *Thus Spake Zarathustra* was to be the result of that timeless "moment," but it is noteworthy that Nietzsche first (in 1883) commemorated the occasion in a short poem of three distichs bearing the title "Sils-Maria":

Hier sass ich, wartend, wartend,—doch auf nichts,
Jenseits von Gut und Böse, bald des Lichts
Geniessend, bald des Schattens, ganz nur Spiel,
Ganz See, ganz Mittag, ganz Zeit ohne Ziel.
Da, plötzlich, Freundin! wurde Eins zu Zwei—
—Und Zarathustra ging an mir vorbei . . .[32]

> Here I was seated, waiting—yet expecting nothing,
> Beyond good and evil, savoring now the light,
> Now shadows, all a pure game,
> All lake [*or* sea], nothing but noon, only time without aim.
> Then, suddenly, dear friend, one became two—
> —And Zarathustra came into my view . . .

This ecstatic vision is reflected in the longer poem ("From High Mountains") appended as an aftersong to *Beyond Good and Evil*. Beginning with the words "Midday of life! Oh, time to celebrate," the poem concludes with the announcement of the advent of Zarathustra, the midday friend (or friend of midday), and, again, with the statement that it was at noon that one turned into two:

Der Mittags-Freund—nein! fragt nicht, wer es sei—
Um Mittag war's, da wurde Eins zu Zwei . . .

It was then that Nietzsche, as his sister recorded, decided to reveal the doctrine of the eternal return through the figure of Zarathustra, and among the papers of that period is a page bearing words that suggest the first definite plan of the masterwork: "Midday and Eternity: Guide-Posts to a New Way of Living." And beneath this: "The sun of knowledge stands once more at midday; and the serpent of eternity lies coiled in its light—; It is *your* time, ye midday brethren."[33]

In the masterwork itself, solar imagery and the solar cycle serve as the main metaphorical device. The opening references are to sunrise and sunset in the key of the archetypal symbolism of rebirth, dying, and resurrection. It is with the blessing of the sun that Zarathustra descends (following the pattern of the sun) to the valley of ordinary men, his mission being to prepare them for the great midday. But he himself must first pass through the hour of crisis which is also the time of the revelation of being and eternity. At perfect noontide, with the sun directly above his head, Zarathustra lies down to sleep; yet his soul and his eyes remain awake. And in the stillness he says unto his heart: "Hath not the world now become perfect? . . . O happiness! O happiness! Wilt thou perhaps sing, O my soul? But this is the secret, solemn hour, when no shepherd playeth his pipe. Take care! Hot noontide sleepeth on the fields. Do not sing! Hush! The world is perfect."[34] The noonscape, with its echoes of the ancient dread recorded by Theocritus—midday as the hour of Pan—is here a perfect fusion of actual experience and metaphorical (and metaphysical) significance. Timelessness or eternity *is* felt: "What hath befallen me: Hark! Hath time flown away? Do I not fall? Have I not fallen—hark! into the well of eternity?" Then, upon waking fully from this trancelike sleep and reeling with the intoxication of the experience, Zarathustra yearns to be recaptured, enraptured again: "When, thou well of eternity! thou joyous, awful, noontide abyss! when wilt thou drink my soul back into thee?"

That what is involved here is a mystical experience or at least an ecstasy and a mystical yearning can hardly be doubted. But the noontide abyss into which Zarathustra wishes to be reabsorbed is not the transcendental Other of traditional religions. Nor is it a pantheistic God. The image of verticality (the well of eternity) precludes that. Rather, I think, it is eternity as the well of perfect latency and potentiality. The additional image of midday perfection being "round and ripe" suggests that the time for fruition is imminent. This is perhaps the source of the joy or happiness that Zarathustra feels in "the secret, solemn hour, when no shepherd playeth his pipe." He would not break the spell at this moment, but neither can this perfect stasis of latency long endure. Nonetheless, when the time for the actualization of potentiality comes, the great midday will prove to be a morning—a morning, that is, when man has already come of age. This is the meaning of the startling if not perplexing equation made by Zarathustra's last words in the book: "This is *my* morning; *my* day beginneth; *arise now, arise, thou great noontide.*" In *The Twilight of the Idols*, we read the optimistic announcement: "Noon: moment of the shortest shadow; end of the longest error; high point of humanity. INCIPIT ZARATHUSTRA."[35]

It would be presumptuous to think one could deal adequately on this occasion with Nietzsche's difficult concepts of eternal return and the superman (or "overman"), and to find a simple formula for them is not possible. It is enough for us to have indicated that these two pivotal themes of his thinking (in which the superman is he who knows and embraces the doctrine of eternal return) are strictly connected with the intuition of timelessness and fullness experienced by him at midday. Thus he has written that in existence there is always an "hour" in which first one, then many, and finally all men are illuminated by the mightiest thought of all—that of the eternal return—and every time this occurs it is the midday hour of humanity; and for this reason too, he noted, "When I had created the superman, I ordered around him the great veil of becoming and I caused the midday sun to shine upon him."[36]

There is yet another text, from *Human, All Too Human*, that is of much interest to us. Paragraph 308, entitled "At Noontide," is a meditation on life in which Nietzsche applies the allegory of the diurnal solar cycle to the life of man. Inasmuch as the passage was written in 1879, it reveals that he had indeed known a noontide ecstasy with its sensation of timelessness before his experiences at Sils-Maria and Portofino and well before the writing of *Zarathustra*. Indeed, it is perhaps this earlier experience (which could have been repeated) and passage that nourished the midday theme and imagery of the later masterwork:

> He to whom an active and stormy morning of life is allotted, at the noontide of life feels his soul overcome by a strange longing for a rest that may last for months and years. All grows silent around him, voices sound farther and farther in the distance, the sun shines straight down upon him. On a hidden woodland sward he sees the great God Pan sleeping, and with Pan Nature seems to him to have gone to sleep with an expression of eternity on their faces. He wants nothing, he troubles about nothing; his heart stands still, only his eye lives. It is a death with waking eyes. Then man sees much that he never saw before, and, so far as his eye can reach, all is woven into and as it were buried in a net of light. He feels happy, but it is a heavy, very heavy kind of happiness. —Then at last the wind stirs in the trees, noontide is over, life carries him away again, life with its blind eyes, and its tempestuous retinue behind it—desire, illusion, oblivion, enjoyment, destruction, decay. And so comes evening, more stormy and more active than was even the morning. —To the re-

ally active man these prolonged phases of cognition seem almost uncanny and morbid, but not unpleasant.

Here the actual experience of noontide is more readily separable from the allegory it is meant to serve, and we can perhaps see in it a closer approximation to such experiences of timelessness as are to be found in the Hindu tradition. But if the moment of midday beatitude seems all the more a sort of nirvana, that is also because in returning to the allegorical dimension at the close of the passage, the life to which man is called back following the noontide pause of fullness is judged negatively in terms that suggest Schopenhauer and Hindu speculation. Thus where one would expect a diurnal cycle allegorized into the human life cycle to end in a serene sunset, Nietzsche, on the contrary, speaks of an evening that is even more stormy and demanding than morning. The calm lies only in the pause and light of noontide. But it is a calm like no other: a death with waking eyes, a heavy kind of happiness in which one has a mystic intuition of truths undisclosed in the midst of life. Perhaps not at all strangely, Nietzsche notes that it is the truly active man—the man caught up by movement—who best appreciates the noontide immobility and the knowledge inherent in it. But as the end of his noon piece makes clear, the ambiguous character of the encounter is ever present, for such states of noontide cognition are "unheimlich und krankhaft, aber nicht unangenehm."[37]

Aside from any philosophical symbolism that attaches to Nietzsche's speculation on midday, his encounters with noontide represent a profound experience of nature mysticism and an insight into nature's secret life. For this reason, and because in the later chapters of this study we shall find it fruitful, even necessary, to refer to his experience, we may end the present discussion of him by quoting one of his most telling poetic accounts of midday ecstasy—the lyric "Nach neuen Meeren" ("Toward New Seas"):

> Dorthin—will ich; und ich traue
> Mir fortan und meinem Griff.

> Offen liegt das Meer, ins Blaue
> Treibt mein Genueser Schiff.
>
> Alles glänzt mir neu und neuer,
> Mittag schläft auf Raum und Zeit—:
> Nur dein Auge—ungeheuer
> Blickt mich's an, Unendlichkeit!g 38

In the vast noontide sea of light and silence, Midday (the Absolute personified as a god) "sleeps" on space and time, and only the limitless or monstrous eye of Infinity looks upon the poet. But *limitless* and *monstrous* as words are not wholly satisfactory in translating *ungeheuer* in this context. The "eye" of Infinity that has transfixed the poet and holds him in thrall is the subjective feeling of the *uncanny*, the sentiment of numinous awe that has invaded Nietzsche. Accordingly, the word is more appropriately rendered by *awesome* or *awful*.39 Finally, it is noteworthy that the (metaphorical) ship that charts these new seas of thought and feeling is said to be Genoese. That may not be important to some who, in translating the piece, have preferred simply to omit the attribute. But for us it has its interest. Nor does this lie only in the fact, important as it is, that Nietzsche felt himself to be a new Columbus. (Among his poems is a lyric entitled "The New Columbus" in which he portrays himself as forever gazing into the blue and forever enthralled by distance.) Equally relevant is the fact that he felt himself to be a man of the south, and as much of Liguria as of Greece. Genoa was where he spent most of 1881 (the summer of which he passed at Sils-Maria) as well as the winter and early spring of 1882 and 1883. Part one of *Zarathustra* was written in Rapallo, and we have noted that the midday ecstasy

---

g There!— there I would go, and I trust
 In my self henceforth, the till in my hold.
 The sea lies vast, and into the blue
 My Genoese ship now makes bold.

 All has a brightness, new and newer,
 Midday sleeps on space and time.
 Your eye alone—awesomely,
 Fixes on me, Infinity.

recorded in "Sils-Maria" is also an account of an experience he had in Portofino. This will not seem irrelevantly erudite when we consider that in the twentieth century a large part of the emblematizing literature on the themes of the sun and midday has come from writers of Liguria.

Before bringing these introductory remarks to a close, it is essential to note that the Christian tradition, which gives ample testimony to the ambivalence of midday, has itself resolved the ambiguity in a sense that on the whole is more positive than negative. Besides the "midday demon" motif, Christian writers were mindful of the Old Testament account (Gen. 18:1) that it was midday when Abraham received the three angels, which Christians interpreted as an epiphany of the Trinity. Adam and Eve, it was also held, partook of the forbidden fruit at that fateful hour. But the most important event of all to be associated with the three hours par excellence of noontide was the agony of Christ on the cross. Among the most significant descriptive features recorded by the Gospels concerning that tremendous midday is the obfuscation of the sun. Evidently not the result of an eclipse, the cause for this phenomenon has been much discussed. "But if the physical cause of the darkness remains mysterious," writes Daniel-Rops, "its supernatural significance is plain; 'Day of doom, says the Lord God, when there shall be sunset at noon, and earth shall be overshadowed under the full light' [Amos, 8:9]."[40]

In its encounter with the sun cult of antiquity, Christianity, refusing to compromise its faith in a God who was the creator of the sun and all other celestial bodies, brought about what Hugo Rahner has called "the dethronement of Helios." By this is meant "nothing less than the most brusque and determined correction of all Stoic pantheist, or Platonic mystical, devotion to the sun into transcendent monotheism."[41] At the same time, however, the symbolical value of the sun as an image of the Divinity was not discarded, but, on the contrary, was appropriated to the person of Jesus Christ, the "True Sun," as the church fathers were to call him. Indeed, for Christians the "sun of righteousness" which Malachias prophesied would arise (Mal. 4:2) was no other than Jesus Christ. Now although in Christian solar symbolism it is sunset and sunrise that are most often invoked, the noontide agony of the "sun of righteousness" could not but make midday hallowed. It was only natural, then, that noon should have come to be regarded by Christians as a time especially propitious for prayer. Already by the third century, midday—the hour of sext—was considered to be as solemn and important an hour for prayers as were tierce and none. The later centuries of the Middle Ages, moreover, saw several attempts by Christian poets to narrate the whole of the Passion in terms of the canonical hours, with sext as the hour at which Christ mounted the cross and none the hour at which he expired.[42] Connected with that most solemn event is the great midday encounter of Paul on the road to Damascus when, blinded by the dazzling light of glory, brighter than the physical sun (though evidently manifesting itself by way of it), the revelation of Jesus was made to him (Acts 22:6-11; 26:12-16). At a distance of some seventeen centuries we may say that the same connection applies to Milton's Samson Agonistes whose cry—"O dark, dark, dark, amid the blaze of noon"—is the richer in tragic relevance because the physical reality of blindness is secondary to, and a symbol of, a spiritual drama that has reached its high noon, the hour of the crisis of clarity. Milton, moreover, went so far as to structure the temporal dimension of *Paradise Lost* on the poles of noon and midnight, with midday figuring centrally as the time for most of the critical moments in the drama of the Fall.[43]

In a similar way midday is used to symbolize the crisis of guilt and conscience in Coleridge's "The Rime of the Ancient Mariner." Whatever the several layers of meaning may be in this celebrated poem, it is clear that it is a retelling of the Christian drama of a soul that passes from guilt and punishment to repentance, expiation, and redemption. It is after the Mariner has killed the Albatross (and one can hardly miss the bird's association with Christ), and, more specifically, the murder has been accepted by the other mariners, that the tropical sun appears at noon as a hostile force. When the sun had risen gloriously "like God's own head" on the morning after the night of the murder, the ship's crew felt reassured and even congratulated the Mariner on his deed. But after favorable winds throughout the morning, at noon a dead calm comes over sky and sea, and the ship is unable to move:

> All in a hot and copper sky,
> The bloody Sun, at noon,
> Right up above the mast did stand,
> No bigger than the Moon.
>
> Day after day, day after day,
> We stuck, nor breath nor motion;
> As idle as a painted ship
> Upon a painted ocean.
>   (Part II, stanzas 7-8)

Although the second of the above stanzas indicates that the inertness of ship, air, and water continues round the clock for many days, we picture the scene as being under a perennial, relentless high-noon sun, an impression strengthened by the theme of awful drought that is developed in the remaining stanzas of this part of the poem. The bloody midday sun here may be God seen in his wrathful aspect rather than in his glory, and yet a symbolic connection with the noontide agony of Christ must surely suggest itself. Christ the victim and Christ the avenger perhaps unite in this midday sun that has "stuck" the unregenerate ship and its crew to the ocean. In this respect, it is not wrong to see in the image a reminiscence or a version of the biblical *daemon meridianus*. Interestingly enough, this image returns later in the poem when, after the Mariner's repentance and redemption, the ship is once again sailing under the force of a "roaring wind" (the Polar Spirit in the poem, but surely with some suggestion of the Holy Spirit) that does not physically reach the ship, the high-noon sun once more "fixes" it in a crisis of immobility:

> The Sun, right up above the mast,
> Had fixed her to the ocean.
>   (Part V, stanza 21)

The Mariner's earlier recognition of the beauty and sanctity of God's creatures had liberated him from the first "midday crisis," and now a fuller contrition and repentance for the offence against God delivers him from this second stasis. The reconciling spirit energizes the ship once more until restoration is complete.[44]

We know that both within and without the context of religious symbolism, the midday sun is often associated with the idea of glory. Outside the context of Christ's agony, the church fathers, such as Saint Ambrose, could speak of midday as the time when the Divine Light is in its fullness, and we will find Dante advancing a theory for the hour of the Passion precisely on those grounds. This symbolical relationship between deity and midday is particularly strong in the Christian tradition where such expressions as "glorious noon" and "eternal noon" are ways of speaking of the effulgence of God in his essence or of the light of glory in Paradise. Such light, as Dante, among others, observed, cannot be looked into directly, and when in the seventeenth century Henry Vaughan spoke of the moon as a sphere of light into which man can gaze and recognize the Divinity, he saw it as a lesser but tolerable image of God's "glorious noon."[45] Both in God and in the physical sun at midday there is "a deep, but dazzling darkness," to use another phrase from Vaughan's poem. In terms of the Deity, this is the obscurity that surrounds the most incomprehensible of all beings, an idea that Edmund Burke spoke of in illustrating how the effect of the sublime is produced by "a light which by its very excess is converted into a species of darkness."[46] The idea of the impossibility of "seeing" into the Deity (as of looking into the sun) is, of course, a commonplace, but we shall find the phenomenon on which it rests—that of an excessive and intolerable light that obscures rather than illumines—in a variety of midday contexts in the later chapters of this study.

In the light of this Christian tradition, we may take note of the meditation on the hours of the day by the modern Catholic theologian Romano Guardini and the unique place he gives to midday because of its mystical lure. "Though each hour of the day has its own character, three hours stand out from the rest—morning, evening, and half way between them, noonday, and have an aspect distinctively their own."[47] In keeping with the archetypal significance of the sun at dawn and at sunset, Guardini observes that each morning is a revelation and a reenactment of the mystery of birth bringing us an impulse of fresh energy, whereas evening reveals the mystery of death and brings us a sense of the past being past. Halfway between the rising and the setting sun, when the day is at its height, comes "a brief and wonderful moment" (p. 97). Though midday is a pause, it is not a moment of weariness: "our strength and energy are still at the full, for noonday is the pure present" (p. 98). It is the most sacred hour because it holds the greatest mystery—the Absolute in which time and space are no more. That Guardini is talking also (or first) about a physical noontide (albeit with metaphysical implications) is made clear by his observation that while the "deepness" of midday goes unperceived in the bustling city, it surrounds us in the countryside, among cornfields and quiet pastures, when the very horizon is glowing with heat. Then we stand still, and time falls away: "Eternity confronts us; time waits and holds its peace" (p. 98). Here then is a mystical encounter with midday in a wholly positive sense. Noontide is felt by Guardini as a moment of wonder and fullness that carries a promise of expectation. But how different a midday expectation from Nietzsche's!

The possible variations on the midday theme are hardly limited to the kinds cited in these introductory pages, but enough has been said to allow us to go on to our discussion of the topos in Italian literature. Our consideration of the subject in the Christian tradition, moreover, is an especially appropriate prelude to the first of the Italian authors in whom the image of midday figures significantly.

I. From Dante to Pindemonte

> Le soleil ni la mort ne se
> peuvent regarder fixement.
> (*La Rochefoucauld*)

For those who have only normal or "natural" vision, La Rochefoucauld's maxim is all too true. Dante himself had written that the sun has two properties in common with arithmetic: its light "informs" all other stars, and the human eye cannot gaze into it.[1] But for the truly spiritual man it is different. Within the *Divine Comedy*'s framework of a narration of the journey in the afterlife to God, Dante's ascension from the earthly to the celestial Paradise is intimately connected with the unshadowing sun at its zenith. Exactly at midday—"E più corusco e con più lenti passi / Teneva il sole il cerchio di merigge" (*Purgatorio* XXXIII, 103-104)—Dante is finally made whole again and restored to a state of perfect innocence and perfect justice. ("Midi le juste," said Valéry in a different context, but not entirely without applicability here.) And following his ritual ablutions in the streams of Lethe (forgetfulness of evil deeds) and Eunoe (restoration of memory of good deeds), it is still midday when Beatrice looks up into the sun (symbol of the Divinity), and Dante, gazing first into the reflected sunlight in Beatrice's eyes, acquires the power to look directly into the plentitude of light that streams down perpendicularly from above. Infused with this new spiritual energy (i.e., sanctifying grace), Dante begins to rise into the celestial Paradise, the final phase of his mystical journey (*Paradiso* I, 43-53).[2]

For Dante, as for other religious spirits before and after him, especially in the Christian tradition, the midday sun is the image of the Divine Splendor. Indeed, one is tempted to say that in the *Divine Comedy* it *is* the Divine Splendor. In the *Convivio* Dante had written that there is no physical object more worthy than the sun to signify God (cf. Saint Francis's "Canticle of the Creatures"), inasmuch as it is not only self-illuminating, but also illuminates all other heavenly and earthly bodies: "Nullo sensibile in tutto lo mondo è più degno di farsi essemplo di Dio che 'l sole; lo quale di sensibile luce sé prima e poi tutte le corpora celestiali e le elementali illumina" (*Convivio* III, xii, 7). Even more important for us is his digression on the four parts of the day and the corresponding canonical hours. Midday (i.e., noon sharp) is said to be the "noblest" hour of the day, and the most "virtuous" (*Convivio* IV, xxiii, 12-16). The principal reason for this exalted position of the noon hour lies in the fact that the meridian marks the maximum point (the zenith) of ascendancy in the diurnal arc or course of the sun. It is the same with the arc or course of man's life. For this reason Christ chose to die in the fullness of life—his meridian (i.e., at thirty-five years of age)—and at the solar hour of midday, when the physical sun was at its highest and its fullest strength.[3] Saint Ambrose had observed that the splendor of the Divine Light is at its fullest at midday. Even more pertinent is the fact that he associated the idea of midday with the Sun of Justice, noting that the just man carries midday within himself; it is midday for those upon whom the Sun of Justice shines: "Habemus ergo in nobis meridiem. Meridies est ei cui justitiae sol refulget."[4] In Eden at the meridian of his own life (see *Inferno* I, 1), and finding himself with newly acquired perfect justice, Dante rises toward Christ, the Midday Sun of Justice.[5]

The emblematic value given to the midday sun as a symbol of God's justice and glory is actually anticipated early in *Purgatorio*. This occurs when the pilgrim Dante meets Belacqua among those souls who are obliged to spend time waiting in the Antepurgatory before being allowed to start the actual purification of their sins on Purgatory's seven punitive terraces. The waiting period imposed upon these particular souls is the result of their having come to repentance and a reconciliation with God only *in extremis*. Now, in the shade of a massive boulder where they have sought refuge from the sun's rays, these lounging souls appear as the very image of physical laziness and weariness, especially Belacqua (known to

Dante on earth during his mortal life) who sits clasping his knees and holding his face down between them. In the previous canto (III) Dante had applied the image of sheep explicitly to the souls in Purgatory, and the aptly applied metaphor is a constant in this realm where the souls tend to move together in flocks. The picture of the negligent souls that Dante now sees suggests the image of sheep resting motionless in the shade at noontide:

> Ed ivi eran persone
> Che si stavano all'ombra dietro al sasso
> Come l'uom per negghienza a star si pone.
> E un di lor, che mi sembiava lasso,
> Sedeva e abbracciava le ginocchia,
> Tenendo il viso giù tra esse basso.[a]
> (*Purgatorio* IV, 103-108)

Since Dante's Purgatory is situated on the earth and therefore has its diurnal cycle, these souls could have been met at any hour in the area of Antepurgatory. Hence it is a sign of the emblematic value of midday that Dante has staged his encounter with them during that part of the day that is commonly and spontaneously associated with a pause in the activity of men and nature. The condition of spiritual laziness or sloth that was theirs in earthly life is figured in these sheeplike souls who are at rest in the shade, out of the midday sun which is the symbol of God's justice and glory. When Dante wonders why Belacqua is just sitting there rather than making his way up Mount Purgatory, the latter makes it plain that he will not leave the shade to attempt the climb, for he would not, in any case, be permitted to begin his purgative experience; and so, why bother?—"O frate, l'andar su che porta?" But not so the pilgrim Dante who understands Virgil's pointed reference (at the end of the canto) to the fact that it is midday—"vedi ch'è tocco / Meridian dal sole"—to be an ad-

---

[a] And there were persons lounging in the shade behind the rock, even as men who settle themselves to rest for laziness; and one of them, who seemed to me weary, was sitting and clasping his knees, holding his face low down between them. (Trans. C. S. Singleton, *Purgatorio*, Princeton, N.J., 1973, p. 41.)

monition to lose no part of the day in continuing the climb to God's glory. Virgil's reference indicates both the actual physical hour and the goal of Dante's journey. And in contrast with the negligent souls fixed in the image of a slothful noontide siesta, the pilgrim moves out into the high-noon sun to continue his ascent.

The bucolic image of sheep resting at noon in the shade, which is only implicit in the passage just discussed, is explicitly employed as a simile later in the *Purgatorio*. Having passed through the seventh and last punitive terrace of Purgatory, the pilgrim Dante, after a few steps further up the mountain, finds that he and his guides (Virgil and Statius) must once again stop for the night because of the law that forbids any climbing after sundown. Settling down to rest, the weary pilgrim now "ruminates" (as line 91 has it) on the day's events. Dante here compares himself with goats who after a morning of wild frolicking have come to rest in the shade while the midday sun blazes:

> Quali si stanno ruminando manse
> Le capre, state rapide e proterve
> Sopra le cime avante che sian pranse,
> Tacite a l'ombra, mentre che 'l sol ferve,
> Guardate dal pastor, che 'n su la verga
> Poggiato s'è e lor di posa serve.[b]
> (*Purgatorio* XXVII, 76-81)

It is a picture of a placid noontide, complete with the presence of the goatherd caught in a perennially true moment of leaning on his staff as he watches over the flock.[6] But more than a description of idle pastoralism is intended here. Coming at a time when Dante has been making vigorous efforts to climb but now must halt, the image creates the sense of a vast pause or suspension. Yet it is interesting that the image of a bucolic noontide pause should be used to describe the mood and the hour of evening by the poet who, as we have already seen,

[b] As goats, which have been swift and wayward on the peaks before they are fed, become tranquil as they ruminate, silent in the shade while the sun is hot, guarded by the shepherd who leans upon his staff and tends their repose. (Trans. C. S. Singleton, *Purgatorio*, p. 295.)

earlier in the climb up Mount Purgatory did not hesitate to go forth under the sun during the actual hour of midday and who soon after the metaphorical noontide just described (the third and final night on Purgatory) was to leave even the most beautiful of pastoral oases (Eden)—typically the ideal midday retreat—in order to rise to the glory of eternal noon.

In the more mundane eyes of Boccaccio's blithe band (*lieta brigata*) of seven women and three men of the *Decameron* who have fled plague-stricken Florence and retired into the countryside, noontide with its torrid heat and intolerable light calls for a retreat of its own (thus a retreat within a retreat) that consists of a nap followed by a longer period devoted to the narration of stories void of traditional religious values but not always without a moral intent. To this purpose, shortly after the *ora nona* has "struck," the group seeks a spot out of doors where it will be protected from the midday sun. It is a nicely idealized if not magical space: a meadow with luscious green grass where a soft breeze conveniently blows and olive trees supply the shade. The sun's rays are unable to invade the refuge: "né vi poteva [i.e., *penetrava*] d'alcuna parte il sole." The phrase is significant, for it seems to suggest that along with the actual physical sun all extraterrestrial concerns are excluded.[7]

Though the rays of the noonday sun may not penetrate there, the group can see that the sun is high. The silence of the hour is broken only by the sound of the cicadas coming from the olive trees, a detail that, while it is characteristic of midday settings in southern lands, also has literary sources in Theocritus and Virgil (poets of the south). These ancient sources have doubtless contributed to making cicadas a constant in literary noonscapes down to our own epoch. Here the members of the *lieta brigata* sit upon the grass in order to beguile the hottest part of the day by telling stories—sad and gay—of the defeats and triumphs of earth-bound creatures. Pampinea, the acknowledged leader of the group sets the stage:

> Come voi vedete, il sole è alto ed il caldo è grande, né altro s'ode che le cicale su per gli ulivi, per che l'andare al pre-

sente in alcun luogo sarebbe senza dubbio sciocchezza. Qui è bello e fresco stare . . . [e] novellando, il che può porgere, dicendo uno, a tutta la compagnia che ascolta diletto, questa calda parte del giorno trapasseremo.[c][8]

Each day for ten days the pastime is repeated, and on each occasion there are references to the time or the position of the sun and, in particular, to the heat of the hour. The curious but significant effect of this repetition is to lend a quasi-ritualistic character to a mundane mood and activity. There is built up the sense of a deliberate opposition of the *locus amoenus* (in which the storytelling takes place) against the menace of a hostile moment of nature. The storytelling itself might almost be a magical rite. It is all very urbane, of course, and who could argue with what seems to be so rational a suggestion. As Pampinea says, the sun is high, the heat stifling, and all things are at rest (only the sound of the cicadas in the olive trees breaks the silence), so that it would certainly be foolish to go anywhere at this hour. Thus one might prefer to speak here of a secular analogue to a primitive or religious behavioral pattern. The pattern remains clear, though Boccaccio has employed it with his own dual purpose: he has made it serve an aesthetic end in the creation of a narrative structure, and, closely related to this aim, he has sought to desacralize midday, which serves his secular ethic in the storytelling. The noontime telling of tales has been substituted for the Church-prescribed office for the hour of none. A human space, a totally "earthly" paradise has shut out the direct rays of that midday sun which has symbolical connections with the Divinity and, what is even more pertinent here, with the "destruction that wasteth at noonday"—the raging pestilence from which the *lieta brigata* has sought to escape.[9]

The motif of setting a group of storytellers in a shady retreat during the hot midday hours had been used earlier by

[c] As you see, the sun is high, and the heat is intense; nor is anything to be heard save the cicadas upon the olive trees. And so, to go anywhere at this time would certainly be foolishness. It is beautiful and refreshing to pause here . . . [and] with now one and then another of us telling stories, which can give pleasure to the whole company listening, we will pass this hottest part of the day.

Boccaccio in his pastoral romance *Ameto* where the nymph Lia makes much the same invitation to her companions as does Pampinea to hers.[10] Of more interest, however, is the development the *Ameto* brings in verse to the topos of the shepherd-swain's invitation to his nymph to come out of the heat of the noonday sun and into a shady retreat—a *locus amoenus*—where he awaits her with precious fruits and gentle animals. With these verses Boccaccio helped to inaugurate a long tradition of pastoral midday eroticism of the kind that was to be particularly fashionable in the eighteenth century and was eventually to give us the midday fauns of Mallarmé and D'Annunzio. The topos allowed for a description of midday in a country setting, emphasizing its vexatious, negatively perceived effects but also including something of the inviolate character of the hour.

The swain's song begins with references to the position of the meridian sun under whose perpendicular rays the shadows that might offer shelter are reduced to a minimum. A gentle breeze invites men at that hour to flee from the sun and to seek a refuge in shady bowers while the sun reigns like a sky god "feeding" on land and sea:

> Febo salito già a mezzo il cielo
> Con più dritto occhio ne mira e raccorta
> L'ombre de' corpi che gli si fan velo;
>   E Zeffiro soave ne conforta
> Di lui fuggire e l'ombre seguitare
> Fin che da lui men calda ne sia pórta
>   La luce sua, che nell'umido mare
> Ora si pasce, e in terra pigliando
> Il cibo quale a sua deità pare.[d][11]
>
>   (1-9)

---

[d] Phoebus having risen already to the meridian
With straighter eye looks on us and shortens
The shadows of bodies that veil his light;
And soft Zephyr invites us to
Flee from him [Phoebus] and seek the shade
Until he yield less hot his light to us,
Which now feeds on the liquid sea
And feasts on earth as pleases its deity [Phoebus].

All animals have gone into their lairs where they "ruminate" on what they had eaten in the morning, and the idea of a suffering nature is evoked in the image of flowers wilting in the oppressive heat: "E ogni fiera ascosa, ruminando / Quel c'ha pasciuto nel giovane sole, / Tien le caverne, lui vecchio aspettando. / / Fra l'erbe si nascondon le viole / Per lo venuto caldo, e gli altri fiori / Mostran, bassati, quanto lor ne dole" (10-15).[e] The shepherds have guided their flocks away from the open grazing fields to shaded areas (16-18), and an absolute quiet has stilled the voices of the forest: "Taccion le selve e tace ciò che in quelle / Suol far romore" (19-20). But though all other forms of life seek refuge in the shade, the shepherd's nymph, reluctant to rest from the hunt, wanders alone in the torrid landscape: "E ciascheduna cosa i blandimenti / Ora dell'ombre cerca; ma tu sola, / Lia, trascorri per l'aure cocenti" (28-30). As he continues his plea for her to come to his retreat, Ameto compares the nymph to beautiful restorative aspects of nature. In this passage, the oppressive midday hour becomes emblematic of the distressful passion of the shepherd-swain, and in this sense Boccaccio very likely owes something to Virgil's second eclogue. Though his swain has sought out the shade while Virgil's Corydon cannot do so, for both suitors noontide has an erotic value.[12]

No less important in the development of the mythology of midday eroticism in Western literature is the motif with which the prose narration of the *Ameto* opens. After a successful morning chase in a lush mountain forest, the young hunter has descended to the foot of the mountain where, at noon, he pauses to rest under a leafy tree not far from a stream. Hearing a more than human voice that sweetly sings a song that is unknown to him, and finding it to be coming from the bank of the stream, the enchanted Ameto can only think that divinities have made their appearance at that hour. After making his way to the stream, he espies a group of maidens (*giovinette*) in varying degrees of dress, some bathing, some

---

[e] And each hidden animal, ruminating on / What it had eaten under the early sun / Keeps to its lair waiting for him [the sun] to grow old. // The violets shrink into the grass / Because of the heat that has arrived, and the other flowers, / Bent, reveal how much they are grieved.

sitting on the grass rich with flowers. At this sight Ameto experiences a sense of awe, accompanied by terror at the thought that he might suffer the fate of Actaeon. But Boccaccio, significantly enough, supplies a happy ending to the episode he has borrowed from Ovid, for here the nymphs welcome the young hunter into their midst. And there Ameto is soon at his ease, so that any element of religious awe that Boccaccio, in appropriating the Ovidian account, may have wished to suggest as part of his hero's terror is quickly undercut and dissipated. Despite the attempt (somewhat awkward if not grotesque) to allegorize the sensual nymphs of the *Ameto* into Christian virtues, in this initial episode midday has been secularized, so to speak, no less than was to be the case in the later episode of the *Decameron* discussed above.[13]

As important as Boccaccio's adaptation is, Ovid's tale of Actaeon's fatal midday nympholepsy was echoed with even richer psychological implications in one of the more erotic fantasies of the storyteller's great contemporary, Petrarch. The following scene is the closing amatory metamorphosis of the canzone "Nel dolce tempo de la prima etade" ("In the sweet time of my youth"):

> I' segui' tanto avanti il mio desire,
> Ch'un dì, cacciando sì com'io solea,
> Mi mossi, e quella fera bella e cruda
> In una fonte ignuda
> Si stava, quando 'l sol più forte ardea.
> Io perché d'altra vista non m'appago,
> Stetti a mirarla, ond'ella ebbe vergogna,
> E per farne vendetta o per celarse,
> L'acqua nel viso co le man mi sparse.
> Vero dirò, forse e' parrà menzogna,
> Ch' i' senti' trarmi de la propria imago,
> Et in un cervo solitario e vago
> Di selva in selva ratto mi trasformo,
> Et ancor de' miei can fuggo lo stormo.[f]
> (147-160)

[f] I followed after my desire so far
That one day, while hunting as was my wont,

Applying the metaphor of hunter to himself, the poet is pictured as having come one day upon the beautiful and disdainful Laura (to whom the metaphor of "beast" is applied) bathing naked in a stream, precisely at that moment when the (midday) sun was burning at its fiercest—"quando 'l sol più forte ardea." Discovering herself espied in close proximity at so intimate a moment by her hunter-suitor (or so that fantasy would have it), Laura splashes water into his face (as Diana did to Actaeon), whereupon Petrarch feels himself transformed into a stag (as Actaeon was in fact) who races through the forest because he is chased by his own hounds. According to the most reasonable explanation to be culled from the many commentaries of the *Canzoniere*, these hounds are the allegorical representation of the poet's persistent desire and his remorse, perhaps his torment at the thought that he has offended his lady and may not have her pardon. Again, the importance of the text for us lies in the fact that in it and in the episode from Boccaccio's *Ameto* we are witnessing the beginning in a modern European language of an aspect of midday mythology—the association between noontide and erotic passion—that was to continue to thrive and, for that matter, was to reach its greatest poetic significance in the literature of the last century or so. That this tradition has its chief literary precursor in Ovid can come as no surprise, though we could hardly forget Virgil's role. What may yet be pointed out here is that Petrarch's passage is more "faunesque" than either Boccaccio's or Ovid's.

To begin with, neither Ameto nor Actaeon is motivated by

I set out, and that fair and cruel beast
In a fount, naked
Stood, when the sun burned at its highest.
And I, who by no other sight am satisfied,
Kept gazing at her, whereat she felt abashed,
And, either to take revenge or to hide herself,
With her hands she splashed water on my face.
Truth to tell, though a lie it may appear,
I felt myself drawn from my own form,
And I am transformed suddenly into a solitary stag
Wandering from wood to wood.
And even now I run from my pack of hounds.

love in their similar (up to a point) adventures, although the former's different and fortunate fate eventually casts him in the role of lover. Whereas both these young hunters merely chance upon their respective groups of nymphs, Petrarch, really more of a faun than a hunter in the encounter he has fantasized, has consciously pursued his "desire" with a strong sensual appetite: "I' segui' tanto avanti il mio desire." In a sexual sense, faun and hunter are almost interchangeable, except, of course, in the tradition in which the hunter, as a devotee of Diana, is steadfastly opposed to the dangerous charms of Venus. And the hunter may reveal more human traits than the faun. Yet one might think Petrarch too timid to be the one or the other since, in the end, he does no more than gaze at his prey: "Io, perché d'altra vista non m'appago, / Stetti a mirarla." But how long and what longing in that gaze! It is not at all amiss to see in this Petrarch a forerunner of the midday fauns of, say, D'Annunzio and Mallarmé which are to claim our attention later on. Nonetheless, if, in the passage under examination, Petrarch seems to share a common ground of midday eroticism with Boccaccio, it is also true that his attitude of faun/voyeur contains the hint of a quasi-religious (or idolatrous) sense of awe which connects his fantasy more authentically with the nympholepsy of the Ovidian account and that of antiquity in general.[14]

It is perhaps a matter of nuance, but the difference can be detected, I think, even in two lyrics by Boccaccio that also build on the Actaeon motif and reveal the tendency to merge classical and contemporary trends in the development of a new (secular) mythology of midday nympholepsy. The sonnet "Il Cancro ardea, passata la sest'ora" ("The Crab was aflame, with noon just struck") shows us the sun on high and the beloved surrounded by other maids in a shady spot by the sea while the poet who espies them is so enchanted that he is as motionless as the rock behind which he is hidden. More interesting and closer to Petrarch's stanza is the sonnet "Guidommi Amor, ardendo ancora il sole" ("Love led me, while the sun was yet burning high") in which Boccaccio shows himself "led by love" (cf. "I' segui' tanto avanti il mio desire") while the sun is still on high, to a myrtle grove from which is heard beautiful singing (cf. the *Ameto* scene). Entranced, he thinks that it must be "an angel, perhaps, or a nymph, or goddess singing, in this *locus amoenus* [his phrase is *loco eletto*], of the loves of ancient times":

> "Angela forse, o ninfa, o dea
> Canta con seco in questo loco eletto"
> Meco diceva "degli antichi amori."
>
> (9-11)

The profanation here also involves the setting and the figure of Dante's Matelda who sings and gathers flowers in a *loco eletto* (Eden), itself a *contaminatio* but weighted on the side of Christian spirituality (*Purgatorio* XXVIII, 77). Despite the gentility of Boccaccio's more ambiguous female figure, the "ancient" loves that she sings of in her noontide retreat are without doubt Ovidian in character with little or no real Christian overtones, and the sense of devotion or awe that the poet wishes to suggest in connection with this angel-nymph-goddess herself, if present at all, is surely less tremulous than what we find in Petrarch's scene.[15]

Returning to Petrarch, we note that the Ovid-inspired stanza of his canzone has a parallel in a short piece where the story of Actaeon is again clearly an influence, though the allegorized motif of the hunter and his fate are not developed in it. This is the enchanting yet somewhat roguish madrigal that follows:

> Non al suo amante più Diana piacque
> Quando per tal ventura tutta ignuda
> La vide in mezzo de le gelide acque,
> Ch'a me la pastorella alpestra e cruda
> Posta a bagnar un leggiadretto velo,
> Ch'a l'aura il vago e biondo capel chiuda
> Tal che mi fece, or quand'egli arde il cielo,
> Tutto tremar d'un amoroso gielo.[g]
>
> (*Canzoniere*, LII)

---

[g] Diana pleased not her lover more,
When by rare chance he saw her

The standard interpretation of this lyric would have us see Petrarch more entranced by the sight of his "shepherdess" in the humble act of rinsing a veil that is used to keep her golden hair in place than was Actaeon when he beheld Diana bathing in the nude. Grammatically, of course, that is the most if not the only "legitimate" reading, although to be content with it is, I think, to miss the fuller meaning of the poem. *Velo* is a well-known Petrarchan metaphor for the body, and indeed some early commentators, undaunted by the apparent syntactical difficulty posed by the sixth line, interpreted it in this sense in the present case. Surely there is a double-entendre here. To begin with, the word play, frequent enough in the *Canzoniere*, by which *l'aura* = *Laura* should leave no question about the real identity of the female figure. Laura is a shepherdess because the poem is a madrigal, and rustics had to populate the genre at that time, as was true of the genre of the *pastourelle* itself. But she is no less totally nude here (in the "second" sense of the poem) than was Diana *tutta ignuda* when seen by Actaeon. Indeed, she is in much the same pose that was hers as the "fair beast" in the canzone "Nel dolce tempo de la prima etade" where "In una fonte ignuda / Si stava." And in both cases the sun as libido symbol is burning with its most intense force.

By departing from Ovid and portraying Actaeon as the lover of Diana, Petrarch heightens the poem's erotic suggestiveness. And this, along with the implied comparison between his "humble" Laura and the august goddess herself, enriches the closing conceit—this, too, typically Petrarchan—by which the poet is said to tremble with an erotic chill—*amoroso gielo*—precisely at the time the midday sun blazes down upon him. Without doubt, Petrarch had a remarkable penchant for fetishistic indirection. Nonetheless, the amorous chill that causes him to tremble seems more commensurate with the

> Quite naked 'midst the gelid waters,
> Than did me the harsh and cruel shepherdess
> Intent on bathing a charming veil
> That would to the breeze her fair blond hair deny.
> [That would protect Laura's fair blond hair.]
> Such that it made me, even as the heaven blazes,
> Tremble all over with an amorous chill.

sight of something more immediately palpable (in desire) than a garment.[16] But for all the mischievousness in the poem, there is perhaps still a residue of awe to be felt in that chill, and one may speak here, too, of a fusion of the sacred and the profane. Certainly it is in part this that makes Petrarch's experiment with the rustic genre of the madrigal so different from the genre of the *pastourelle* as it is usually found in the medieval tradition—even, say, in Guido Cavalcanti's famous example—where the shepherdess offers the occasion for an uncomplicated, undramatic sexual conquest or, in the case of a rebuff, for a harmless hour of flirtation. It is rather something of the trembling attitude expressed by the Cavalcanti of the *dolce stil nuovo* poems that Petrarch has brought to the madrigal and his vision of the divinity of the feminine form. We ought not to forget that Diana was a goddess.

It is a quite different midday mood that Petrarch evokes in his famous Latin treatise *De vita solitaria* where the author's allegorizing tendency takes a more orthodox moral direction and, interestingly enough, the reflections on midday occur in the context of a meditation on the various parts of the day. Limiting ourselves to this midday section, we may note first that Petrarch takes as his point of departure the idea that man is an unquiet creature, especially if he dwells in the city and in the society of other men. The wise man is he who retires into the country and into himself as much as possible and who says his devotions at the appropriate times of the day. At the approach of noon, as the sun nears the zenith and begins to burn more intensely, he will slowly return home with prayers to the effect that all "flames" of strife and the "heat" of passion found in ambitious and unscrupulous men not descend upon him. His desire is for Juvenal's ideal of a tranquil mind and a healthy body. Such a man uses his time and the noon hour more wisely than do others (I, ii, 2). As part of the midday portion of the day there is time for the noon meal, which for the retiring man will be judiciously frugal. The moralizing of midday continues in the postprandial observations on the contrast between the anxious, avaricious man and the calm, unambitious, retiring man. With the sun at the zenith and at its greatest strength, the restless man burns (*estuat*, as does the midday sun itself, of course, but Petrarch has transferred the term to the ambitious man) and with deceit in his heart hastens frantically so as not to lose any chance for more gain, and so as not to sink into "torpor." A perverse mind brooks no delay in trying to realize success. Neither siesta nor noon devotions are for such a one. The retiring or solitary man, on the contrary, does nothing in haste, least of all at noontide. He is mindful of the flow of time, and yet midday, evidently because of its apparent impression of the slowness if not the suspension of the sun's diurnal course, arouses in him a desire to be where there is no flux of time and no fear of death. Hence he again moves his lips in prayer, asking not for the serene sunset of a single day but of a whole existence (it is the motif of the parallel between the diurnal solar cycle and the human life cycle) and the reward of a glory that has no sunset (suggesting the vision of Paradise as a perennial midday glory).[17]

Within this meditation, then, we find a revealing shift in the writer's perception and emblematization of midday. Noontide appears first as a raging blaze that corresponds to the intense and restless ambition that torments the unspiritual man, whereas at the end of the meditation it is experienced as a vast but serene motionless expanse of solar splendor that for Petrarch, no less than for the "transhumanizing" eyes of Dante, is a symbol of God's glory in eternity. To the degree that the nature of these two noontides depends on the particular moralizing point Petrarch wishes to make, it partakes of a subjective quality, but in either case it has its basis in the perception of a true value in the natural phenomenon itself. According to the quality of the spiritual value or reality that he wishes to dramatize, Petrarch moves from the negative to the positive pole of midday.

We have already seen enough to know that the midday topos can occur at any time in a writer's work, and although noontide is, of its nature, ambivalent, or perceived to be so, it may be experienced and used symbolically as a wholly negative or a wholly positive value. Thus the negative overmastering features of a summer midday were used by Ariosto when he wished to dramatize and allegorize the difficulty of the path to virtue. Under the perpendicular rays of a vehement noonday sun—"nel più intenso ardor del mezzo giorno"—after struggling through a terrain that is reminiscent of Dante's "selva selvaggia e aspra," a weary Ruggiero arrives at a parched desert strand between mountains and sea:

> Su la fervida nona in una spiaggia
> Tra 'l mare e 'l monte, al mezzodì scoperta,
> Arsiccia, nuda, sterile e deserta.[h]
> (*Orlando Furioso*, VIII, xix, 6-8)

(Here too the liturgical *nona* is the term used to refer to the heart of the midday hours.) It is along this arid, scorched stretch of land that Ruggiero must proceed toward the domain of Logistilla. The description that takes up the whole succeeding octave is a marvel of Ariostesque art and as efficacious a depiction of a forbidding midday landscape as one could hope for:

> Percuote il sole ardente il vicin colle;
> E del calor che si riflette a dietro,
> In modo l'aria e l'arena ne bolle,
> Che saria troppo a far liquido il vetro.
> Stassi cheto ogni augello all'ombra molle:
> Sol la cicala col noioso metro
> Fra i densi rami del fronzuto stelo
> Le valli e i monti assorda, e il mare e il cielo.[i]

Here where air and sand seem to be liquefying in the intensity of the light and heat of a blazing midday sun, all living things

---

[h] In burning noontide to a shore,
Between the sea and the mountain, opened to the south,
Scorched, barren, sterile, and deserted.

[i] The blazing sun beats on the nearby mountain;
And with the heat that is reflected back
Air and sand boil in such a way
That it would more than suffice to melt glass.
All birds are silent in the gentle shade:
Only the cicada with tedious rhyme
Midst the thick boughs of leafy trees
Fills vales and hills, and sea and sky, with deafening din.

are motionless and silent. All, that is, save the cicadas whose monotonous, persistent refrain seems deafening and maddening as it pervades the vast stillness of space all around. This is one of those cases in which the chirr of the cicadas is not to be understood as a mere annoyance of no great import, much less an element of idyllic or pastoral calm. The adjective *noioso* refers to the exasperation experienced by the subject (Ruggiero) exposed to the fierceness of noontide, and the cicadas' piercing note is rather the acoustical impression that seems almost to be an effect created by the highly charged tension of the "silent" hour of crisis. Ariosto's noonscape is not just an incidental virtuosic piece, but, on the contrary, a superb poetic objectification (objective correlative, if one likes) of a psychological condition and the spiritual struggle of a soul which in order to acquire virtue must pass through the crisis provoked by a hostile power.[18]

Hence it is significant that in the poem's central and most famous episode, the hour of crisis and revelation comes for the paladin Orlando at noon:

> Il merigge facea grato l'orezzo
> Al duro armento e al pastore ignudo;
> Sí che né Orlando sentia alcun ribrezzo,
> Che la corazza avea, l'elmo e lo scudo.[j]
>
> (XXIII, ci, 1-4)

It is in keeping with Ariosto's pervasive irony by which the ambitions and desires of man are seen to be or to become reversals of themselves that the shady grove—the usually reliable refuge from noontide's destructive light and heat—turns out to be the setting for the encounter with a truth that Orlando cannot withstand and to which he will succumb, falling into a derangement that is only matched by (if it is not a symbol of)the riot and delirium of midday:

> Quivi egli entrò per riposarsi in mezzo;
> E v'ebbe travaglioso albergo e crudo,

[j] Midday made dear the shade
To hardened flock and naked shepherd;
So that Orlando certainly felt no chill,
He who bore armor, helmet, and shield.

> E più che dir si possa empio soggiorno,
> Quell'infelice e sfortunato giorno.ᵏ
>> (XXIII, ci, 5-8)

The refuge motif is introduced by Ariosto with a reference to shepherd and flock, the figures traditionally connected with the image of an idyllic retreat from midday. Though he is no shepherd, Orlando here belongs to the family of Corydon who can find no relief from the blaze of noontide but, on the contrary, finds his erotic passion mirrored and increased by it. Of course, he is a grandiosely hyperbolized version of Virgil's swain.

For the real idyllization of the motif of midday eroticism in continuation of Boccaccio's efforts in this vein we must turn to Jacopo Sannazaro in whose immensely influential pastoral romance *Arcadia* noontide becomes supremely the pastoral hour. His land of Arcadia, writes one critic, "most often is a place of glorious and sensuous beauty, seen either in a noontide blaze of light or by the soft glamour of the moon."[19] But there is much more of the noontide blaze than moonlight in the work. The very first song is sung at midday by Ergasto in a *locus amoenus*, a spot where the sun is made tolerable, even delightful, by being filtered through leafy trees, and it is a song of unrequited love. (We may note in passing that the Theocritean interdiction on piping at noon does not hold here.) But what is of most significance in the song is that part that tells of the circumstances in which the lovesick shepherd became enamored. One day while leading his flock to drink at noon, Ergasto beheld a lovely shepherdess in the midst of a stream, beneath the burning sky:

> Menando un giorno gli agni presso un fiume,
> Vidi un bel lume in mezzo di quell'onde,
> . . . .
> Io vidi prima l'uno e poi l'altro occhio;

ᵏ There he entered into its depth to rest,
 And found an anguished and cruel abode instead,
 And a more merciless stay than words can say,
 That unhappy and ill-fated day.

> Fin al ginocchio alzata al parer mio
> In mezzo al rio si stava al caldo cielo;
> Lavava un velo in voce alta cantando.
> Oimè, che quando ella mi vide, in fretta
> La canzonetta sua spezzando, tacque:
> E mi dispiacque, che per più mie' affanni
> Si scinse i panni, e tutta si converse.[1]
> (61-62, 71-78)

As in Petrarch's madrigal "Non al suo amante più Diana piacque" upon which this episode clearly draws, the protagonist here has evidently seen more than the commentators seem to realize.[20] This "shepherdess," too, is bathing in the stream and has little enough to do with laundering. She would hardly have to be standing knee-deep in water to wash a veil. Sannazaro got Petrarch's point in the ambiguous word *velo*, and he has repeated the erotic joke, not, however, without an additional heavy dose of roguishness. In his little scene, *velo*, besides being susceptible to the double meaning veil = body, is probably more specifically a veiled allusion to the pubic region. And as with Petrarch's madrigal, the notation on the hot noon sky above takes us back to Ovid's scene of Diana bathing and Actaeon's chance view of her. Thus we can understand why, after she has noticed Ergasto gazing at her, the maid stops her singing abruptly and, to the shepherd's extreme chagrin, hastily lowers her dress which had been raised and perhaps clasped around her *waist*. The words "Si scinse i panni" makes this last point plain enough. The focus on the waist, moreover, is continued in the very next line:

[1] One day while leading my flock by a river,
I saw a fair light in the middle of the waters,
. . . .
I saw first one and then the other eye;
With skirts raised to her knees, it seemed to me,
She stood in the middle of the river under the hot sky;
She was washing a veil while singing aloud.
Alas, that when she saw me, in a hurry
Breaking off her pretty song she became silent:
And it grieved me, that to my greater anguish
She lowered her skirts and covered herself wholly.

> Poi si sommerse ivi entro insino al cinto;
> Tal che per vinto io caddi in terra smorto.[m]
>
> (79-80)

As though having covered herself by lowering her dress were not enough, the shepherdess immerses herself up to her *waist* in an instinctive act of concealing that part of her that had been exposed to Ergasto's sight. The shepherd's distress is such that he falls in a swoon.

I have given what seems to me to be the most plausible reading of this account. It is possible, however, that Sannazaro's text is a rather interesting example of a *contaminatio* of two images or literary traditions: one medieval and the other classically paganizing. That the two should join or the one (the classical) be superimposed over the other (the medieval) under the libido symbol of the blazing midday sun makes a word about this matter appropriate here. To see, in the first part of the passage, a shepherdess standing with her dress merely tucked up a bit at the waist so as to keep it at knee level is not necessarily wrong. In fact, one can reasonably argue that it is the first or "correct" image, for the word *alzata* in the lines that place the maid in the midst of the stream—"Fin al ginocchio alzata al parer mio / In mezzo al rio si stava al caldo cielo"—can mean *with garments raised* (that is, then, with skirts lifted up to her knees). This is the meaning some of the early commentators on Dante give to the word in the phrase *trescando alzato* (*Purgatorio* X, 64) where it is used to describe the action of King David dancing "with garments girded up." If this is the meaning in Sannazaro's passage, then the shepherdess is indeed in the act of washing a garment—literally, a veil. (We need not seek to rebut this with the "realistic" or literal-minded argument that in medieval and Renaissance times a veil was more than likely of precious silk and therefore unlikely to be the possession of a simple "shepherdess.") But in the last part of the passage the image is clearly that of a "nymph" who has been bathing, and in true Ovidian fashion

---

[m] Then she submerged herself there up to her waist;
So that overcome I fell lifeless to the ground.

when she sees herself espied she quickly lowers her skirts (tucked up till then at her waist if not draped over her shoulder) and, almost at the same time, she immerses herself in the water. Moreover, this latter image, that of the shepherdess as nymph, is really the dominant one. Even if we prefer to see no more than a laundering shepherdess in the first part, it is clear that in placing her in the *midst* of the stream Sannazaro has done so in anticipation of the final gesture of immersion. The water proves to be deep enough for her to do that, and in any case one need not go beyond the edge of even a shallow stream to wash a veil. But it is the Ovidian reminiscence of the heat of the hour that is also telltale, for it is something that would have alerted a reader of Sannazaro's time to a meaning that might not otherwise be immediately apparent. Finally, it is (to me) farfetched to think that a poet who was so instrumental in introducing classically paganizing themes and images (many of them erotic) into modern European literature should have his shepherd swoon because he has been deprived of the sight of a shepherdess' calves.

But the *contaminatio* referred to is symptomatic and important. The episode under discussion may well be the most extreme case of midday voyeurism in all Arcadia, and it has special significance for us because in the context of Sannazaro's work it serves to show that "real" maids have taken over the role of nympholeptic visitants or visions, a development that was already under way with Boccaccio and Petrarch. In the *Arcadia* the tendency becomes still clearer with the subsequent references that establish noon as the true psychical and sensuous atmosphere of the work. In the second chapter midday is again the setting as Sincero leads his sheep to a shady bower (where, incidentally, he hopes also to find a gentle breeze blowing). On his way he meets the shepherd Montano who as he drives his flock before him makes sweet music with his pipe. Sincero's courteous greeting to him takes the form of an exhortatory wish "that benevolent Nymphs may lend attentive ears to his singing" and that his lambs may be preserved from wolves: "le benivole Nimfe prestino intente orecchie al tuo cantare." Benevolent nymphs are one thing, but vengeful ones are another. The "unworthy eyes" of the shepherds must be protected from them as well as from Diana bathing naked and woodland Faunus (a Roman version of Pan) when he returns weary from the hunt at midday, crossing the open fields and raging under the violent sun. This, in chapter three, is part of the prayer raised by the priest in the temple of Pales, goddess of the shepherds:

> Nè consentire, che gli occhi nostri non degni veggiano mai per le selve le vendicatrici Nimfe, nè la ignuda Diana bagniarse per le fredde acque, nè di mezzo giorno il silvestre Fauno, quando da caccia tornando stanco, irato sotto ardente sole transcorre per li lati campi (p. 72).[n]

The prayer is a fairly literal borrowing from Ovid's *Fasti* (IV, 759-762), except that Sannazaro has supplied the adjectives *vengeful* and *naked* and the reference to the shepherds' "unworthy eyes," evidently in order to communicate a sense of religious awe. At any rate, just before entering the temple, Sincero had been much delighted with an external mural painting which portrayed a group of naked nymphs being chased by four satyrs. And, in chapter four, it is under a high-noon sun that the "shepherdesses" are specifically compared to Naiads and Napaeans—river and valley nymphs. It is not necessary to trace all the occasions in which noontide serves in the *Arcadia* as the hour for encounter or singing. The lament raised at the end of the book to the effect that nymphs and satyrs are no longer to be found in the woods and that shepherds are without song need hardly be taken too seriously in view of the fact that the *Arcadia*, in song and word, has perhaps done more than any other single work of literature to put "shepherdessess" and "shepherds" on a par with those divinities, though the author's timid males in particular are more like their mythological counterpart in desire than in act. But this last feature has its own interest for our theme. If

---

[n] Do not permit our unworthy eyes ever to look upon the vengeful nymphs in the woods, nor to see naked Diana bathing in the cold waters, nor sylvan Faunus at midday when, returning tired from the hunt, irate under the blazing sun he crosses the open fields.

the pastoral world of Arcadia expresses an aspiration for a realm of blessed repose, the theme of unrequited love, which is an integral part of the pastoral tradition in Italy, supplies the element that keeps alive the tension or repressed energy that can be felt even in this noontide atmosphere. Finally, it can hardly be a fortuitous occurrence that it is noon (in chapter ten) when Sincero and his fellow shepherds are led by the holy priest into the sacred grove that has remained inviolate through the centuries and are there initiated into the secrets and the history of pastoralism.

The midday backdrop is a common enough feature in the idyllico-amatory poetry that was to become so widespread in the seventeenth and eighteenth centuries. The poets of the baroque age deserve mention because of the special quality of the imagery in their noonscapes. The first quatrain of a sonnet by the exuberant pen of Giambattista Marino, for example, describes a meridian sun whose refulgence causes the motionless sea to appear as an extension of the sky:

> Or che l'aria e la terra arde e fiammeggia,
> Né s'ode Euro che soffi, aura che spiri,
> Ed emulo del ciel, dovunque io miri,
> Saettato dal sole, il mar lampeggia.°

From here, the poet goes on to invite his nymph to retreat with him into the *locus amoenus* beneath the cool shade of a large leafy tree on the bank of the waters. It is the same topos that Boccaccio introduced into the verses of the *Ameto*, though Marino develops it with greater economy despite the typical baroque conceits he employs in the imagery.[21]

One of Marino's followers, Bernardo Morando, offers a sonnet—"No more with kindly rays and gentle beams"—that is almost wholly given over to describing the midsummer midday sun drying up rivers and meadows and scorching the fields. All creatures of the animal kingdom seek in vain for

---

° Now that air and earth burn and blaze,
 And Eurus is not heard blowing, nor gentle wind to breathe,
 And emulous of the sky, wherever I look,
 The sea, darted by the sun, flashes.

respite as the sky seems to rain down a stream of fire that engulfs the world:

> Par che diluvi il cielo influssi ardenti
> E in pelago di fiamme il mondo avvampi.[p]
> (7-8)

In considering possible ways to find relief from the fiery drought, the poet excludes love because, as he suggests, love "burns" its practitioners (or victims) with the same intensity as the summer sun. Unfortunately, this interesting parallel is suddenly dropped as the poet goes on, in the final line, to an anticlimactic and almost nonconsequential conclusion—relief will be found in wine.[22] The promising topos that equates the cruel heat of midday with love's torment, hinted at in Morando's poem, goes back, as we have seen, to Virgil's second eclogue and to a passage from Boccaccio's *Ameto*.

Another Marinistic version of the topos worth noting is Girolamo Fontanella's "Già la tremola spica in mezzo i campi" ("Already the tremulous spike 'mid the fields"). Like Morando's poem, this too is given over almost entirely to a description of the destructive heat of a midsummer noon. Again the ubiquitous cicada is heard, and amid a series of hyperbolic conceits in which the parched earth is said to be a burning tomb, the image of fiery heat colors the whole landscape and the poem.[23] Even streams and rivers "burn." Only with the last line, where the *point* of the poem is made, do we learn that the conflagration of nature in this cruel season and hour are a metaphor for the burning love that, though it consumes the poet, cannot melt the icy heart of Phyllis:

> Spira foco l'erbetta e fiamma il fiore,
> Arde il fiume, arde il rio, ferve la sponda;
> Solo ha Filli mia di ghiaccio il core.[q]

---

[p] The sky seems to pour burning emanations
And the world flares up in a sea of flames.

[q] The tender grass breathes forth fire and the flower flames,
As the river burns, so burns the stream, the bank is scorched;
Phyllis alone retains a heart of ice.

Undoubtedly, in the imagery of the foregoing examples—above all in the last of them—one meets with the extravagant cerebral play that gluts so much of Italian seventeenth-century verse (i.e., the Marinistic vein) and cloys rather than satisfies. Yet it needs to be said that the subject of noontide is one that seems to elicit hyperbolic expression in writers of any period. Even Ariosto's verses reveal this characteristic, and we will find it to be so time and time again in writers of the succeeding ages, especially those of the nineteenth and twentieth centuries. The plausible explanation for this would seem to lie first of all in the strong reaction invariably provoked by the violence of midday's invading force on the human psyche. At the same time, however, some authors, both before and after the *concettisti* of the age of the baroque, seize upon the opportunity the topos offers for the creation of intense images in order to make a statement about the self or the human condition. It is this profounder ethical realism or metaphysical implication—whether in a negative or positive sense—that is lacking in the baroque fantastication almost exclusively concerned with exploiting the motif for the purpose of virtuosic display and the turning of a startling conceit.

The motif of the noontide retreat—or, it would be better to say, the reatreat from midday—is the chief direction taken by the topos in the eighteenth century, although within this limit there is important variety. Many instances of midday occur in poems that take their title from the summer season, a not surprising fact in view of the symbolic and archetypal equation that obtains between the season and the hour, a matter touched on at the beginning of the introduction. Precisely because the century gave rise to an exceptionally rich development of poetry of the seasons, it is worthwhile to pause on a matter of interest to our theme: outside of the cyclic poems on the seasons, where a place for it was obligatory, summer was much less often taken as a subject by poets than spring and autumn.[24] Just as winter was a relatively unsung season, because of its unpleasant associations with hardships, meteorological severity, and even chthonian implications, so too summer, especially in the southern climes, could be forbidding because of the opposite natural phenomenon of a sun turned cruel, pouring down debilitating heat and relentless light. Concomitantly, of the four principal time divisions of the day, midday (or noontide) is the one least celebrated by poets outside the context of poems making use of the pattern of the diurnal cycle. Paul Van Tieghem notes that in eighteenth-century nature poetry the sun is invariably described either as rising, or, more often, as setting.[25] This suggests not just a predilection that derives from conscious or unconscious archetypal associations, but a deliberate eschewal of the depiction of the midday hours in which the sun is at or near its zenith. The same preference or prejudice is to be noted in painting. Indeed, in his *Polygraphice*, which saw eight editions between 1672 and 1701, William Salmon gave precise guidelines in this sense: "And if you express the Sun, let it be as rising or setting, and as it were behind or over some hill or mountain."[26] To be sure, the actual depiction of the sun at the zenith in all its refulgence would hardly be possible in a directly representational art. But the advice given by Salmon seems to betray a bias that stems from more than just a realistic or practical principle. That the midday sun was represented directly (in a manner of speaking) in the verse of the eighteenth century we know from the descriptive poetry of James Thomson and others who were among the determining forces in the development of a new feeling for nature in Europe, but even a brief look at these writers' references will reveal the presence of a negative attitude toward the midday hour.

It has been rightly said of Thomson's *The Seasons* that "the whole poem gathers significance from the conception of all nature as revelation of God."[27] In the section *Summer* (which is structured on the main parts of the day) Thomson himself wrote "Great are the scenes with dreadful Beauty crowned," and "Deep-roused, I feel / A sacred terror, a severe delight / Creep through my moral frame" (540-542). However, this *frisson* of the sublime and the sentiment of the numinous are experienced by the poet not in the "undistinguished blaze" and "all-conquering heat" of the "raging noon" he has so dramatically described (432-455), but rather in the "midnight depth" of the shady grove into which he has retired seeking refuge. This is the grove of meditation, that is, of an activity not possible in "the bright severity of noon." In keeping with his tendency to allegorize the various faces of nature in philosophical or theological terms, Thomson's noonscape equates the deep cool shade first with equanimity and serenity and then with numinous presentiments, whereas naked midday is made to stand for the restlessness and torment of the unwise and unvirtuous world that "unsatisfied and sick tosses in noon" (464). Raging noon is "a jarring world with vice inflam'd" (468). Such a moralization of midday is not new in itself, for we recall that Petrarch in his meditation proposed the same symbolic correspondence between a meteorologically intemperate noon and the ambitious man driven to restless and sinful activity. But Thomson reveals a fascination in the natural spectacle that is important, and even the retreat, in his case, is into a natural setting. Thus notwithstanding the negative moral associations he attaches to it in this part of the poem, Thomson's more circumstantial description of a noontide where "a dazzling deluge reigns" and "distressful Nature pants" has its own inherent grandeur and sublimity.

Despite a conscious shifting of emphasis from the aesthetic of the sublime (characteristic of Thomson) to a more utilitarian intent and a taste tending toward *la belle nature*, the context of another series of *Saisons* allowed even the French poet Jean-François de Saint-Lambert in *L'été* (with echoes from Thomson) to evoke effectively the brutal heat, cruel light, and sense of languor connected with a summer noontide. In his noonscape, too, the sun rains down fire and

> Tout brille confondu dans la lumière immense.
> La campagne gémit sous les rayons brûlants.[r]
> (169-170)

[r] Everything sparkles merged in the immense light.
The countryside moans under the burning rays.

A circumstantial genre description shows man, animal world, and vegetation in a state of languor in the midst of a vast stasis where

> Tout est morne, brûlant, tranquille; et la lumière
> Est seule en mouvement dans la nature entière.ˢ
>
> (200-201)

The conventional but archetypal retreat to a cool shady forest that follows by way of contrast not only is in line with the pattern of Thomson's poem, it also carries the same connotations of the numinous and the sublime.[28] The *forêt sacrée* instills a sensation of "agréable horreur," and "Le plaisir que j'éprouve est mêlé de terreur." Again we note that it is not in the immense still brightness of absolute midday that Divinity is revealed, but here in the "calme universel" of the shady primeval forest that "Tout semble autour de moi plein de l'Être suprême." And again raging noon seems to bespeak the Absolute in its negative character of menace and destruction.

Noonscapes sometimes tend to take on the character of a hymn to the sun, and in this respect the voice of Ossian—another influential guide in the formation of a new feeling for nature—should be heard here in the Italian version of Melchiorre Cesarotti. In a passage that is indeed a hymn to the sun, there is a brief allusion to the *terribilità* and the threatening Gorgon face of the sun which is surely a reference to high noon:

> Sole del ciel, quanto è terribil mai
> La tua beltà, quando vapor sanguigni
> Sgorghi sul suol, quando la morte oscura
> Sta ne' tuoi crini raggruppata e attorta!ᵗ
>
> (*Temora*, II)

ˢ All is sad, ablaze, calm; and the light
   Alone is in motion in the whole of nature.
ᵗ Sun of heaven, how vastly terrible
   Is your beauty, when blood-red vapors
   You spout upon the earth, when dark death
   Crouched and writhing is in your mane.

Cesarotti's brief comment on this passage to the effect that it may refer to a miasmatic infection is interesting ("Par che accenni il tempo di qualche infezione").[29] And indeed it seems that the "primitive" bard Ossian betrays, by way of Macpherson and Cesarotti, a biblical reminiscence of considerable importance: the *daemon meridianus*, or the pestilence and "the destruction that wasteth at noon."

Although the use of a distressful midsummer noonscape as a decorative foil to an idealized, rarefied landscape could allow, and perhaps called for, an element of realism in the representation of noontide, eighteenth-century Italian descriptive poetry tends to eschew the sublime and suggestions of *terribilità* that came to be associated with that season and hour. The direction of Italian Arcadians was clearly toward an aesthetic of the *piacevole* and the reduction of nature to *la bella campagna* serving as a backdrop for erotic gallantry or pleasant reveries.[30] Nonetheless, the cases in which a midsummer noontide appears as a theme are not wholly without effective touches of realism and a certain negative grandeur. Even for the Arcadians, at the hour of midday nature still asserts itself as an aggressive, overmastering protagonist. This is the case, for example in a poem entitled simply "L'estate" ("Summer," 1724) by Pietro Metastasio, the major Arcadian poet of the age. Although this long *canzonetta*, which predates the vogue of Thomson, Saint-Lambert, and other influential non-Italians, describes the negative aspects of summer in general, the description inevitably suggests noontide or the hottest hours of the day. Indeed, the poem is an excellent illustration of the fact that the true hour of midsummer is noon. The fiery sun liquefies the sands: "E già sotto al raggio ardente / Così bollono le arene, / Che alla barbara Cirene / Più cocente il sol non è;" a vast drought marks the landscape; a weary, perspiring reaper lies sleeping while an equally lifeless dog languishes beside his inert master; a bull (pastoral symbol of erotic energy) who earlier had been prancing and butting tree trunks now lies meekly by a stream, languidly lowing in the direction of an "enamored" cow who replies in kind; fearful of the scorching sun no bird is on the wing; the nightingale becomes silent, yielding to the shrill cicadas in the beech trees; serpents in new skins sun themselves. For all the Arcadian coloring and lilting rhythm of the verses, the description offers us an extended genre sketch with realistic notations of the countryside at noon. It is against this background that the poet entreats Phyllis to retreat with him to a shady spot which—such is this Arcadian pastoral oasis—is protected not only from the invading sun but also from anything so uncouth as a real shepherd tending sheep ("Né pastor greggia importuna / Vi conduce a pascolar").

In Metastasio's poem, as in those of other Arcadians on the same subject, the distress of nature during a summer noontide continues to function as a metaphor or mirror for the poet's erotic passion, albeit in a somewhat oblique way. Here, at any rate, love (in the person of a compliant Phyllis) together with a more amenable nature having the standard Arcadian trappings are set up in order to neutralize the effects (or the thought) of that disturbing and disagreeable season and hour.[31] One sees that the poem is structured on a contrast, if not a tension, between the harsh realistic circumstances of country life—emblematized by the summer noontide—and an idyllized vision. The escape from naked noon by seeking refuge in a *locus amoenus* is an Arcadian variation of the pastoral, but no less authentic a version than is the desire to escape from the city or the court into the countryside. We have seen that it goes back, in Italian literature, to Boccaccio's *Ameto* and the *Decameron*.

As a statement of the close relationship between sultry midday and erotic pursuit, a poem ("L'estate") by Metastasio's contemporary Carlo Innocenzo Frugoni shows us that Arcadians could be as witty as the Marinisti while rejecting the convoluted metaphors of the latter. Here it is Love who knocks directly at the poet's door and asks for shelter from the torrid noontide that consumes him:

> Apri, mi dice Amore,
> Teco dal dì focoso
> Mi venni a riparar;

> Apri la tua capanna:
> Il fervido meriggio
> Vedi, come m'affanna
> Come mi fa languir.[u]
> (6-12)

This amounts to a direct equation between midday torpor and erotic languor. Love, however, has evidently asked only for a brief respite, and he goes on to announce that he must continue his search for Dori even now under the sun that blazes from the meridian, while shepherds and their flocks do not dare leave hut and fold. But is there anything one would not suffer in pursuit of so sweet a nymph?

> Sebben nel ciel fiammeggia
> Alto il Titanio lume,
> Né pastorel né greggia
> Osa lasciar l'ovil;
> Dori per rinvenire,
> Fenderò l'aure ardenti:
> Che non si può soffrire
> Per ninfa sì gentil?[v][32]
> (89-96)

Fortunately, Love's perceptive eyes allow him to see that Dori is in the poet-shepherd's heart. It is then an easy task for him to shoot his arrow at her! However frivolous this may seem

---

[u] Open, says Love to me,
I have come to you for shelter
From the fiery day.

Open your hut:
See how the searing midday
Torments me and
How it makes me languish

[v] Although the Titanic light
Flames high in the sky,
And neither shepherd nor flock
Dares to leave the fold,
In order to find Dori
I will cleave the burning air.
What may one not put up with
For so lovely a nymph?

on the surface, such a reduction of Corydon's noontime erotic distress (in Virgil's eclogue) to amatory gallantry yet reveals something about the age's attempt to neutralize the forbidding face of midday.

Despite the growing popularity of Thomson and even of Ossian, it is this "Metastasian" mood and manner, with its overtly hedonistic intent, that we find also in the later Arcadians of the century. Of these the most interesting figure in connection with our theme is Giovanni Meli, one of Italy's many writers to use a dialect (here, Sicilian) rather than Italian. Meli's depiction of noon occurs in yet another poem on summer ("L'està") which in turn has its place in the context of a four-seasons cycle under the title *La Buccolica* (*Bucolic*). One of the main themes of *La Buccolica* as a whole is the desire for idyllic serenity in a world ruled by love. In the "Primavera" section love figures as a universal law of nature, and spring is the sweet season of awakening to the surge of erotic energy.[33] Love is a driving, vital force experienced as a "certu focu dilicatu" ("certain delicate fire"), and there is a harmonious relationship between man and an almost humanized nature. The same concept of love as the necessary vital drive and law of nature continues into "L'està," but now spring's gentle verdant landscape gives way to a Sicilian countryside scourged by a vehement sun that corresponds to the raging erotic fire and drought in the heart of the lover. "Aju in pettu àutri ciammi ed àutri vampi; / Un nonsocchì, chi prima fu gentili, / E 'un appartau chi un duci batticori, / Quantu ora è amaru, ohimè! quant'è crudili!" (24-27).[w] So laments a lovesick, shade-seeking Tityrus who notes that it is the hour of fiery high noon—"mentri chi d'intornu / Regna lu suli, e tuttu brucia ed ardi"—and goes on to observe that as sheep and kine move toward the shade and birds rest wearily in their nests, only the cold serpents expose themselves to the sun's burning rays. Here Tityrus pauses to listen to the piping and singing of Tyrsis who (in a *canzonetta*) gives a more cir-

[w] In my breast I carry other flames and other blazes; / A certain feeling, which at first was pleasant, / And caused me only a sweet palpitation, / But now how bitter it is, alas! how cruel.

cumstantial series of genre sketches of the midday scene, culminating in the picture of a fierce luminosity in which a blasted nature is reduced to painful immobility:

> Li venti chiù nun ciàtanu,
> Nè chiù lu voscu scrusci,
> Ma movi l'ali musci
> Un zefiru chi c'è.
>
> S'infocanu li vàuci
> Sutta l'ardenti lampa,
> Chi scarmuscisci e allampa
> L'irvuzza virdi, ohimè![x]
> (110-117)

Tyrsis's song goes on in conventional fashion to invite the maid Licori to a shady *locus amoenus*: "C'è un fonti 'mmenzu all'àrvuli, / Chi l'umbri si nutrìca; / Quannu lu suli pica, / Lu friscu è tuttu ddà" (142-145).[y] Although the retreat from nature in its oppressive, hurtful mood is itself both a natural (and sensible) reaction and an ancient literary motif, it is symptomatic of the tyranny of the Arcadian aesthetic and vision that the greater part of Meli's *canzonetta* exploits this motif of the escape from raging noon in order to describe love's pastoral oasis.

A more interesting insight into the "natural" aversion to midday and the eighteenth century's particular mode in expressing it can be found in two writers whose works, while partaking of Arcadian features, belong more intimately to the preromantic current of that time. These are Aurelio De' Giorgi-Bertola and Ippolito Pindemonte. Thus in an introductory letter to his summer poem, "L'estate," Bertola himself tells us that his ventures into the midst of nature were

---

[x] The wind no longer blows,
  No longer is there rustling in the woods,
  But a soft breeze wafts its light wings.
  The valley slopes become aflame
  Under the burning light
  That wastes and dessicates the tender grass, oh woe!

[y] There is a fount in the midst of the trees, / Which nourishes them for itself; / When the sun is directly above, / Coolness remains constant there.

made with the poetry of James Thomson in hand and that in his own poems on the seasons he has been guided by his illustrious predecessor.[34] Equally significant is his reference to the fact that most of the poets who have dealt with the seasons have done so almost as a pretext for the writing of amatory verse. For his own part, he will not touch on love because he would keep nature prominently before us in its true colors. This attitude seems clearly to suggest a dissatisfaction with the Arcadian manner. In the poem itself, Bertola traces the pattern of the diurnal course of the sun from morning to midday and evening, and, in doing so, he too, like Thomson, notes that nature undergoes a change from gentleness and beauty in the spring to opulence, sublimity, and grandeur in the summer. But noontide is seen by him only in generic terms and not in a very destructive mood. Hence there is little enough of Thomson here. Though the sun at noon is majestic, it is a "conquistator benefico" ("benign conqueror"), and a fleeting reference to the suffering of nature at that hour serves only to introduce the motif of the invitation to retreat to a shady bower: "Or che il terren d'intorno / Sotto al meriggio geme, / Arrestati, riposati; / Nel gran calor del giorno / L'ombra cerchiamo insieme."[z] Alas, the further invitation is neither to Arcadian dalliance nor to Socratic dialogue, and least of all to Thomsonian meditation.[35] Rather, in what can only be described as a spiritual and artistic letdown (even in the context of Bertola's mediocre verse), the poet suggests that a nap is in order.

It is a curious but revealing fact that in his very readable prose sketches of nature, Bertola writes enthusiastically and eloquently of morning and sunset but does not touch on midday.[36] And yet he dedicated a poem to the theme of noon in the context of a cycle on the four parts of the day. The author's dedicatory letter acknowledges the popularity of the subject of the four parts of the day, especially in French poetry. As a claim to originality, however, it also points out that this new cycle is different inasmuch as it connects the

---

[z] Now that the land all around / Suffers under the midday sky, / Stop here, and rest; / In the great heat of the day / Let us seek the shade together.

theme with a setting by the sea.[37] But Bertola's "Mezzogiorno" ("Midday") has little to say about midday. Its aim is to show that even at noon the seaside offers sights and activities no less pleasant than those of the countryside: "Ha sul meriggio ancora / I suoi diletti il mar" (8-9). The only notation on the character of the hour is a conventional reference to the scorching hour ("cocente giorno," 37), relief from which can be had in a sea grotto, a convenient marine substitute for the thick forest and shady pastoral arbors that inlanders revert to. Again, however, there is no turning to philosophical reflection.

More instructive even than Bertola in the matter of aesthetic and psychological aversion to midday is Ippolito Pindemonte. Author of a diurnal cycle in verse—"Le quattro parti del giorno" ("The Four Parts of the Day")—included as part of his *Poesie campestri* (*Poems of the Country*) in 1795, he published the poems in conjunction with a series of prose meditations (*Prose campestri*, *Prose Pieces of the Country*) on the pleasures of solitude for a contemplative country gentleman. As in the case of his friend Bertola's prose sketches, Pindemonte's prose makes specific references to morning (or sunrise), evening (or sunset), and even to night—all with symbolic intent—as welcome moments conducive to reflection:

> Una delle più rare scene, che la campagna ci offra, è quella del Sole nel suo tramontare. Ella m'è ancor più cara di quella del Sol nascente, forse in grazia d'una di quelle considerazioni, che si fanno quasi senza avvedersene. Il Sole, che nasce, sappiamo che rimarrà con noi per alcune ore: quello, che muore, nol rivedremo che il giorno appresso. Ora non è egli così d'ogni cosa, che allora ci par più preziosa e grande, che ci sfugge e abbandona?[aa][38]

[aa] One of the choicest scenes that nature offers us is that of the Sun at its setting. The scene is dearer to me than that of the rising Sun, perhaps because of one of those reflections that we make almost subconsciously. We know that the Sun that rises will stay with us for some hours; that which dies we shall not see again until the next day. Now is it not the same with all things, that they seem greater and more precious to us when they slip from us and abandon us?

Shortly afterward, in this same preromantic vein, Pindemonte again points to the rising and setting of the sun, and also to the nocturnal sky with its moon and stars, as the moments in which nature evokes a sympathetic response in the sentitive soul. Those unmoved by these spectacles of nature are to be pitied: "Trista cosa a pensare che . . . un uomo vivo . . . non sia mai desto quando nasce il Sole, e desto egli dorma quando tramonta; e che a lui non piaccia la Luna, se non perchè gli scusa una lampada; e niente a lui dica, mai niente, la stelleggiata volta notturna."[bb][39] Again, the absence from the prose of any reference to the sun at its meridian is all the more significant in view of the fact that in the poems, to which the *Prose campestri* serve as a sort of long preface, the motif does appear. As in the case of Bertola, one can reasonably assume that its appearance in the poetry was dictated by the prescribed pattern for representing the four parts of the day. A look at the section corroborates this impression that he deliberately shunned the noontide period.

Indeed, the "Mezzogiorno" portion of "Le quattro parti del giorno" testifies rather clearly to an avoidance of a direct encounter. In the section on morning—"Il mattino"—the poet greeted the rising sun with an act of devotion, hailing it as the great custodian of nature and the visible image of God ("Io ti saluto e inchino, o di natura / Custode e ad occhio uman visibil Dio"); and in the section on evening—"La sera"—the setting sun contemplated directly by him figures as the image of the approaching close of life, a thought it inspires in a gently melancholy way by virtue of the magical charm of the soft pink of its dying rays (stanza I). But from the very opening of the midday section of the cycle the sun is allowed to appear only filtered through the enmeshed overhanging foliage of a thick grove of trees. The invading, vanquishing blaze of noon thus appears only indirectly in the fifteen octaves of the poem. Yet, for a moment at least, the very deliberateness with which

---

[bb] It is sad to think . . . that a living man . . . is never awake when the Sun rises, and, after awaking, that he sleeps when it sets; and that the Moon does not please him except for the reason that it saves him the use of a lamp; and that the starry nocturnal sky says nothing to him, absolutely nothing.

Pindemonte seeks to neutralize the hour suggests he was aware of an inimical force. Inviting the reader to linger in this shady spot by the banks of the river, the poet notes that the very act of gazing into the cool waves tempers the heat of the hour. And in this idealized spot a softly caressing but fresh breeze is also present as a restorative. Any tension that is intimated in the contrast between raging noon and the protected area of the refuge is quickly dissipated as Pindemonte relaxes into a bucolically serene landscape of withdrawl conducive to his meditation on the moral and utilitarian lesson that nature offers. Nonetheless, although this invitation is on a higher plane than what Bertola is able to extend to his readers as midday entertainment, it is still a far cry from the grandiose noontide atmosphere (even in the retreat) that leads to Thomsonian reflection. In conclusion, then, it may be said that for Pindemonte midday is perceived almost wholly as a negative spot of time that disturbs the serenity that this poet, in keeping with the dominant trend of his age, looks for in a tamed and idyllized nature. To most of that age one could apply Valéry's thought (but without the drama that led him to it) that "Midi . . . convient à soi-même," and, perhaps even more, the maxim by La Rochefoucauld with which we opened this chapter: "Le soleil ni la mort ne se peuvent regarder fixement."[40]

II. The Nineteenth Century

Il sol sa l'ombra, ma non l'ombra il sol.
(*Arturo Onofri*)

Although the motif of a retreat from the naked face of midday into a shady *locus amoenus* was not to be abandoned, the nineteenth century reveals a marked predilection for face-to-face encounters or for a meditation on the mystery of noontide in its own light. But a divergence from the previous age's typical attitude toward midday is found also in the idealization of the hour itself. For example, Arcadian midday dalliance and preromantic meditation, both involving a retreat to shade, may give way to a revival of ancient nympholepsy in the form of a nostalgic evocation of a lost Eden. This is what we find in the romanticizing neoclassicism of Ugo Foscolo at the outset of the century. In the episodic poetry of *Le Grazie* (*The Graces*), with its dream of a superior world of the spirit, one of the shortest and most incantatory fragments evokes a pagan vision of utter serenity. From his refuge on the hill of Bellosguardo, looking out toward Florence at noon when the air is still and silence reigns, the poet hears the piping of a faun who is calling his flock to the cool waters of a pastoral oasis:

> Io dal mio poggio
> Quando tacciono i venti fra le torri
> Della vaga Firenze, odo un Silvano
> Ospite ignoto a' taciti eremiti
> Del vicino Oliveto: ei sul meriggio
> Fa sua casa un frascato, a suon d'avena
> Le pecorelle sue chiama alla fonte.[a]
> (II, 396–402)

[a] From my hillock
When the winds are quiet amid the towers

The distinction between reality and the dream is not dramatically posed as is so often the case in Foscolo's poetry and in that of the Italian Romantics who follow him but seems simply to be obliterated. And yet, while the juxtaposition of the faun (or Silvanus) and the Christian anchorites—"taciti eremiti"—in the convent of Monte Oliveto who are unaware of his presence (he is an "ospite ignoto" to them) does not make for a disturbing polemical thrust, it does establish a contrast between the present world of reality, which has shut out such mythical creatures with all they stand for, and the classically idyllized pre-Christian past evoked by the poet in a sort of revery that is very much like a memory.

It is this idealistic and serene vision of an age when men believed in life-enhancing illusions and in the harmony between man and nature, that the hero of Foscolo's youthful epistolary novel *Ultime lettere di Jacopo Ortis* (*The Last Letters of Jacopo Ortis*) evokes in a noontide revery on the banks of a lake:

> O Lorenzo! sto spesso sdraiato su la riva del lago de' cinque fonti: mi sento vezzeggiare la faccia e le chiome dai venticelli che alitando sommovono l'erba, e allegrano i fiori, e increspano le limpide acque del lago. Lo credi tu? Io delirando deliziosamente mi veggo dinanzi le Ninfe ignude, saltanti, inghirlandate di rose, e invoco in lor compagnia le Muse e l'Amore; e fuor dei rivi che cascano sonanti e spumosi, vedo uscir sino al petto con le chiome stillanti sparse su le spalle rugiadose, e con gli occhi ridenti, le Najadi, amabili custodi delle fontane. —*Illusioni*! grida il filosofo. —Or non è tutto illusione? tutto! Beati gli antichi che si credeano degni de' baci delle immortali dive del cielo.[b1]

Of beautiful Florence, I hear a Faun
Unknown guest of the silent anchorites
Of neighboring Oliveto: He at noontide
Makes his home in a leafy bower, with his oaten flute
He calls his sheep to the spring.

[b] O Lorenzo! I often lie stretched out on the bank of the lake of the five sources: I feel my face and hair caressed by the gently blowing breezes that stir the grass, gladden the flowers, and ripple the clear waters of the lake. Can you believe it? In a sweet delirium, I see naked nymphs dancing before me,

Though specific mention of the hour is not made in this passage, there can be no doubt that this is that midday nympholepsy which, as we noted earlier, was spoken of frequently by the ancients themselves. There is, however, one very important difference: Foscolo has left out all intimations of dread or terror and the negative possibilities that the ancients associated with the phenomenon and that even Boccaccio (though hardly with real religious awe) felt it necessary to acknowledge in the scene from *Ameto*.[2] What is left is a nostalgically neoclassicizing midday eroticism without tension, a feature that differentiates this vision from such subsequent erotic nympholepsy (poised between dream and reality or, again, evoked in a zone between dream and memory) as we shall find in Leopardi, Mallarmé, and Ungaretti.

While it is true that in the context of Foscolo's novel the vision is consciously contrasted with the bleakness of reality, it should be noted that reality impinges not during the revery itself but rather at a later moment, in the act of recalling the revery and writing about it. It is only then that Foscolo's hero, anticipating the scoffing challenge of hard-headed realists, is provoked into defending it. The midday vision itself, however, is represented as a tensionless experience.[3] And this, significantly enough, is essential to the larger, polemical purpose for which the author has indeed brought the topos into play. When we take this vision of noontide nympholepsy together with the attack the hero makes against the "philosophers" who would seek to dismiss it as a useless sentimental indulgence in illusions, we recognize that it figures as an emblematic statement of a refined but radical primitivism. In this sense the episode, brief as it is, has considerable importance in the economy of the novel. Coming almost at the halfway mark, it dramatizes the central theme of the work

---

wreathed with roses; and along with them I invoke the Muses and Love. And from the rivulets that fall resoundingly and frothily, I see the Naiads, sweet guardians of the founts, emerge up to their breasts, with their dripping locks strewn over their dewy shoulders and eyes sparkling with laughter.—Illusions! The philosopher cries out.—But is not everything an illusion? Everything! How blessed were the ancients who considered themselves worthy of the kisses of the immortal goddesses of heaven.

(and of the Romantic spirit in general), that is, the conflict between the real and the ideal and the superiority of the latter. Yet Foscolo's implementation of the midday motif in neoclassic garb is not a case of naive escapism. By it he contributes to the myth that mankind in antiquity was happier than modern man, but insofar as that happier condition is sensed as having its cause in a spontaneous and harmonious relationship with nature—and also in a religious respect (without dread) for the beautiful forms of nature—the myth has ethical value. The value would be real even if one were to limit it by insisting that Foscolo's evocations partake of the Romantic predisposition to set up the dream as a palliative or restorative to the pain brought by reality. For it was a very crass as well as real world that offended the poet. Thus it should not seem odd that the most serene visions of midday—even of midday eroticism—come from the writer who is Italy's foremost example of the restless, tormented Romantic spirit.

However serene Foscolo's midday evocations may be, the paganizing value in them is real enough, and on that account they could not have found favor with Alessandro Manzoni.[4] On the other hand, it is this most self-possessed of Italy's Romantics who supplies us with a contrasting image of a fierce summer midday sun, used as a term of a simile to describe a more violent erotic mood. For in addition to not being a prude, and despite his belief that too much had been written about love, Manzoni in his own works penetrated into the depths of passion and the female heart with an insight and delicacy unmatched by any Italian writer after him. As the tragedy *Adelchi*, the undisputed masterwork of Italy's Romantic theatre, is the most Romantic of Manzoni's works, so Ermengarda, the queen repudiated by Charlemagne, is the author's most genuinely Romantic heroine. (The fascinatingly lurid figure of Gertrude in *I promessi sposi* has something of the eighteenth-century Gothic tale about her.) It is a most interesting but, as far as I know, uncommented-on fact that the great chorus on Ermengarda's death draws metaphors from the three principal moments of the diurnal solar cycle in order to objectify the spiritual drama of the ever-enamored queen. In the first moment, her passion is said to find relief in thoughts of divine love, a condition that is likened to the restorative effect brought to parched grass by the gentle dew that accompanies the soft light of dawn (61-72). But like the sun, Ermengarda's passion—her memories will give her no respite—rises again and, returning to its zenith, scourges her with the implacable fury of a breezeless, torrid high noon that soon scorches the newly revived blades of grass:

> Ma come il sol che reduce
> L'erta infocata ascende,
> E con la vampa assidua
> L'immobil aura incende,
> Risorti appena i gracili
> Steli riarde al suol;
> Ratto così dal tenue
> Obblìo torna immortale
> L'amor sopito, e l'anima
> Impaurita assale,
> E le sviate immagini
> Richiama al noto duol.[c]
>
> (73-84)

This is not, as some commentators think, the sun only as it rises and appears above the horizon. To be sure, the past participle in the phrase *erta infocata* very likely refers to the red color of the sky announcing the imminent appearance of the sun itself. But it is to be noted that the poet is careful to indicate that the sun has returned ("il sol reduce") and already as-

---

[c] But as the sun which has returned
Climbs its enflamed incline,
And with its relentless blaze
Inflames the motionless air,
And burns back to the ground
The delicate stems that had recently revived;
    Just as swiftly, from a tenuous
Forgetfulness love that had recessed returns
Undying and assails
The frightened soul,
And brings back the diverted images
To her well-known suffering.

cends its "enflamed path." In particular, the implacable fire ("la vampa assidua") that "burns" the "motionless" air ("l'immobil aura") is an unmistakable sign of the destructive sun of a raging summer noon, evoked, as in the case of Virgil's second eclogue, to figure the erotic passion. What Manzoni has done is to telescope the two "moments" of sunrise and midday in order to emblematize the dramatic daily return of Ermengarda's passionate memories and the swift course they follow in reaching their cruel zenith. The idea that a diurnal solar pattern is the emblematic structure of the chorus is strengthened by the poet's use of the image of sunset at the close after the reference to the final, irrevocable turning of Ermengarda's thoughts to God in her dying moments. At the end of the storm of the queen's life, as at the end of a tempestuous day (the meteorological metaphor has been appropriately modified), there appears a setting sun whose reddish rays, breaking through the dissipating clouds, are interpreted in terms of Christian hope as the promise of a succeeding "day" of eternal calm and peace.[5]

Of the three major figures of the Romantic age, it is Italy's greatest modern lyric poet, Giacomo Leopardi, who reveals the most frequent and most significant absorption with the midday motif. He is, we may say, a pivotal figure in the history of our theme, for he both summarizes some of the main features of earlier midday mythologizing and points the way to a profounder sounding of noontide that was to influence later writers. Already at the age of eleven, in a series of five poetic exercises (*canzonette*) on the theme of the countryside that reveal he was even then familiar with both the classical idyll and eighteenth-century treatments of the subject, Leopardi wrote of the seasons and the parts of the day. The fourth poem of the group, "La campagna" ("The Country"), is a wholly idyllized view of summer at morning and noon. Industrious field hands rise with the sun and work happily through the morning. Midday follows bringing with it a satisfying pause. No sense of solar oppression or dread here. As the sun now shines with greater brilliance, the workers retreat to the shade of a large tree where they partake of their frugal lunch. But they remain a happy group—"Felice turba rustica"—living in a healthy, uninquiring relationship with a benign nature and, one assumes, an equally benign landowner.[6] This early poetic exercise on the theme was itself preceded by a passage in prose entitled "Descrizione del Sole per i suoi effetti" ("Description of the Sun as Seen in its Effects"). Here the sun is said to double its heat as well as its light at midday; yet it is meltingly sweet to see the peasants halt their work for the noonday pause. In their life free from treachery and filled with peace, these peasants are more blessed than the great rulers of the earth![7]

The interest in the midday hour was to acquire a new dimension and profounder insight in the adolescent Leopardi who included a chapter on the topic ("Del Meriggio," "On Noontide") in his erudite compilation, *Saggio sopra gli errori popolari degli antichi* (*Essay on the Popular Superstitions of the Ancients*, 1815). That chapter opens with an idyllic noonscape that does not seem psychologically or ethically more complex than the vision of the eleven-year-old boy, although, of course, besides revealing some new elements in the scene described, it is more sophisticated in its formulation:

> Tutto brilla nella natura all'istante del meriggio. L'agricoltore, che prende cibo e riposo; i buoi sdraiati e coperti d'insetti volanti, che, flagellandosi colle code per cacciarli, chinano di tratto in tratto il muso, sopra cui risplendono interrottamente spesse stille di sudore, e abboccano negligentemente e con pausa il cibo sparso innanzi ad essi; il gregge assetato, che col capo basso si affolla, e si rannicchia sotto l'ombra; la lucerta, che corre timida a rimbucarsi, strisciando rapidamente e per intervalli lungo una siepe; la cicala, che riempie l'aria di uno stridore continuo e monotono; la zanzara, che passa ronzando vicino all'orecchio; l'ape, che vola incerta, e si ferma su di un fiore, e parte, e torna al luogo donde è partita; tutto è bello, tutto è delicato e toccante.[d][8]

[d] Everything sparkles in nature during the midday period. The farm worker who takes his rest and food; the oxen, lying down and shrouded by

As with the earlier (1809) noonscapes, midday here inspires neither dread nor distress. Greater attention is given to the scene, but despite a potentially negative detail or two (e.g., the shrill cicadas), the hour and the setting convey a sense of tranquillity and even of a joyful value in nature. The mood or affective quality associated with nature is declared in the words *delicato e toccante* used in their eighteenth-century sense of *tender and touching*, and there is a sense of luxurious torpor or languor suggested by the few signs of reduced motion and life that do exist in this genre piece. But this idyllic noontide, so thoroughly bereft of any intimation of the uncanny or the supernatural, indeed, of any tension, is meant to function as an anticipatory but contrasting vision setting off the subsequent long discussion on midday as a time of bewilderment, beginning with the comment: "Who would think that for the ancients midday was a time of dread if they themselves had not taken the trouble to inform us about it with care?"[9] Accordingly, there follows a series of references, with many duly quoted passages from classical, biblical, and early Christian writings, to midday as the hour of Pan and "Panic" terror, to the midday demon, to the apparition of gods and goddesses at noon, etc., all given as evidence that the ancients considered that time of day with a sense of religious awe and dread: "È dunque evidente che gli antichi aveano del tempo del meriggio una grande idea, e lo riguardavano come sacro e terribile."[10] All of which the young Leopardi—at sixteen still unshaken in his faith in reason and Christianity's revealed truths—registers as superstitions which modern enlightened man has fortunately expunged from his experience! But one

---

flying insects, flailing themselves with their tails in order to chase them away; from time to time they lower their snouts on which thick drops of sweat glisten continuously, and lazily, with long pauses, take a mouthful of the fodder scattered before them; and the thirsty flock of sheep that crowd together with lowered heads and huddle under the shade; the lizard that runs timidly to hide itself again, slithering quickly and at intervals along a hedge; the cicada that fills the air with a steady monotonous stridor; the mosquito that buzzes by one's ear; the bee that flies uncertainly, stops on a flower, sets off again, and returns to the spot it started from. Everything is beautiful, everything is tender and touching.

would not be wrong in detecting a very real attraction to those "popular" superstitions.

Certainly, it was not long, we know, before a disenchanted Leopardi was to lament the loss of these and other illusions or "errors" of the age of fable. Yet the rationalist in him and his low esteem for modern man always kept him from any serious attempt to reactivate or renew them in a mythical way. It is in keeping with his unyielding rationalism and pessimism that in his mature verse the only evocation of midday as a time when sylvan deities and the goddess Diana appear occurs in the poem "Alla primavera" which, as its subtitle—"o delle favole antiche"—suggests, is a nostalgic farewell to the happy age of fable:

> Già di candide ninfe i rivi albergo,
> Placido albergo e specchio
> Furo i liquidi fonti. Arcane danze
> D'immortal piede i ruinosi gioghi
> Scossero e l'ardue selve (oggi romito
> Nido de' venti): e il pastorel ch'all'ombre
> Meridiane incerte ed al fiorito
> Margo adducea de' fiumi
> Le sitibonde agnelle, arguto carme
> Sonar d'agresti Pani
> Udì lungo le ripe; e tremar l'onda
> Vide, e stupì, che non palese al guardo
> La faretrata Diva
> Scendea ne' caldi flutti, e dall'immonda
> Polve tergea della sanguigna caccia
> Il niveo lato e le verginee braccia.[e]
>
> (23-38)

[e] Once to fair nymphs the streams were an abode,
Calm abode and mirror
Were the limpid fountains. The arcane dancing
Of immortal feet shook the precipitous ridges
And the arduous woods (now the desolate
Home of winds): and the shepherd who into
Uncertain midday shade and to the flowery
Edge of rivers led
His thirsting lambs, heard the shrill song [piping]

It is hardly necessary to note that this vision, especially when taken in its context, is incomparably more complex in aesthetic, affective, and psychological values than the earlier Arcadian-inspired noon pieces of Leopardi himself or of his eighteenth-century predecessors. Here too, at the center of the vision, is a shepherd leading his flock to a shady retreat and stream.[11] But how much richer is the life of this shepherd and how much more real is the desire of the poet to identify with him in hearing the voice of the fauns and, still more, in looking about for Diana who, he knows, should be there bathing. The vision evokes a sense of something sacred, but still without dread; an evocation, rather, of awe and marvel. Though more circumstantial in its depiction, the quality of its mood of nympholepsy without terror is of the same kind as that which permeates Foscolo's marvelous fragments from *Le Grazie* and the *Ultime lettere di Jacopo Ortis*, except that Leopardi's passage also conveys a poignant sense of the irretrievability of a lost pastoral Eden, which Foscolo, on the other hand, seems for a moment to have fully recovered. Foscolo's visions, we recall, are given as experiences lived by the poet himself in the present tense, whereas Leopardi's evocation refers the experience to the third person and has all the verbs in the past tense. Indeed, it is Leopardi's passage, especially when seen in its fuller context where it figures as the vision of a prelapsarian condition that has been forever lost, that is the more specifically primitivistic and that more programmatically, if poignantly, develops the myth of the happier and healthier state of man in antiquity on the supposition that the ancients' belief in what modern man has repudiated as superstitions or illusions—the *errori popolari*—kept them in the condition that nature intended for them. More surprising, perhaps, is the fact that Leopardi's vision of noontide nym-

---

  Of sylvan fauns resound
  Along the banks; and he saw the waters
  Tremble, and marveled that unseen to him
  The quivered Goddess
  Descended into the warm waters, and cleansed
  Her snowy flanks and virgin arms
  From the unclean grime of the gory game.

pholepsy reveals a higher degree of erotic value than does Foscolo's. The reference to Diana is clearly in the line that comes directly from the Ovidian tale of Actaeon.[12]

But now the ill-fated hunter has been replaced by a shepherd who is in no danger of being punished. Nor, indeed, does the shepherd actually see the naked goddess. All this removes any sense of dread or apparent tension that might otherwise have been carried over from Ovid's account. Yet there is a more tremulous eroticism of secret desire present in the figure of this shepherd who seems to have come to the midday retreat as much in the hope of observing the ablutions of Diana as to bring his flock to drink. And is there not a certain ambiguity in the word *stupì* which perhaps suggests more disappointment than surprise in the shepherd because the goddess has not appeared or remains unseen by him? Furthermore, there is, I think, something like Romantic irony at work in these lines. That is, at the very center of the Edenic vision stands a protagonist who is denied the realization of his heart's desire no less than is the poet who has nostalgically evoked it. This being so, the relationship between this shepherd and the poet is one of identity. But though Leopardi stands both inside and outside his creation, there is no sardonic or capricious shattering of the vision itself, and no shift in its mood of incantatory nostalgia either without or within. Less overtly faunesque than the Petrarchan fantasy that also drew subtly from the Ovidian fount, Leopardi's passage nonetheless evokes a complex atmosphere of midday eroticism that, even more than Petrarch's poem, calls to mind Mallarmé's justly celebrated poem "L'après-midi d'un faune."[13]

As enchanting and poignant as the vision from "Alla primavera" is, there is a yet more remarkable noontide experience to be found in Leopardi. Presented as an actual encounter, it is wholly different from the "Alla primavera" passage and marks an even more radical departure from the Arcadian idyllizing of midday and nature into an ideal landscape or pleasance. Its unique character is further highlighted by the fact that it is built into the schema of a poem on the major parts of the day, a genre on whose popularity we have commented earlier in this study. That genre was itself connected, as in the case of Pindemonte, with the theme of the *beata solitudo* of which the second stanza (the *meriggio* section) in Leopardi's "La vita solitaria" ("The Solitary Life") represents a most extraordinary variation. The experience described therein takes place under a midday sun that neither vivifies nor blasts the earth, but silently reflects a still image of itself in the motionless waters of a lake on the banks of which the solitary poet sits without stirring:

> Talor m'assido in solitaria parte,
> Sovra un rialto, al margin d'un lago
> Di taciturne piante incoronato.
> Ivi, quando il meriggio in ciel si volve,
> La sua tranquilla imago il Sol dipinge,
> Ed erba o foglia non si crolla al vento,
> E non onda incresparsi, e non cicala
> Strider, nè batter penna augello in ramo,
> Nè farfalla ronzar, nè voce o moto
> Da presso nè da lunge odi nè vedi.
> Tien quelle rive altissima quiete;
> Ond'io quasi me stesso e il mondo obblio
> Sedendo immoto; a già mi par che sciolte
> Giaccian le membra mie, nè spirto o senso
> Più le commova, e lor quiete antica
> Co' silenzi del loco si confonde.[f]
>
> (23-38)

---

[f] At times I sit in a secluded place,
Upon a mound at the edge of a lake
Crowned with mute trees.
There, when midday displays itself in the sky,
The Sun depicts its tranquil image,
And neither grass nor leaf falls in wind,
No wave ripples, and no cicada
Chirrs, nor does any bird flutter in the boughs,
Nor butterfly [insect] buzz, neither sound nor movement
Near or far is heard or seen.
Deepest stillness reigns over those banks;
So that sitting motionless I well-nigh forget
Myself and the world; and already it seems my limbs

How different this midday scene and mood not only from the nostalgically pagan noonday dream of "Alla primavera" but even from the idyllic noonscape painted by Leopardi at the outset of the *meriggio* chapter of the *Saggio sopra gli errori popolari degli antichi*. The contrast is all the more striking in that the *Saggio* passage and the stanza from "La vita solitaria" mention several of the same elements. But whereas in the prose piece those elements are given as existing realities and reveal the presence of a degree of life—a series of reduced movements and sounds suggesting a pastoral or bucolic moment of sweet repose—the poem obliterates them and any suggestion of conventional pastoral *otium* by enumerating them in a series of negatives that refers to the total absence of all sound and movement. Here, in short, is an absolute stasis in the truest sense. There is neither sound nor motion in the grass and trees, for it is utterly windless; the lake itself is without a ripple; no bird flutters, no butterfly sports, and no mosquito or bee buzzes.[14] Now not even the cicada is heard! Most curious, and significant, is the absence of the theme of the oppressive scorching midday sun, for that theme in itself would intimate a sense of life in nature, suffering life, but life nonetheless. So too it would call attention to the "force," however negative, of the sun and thereby take away from the impression of total immobility. While Leopardi's evocation may imply the heat of noontide, it deliberately avoids any reference to it in order to focus on the absence of life. Nor is there any specific mention of a dazzling, blinding light, for much the same reasón. Thus it is as though the whole scene were bathed in the light of a midday sun without glare and without warmth. This is purposely not a violent or aggressive sun, and indeed Leopardi is careful to note that it is a calm image (*tranquilla imago*) of the sun that is reflected in the motionless waters of the lake. For here silence and stillness reign absolutely. And yet, we note, still no dread! Attuning himself to the setting, the poet *feels* himself being absorbed into a

---

Lie released, no spirit or feeling
Stirs them more, and their ancient [original] stillness
Merges with the silence of the spot.

moment of timelessness, all traces of consciousness and sentiency drained from him as he becomes one with the infinite stillness of this strange midday.[15]

In this most remarkable of noon pieces the hour of Pan seems to be entirely without the hushed sense of that august god's presence. And Leopardi's nature and sun at midday are quite unlike what Shelley spoke of in his "Lines Written among the Euganean Hills." In the English poet's midday, although the plains below lie silent and the air is windless, the mountains around him, all living things, and with them his own spirit (cf. Leopardi's *spirto*)

> Interpenetrated lie
> By the *glory* of the sky.

In his account, Leopardi deliberately avoids the expansive style. There is no rhapsodic feeling, not even an intimation of a "deeper meaning" that a nature mystic might claim to experience "while gazing at the sky in the azure noon."[16] Rather, we are confronted with a vast deadness into whose immobility and silence the poet has been released.

Writing on classical antiquity's use of the midday motif, Thomas G. Rosenmeyer has observed that "The noon-day cancellation of *kinēsis* will, if the poet wishes, turn into a full-fledged cancellation of life. Then the quasi-death becomes a true death, and the pastoral ripens into a dirge. Antiquity was comparatively reluctant to avail itself of this extension of the notion of paralysis into the notion of extinction."[17] What is meant here is the real death of someone and the development of the pastoral elegy, but I shall not be misappropriating Rosenmeyer's apt phrasing if I borrow it to describe what is evoked in Leopardi's single stanza without elegiac intent. In place of pastoral peace and *otium*, this midday stasis (with its release from time) is experienced as an ideal or metaphysical emptiness or nothingness. Leopardi's *meriggio* stanza thus creates a radically personal *locus amoenus*. His absorption into the *antica quiete* may still be thought of as belonging to the benedictional mode of pastoral ("La vita solitaria" presupposes and develops the most extreme contrast between society and the poet), but it is hardly Wordsworthian, and any true Arcadian would flee from it in horror. Perhaps even more than in the case of "L'infinito" ("The Infinite") where there is a strong suggestion of luxury or voluptuousness in Leopardi's surrender into the sea of boundless silence (and, accordingly, a suggestion of the expansive style), the "Vita solitaria" passage describes a state of nirvana—at least in the psychological and experiential sense. For here the experience is not, we have noted, an ecstasy but the muting of all emotions and the recovery of a condition of *ancient*, that is, original, quiet and absolute solitariness.[18]

The stasis of Leopardi's *meriggio* is so absolute as to exclude any hint of a mere temporary suspension of life or of a repressed energy suggestive of indeterminate potentiality. There is, however, an almost litanylike effect in the recital of the negatives that cancel out, one by one, all possible signs of life (i.e., motion and sound) so that there remains only an inviolable primordial anesthesia into which the poet is totally absorbed. This quasi-liturgical chant, coupled with the hint that the experience is cultivated by the poet ("*Talor* m'assido in solitaria parte") suggests an almost ritualistic enactment. If the enchantingly nostalgic midday from "Alla primavera" looks forward to "L'après-midi d'un faune," the *meriggio* of "La vita solitaria" anticipates and almost seems an answer to still another remarkable French poem on midday—Leconte de Lisle's "Midi" with its noontide revelation that at the core of existence lies "le néant divin," the divine void.

We shall have other occasions on which to refer to Leconte de Lisle's "Midi," especially in connection with Ungaretti and Montale. Indeed, because it may well have been an influence second only to Leopardi and D'Annunzio in those poets' emblematization of midday in an existential key, we may say a word more about it here in relation to the *meriggio* in "La vita solitaria." There are, of course, significant differences between the two noonscapes. For one thing, the French poet uses some of the more traditional elements found in descriptions of noontide although the poem is no less fascinating for that. We may note especially the emphasis on fiery heat and the reduced sense of life, along with the glare of light. The poem evokes an atmosphere of oppressive sultriness and vast torpor. Like Leopardi, however, Leconte de Lisle invites us (though more programmatically) to an absorption into the vast deadness or nirvana ("le néant divin") which is revealed in and by the implacably consuming sun itself. But there is not in his poem a neutralizing of all emotion. The poem's last three stanzas are especially relevant here:

> Homme, si, le coeur plein de joie ou d'amertume,
> Tu passais vers midi dans les champs radieux,
> Fuis! La nature est vide et le soleil consume:
> Rien n'est vivant ici, rien n'est triste ou joyeux.
>
> Mais si, désabusé des larmes et du rire,
> Altéré de l'oubli de ce monde agité,
> Tu veux, ne sachant plus pardonner ou maudire,
> Goûter une suprême et morne volupté,
>
> Viens! Le soleil te parle en paroles sublimes;
> Dans sa flamme implacable absorbe-toi sans fin;
> Et retourne à pas lents vers les cités infimes,
> Le coeur trempé sept fois dans le néant divin.[g]

The ironic, nay, the sardonic paradox proposed here is that the experience and contemplation of this metaphysical nothingness acts as a restorative for man who, now "replenished" by it, can return to the infected city and the indifference of the world armed with a superior "indifference" or impassivity.[19]

---

[g] Man, if, with your heart filled with joy or bitterness,
You should pass through the radiant fields at midday,
Flee! Nature is empty and the sun consumes:
Nothing is alive here, nothing is sad or joyful.

But if, disenchanted with tears and laughter,
Thirsting for forgetfulness of this restless world,
And no longer knowing how to forgive or to curse,
You desire to taste a supreme and dreary pleasure,

Come! The sun will speak to you with sublime words;
Absorb yourself infinitely in its relentless flame;
Then return with slow steps to the lowly cities,
Your heart drenched seven times in the divine nothingness.

Returning to Leopardi, it can be said that his variegated experience with noontide will often suggest itself to us as a touchstone for evaluating the poetry of midday in later writers yet to be discussed. In this connection, his lyric "L'infinito" was even more of an influence than those poems of his we have analyzed in detail. Although I believe that this, the most famous lyric of modern Italian poetry, is itself the account of a noontide experience, the absence of any overt time reference in it would make an argument in support of such an interpretation extremely lengthy and perhaps unnecessary here. But it is clear to me that many of the interesting midday poems of subsequent writers are to a great degree directly referable to Leopardi's "L'infinito." I have in mind of course those cases in which noontide is associated with the idea or impression of infinity or eternity.[20] This is not to say that such poems and the experience they record would never have arisen without the Leopardian precedent. And, certainly, in the best of them there are significant differences. But in an ideal sense they are, in one way or another, versions, however variant, of that matchless lyric. Only the later midday mythology of Gabriele D'Annunzio can be said to have exercised an equal influence on the literary treatment of the theme. Thus in many instances in the remainder of this study, the reader should be alert to explicit or implied comparisons with this poem as well as with the passages from "La vita solitaria" and "Alla primavera." For this reason and for the convenience of readers who may not recall in detail the poem's imagery and thought, I offer it here with a literal translation, but without further comment:

> Sempre caro mi fu quest'ermo colle,
> E questa siepe, che da tanta parte
> Dell'ultimo orizzonte il guardo esclude.
> Ma sedendo e mirando, interminati
> Spazi di là da quella, e sovrumani
> Silenzi, e profondissima quiete
> Io nel pensier mi fingo; ove per poco
> Il cor non si spaura. E come il vento

> Odo stormir tra queste piante, io quello
> Infinito silenzio a questa voce
> Vo comparando: e mi sovvien l'eterno
> E le morte stagioni, e la presente
> E viva, e il suon di lei. Così tra questa
> Immensità s'annega il pensier mio:
> E il naufragar m'è dolce in questo mare.[h]

Because the midday theme recurs with increasing frequency throughout the nineteenth century, it will be well to consider briefly some of the more interesting examples in minor authors before pausing at length on those important figures in whom it has a significant place.

The four sonnets making up the *Scene villesche* (*Country Scenes*) of Agostino Cagnoli were worthy contributors to the continuing popularity of the diurnal solar cycle. Although the idyllic and melancholy languor of much of Cagnoli's verse often seems to echo Leopardi and Pindemonte, in these poems on the four parts of the day his own strong inclination toward realistic description expressed in an almost technical lexicon takes this poet unequivocally beyond the Arcadian manner. This is evident in the sonnet on midday ("Il mezzogiorno"), which as a genre piece is precise in its depiction of noontide in the country, but is almost wholly devoid of subjective impressions or emotions and is certainly without metaphysical suggestiveness:

> [h] Ever dear to me has been this lonely hill,
> And this hedge that takes so great a part
> Of the ultimate horizon from my view.
> But sitting here and gazing, boundless
> Space beyond it, and uncanny
> Silence, and unfathomable quiet
> I evoke (feign) within my mind; whereat well-nigh
> My heart is gripped with fear. And as the wind
> Rustles through these leaves, that
> Infinite silence to this sound
> I do compare: and there come to mind the eternal,
> And the dead seasons (ages), and the present
> Living one, and its voice. Thus within this
> Immensity my thoughts are drowned:
> And sinking is sweet to me in this sea.

> S'infuoca l'ora meriggiana; ed ecco
> Di mezzo al ciel più grande il sole irraggia.
> Ogni campo si fa squallido e secco,
> E par che al suol fiamma dall'aere caggia.
> Foglia non crolla, e muto alla selvaggia
> Ripa l'augel s'immacchia, e liscia il becco.
> Stridono solo dall'aperta frasca
> Le noiose cicade in su lo stecco.
> All'ombra delle querce il bue stramazza;
> Cercan le pecorelle una spelonca:
> L'oca ad un fosserel l'ali starnazza.
> E il mietitor, che a un rezzo il fiasco cionca
> E terge il crine che in sudor gli guazza,
> Lento s'addorme sulla spiga tronca.[121]

There is nothing sentimental in this picture, and no pastoral intent or nostalgia informs it. Perhaps its single conventional term is the adjective *noiose* which suggests that the shrill of the cicadas is perceived as an irritant (cf. Ariosto's noon piece). The phrase *Foglia non crolla* is straight from Leopardi's "Vita solitaria" *meriggio* ("Ed erba o foglia non si crolla al vento"), and yet the atmosphere and mood of the poem are anything but Leopardian. Equally removed from the Arcadian mode, Cagnoli's noonscape is a genre piece in the strict sense of the word, and in its unemotional presentation of the distressful hour of midday in the country it anticipates the veristic manner that was to flourish later in the century, except that it

[i] The meridian hour is inflamed; and now
From the zenith the sun more greatly irradiates.
All the fields become bleak and dry,
And it seems that to the ground flames fall from on high.
No leaf stirs, and silently the birds repair
To the woodsy bank, and preen themselves.
Only the monotonous cicadas from the twigs
Of the extended branches stridulate.
In the shade of the oaks the ox collapses;
The sheep look for a cave:
The goose flaps its wings in a stream
And the reaper, who guzzles his flask in the shade
And wipes his hair which drips with sweat,
Slowly dozes off on the cut ears of wheat.

shows little if any of the secret human sympathy the *veristi* inevitably reveal despite a professed poetic of total removal of the author from the world he describes.

It is quite distinctly a quasi-veristic mode that we find in the landscape setting of the sonnet *"Dies"* ("The Day") in which Olindo Guerrini (Lorenzo Stecchetti), via a more rapid but intense impressionism, describes a midday in which the Arcadian motif of the invitation to a shady retreat or pleasance for amatory dalliance is revived:

> Il sole brucia implacabile, uguale,
> Le stoppie gialle del pian vaporoso,
> L'azzurra volta del ciel luminoso
> Riflette in terra la fiamma estivale.
> Non move foglia. La vita animale
> Langue in un grave sopor neghittoso:
> Turba la pace al meriggio affannoso
> Solo un molesto frinir di cicale.
> Sull'erba verde, nel bosco frondoso,
> Fresco t'ho fatto di fiori un guanciale
> E tu vi adagi le membra al riposo.
> Dormi discinta nell'ombra ospitale
> Ed io contemplo con l'occhio bramoso
> L'onda del petto che scende e che sale.[j22]

Here too a mild echo from Leopardi may be heard in the phrase *Non move foglia*, and again, but without the suggestion of tenseness, we hear the refrain of the cicadas as an irritant

---

[j] Implacably and equally the sun burns
 The yellow stubble of the hazy plain;
 The blue vault of the bright sky
 Reflects the summer flame to earth.
 No leaf stirs. The animal world
 Languishes in a heavy, lazy drowsiness.
 The calm of the breathless noon is disturbed
 Only by the irritating chirr of cicadas.
 On the green grass, within the leafy woods,
 I have made you a cool cushion of flowers
 And there you ease your limbs in rest.
 You sleep ungirt in the hospitable shade
 And I gaze with longing eyes
 On your swelling breast that falls and rises.

("molesto frinir"). In the sestet, however, the atmosphere of midday sensualism belongs to neither the Arcadian nor the veristic manner, but rather, on a smaller scale, to the dreamlike eroticism of Mallarmé's "Faune," and it anticipates certain faunesque visions of D'Annunzio, Villaroel, and even, as we shall see, of Ungaretti.

The light, heat, and stillness of a summer midday are evoked with impressionistic intensity in the short lyric by an even more minor poet, Domenico Milelli:

> Bianca ne l'aria immota
> Passa l'estate e splende;
> Adugge i campi e incende
> Le vie della città.
>
> Color d'argento al sole
> Ne la gran luce il mare
> Come senz'onda pare
> E scintillando sta.
>
> Arde il meriggio, fuma
> Il sollione intorno,
> Tace nell'afa il giorno
> Come in immenso avel:
>
> E non rumor lontano
> D'ala o fruscìo di fronda;
> Vampa stagnante è l'onda,
> Arco d'incendio è il ciel.[k23]

Here the images may be said to partake of baroque and decadent characteristics, especially in the last two stanzas: in the suffocating white heat of noon, nature seems to be a vast si-

[k] White in the motionless air
Summer passes and shines,
It desiccates the fields and emblazes
The streets of the city.

Color of silver under the sun
The sea in the great light
Appears to be without waves
And sparkling lies.

Midday burns, the scorching
Heat smokes all around,
The day is silent in the sultry air
As in an immense tomb:

And no sound in the distance
Of wing or rustling of branches;
The sea is a stagnant blaze,
The sky is a vault of fire.

lent tomb, the motionless sea a stagnant flame, and the sky a vault of fire.

On the other hand, the equally short poem of Pompeo Bettini presents a series of impressions that creates a sense of quasi-stasis in which there is no hint of oppressive heat, but a diminishing of the rhythm of life and nature and, above all, the presence of a quality of light that suggests a deeper life and moves the poet to a contemplative ecstasy and mystical awe:

> Rintocca il mezzogiorno;
> L'aria è nitida e sgombra;
> Son tranquilli i rumori
> E luminosa è l'ombra.
>
> Le vaghe lontananze
> Splendon con fissità:
> Si bilancia quest'attimo
> Fra doppia immensità.
>
> Fruscìi sommessi, fremiti
> D'acque correnti, prati
> Ebri di fiori, ed aliti
> Di venti smemorati
>
> Non interrompono l'estasi
> E il silenzio profondo . . .
> O viva e sacra luce
> O stupore del mondo![1]

Of particular interest in these verses is the merging of the silence and light into one sensation and the idea that time itself is suspended between past and present: "Si bilancia quest'attimo / Fra doppia immensità." It is the experience of

---

[1] Midday sounds;
The air is sharp and clear;
Noises are calm
And the shade is bright.

The indistinct distances
Radiate with intensity:
This moment is balanced
Between a double immensity.

Subdued rustling, tremor
Of flowing water, meadows
Drunk with flowers, and breath
Of distracted winds

Do not disturb the ecstasy
And the deep silence . . .
O living and sacred light
O wonder of the world!

timelessness, and with it, in this moment when the light has obliterated all shadows ("E luminosa è l'ombra"), comes the ecstatic sensation of a living glory.[24]

There are several midday evocations in the poetry of Giacomo Zanella, but the following sonnet is perhaps the most suggestive of them for us because of its connection with the theme of noonday nympholepsy:

> Solinga nell'ardor meridiano
> La campagna tacea: l'adulta spica
> Lieve ondeggiando nell'immenso piano
> Sul gracil si reggea stelo a fatica.
> Non Satiri bicorni, non Silvano,
> Che in quest'ora atterrian la gente antica,
> Ma Ruth vider questi occhi, la pudica
> Spigolatrice, fra il maturo grano
> Alta e bella passar. Si confondea
> Colle spighe la chioma: l'azzurrino
> Fiore del ciano nelle luci avea:
> Ma sulle guance, che celar volea
> Inchinandosi a terra, il porporino
> Fiammeggiar del papavero ridea.[m][25]

Beneath the fiery sun of midday, the whole countryside lies uninhabited and pervaded by silence; endless fields of wheat undulate softly under the weight of their ripeness. In the midst of this vast stillness suggestive of something sacred, the poet has a vision not of sylvan deities and satyrs such as pagan

---
[m] Solitary in the burning noon
The countryside was silent: the mature spikes
Waving lightly in the immense fields
Barely supported themselves on slender stalks.
Not two-horned Satyrs, not Sylvanus,
Who terrified the ancients in this hour,
But Ruth my eyes beheld, the modest
Gleaner, tall and beautiful, passing by
In the midst of the ripe wheat. Her hair
Merged with the spikes: the pale blue
Of cornflowers was in her eyes:
But on her cheeks, which she sought to hide
By stooping to the ground, the ruddy
Flaming of the poppy was laughing.

antiquity experienced and feared in that mysterious hour, but of the biblical figure of Ruth—chaste, tall, and beautiful—gleaning silently and alone in the fields of wheat and appearing as the true spirit and embodiment of the enchanted noontide hour. In explicitly opposing his figure of shy Ruth to the pagan evocations of midday nympholepsy, Zanella may also have had in mind both Foscolo's revery in *Jacopo Ortis* and Leopardi's vision in "Alla primavera." Nonetheless, in the economy of his sonnet the polemical thrust is not obtrusive but poetically functional.[26]

There are other midday evocations by minor poets of the second half of the nineteenth century that could properly be considered here. In poems that are surely "variants" of Leopardi's "L'infinito," Antonio Fogazzaro, for example, knew the sense of strange stillness ("riposo arcano") of midday in the Alps ("Quiete meridiana nell'Alpe," "Noontide Quiet in the Alps"), and Edmondo De Amicis was likewise absorbed by the silencing of all things during that hour when "una sovrana / Pace sembra regnar nell'infinito" ("A supreme / Peace seems to reign in the infinite," "Mezzogiorno"). Giulio Salvadori could feel the waves of the sea sparkling under the rays of the midday sun to be enacting a "danza / D'immensa esultanza" ("dance / Of immense jubilation," "Calma"). Giovanni Camerana, Giovanni Marradi, Emilio Girardini, and Enrico Panzacchi are other poets who have left their impressions of the hour. But all these and more may be foregone here in favor of a discussion of the far more significant image of midday in the work of Italy's greatest post-Manzonian narrator, Giovanni Verga. The first of the examples from him, moreover, may fittingly claim our attention at this point between Zanella's evocation of Ruth, the solitary reaper at midday, and a similar evocation by Carducci to which we shall later turn.

The ancient Sicilian Theocritus and the medieval legends of malefic and erotic nymphs or noonday demons are matched by the modern Sicilian writer. In Verga's novella "La lupa" ("The She Wolf"), which I am tempted to call a pastoral tragedy, the gaunt female protagonist, felt by the other women of the village to possess demonic powers ("Le donne del villaggio si facevano la croce quando la vedevano passare"), appears as an isolated figure who alone dares to walk through the sun-scorched fields in the hottest hours of the day, siesta time for all except the evil spirits. The sensual passion that drives her and that will eventually lead her to self-destruction is symbolically mirrored by the cruel noontide sun that consumes the countryside:

> *In quell'ora fra vespero e nona, in cui non ne va in volta femmina buona*, la gnà Pina [*la Lupa*] era la sola anima viva che si vedesse errare per la campagna, sui sassi infuocati delle viottole, fra le stoppie riarse dei campi immensi, che si perdevano nell'afa, lontan lontano, verso l'Etna nebbioso, dove il cielo si aggravava sull'orizzonte.[n][27]

While this passage reflects the survival in folklore of beliefs that go back to antiquity and medieval superstitions concerning nympholeptic visitations and evil spirits that roam (and we note that Verga's verb is *errare*) at noontide, there is something in Verga's protagonist that is also suggestive of a modern (existentialist) condition. For though *la Lupa* strikes a superstitious dread and exercises a sexual tyranny over others, she is herself a tragic figure, restless, unappeasable, and more tormented than tormentor. In terms of her own inner life she is not just the midday demon or succubus she is for others, though she may herself feel cast in that role. She is as much a victim of the vehement midday sun (the libido symbol of her passion) with which she has an ambiguous relationship or identification and by which she is driven and conquered as she is its apparent personification. Like the midday sun that ravages the countryside, *la Lupa* consumes and "devours" the sons and husbands of the village women: "Ella si spolpava i loro figliuoli e i loro mariti." The story of her last and fatal

---

[n] In that hour between vespers and none, when no good woman goes about, *gnà* Pina [the she wolf] was the only living soul to be seen wandering through the countryside, over the red-hot stones of the paths, amid the parched stubble of the immense fields that stretched out lost to sight in the sultry heat, far off toward hazy Mount Etna, where the sky lay heavily on the horizon.

passion, the incestuous sexual conquest of her son-in-law, Nanni, is situated in the fields at noontide (she wakens him from his siesta sleep for the occasion). Throughout the long period of the affair, in fact, noontide remains their trysting hour. And when, finally, she walks undauntedly toward him in their last meeting, the ax the distraught Nanni (convinced he is "bedeviled") raises against her is seen glistening in the fierce brightness of the midday sun. It is with this image that the novella ends.[28]

Anyone familiar with Verga will have in mind some scene or other of his in which a drought-stricken, vast expanse of Sicilian landscape is pictured as suffering under the blasting sun of high noon. But other than the episode just discussed, the most striking of such scenes for us occurs in the novel *Mastro-Don Gesualdo*, striking especially for the parallel it offers in a veristico-symbolic key to the figure of *la Lupa*. The master builder Don Gesualdo, relentless in his drive for material success, is like the "she wolf" in that he, too, walks restlessly during the midday hours. With him, however, it is a matter of attending to business and overseeing his workers. Unwilling to pause even for lunch, he makes his way through the countryside under a blistering sun which would bring calamity to most persons exposed to it: "un sole che scottava, da prendere un malanno chi andava per la campagna a quell'ora."[29] This is the midday sun of the Psalmist that brings pestilence or fatal sunstroke. The connection between the noontide demon and Gesualdo is further hinted at in the words of an old man surprised to see him arriving at that hour in the town, which is perched on a hill that the builder has had to climb with his mule: "O dove andate vossignoria a quest'ora? . . . Avete tanti denari, e vi date l'anima al diavolo!" (p. 553).° The expression is metaphorical, but coupled with the reference to the time of day (the scorching hour of midday) and the residue of superstitious belief that survives in the speaker, its suggestive intent is unmistakable. This intent is heightened when a fellow builder with whom

° Oh, where is your Lordship going at this hour? . . . You have so much money, and still you give your soul to the devil?

Gesualdo has conferred in the town compliments him for his business shrewdness by referring to him as a "devil" and by suggesting (again in an expression that lies between metaphor and superstition) that he, Gesualdo, has spoken with the devil: "Ah! ah! . . . siete un diavolo! . . . Vuol dire che avete parlato col diavolo" (p. 553). Again Don Gesualdo will not stop to eat, but goes on under the high sun leading his exhausted mule through the suffocating atmosphere of a blasted, shadowless noonscape where the sun, as Verga's image has it, beats upon his head with the force of the sledgehammers used by his men who are working on the road of Camemi:

> Pareva di soffocare in quella gola del Petraio. Le rupi brulle sembravano arroventate. Non un filo di ombra, non un filo di verde, colline su colline, accavallate, nude, arsicce, sassose, sparse di olivi rari e magri, di fichidindia polverosi, la pianura sotto Budaturo come una landa bruciata dal sole, i monti foschi nella caligine, in fondo. Dei corvi si levarono gracchiando da una carogna che appestava il fossato; delle ventate di scirocco bruciavano il viso e mozzavano il respiro; una sete da impazzire, il sole che gli picchiava sulla testa come fosse il martellare dei suoi uomini che lavoravano alla strada del Camemi (p. 554).[p]

But his workers are discovered by Gesualdo to be lying prostrate here and there in the ditch, as though they had been felled by the ferocity of the sun. Unlike their employer, they are no match for the rage of midday. Gesualdo, on the other hand, can now be seen for what he is—not so much a force able to resist the sun but its demoniacal agent or counterpart. Surely, to the workers he has angrily awakened he appears in

---

[p] It was suffocating in that gorge of Petraio. The barren cliffs seemed red hot. Not a bit of shade, not a blade of grass, hill upon hill, heaped up on one another, bare, parched, stony, with a scattering here and there of scrawny olive trees and dusty prickly-pear plants, the plain below Budaturo like a heath scorched by the sun, the dark mountains in a misty distance. Some scavenger crows rose up croaking from a carrion that lay stinking in the ditch; gusts of the southeast wind burned one's face and cut one's breath; a maddening thirst and the sun beating on his head like the hammering of his men who were working on the road of Camemi.

such a guise: "Vedendolo con quella faccia accesa e riarsa, bianca di polvere soltanto nel cavo degli occhi e sui capelli; degli occhi come quelli che dà la febbre, e le labbra sottili e pallide; nessuno ardiva rispondergli" (p. 554).[a] With his thin, pale lips and his eyes aflame with fever, Gesualdo seems the incarnation of the cruel sun visiting the earth with pestilence and death. He is, at this moment at least, the noontide devil. Lest this interpretation seem excessive, let us reflect on the image that closes the episode. Like Nanni helplessly yielding to *la Lupa*'s devouring midday sexuality, the workers do not dare to answer Gesualdo, but silently return to their hammering. (In both cases the protagonist invades the siesta hour.) There follows a reference to the carniverous scavenger crows (mentioned once already in the passage quoted above) who are seen circling above in the "implacable" sky. An old man among the workers raises his dusty face and looks at the crows with burning eyes, as though (and the comment is Verga's) he knew what they wanted and was resignedly awaiting them: "I corvi ripassarono gracidando, nel cielo implacabile. Il vecchio allora alzò il viso impolverato a guardarli, con gli occhi infuocati, quasi sapesse cosa volevano e li aspettasse" (pp. 554-555).

The episode under consideration emblematically characterizes the protagonist and the world in which he moves. For like the midday sun, Gesualdo throughout the novel is implacable in his drive to acquire wealth and property in a hostile world, and cruel if need be to the point, as here, of pushing his workers to their death under the burning sun. It is in this context that he takes on the features of a noontide demon. But, again as in the case of *la Lupa*, this demon is also Gesualdo's own rabid passion of which he is the victim. He is himself driven and consumed by a feverish ambition which is reflected in the violent but arid noontide, an emblematical relationship that we have seen in the midday meditations of Petrarch and James Thomson.[30]

[a] Seeing him with his face flushed and scorched, white with powder only in the hollow of the eyes and on his head, his eyes aflame as though burned by fever, and his lips thin and pale, no one dared to reply.

For the most part we are far from such negative noontide violence in the writings of Giosue Carducci, where it is rather the splendor and glory of the midday sun that illuminate more than one scene. In considering the role of midday in Carducci, we may begin with the idyllic and nostalgic evocation of "Idillio maremmano" ("Idyll of the Maremma"). Here, at the center of the world-weary poet's vision of a simple and healthy life in communion with nature, which might have been his, is the figure of a young woman who strides "alta e ridente" along the furrows of fields of wheat. Carducci's "bionda Maria" may remind us somewhat of Zanella's Ruth at midday, except that Maria is clearly a pagan poet's vision of a nature goddess of health and fertility, a nostalgic but vigorous nympholepsy. The nigh-noon sun of midsummer with its heat and light bathes her in glory as in an act of homage, and she moves Juno-like in it as in her natural element:

> . . . . e a te d'avante
>
> La grande estate, e intorno, fiammeggiava;
> Sparso tra'verdi rami il sol ridea
> Del melogran, che rosso scintillava.
>
> Al tuo passar, siccome a la sua dea,
> Il bel pavon l'occhiuta coda apria
> Guardando, e un rauco grido a te mettea.[r31]
>
> (24-30)

An even more openly paganizing classical midday scene is at the center of the second of the three odes of "Primavere elleniche" ("Spring in Hellas"). In this hymn to love the poet invites his beloved to an imaginary voyage to a Theocritean Sicily "where the shepherd Daphnis sang divine songs amid

[r]
> . . . and before you,
>
> And all around, the great summer blazed.
> The sun was laughing scattered through the green
> Boughs of the pomegranate tree that sparkled red.
>
> When you passed by, the beautiful peacock, as though
> Looking at its goddess, opened its eye-splendored tail
> And hailed you with a strident cry.

the fountains" (27-28). There, with the magic of his verse he will enrapture her, and in the midst of the noontide calm and leisure, at that hour when light and silence pervade all of nature, he will evoke the presence of the swift-footed sylvan nymphs:

> Ti rapirò nel verso; e tra i sereni
> Ozi de le campagne a mezzo il giorno,
> Tacendo e refulgendo in tutti i seni
> Ciel, mare, intorno,
>
> Io per te sveglierò da i colli aprichi
> Le Driadi bionde sovra il piè leggero.[s32]
> (41-46)

How emblematic of refuge into a world of calm, happiness, and harmony with nature this theme of midday nympholepsy was for Carducci is evidenced by the fact that the same invitation and evocation are at the center of what still remains his best-known poem—"Davanti San Guido" ("Passing by San Guido"). As in "Idillio maremmano" here too the theme is that of the pastoral opposition between the simple rural life close to nature and the active, care-filled life demanded by the city. As the poet returns by train to the city and his obligations as a man of the world, the cypress trees familiar to him from his childhood seem to invite him to stay, offering the promise of innocent pleasures and repose. It has become fashionable of late among critics to belittle this poem, but there can be no doubt that the three stanzas containing the nympholeptic evocation are among Carducci's finest poetic achievements. It is a vision of pagan bliss invoked in one sentence that carries over three quatrains, syntactically one of the most amply constructed sentences of Italian poetry in the second half of the nineteenth century:

---

[s] I will steal you away with my verse; and midst
The placid indolence of the fields at noon,
Silently shining in all breasts
The sky and sea, around,

For you I will summon from the sun-bathed hills
The blond dryads fleet of foot.

> Rimanti; e noi, dimani, a mezzo il giorno
> Che de le grandi querce a l'ombra stan
> Ammusando i cavalli e intorno intorno
> Tutto è silenzio ne l'ardente pian,
>
> Ti canteremo noi cipressi i cori
> Che vanno eterni fra la terra e il cielo:
> Da quegli olmi le ninfe usciran fuori
> Te ventilando co 'l lor bianco velo;
>
> E Pan l'eterno che su l'erme alture
> A quell'ora e ne i pian solingo va
> Il dissidio, o mortal, de le tue cure
> Ne la diva armonia sommergerà.[133]
>
> (53-64)

First we have the evocation of the midday hour as a time of stillness and fierce heat over a vast expanse in which arcane sentiments and voices seem to float, then the sylvan nymphs who fan the poet. Finally there is Pan, not asleep at noontide and not the *daimon* causing terror, but Pan the Eternal, personification of a pantheistic concept of the universal harmony of nature that is revealed in the sacred hour of midday and into which the care-worn individual can sweetly merge.

There are other midday references in Carducci. "Elegia del Monte Spluga" (1898) once again evokes, as in an atmosphere between dream and reality (cf. Leopardi, Foscolo, Chenier, Mallarmé), a classically nympholeptic midday in which, however, a Nordic Lorelei also appears (1-12). And leaving

---

[t] Stay: and tomorrow at noon
   When in the shade of the great oaks
   The horses stand muzzle to muzzle and all around
   Everything is silent in the burning plain,

   We cypresses will sing to you the chorus
   That wafts eternal between earth and sky:
   From those elms the nymphs will come forth
   Fanning you with their white veils;

   And Pan the Eternal who goes along the solitary heights
   At that hour and all alone over the plains,
   Will submerge the anguish of your cares,
   Oh mortal, in the divine harmony.

the classical and paganizing world, the solemn evocation of the medieval Alpine commune in "Il comune rustico" ("The Rustic Commune") acquires a quality of fixity and stunning intensity by virtue of the poem's final image in which we learn that the midday sun has illuminated the scene:

> A man levata il popol dicea Sì.
> E le rosse giovenche di su 'l prato
> Vedean passare il piccolo senato,
> Brillando su gli abeti il mezzodì.[u][34]
>
> (33-36)

In "Fuori alla certosa di Bologna" ("Outside the Charterhouse of Bologna"), the sun at its zenith figures as the symbol of the joy and intensity of life in opposition to the symbols of death (as extinction of the self) represented by the tombs of the Carthusian cemetery the poet has just visited. Under that blazing midday sun flooding the earth with a "kiss" of light, the cicadas' "song" is not an irritant but a paean to summer, and even the dead, in the poet's mind, seem to invite the living to love one another. The noonday sun is here equated with the eternal splendor of love. In this vein, however, Carducci's most exalted paean to the midsummer midday sun and to the sense of a rich immersion of the self in nature at the hour of Pan occurs at the beginning of one of his best-known prose compositions, *Le risorse di San Miniato al Tedesco* (*The Resources of San Miniato al Tedesco*). And here the poet's cue is taken from the ubiquitous and (for him) much maligned cicadas whose persistent shrill filling the air is interpreted as the audible voice of the irrepressible energy and joy of all of nature, eternally young and drunk with the light and heat of the sun:

> Come strillavano le cicale giù per la china meridiana del colle di San Miniato al Tedesco nel luglio del 1857. . . . Io non ho mai capito perché i poeti di razza latina odiino e ol-

---

[u] With hand raised high, the people said "Yes."
And the red heifers from the meadow
Saw the small senate pass by,
As midday shone brightly on the fir trees.

traggino tanto le cicale. . . . Poi tutto un gran coro [di cicale] che aumenta d'intonazione e d'intensità co 'l calore e co 'l luglio, e canta, canta, canta. . . . Nelle fiere solititudini del solleone, pare che tutta la pianura canti, e tutti i monti cantino, e tutti i boschi cantino: pare che essa la terra dalla perenne gioventù del suo seno espanda in un inno immenso il giubilo de' suoi sempre nuovi amori co 'l sole.[v35]

In this pantheistic nirvana—the metaphor of nirvana is Carducci's own—of light and exultation, which is in fact the sensation of an intense life, Carducci "drowns" in a willing surrender of the self's identity and its cares in order to become at one with the pulsating life of the All of nature, and the very body of the poet seems to be of the essence of the cicadas' wild song:

A me in quel nirvana di splendori e di suoni avviene e piace di annegare la coscienza di uomo, e confondermi alla gioia della mia madre Terra: mi pare che tutte le mie fibre e tutti i miei sensi fremano, esultino, cantino in amoroso tumulto, come altrettante cicale.[w36]

It would be difficult to find a more extreme contrast than that between the noontide vision and sensations recounted by Carducci in this passage and the *meriggio* of Leopardi's "Vita solitaria." In a strict sense, to be sure, the term *nirvana* does not apply to either noon piece, but as a metaphor it is more suited to characterize the earlier poet's experience. Leopardi,

[v] How the cicadas stridulated down along the slope of the hill of San Miniato al Tedesco under the midday sun in July 1857. . . . I have never understood why poets of Latin descent so greatly hate and insult the cicada. . . . Then a whole large chorus [of cicadas] that increases in intonation and intensity with the heat of July, and sing, sing, sing. . . . In the fierce solitude of the midsummer sun it seems as though the whole plain sings, and that all the mountains sing, and all the forests sing: it seems that from the perennial youth of its bosom the very earth expands into an immense hymn the celebration of its ever new love with the sun.

[w] In that nirvana of splendor and sounds I have the pleasurable experience of drowning my human consciousness and of merging with the joy of my mother earth: I feel that all my nerves and all my senses quiver, exult, sing in an amorous tumult like so many cicadas.

we saw, is released from sentiency and the consciousness of self into a metaphysical nothingness emblematized by the perfect stasis of his noonscape. On the other hand, Carducci's senses are literally thrilled and set to vibrating by an exuberance that throbs in the very heart of hot midday's fierce silence—"Nelle fiere solitudini del solleone." In a moment of Panic inebriation and expansion, Carducci is "released" precisely from the anguish of the thought of the nothingness that follows death, an anguish symbolized by the image—frequent in this writer—of the cold silence of the tomb: "Non è vero che io sia serbato ai freddi silenzi del sepolcro! io vivrò e canterò, atomo e parte della mia madre immortale."[x][37]

It is quite possible that Carducci's use of the metaphor of drowning to speak of the surrender of the self may be an echo from Leopardi's "L'infinito," although it is a common enough image in the writings of religious mystics. Again, however, where Leopardi drowns voluptuously in a sea of infinite silence—"E il naufragar m'è dolce in questo mare"—Carducci drowns in a sea (or "nirvana," as he puts it) of luminosity and sounds—"nirvana di splendori e suoni." These meridian "sounds" are first of all the actual chirring of the cicadas, but also, it should be noted, the metaphorical yet exultant "singing" of all of nature—fields, mountains, and forests. What may be involved here is the acoustical impression that the very absoluteness of midday's silence seems at times to arouse in an absorbed spectator. It is a psycho-aural phenomenon that we have referred to already, and we shall soon meet with it again.

But the experience of the midday sun as an ambiguous and even negative demonic power of nature was not unknown to Carducci. This is most evident in the short lyric "Davanti una cattedrale" ("In Front of a Cathedral"), as sardonic a poem as any written by the *Scapigliati* (i.e., Italy's *poètes maudits*) contemporary with him. Here the images of the sun and tombs, normally used by the poet as terms of an opposition between life and extinction, appear in an ambivalent relationship:

[x] It is not true that I am destined for the cold silence of the tomb! I will live and sing, particle and part of my immortal mother.

Trionfa il sole, e inonda
La terra a lui devota:
Ignea ne l'aria immota
L'estate immensa sta.

Laghi di fiamma sotto
I domi azzurri inerte
Paiono le deserte
Piazze de la città.

Là spunta una sudata
Fronte, ed è orribil cosa:
La luce vaporosa
La ingialla di pallor.

Dite: Fa fresco a l'ombra
De le navate oscure,
Ne l'urne bianche e pure,
O teschi de i maggior?[y][38]

A fiercely triumphant summer sun vanquishes the earth and fixes everything in a broiling immobility. Already in the first stanza an ambiguity or irony is suggested by the attitude of devotion that the earth is said to have toward the sun, for in point of fact the earth has succumbed to the sun. The second stanza makes it clear that this is specifically an urban

[y] The sun triumphs, and floods
The earth that is devoted to it:
Afire in the motionless air
Summer hovers immense.

The abandoned and inert
Squares of the city
Seem lakes of flames
Beneath blue domes.

There, suddenly a sweaty
Forehead emerges, and it is a horrible sight:
The misty light
Gives it a yellow pallor.

Say: Is it cool in the shadow
Of the dark naves,
Within the pure white urns
Oh skulls of our ancestors?

noonscape (itself a rarity), and the deserted squares of the city (a sure sign it is noontide) appear as lakes of motionless fire beneath a deep blue sky. In the third stanza the sense of noontide oppression is heightened by the sudden appearance of a solitary perspiring figure. We may take this figure to be the poet himself who is approaching the cathedral in the square. He is rendered grotesque and yellowish in a deathlike pallor by the light that seems to deform and disintegrate all objects. Finally, the last stanza brings a macabre twist to the motif of the midday retreat to a shady refuge. The cathedral before which the poet stands contains cool shade but also the tombs of the dead. It is a place of darkness and so, in a Carduccian view, a place where life is absent. But the derisive, Baudelairean guise in which he poses his question to the dead interred in the cathedral may also be self-mockery. For in this case, at least, the midday sun in which he stands is experienced as the destructive Gorgon.

But let us take leave of Carducci on a more truly solar note. The following Alpine midday in the poem by that title ("Mezzogiorno alpino") is, for all its brevity, among the most highly suggestive evocations of the special sense of timelessness that noontide seems so often to arouse:

> Nel gran cerchio de l'alpi, su 'l granito
> Squallido e scialbo, su' ghiacciai candenti,
> Regna sereno intenso ed infinito
> Nel suo grande silenzio il mezzodì.
>
> Pini ed abeti senza aura di venti
> Si drizzano nel sol che gli penètra.
> Sola garrisce in picciol suon di cetra
> L'acqua che tenue tra i sassi fluì.[z][39]

[z] In the great circle of the Alps, on the granite rock
Bleak and pale, on the shining glaciers,
Serene, intense and infinite
Midday reigns in its majestic silence.

Pines and firs in the windless air
Rise in the sun that penetrates them.
Alone, like a faint sound of a lyre, chirps
The water that has flowed tenuously through the rocks.

One must revert to the category of the sublime in considering this poem which presents the grandiose spectacle of the Alps in the absolute silence and light of midday. In part there is gray granite whose barrenness seems to be the more exposed in the totality of light, in part, the peaks and patches of ice and snow glistening with a dazzling radiance. Sole protagonist here is midday "reigning" over all things in majestic immobility, imparting a light and silence that are the same phenomenon. The adverbial adjective *intenso* refers not to the sun's heat, but to the quality of fixity and absoluteness of the light and silence, just as *sereno* bespeaks their purity while denoting a vision of a cloudless sky, and *infinito* conveys the impression of their timelessness. Below these highest regions, forests of pines and firs stand tall and motionless in the windless air and seem now to be of the substance of the luminous silence that has penetrated and possessed them. The one sound is that of a vein of water playing steadily like a musical instrument. But it is not a wild or intense sound like that of the cicadas. Significantly, the acoustic sensation suggested by *garrisce* is immediately attenuated by the qualifying notation of *in picciol suon*, and like the soft rustling of the wind through the foliage in Leopardi's "L'infinito," its effect is not to break a surrounding preternatural silence but rather to throw that silence (and the majestic setting to which it is attached) into a greater relief, to deepen it, as it were.[40] This effect is heightened by the daring use of the past absolute tense of the important verb *fluì*. The idea or impression that this creates is that the water, even as it flows through and by the stones and rocks, seems continually to have already passed by. The flow of water is an archetypal image of the fluidity of time, and here it signifies the present moment that is continually transforming itself into the past, becoming lost or nullified in the stillness and timelessness (as opposed to never-ending time) experienced in the deep midday stasis. Here then time is recognized less in Plato's sense of a moving image of eternity than as an illusion that vainly seeks to conceal the reality of eternity.[41]

The final word in each of the two stanzas of Carducci's poem has extraordinary value in contributing to the quality of the evocation. The key word *mezzodì* (midday) occurs precisely at the midway point of the poem, at the very end of the first stanza. The word, of course, also refers to the subject of the poem, and as the subject of the sentence occupying the whole stanza, it has been postponed to the very end by the syntactical inversion. With its strong accent on the last syllable, it creates a sense of suspension (the midday pause) and fixes the entire vision of the first part of the poem in a zone of indeterminacy, wonder, and expectation. Likewise *fluì*, the last word of the poem, echoes the acoustic effect of *mezzodì* with its accented last vowel (which creates the illusion of a rhyme) and thereby keeps us suspended in the midday impression of indeterminacy and timelessness.[42] Thus the word *fluì* has an enormously important role in the poem. It functions on one level—the visual—to indicate motion, whereas on another level—the acoustical—it suggests immobility. Such an impression of motion in immobility, or energy in stasis, is one of the ambiguities, perhaps the most important one, that contribute to the mystery of midday.

Giovanni Pascoli was once Carducci's student at the University of Bologna, but as Italy's most authentic if homespun decadent poet he has only surface resemblances to his former master. "Romagna" is generally taken to be among those poems of his that owe most to Carducci. While there is truth in this opinion, Pascoli's nostalgic evocation of the countryside and the village of his birth reveals, in its tone and in the details of the landscape, a character that is unmistakably its own. "Sempre mi torna al cuore il mio paese" ("This land of mine comes ever to my heart," 5); and the vision that returns constantly to the desolate poet is of a "Romagna solatìa" ("Sunny Romagna"), a memory of happiness fixed in the suspension of midday: "Oh! fossi io teco . . . / Gettarci l'urlo che lungi si perde / Dentro il meridïano ozio dell'aie" (13; 15-16).[aa][43] The dieresis on the key word *meridïano* lengthens and expands the line which creates an image of the vast noontide silence in which the child's shout of joy rever-

[aa] Oh! to be with you now . . . / To give out a shout that is lost in the distance / In the noontide indolence of the threshing floors.

berates. It is the hour of the siesta ("meridïano ozio"), and the succeeding verses give us a Virgilian picture of field hands pausing for their simple lunch and of oxen slowly ruminating in the stable. From the various villages in the countryside the church bells signal the hour calling all to shade, rest, and lunch. And the poet as child finds refuge from the dazzling sun and the hottest hours of the day ("quelle ore bruciate") beneath the shade of a mimosa tree, reading fabulous tales of chivalry. Some of the elements are familiar to us as belonging to a long tradition, but Pascoli's sensibility, nourished by Virgil in some important ways, is far from Arcadian.

Even so, it is a markedly different atmosphere that characterizes the noontide of "Dall'argine" ("From the Embankment"):

> Posa il meriggio su la prateria.
> Non ala orma ombra nell'azzurro e verde.
> Un fumo al sole biancica: via via
>   Fila e si perde.
>
> Ho nell'orecchio un turbinìo di squilli,
> Forse campani di lontana mandra;
> E, tra l'azzurro penduli, gli strilli
>   Della calandra.[bb][44]

As with Carducci's "Mezzogiorno alpino," we meet first with visual images that create a scene and mood of absorbed contemplation in a vast stillness into which auditory sensations are then introduced. However, the setting, being less obviously grandiose, is different, and so too, despite a certain likeness, is the final impression we are left with. The marvelous first line with its strategically placed initial word (the verb

---

[bb] Midday rests upon the plains,
   No wing, footstep, or shadow in the blue and the green.
   A wisp of smoke gleams white: gradually
      Threads the air and fades.

In my ears is a turmoil of peals,
Perhaps cowbells of a distant herd;
And, in the midst of the blue, dangling, the shrill cries
    Of the wood lark.

Posa) creates at once the impression that the light of the midday sun has come to rest on the earth and, in so doing, has fixed all things in a profound stasis.[45] With an impressionistic technique of great compression, the second line intensifies this sense of stillness and light by its negation of all signs of life or motion: no bird wings its way through the unbroken expanse of blue sky; no living creature moves along the green; and no shadows are cast in this, the shadowless hour.[46] Lines 3-4 tell us that the only movement is that of a wisp of white smoke slowly rising and dissipating into the sky. And that too is gone. On the one hand, the effect is to create a tension upward (as though to a superior realm); at the same time, we are left with a deeper sense of mystery if not of emptiness. The impression of mystery is increased by the presence of sounds introduced in the second stanza. In itself, a "turbinio di squilli" would seem to indicate a noise violent enough to break the poet's absorption, but just the opposite is true. The fact that the source of the sound is unseen and uncertain ("*Forse* . . .") causes it to be integrated into the contemplation of the mysterious hour. The poet surmises that what he hears is the ringing of cowbells which, coming from a far and unspecified distance, contributes to the idea of a vast space. Finally, there are the shrill sounds that are identified as the wood lark's. Again, however, the bird itself is not seen. Moreover, its piercing cries come not from a brake but are indeterminately situated above in the sky (the wood lark is known to fly at great heights) where they give the impression of being suspended, just as all of nature itself seems to be.

The sounds in Pascoli's lyric represent a notable variation on the motif of the wild chirring of the usually ubiquitous cicadas of noontide.[47] Not such as to shatter the sense of nature's stillness, they are, if I may so speak, "frozen" into the midday immobility. Again, however, they seem to accentuate the stasis or silence by charging it with a tension that suggests not a sense of menace such as we meet with in some of the well-known nature impressions of Pascoli, but an undefinable expectancy. Given as actual sensory perceptions, the sounds seem almost to be another example of the impression or effect that arises from the very intensity and absoluteness of the meridian silence itself—"le fier silence de midi" as Mallarmé refers to it in "L'après-midi d'un faune." This, we have noted, is often the case with those midday evocations in which the deafening or maddening stridor of the cicadas seems really to be a negative subjective perception of the silence reflecting the anxiety of the beholder. It is as though the cicadas' shrill itself belongs to the midday silence. Indeed, as we have seen, it is not unusual to associate an acoustical element (usually negative) with the midday hour (in particular with the sun) even when there are no actual sounds being produced by cicadas or other creatures. We have in fact already observed that Carducci perceived the summer's midday silence as containing a "wild" energy or tension—"le *fiere solitudini* del solleone"—that creates auditory impressions. In his case, however, along with the actual chirr of the cicadas, these impressions are felt unambiguously as a wholly positive value, being nothing less than nature's great paean to life. In Pascoli's deceptively simple "Dall'argine," on the other hand, the apparently familiar sights and sounds of a bucolic noonscape acquire the value of indeterminacy and timelessness, and everything—nature and beholder alike—exists in an ambiguous state of suspension between bewilderment and ecstatic enchantment.

In still another noontide vein, quite unlike either "Romagna" or "Dall'argine," the curious but significant lyric entitled "Gloria" makes use of the motif of the retreat from midday in order to communicate both a typical attitude of Pascoli vis-à-vis involvement in life and a statement of his poetics. Only seven lines, "Gloria" echoes the episode of Dante's encounter with Belacqua which Pascoli allegorizes in a personal and terrestrial sense:

—Al santo monte non verrai, Belacqua?—

Io non verrò: l'andare in su che porta?
Lungi è la Gloria, e piedi e mani vuole;
E là non s'apre che al pregar la porta,
E qui star dietro il sasso a me non duole,

Ed ascoltare le cicale al sole,
E le rane che gracidano, Acqua acqua!^{cc48}

One could wish that the poem's title were "Meriggiare" ("To laze in the noontide shade"), so perfect an illustration is it of the activity (or lack of activity) implied in that word. But the poem would then have lost some of the irony and polemical thrust implied in its actual title. Here Dante's sacred mountain of Purgatory that leads to heavenly glory is now the climb to earthly glory to be attained by vigorous involvement in the business of life. But Pascoli, refusing to play the pilgrim Dante to Carducci's Virgil, is content with the role of Belacqua. Moreover, here too, glory, in a Carduccian sense, is symbolized by the midday sun from which Pascoli prefers to hide, seeking refuge behind the boulder, out of sight and in the shade of a humbler reality. Carducci, we remember, was the solar poet par excellence until D'Annunzio appeared on the scene. Pascoli is the supreme twilight poet *ante litteram*, and his polemic involves a rejection of the oratorical solemnity of magniloquent verses on historical and patriotic themes for which Carducci was so famous. (Carducci's poem "Avanti, Avanti"—"Onward, Onward"—may have been especially in Pascoli's mind.) "Gloria" contains a further irony in those elements, clearly indicative of the midday hour, which Pascoli has added to Dante's scene. To be sure, one would not expect to hear cicadas and frogs in Dante's Purgatory. But the cicadas, we also remember, were celebrated by Carducci who identified with them in the blazing glory of midday and joined them in song. One might think that in Pascoli's poem they have the connotation of a humbler reality. But within the allegorical and ironic context of "Gloria," the cicadas and their stridor are more likely to refer

---

^{cc} —Will you not come up the sacred mountain, Belacqua?—

No, I'll not come: What avails going up?
Glory is far off, and demands hands and feet,
And there they open the door only when beseeched,
While it does not grieve me to stay here behind the rock
And to listen to the cicadas in the sun,
And the frogs that croak "Water, water!"

to Carducci himself and his disciples. Nothing, however, is more Pascolian than those humble frogs whose croaking is heard by the poet as a prayer for rain to bring relief from the aggressive noontide exuberance represented, to be sure, by Carducci, but even more so, Pascoli might already have felt, by Gabriele D'Annunzio.

We must not leave Pascoli without taking note of a case in which the sun (a midday sun to judge from its intolerable and obliterating character) figures as an emblem of a metaphysical void. The analogical equivalence between death and the sun is already hinted at in the title of the short lyric "Morte e sole" ("Death and the Sun"):

> Fissa la morte: costellazione
> Lugubre che in un cielo nero brilla:
> Breve parola, chiara visione:
>   Leggi, o pupilla.
>
> Non puoi. Così, se fissi mai l'immoto
> Astro nei cieli solitari ardente,
> Se guardi il sole, occhio, che vedi? Un vòto
>   Vortice, un niente.[dd49]

The invitation to look into death and see what can be read there is made to himself and to the reader. There is something derisive in the definition of death—presented almost in the form of a riddle—as a lugubrious constellation that gleams in a black sky. The impression of a riddle and the irony are heightened with the clue that death is a "brief word," that is, perhaps, an *easy* word to pronounce, but its meaning remains impenetrable. The easy word cannot be read properly: "Non puoi,"—said somewhat preemptorily. So too death is a

---

[dd] Gaze on death: gloomy constellation
  That twinkles in a black sky:
  Brief word, bright vision:
      Read, oh pupil.

  You cannot. So too, if you ever gaze on
  The motionless star burning in the solitary skies,
  If you look at the sun, eye, what do you see? An empty
      Vortex, a nothingness.

"bright" vision, that is, "clear" enough, yet the mind's eye cannot fathom it. The second stanza draws a comparison with the physical eye which is said to be unable to gaze into the immobile sun burning in the vast solitary sky. This parallels the first stanza's image of death as a constellation shining in a black sky. When looked at in any given moment, the sun will appear immobile, but we know that the motionless sun is so characteristically a noontide impression as to be almost a metaphor (like the cicada's stridor) for midday. Moreover, the sun is at the point of most intense heat (*ardente*) and illuminating power at midday, and the poem's irony hinges precisely on the fact that the sun, which is supposedly the source of light and life and the symbol of illumination, is a power of darkness and both symbol and revelation of death itself. The second stanza's comparison is really an answer to the riddle set forth in the first. When the eye looks into the (midday) sun it sees not light but, as though it were blinded-yet-"illuminated," darkness—a black vortex of nothingness. The meaning of death is equally "clear." Critics do not often talk of Pascoli's irony, but we have seen it on one level in the poem "Gloria." Here in "Morte e sole" he has taken the idea that "Le soleil ni la mort ne se peuvent regarder fixement" and turned it into a sardonically intoned (but none the less tragic for that) existential joke. Or was there not something of that already in La Rochefoucauld's maxim?[50]

III. Gabriele D'Annunzio

Combattemmo sul ciglio degli abissi,
In cospetto del Sole, a mezzo il giorno.
("*Ditirambo d'Icaro*")

Few poets have paid tribute to the sun with a fervor, even frenzy, that can match that of Gabriele D'Annunzio, and for no one more than for him has midday been the hour par excellence of the secret of life. From the time of his precocious collection of verse, *Primo vere*, he presented himself as a passionate devotee of Helios, hymning at noon the glory of existence and, in keeping with the archetypal pattern, modulating his lyre to sweetly elegiac music at sunset:

—O Sole, pronubo fulvo, di gioia datore,
Sacro a gli aedi, a' pampini

Caro, m'odi: se mai canzoni di gloria a' meriggi
Ti dissi, e a' vespri placidi
Meste elegie suavi, deh l'ala de 'l tempo fuggente
Tu indugia . . .[a1]

At the height of his fame (in the 1903 volume *Alcyone*) he declared his aggressive love of glory in terms of an allegorical representation in which glory is acclaimed as the vulture of the sun and himself the prey cruelly yet sweetly seized. As he is carried aloft he raises his face to the sun and, looking through the red membranes of his closed eyelids with a pain that is mixed with joy, he sees the world radiant with his

[a] —O Sun, tawny paranymph, donor of joy,
Sacred to poets, dear to the vine,

Hear me: if ever songs of glory at midday
I sang to you, and in the calm evenings
Sweet sorrowful elegies, ah, hold back the wing
Of fleeing time . . .

blood. It is one of several occasions in which the poet suggests a kinship between himself (his "blood") and the sun (glory) and declares his identity as a solar poet:

> O Gloria, o Gloria, vulture del Sole,
> Che su me ti precipiti e m'artigli
> Sin nel focace lito ove m'ascondo!
>
> Levo la faccia, mentre il cor mi duole,
> E pel rossore de' miei chiusi cigli
> Veggo del sangue mio splendere il mondo.[b2]

Yet the earliest of D'Annunzio's poems using the midday motif suggest not triumph and glory so much as the sense of oppression and aridity, and a vision of a humanity vanquished or threatened with destruction. The representation of this theme is given, interestingly enough, in terms that reflect the veristic tendencies in Italian literature of the time. Thus the poem "Pellegrinaggio" ("Pilgrimage," 1880) is very much like a veristic genre picture of a rural landscape in which a procession of mountain and country folk moves along a seemingly endless road, through fields of burnt stubble that lie beneath a pitiless midday sun fixed in a cloudless, birdless sky: "Sta il meriggio fiammante su l'aride stoppie . . . il sole da cieli deserti le fiamme saetta" ("Flaming midday hangs over the parched stubble . . . from empty skies the sun darts its flames," 1; 22). In this vein, the poem "Solleone" ("Days of the Dog Star," 1880) is worth our attention for a number of reasons. It begins with the evocation of a vast silence of a midsummer noontide in which the sun, again from a cloudless blue sky, relentlessly pours its heat and light upon a parched land of endless fields. The creatures of the earth—a waggoner, his horse and dog—are weary and near collapse. Once more cicadas figure as a negative element in the descrip-

---

[b] Oh Glory, oh Glory, vulture of the Sun,
You who swoop down upon me and claw me
Even in the burning shore where I hide!

I raise my face, while my heart is in pain,
And through the redness of my closed eyelids
I see the world radiate with my blood.

tion, their song being referred to as an irritant—"canta la cicala / La canzone de l'uggia" ("The cicada sings / Its monotonous song"). Curiously, however, in a long digression the poet apostrophizes them as symbols of the endless and joyous energy of nature, and as such they are contrasted with the lot of suffering humanity: "Niuna cura te persegue; a gli uomini / Le vane lotte ed il dolore" ("No care pursues you. Unto men / Vain struggle and grief"). The digression is followed by a brief return to the veristic description. Preceded by a calf and followed by a panting child, a passing peasant woman looks at the poet. This feature not only allows for the introduction of the poet into the scene, but, even as it does so, focuses our attention on him. And indeed it is precisely the figure of the poet himself that is of the greatest import here. For the poem closes with a view of him on the scene as a solitary figure emblematic of man overmastered by a hostile and drought-stricken world that offers no refuge (no shade) and no relief (no water). Before him, through the burnt fields, the white road stretches endlessly with no apparent destination:

> . . . . Ho sete:
> Il sole mi brucia orribilmente il volto.
> Non un ruscello mormorante intorno,
> Non un albero ombroso, nulla! Via
> Dritta si slancia la candida strada
> Fra le siepi riarse; sopra il capo
> Il vasto azzurro senza ombra di nube;
> A 'l guardo campi, campi, campi ancora.[c3]

We must be careful not to read too much into these verses, to see in them, for example, an existentialist sense of man's isolation (or lostness) or an Eliot-like picture of modern

[c] . . . . I am thirsty:
The sun burns my face horribly.
Not a murmuring stream around me,
Not a shady tree, nothing! Far
And straight the white road stretches
Through the parched hedges; above my head
The vast blue without the sign of a cloud;
Before my gaze fields, fields, and still more fields.

civilization as a spiritual wasteland. And yet, although the switch from the veristic depiction of the humble folk to the poet himself suggests that the humanitarian or social-minded impulse is simply a pretext for a literary exercise, it would be wrong to deny that the poem's closing lines in some way anticipate the modern use of the midday motif to emblematize the negativity of existence. For that matter, how frequent in veristic literature itself is the portrayal of a vast scorched landscape (where *stoppie riarse* abound) and a mute suffering humanity under the fierce meridian sun of midsummer! The transposition of the motif from a realistic and humanitarian key to a psychological and existentialist one should hardly surprise us. Indeed, to some extent this shift can be seen in the passage (discussed in the previous chapter) from the novella "La lupa" by the master of veristic literature, Giovanni Verga.

As for D'Annunzio, his poems of the immediately succeeding period in the volume *Canto novo* (1882) continue to show a fascination with the hostile Gorgon face of the midday sun, still painted to a degree in semiveristic terms, but not without features that anticipate the vision of, say, a Montale. Thus in the midst of an "immense burning" and an "immobile, virulent splendor," it is again the exhausted poet himself that we see in search of a shady refuge:

> Io cerco a bocca aperta, avidamente,
> Un po' di rezzo qui sotto le rame:
> Dinnanzi, l'Adriatico silente
> Ha barbagli terribili di lame.[d4]

Another poem depicts a funeral procession under the "immense tragic light" of an oppressive noontide:

> Stagna l'azzurra caldura: stendonsi
> Incendiate da 'l sole, a perdita

---

[d] With mouth agape I look, avidly,
For a bit of shade here under the boughs:
Before me, the silent Adriatic
Has terrible flashes of blades.

> Di vista, le sabbie; deserto,
> Triste, metallico bolle il mare.[e,5]

As in the previous verses, here too the sense of a cutting aridity and menace is conveyed by the impression of the metallic glare of the sea, an impression that we will find later in Montale's most famous noonscape.

Noontide is the setting for another unusual attempt by D'Annunzio to depict (again in a veristic vein) the suffering of the Italian peasant. As in the poem "Solleone," the first two stanzas of this lyric evoke a vast, barren, scorched earth where a sultry immobility and silence weigh heavily:

> È mezzogiorno. La strada allungasi
> Diritta innanzi, larga, bianchissima;
> Da' lati le stoppie bruciate,
> Non una pianta là ne 'l giallore.
>
> Non una voce turba l'inerzia
> De l'afa; ardente comme un incendio
> Sta l'afa. Silenzio. Ai cavalli
> Pende la lingua ne 'l trotto stanco.[f,6]

But in the earlier collection of verse, the poem "Lucertole" ("Lizards") already reveals a relationship between the poet and midday that seems more authentically Dannunzian in character by virtue of its classically pagan inspiration and its erotic, sensualistic orientation. The poem evokes a midday scene in which the poet in faunlike fashion is about to complete his seduction of a nymph only to have her suddenly flee

---

[e] The blue heat stagnates: fired
 By the sun the sands stretch
   Out of sight; desolate,
   Sad, the metallic sea boils.
[f] It is noon. The road extends
 Straight before me, wide, intensely white:
 On its sides the burnt stubble,
 Not a tree there in the yellowness.

 Not a sound troubles the stillness
 Of the sultriness; burning like a fire
 The sultriness weighs. Silence. The horses'
 Tongues hang while they trot wearily.

in fright at the sound of a rustling in the bushes. The poet turns to see a number of lizards issue forth and then scamper away. In the volume *Canto novo* this midday eroticism acquires a richer context and a deeper significance, particularly in section VII of the poem "Canto del Sole" ("Song of the Sun"). Again taking his cue from classical precedents (cf. Mallarmé's "Après-midi d'un faune"), the poet as faun prepares to ambush a nymph:

> Sta il gran meriggio su questa di flutti e di piante
>   Verde-azzurrina conca solitaria;
> Ed io, come il fauno antico in agguato, m'ascondo,
>   Platano sacro, qui fra le chiome tue.
> Quando vedrò la ninfa con pavido passo venire,
>   Chiusa ne' suoi capelli l'agile corpo ignudo?[g][7]
>   (1-6)

Beneath the rain of the golden light that pours down from the midday sun through the forest leaves and upon his head, the trembling expectation of the poet-faun is experienced as a Panic surge aiming at the possession of all of nature in a godlike sexual embrace with the nymph (7-31).

The same desire to merge sensually with nature, a merging to be experienced vicariously by sexual union in a noonscape setting, is the theme of section XII of "Canto dell'ospite" ("Song of the Guest"). But rather than being simply propitious, midday here figures as a demanding, even cruel, absolute lord that holds all of nature enthralled. Accordingly, the classical and Arcadian motif of the noontide retreat to a *locus amoenus* is important to the poem which begins precisely on this note of finding relief from an apparently hostile force:

> Dolce godere e l'ombra e l'aura
> Sotto i ciliegi!—Lungi sta l'arido

---

[g] Great midday hovers over this solitary blue green basin of sea and forests;
And I, like an ancient faun in ambush, conceal myself, oh sacred plane tree, midst your foliage.
When will I see the nymph approaching with fearful step and her lithesome nude body enclosed within her hair.

> Giallore dei liti, e il fiammante
> Al sol di giugno tremulo mare.
>
> Lungi ed intorno le solitudini
> Regna il Meriggio, atroce despota,
> Mentre errano per gli orizzonti
> Cupe caligini di viola.
>
> Dolce godere e l'ombra e l'aura
> Sotto i ciliegi![h8]
>
> (1-10)

Here too, the midday sun finds its way through branches and leaves, now playfully arousing the lovers, now "wounding" them (14-20), until, in a paroxysm of sensual joy, the *locus amoenus* is expanded by desire to include all of nature in its full sublimity as the setting for the enactment of the act of love:

> In alto! In alto! I cieli attingere
> Io voglio teco, aver per talamo
> La nube profonda.
>
> . . . Oh delizia
> Suprema! Il mare, il sole, gli alberi,
> I frutti, una chioma, l'amore,
> La giovinezza, fiamma del mondo.[i]
>
> (29-31; 41-44)

---

[h] How sweet to enjoy the shade and the breeze
Beneath the cherry trees! —Far from me is the arid
Yellowness of the shores, and the tremulous sea
Aflame in the sun of June.

Afar and all around the solitude
Midday reigns, cruel despot,
While along the horizon wander
Dark mists of purple.

How sweet to enjoy shade and breeze
Beneath the cherry trees!

[i] On high! On high! To reach the heavens
With you is my desire, to have for bridal bed
A dense cloud.

As though by the silent command of the midday despot (the sun at the zenith), the poet is, paradoxically, driven to the inebriating joy of Panic immersion.

This same motif appears in a slightly different guise in one of D'Annunzio's earliest prose works, the novella "Fra' Lucerta" ("Brother Lucerta") from the volume *Terra vergine* (1882). In the burning hours of noontide the protagonist, a monk, has the habit of seeking a sensually mystic union with nature by lying facedown upon the earth and appearing almost as part of the ground in a posture that suggests a coital embrace. While in this state, he feels himself to be a particle in the womb of immense nature. A tingling and quivering sensation is communicated to him by the earth, and he has the sensation that his blood, though flowing into infinity rather than to his heart, is yet constantly replenished as though by the fount of a god of Hellas. It is a midday delirium—"ubriacature del sole," as the author says.[9]

The midday sun's exacting lordship is the underlying theme of yet another early poem. In fact the sonnet "Panico" (from the collection *Intermezzo*) is the most interesting and most promising of D'Annunzio's early poems on the midday motif insofar as it seeks to communicate a sense of Panic awe and terror in the description of a noontide calm that yet pulsates with life:

> A questo di salute alito enorme
> Che dal sen de la terra umida emana
> Mentre amata da 'l sol la terra dorme
> Ne la tranquillità meridiana,
> Io ne l'imo de l'essere un informe
> Viluppo sento che si schiude. Strana
> Un'angoscia mi preme. Or quali forme
> Partorirà la stanca pianta umana?
> E l'angoscia m'incalza. E l'infinita

>   ... Oh pleasure
> Supreme! Sea, sun, trees,
> Fruit, locks of hair, love,
> Youth, flame of the world.

Vista de i piani, ed il profumo occulto
Che si eleva da i piani, e lo splendore
De l'aria, e queste immense onde di vita
Che su 'l capo mi passano in tumulto,
Or mi dànno io non so quale terrore.[j10]

The "strange anguish" that oppresses the poet is hardly to be mistaken for a Leopardian sentiment of metaphysical anguish. It refers rather to a new stirring and a call to life, felt by the poet in the very heart of a noontide languor and weariness after a period of excess in sexual luxury. (The poem is the third of fourteen sonnets under the general title of *Animal triste*.) It is as though the poet in the guise of a satiated faun is compelled even against his will to respond to the activation of life that the domineering midday sun as relentless lover demands from the earth and its creatures. But the curious thing here is that the analogy developed in the poem is between the impregnated languid earth (cf. Carducci's "Canto di marzo," "Song of March") as a feminine life-giving principle and the poet-faun. Hence the stirring within the poet is experienced as the urge of an embryo to take on form and issue forth. D'Annunzio is here in the role of generatrix (indeed, of womb) on the level of a purely phenomenal relationship with the sun at the zenith. This is true even if we interpret his experience as the sensation of an impulse to a metamorphosis into one of the many "forms" of nature. In the sonnet's sestet, this impulse gives way to an identification of the poet himself as a

[j] At this huge breath of vigor
That issues from the bosom of the damp earth,
While loved by the sun the earth sleeps
Midst the meridian tranquillity,
Within the innermost of my being I feel
A formless, tangled knot unfold. A strange
Anguish presses upon me. To what forms now
Will the weary human plant give birth?
And the anguish keeps crowding upon me. And the infinite
Vista of the plains, and the hidden scent
That rises from the plains, and the radiance
Of the air, and these immense waves of life
That tumultuously pass over my head
Now cause me a nameless terror.

sort of human sounding board catching and vibrating with the sensually grounded intimations of a life force coursing through the whole of the landscape in the hour of Pan. But in seeking to convert the "anguish" into a sense of demonic dread, the sestet seems almost to belong to a different inspiration or level of experience until we realize that it is still the poet as generatrix who has been visited by the midday god Pan himself.

That the revelation of the midday god could have an ambiguous value and even prove a negatively perceived experience (at least for the weak) was a fact well known to D'Annunzio. The most fascinating example of such an encounter in his work occurs in *Il trionfo della morte* (*The Triumph of Death*), a novel in which the sun appears in its dual aspect of virile life-giving source and pitiless god raining cruel light and destructive heat on mankind. The novel's hero seems to have an atavistic kinship with this god, for at one time he even felt the sun to be at the core of his physical and psychic being. But this relationship has been undermined by a fatal flaw in the hero who has now lost the capacity to "revive the Panic delirium of the first day when he believed he had really felt the sun within his heart." Giorgio Aurispa, who has heard the voices of Wagner and Nietzsche, proves unable to rise to the heights of the superman, and as the crowning act of his failure he will descend into the night of Tristan, forcibly dragging his mistress Ippolita with him as an unwilling Isolde. Significantly, the full revelation of his failure is first made in the encounter with midday, which, as we have seen in the introduction, is the supreme Nietzschean test. The further irony or ambiguity lies in the fact that the hero is fully cognizant of the implication of the encounter. The setting is a secluded beach on the Adriatic where Giorgio and Ippolita are bathing:

> Guardando [at Ippolita], egli aveva negli occhi a tratti scintillazioni quasi dolorose; e la gran luce meridiana gli dava un senso nuovo di malessere fisico misto a una specie di vago sgomento. Era l'ora terribile, l'ora pànica, l'ora suprema della luce e del silenzio, imminente su la vacuità

della vita. Egli comprendeva la superstizione pagana: l'orrore sacro dei meriggi canicolari su la plaga abitata da un dio immite ed occulto. In fondo a quel suo vago sgomento si moveva qualche cosa di simile all'ansietà di chi sia nell'attesa di un'apparizione repentina e formidabile. Pareva egli a sé stesso quasi puerilmente debole e trepido, come diminuito d'animo e di forze dopo una prova sfavorevole.[k11]

This is a passage of remarkable insight into the very core of the secret of the midday encounter and the sense of being overmastered. There is in it, moreover, the rich but bewildering ambiguity peculiar to noonday. On the one hand, we find the intuition that this hour of crisis in which light and silence reign supreme contains the revelation of the emptiness or nothingness of existence; on the other, the sense of a mysterious force on the verge of self-revelation toward which the quasi-abulic hero is attracted but by which he ultimately feels diminished and defeated. And in all this there is the suggestion that the two impressions are one and the same.

There are in the novel several symbolically rich scenes in which the noontide sun figures as the overarching antagonist reigning in a terrible glory over human misery, madness, and death, but we may pass over these in order to consider briefly the meditation on Wagner's *Tristan and Isolde* because of its more immediate connection with the episode just discussed. Coming near the end of the novel, it is meant to serve as a prelude to the final scene of murder and suicide by establishing a sense of mystical *amor fati* in the hero who sees a parallel between his own desire for a return to origins (ultimately death) and Tristan's yearning for eternal night.[12] In his reflec-

---

[k] While looking at her, his eyes at times were filled with scintillations that were almost painful, and the intense midday light caused him a new sense of physical discomfort mixed with a kind of vague bewilderment. It was the terrible hour, the Panic hour, the supreme hour of light and silence, hovering over the emptiness of life. He understood the pagan superstition: the sacred horror of hot summer noontides in a region inhabited by a hidden and pitiless god. In the depth of his vague bewilderment there stirred something similar to the anxiety of one who is waiting for a sudden and formidable apparition. He felt himself almost childishly helpless and fearful, as though weakened in courage and strength after having failed in a challenge.

tion on the scene of Tristan's delirium and death, which includes occasional quoting and paraphrasing of Wagner's text, Giorgio equates the fatal love potion with the sun as an instrument and symbol of infinite yearning. This fusion of the two symbols is made clear by the attention given to the fact that the potion is drunk from a *golden* goblet and is felt as a *liquid fire* that roars through the lovers' veins. However, it is the sun that becomes the dominant libido symbol of the passion that burns and consumes Tristan:

> In nessun luogo, in nessun luogo, ahimé, troverò riposo. La notte mi respinge al giorno, e l'occhio del sole si pasce del mio perpetuo soffrire. Ah come il sole rovente mi brucia e mi consuma! E non il refrigerio d'un'ombra a questa divorante arsura (pp. 343-344).[1]

The personification of both sun and passion in the image of the solar eye that cruelly feeds upon Tristan's suffering, even as it evokes the idea of the intensity of the passion (= suffering), deifies that passion by virtue of being itself a relentless, overmastering god. That it is a midday god (or demon) is suggested by the absence of any shade in which to find relief. Of course, this sun/passion burns *within* Tristan and so may be said to feed upon itself. Thus Tristan's cry against the sun is, like his curse of the love potion, really directed against himself: "Questo terribile filtro, che mi danna al supplizio, io, io medesimo lo composi. . . . Io, io medesimo composi il tossico di questo filtro. E io lo bevvi, a lunghi sorsi di delizia . . . Maledetto sii tu, filtro terribile! Maledetto sia chi ti compose!" (p. 344).[m] The sun of passion, however, is also the source of the suprahuman joy Tristan has known. Its value had been declared earlier in his delirium when he stated that it

---

[1] Nowhere, nowhere, alas, will I find peace. Night rejects me and drives me back to day, and the eye of the sun feeds on my perpetual suffering. Oh, how the fiery sun burns and consumes me! And not the relief of a shade for this devouring fire.

[m] This terrible philter which damns me to torment, it is I myself who have prepared it. . . . I myself have prepared the poison of this philter. And I have drunk it in long draughts of joy. . . . Be cursed terrible philter! Cursed be he who concocted you.

was only since the sun had made its secret abode in their breasts that he and Isolde had experienced a paradisal (literally, a *stellar*) light of happiness: "Da che il sole s'è occultato nel nostro petto, le stelle della felicità diffondono il loro lume ridente" (p. 339). Now that it has completed its work of consuming Tristan from within, this sun is revealed for the supreme ecstatic libido symbol that it is, radiating a blinding light that floods the universe as music. This interpretation is inspired by the synesthetic image of Wagner's text (and its accompanying music) where Tristan, just before dying at the approach of Isolde, claims to *hear* the light. D'Annunzio emphasizes the synesthetic element:

> All'approssimarsi d'Isolda e della Morte, egli credeva *udire* la luce. "Non odo io la luce? Non odono i miei orecchi la luce?" Un gran sole interiore lo abbagliava; da tutti gli atomi della sua sostanza partivano raggi di sole e per onde luminose e armoniose si diffondevano nell'universo. La luce era musica; la musica ere luce (p. 345).[n]

Here, the image of the sun and Tristan have merged. It is from *within* the hero that the solar rays irradiate as luminous music that permeates the universe. Tristan has become expanded into the All—the *Gran Tutto*. The paradox is that this "light" is the desired "night" of nothingness: "Tristano era entrato alfine nell'eterna notte" (p. 345).[o] Isolde too is now transfigured from poisoner and murderess (as D'Annunzio, or Giorgio, sees her) into a being of pure light and joy who, like her lover, dissolves into the mystic gulf—into the Great All. And the meditation closes with Isolde's words translated from Wagner's text: "Nell'infinito palpito dell'anima universa perdersi, profondarsi, vanire, senza conscienza: suprema voluttà!" (p. 346).[p]

---

[n] At the approach of Isolde and of Death, he believed he *heard* the light. "Do I not hear the light? Do my ears not hear the light?" A great internal sun dazzled him; from all the atoms of his being rays of sunlight went forth and spread throughout the universe in luminous and harmonious waves. The light was music; the music was light.

[o] Tristan had entered at last into the eternal night.

[p] To be lost in the infinite beating of the universal soul, to sink into it, dissolve, without consciousness: supreme pleasure!

The episode from *Il trionfo della morte* in which Giorgio is overmastered by the sun has all the authenticity of a firsthand experience of an *échec* in the encounter with the midday demon. But more often than not D'Annunzio shows himself equal to the encounter and "increased" or "expanded" in the tensive hour of Pan, sometimes with such intimations as we have found in his retelling of Tristan's death, although we are more likely to think of him in an aggressive pose. Whatever the case, the midday god ("atroce despota") will forever be a cruel god ("dio immite"), yet a beneficent god nonetheless, though in the joy he brings there can be no room for tenderness or nostalgia. This is the message of which D'Annunzio made himself the champion in introducing the several volumes of his *Laudi del Cielo del Mare della Terra e degli Eroi* (*Songs in Praise of the Sky, the Sea, the Earth, and Heroes*). The introductory poem of 156 lines is pregnantly entitled "L'Annunzio," and the "announcement" is that the poet comes as a herald to proclaim the revelation made to him at midday that "great Pan is not dead":

> Uditemi! Udite l'annunziatore di lontano
> Che reca l'annunzio del prodigio meridiano
> Onde fu pieno tutto quanto
> Il cielo nell'ora ardente! V'empirò di meraviglia;
> V'infiammerò di gioia; vi trarrò dalle ciglia
> Il riso e il pianto.[q13]
>
> (13-18)

At high noon when the revelation (*parola solare!*) was made to him, all of nature was in an attitude of hushed devotion toward the sun. The description of this moment culminates in a stanza that equates the poet with the sun, and even, one may say, with the midday god himself from whom the announcement is heard:

[q] Hear me! Hearken to the messenger from afar
Who brings the tidings of the midday miracle
Wherewith the heavens were completely
Filled in the fiery hour! I will fill you with wonder;
I will inflame you with joy; I will draw from your eyes
Laughter and tears.

Tutto era silenzio, luce, forza, desìo.
L'attesa del prodigio gonfiava questo mio
Cuore come il cuor del mondo.
Era questa carne mortale impaziente
Di risplendere, come se d'un sangue fulgente.
L'astro ne rigasse il pondo.
La sostanza del Sole era la mia sostanza.
Erano in me i cieli infiniti, l'abbondanza
Dei piani, il Mar profondo.

E dal culmine dei cieli alle radici del Mare
Balenò, risonò la parola solare:
"Il gran Pan non è morto!"[r][14]

(106-117)

The title "L'Annunzio" is pregnant, of course, because it echoes the poet's real name. But his "Christian" name is no less significant here, and we may be sure that D'Annunzio expected his readers to understand that he was "correcting" an earlier Gabriel's annunciation as a false prophecy. By the same token, the general title *Laudi* echoes the Franciscan lauds of the Middle Ages in a defiantly pagan way. "L'Annunzio" is an exhortation to return to nature, and there is even a polemical thrust at Christianity for having made men deaf to nature's call (125-130).[15] But our main concern is with the character of D'Annunzio's noontide as expressed in the foregoing verses. Silence and light pervade all of nature, but along with them, in the heart of all things, is the sense of a latent primal energy that seems on the very point of bursting

---

[r] All was silence, light, force, desire.
The wait for the miracle swelled my
Heart like the heart of the world.
This mortal flesh was anxious
To shine forth, as if the sun had veined
The heaviness [of my flesh] with a refulgent blood.
The Sun's substance was my substance.
In me were an infinite sky, the abundance
Of the plains, the deep Sea.

And from the summit of the heavens to the roots of the Sea
There flashed, resounded, the solar word:
"Great Pan is not dead!"

into actualization. The sonnet "Panico" already suggested this same characteristic of noontide, and we shall meet with it again in other and greater verses of the poet. Here we may note that at the beginning of an essay on the painter Giorgione, D'Annunzio had referred to it specifically when he wrote that the sense of stasis at the hour of Pan derives from a concentrated passion and a repressed violence: "Soprastava a Venezia una di quelle ore che si potrebbero chiamar paniche, in cui la vita sembra sospesa ma non è, chè anzi la sua immobilità risulta da passione concentrata e da violenza repressa."s16

The verses we have quoted from "L'Annunzio" bespeak a pantheistic sentiment. At the very least there is the sense of an identity of the self with the whole of nature. Though one may deny a theological interpretation to D'Annunzio's midday encounter, it is not possible to deny that it involves a clear case of a perception of a concentration of all energy and of all nature in the self. For a moment individual being has been transcended or has merged into a universal self. The poet is identified with Pan. With that identification, it is true, he is ready to plunge into multiplicity and to celebrate the infinite forms (or "members") of the god.[17] In what Italian critics refer to as D'Annunzio's panism there is now a sense of confidence in which the self is declared to be commensurable with all the phenomenal world.

In connection with this last point it can be instructive and perhaps not as digressive as it might at first seem if at this point we pause to take note of a poem by the English writer with whom our poet shows the greatest affinity. Algernon Charles Swinburne's work was known, admired, and in some cases "imitated" by D'Annunzio, and the long noon piece entitled "A Nympholept" (1894) may well have influenced the latter's midday mythology, though it would certainly be wrong to think of it as having had a formative influence. But even if one prefers not to speak of a direct influence in this

---

[s] Over Venice there hovered one of those hours that can be called Panic, in which life seems suspended but is not, for on the contrary, its immobility results from concentrated passion and repressed violence.

case, Swinburne's themes, images, mood, and, to a degree, the intonation and verbal excesses are, from an Italian point of view, quite "Dannunzian" and so may properly serve as an interesting touchstone in our consideration of the Italian poet.

Intended to describe the splendid oppression of nature, "A Nympholept" is an amazing nature poem by any standard. Besides bringing us as deep into the heart of midday as the texts of the most audacious sounders of that hour, it traces the whole arc of noontide (or man's reaction to it) from its negative to its positive pole. The first two lines of the poem refer to that midday phenomenon in which silence and light may be spoken of in terms of one another, and either or both may be seen and "heard":

> Summer, and noon, and a splendour of silence, felt
> Seen, and heard of the spirit within the sense.

That the noontide stasis is highly charged with the tension of energy and latency is indicated in line 50, "But the silence trembles with passion of sound suppressed," which also confirms the experience of a midday silence so deep that it may create its own audible impression. The bewilderment experienced in the ambiguous atmosphere of midday which circles man round with "rapture or terror," with "hope" and "dread," is summarized in these two lines:

> Is it love, is it dread, that enkindles the trembling noon,
> That yearns, reluctant in rapture that fear has fled?
>
> (78-79)

Though noon "pervades, invades, appals" (83), the presence of Pan is felt as a fear so "deep" and "sacred" that it is "wellnigh sweet" (92-93). And here indeed is a feature that is also characteristic of D'Annunzio's noontide encounters. The fear or dread is not really dissipated entirely at any time, but rather becomes absorbed into what might ordinarily be thought of as its opposite. We are dealing, so to speak, with an experiential oxymoron. This important motif is also present in the treatment of the poet's attraction to the visionary maiden, a figure who is not so much a surrogate as an epiphany of Pan or of the noontide mystery itself. Noon, Pan, and the maiden are ultimately one and the same, a triune divinity that is nature revealing itself at midday. At the poem's climax, as he looks into the maiden's eyes, the poet notes that "her eyes embolden / Fear, till it change to desire, and desire to delight" (216-217). The progression is typical of the mystical experience whether it be in an orthodox religious context or in an atheistic one such as that in Leopardi's inexhaustible "L'infinito."

All the lines we have quoted are pregnant and brilliant, but Swinburne's notorious obsession with words vitiates even this often admirable poem, and it would be tedious to follow him in all the verbal vagaries of his dithyrambic celebration of Pan. We need only observe further that in the end the feeling of dread and menace yields entirely to what is clearly an ecstasy:

> The terror that whispers in darkness and flames in light,
> The doubt that speaks in the silence of earth and sea,
> The sense, more fearful at noon than in mid-most night,
> Of wrath scarce hushed and of imminent ill to be,
> Where are they? Heaven is as earth, and as heaven to me
> Earth: for the shadows that sundered them here take flight;
> And nought is all, as am I, but a dream of thee.

Though the second person pronoun *thee* (the very last word of the poem) is addressed specifically to the visionary maiden, it is an ambiguous referent that applies equally to Pan, noon, and, of course, to the all of nature that is implied therein. The ecstasy or the pantheistic experience of absorption of the self into the all is one in which the self is clearly annihilated—"And nought is all, as am I, but a dream of thee"—and as this most ambiguous of lines would seem to suggest, the all may indeed be nothingness or the Absolute perceived negatively. The atmosphere in which this revelation occurs is the epitome of noon. The absence of shadows and the equality of the light throughout obliterates the distinction between heaven and earth, creating the impression of an undifferentiated luminosity in which all things are transfigured in an immanent glory.

And the whole, of course, is permeated with silence. It is a silent glory.

In returning directly to the Italian poet we can say that the sense of infinite latency and expectancy at the core of nature and the self is perhaps the most typical feature of D'Annunzio's midday encounters. It is connected with the sensation of an absolute suspension in which timelessness is experienced. This is the case especially in a passage from the long "hymn" *Laus Vitae* where the midday stasis is experienced as a "pausa infinita," and eternity actually appears as a quality in things—a quality that is *seen*, as it were ("L'occhio solo / Era vivo e veggente"), and *felt*. In sight of Mount Parnassus, the boat in which the poet and his companions have been sailing over Grecian waters slackens as a vast noontide calm descends:

> Cadde il vento. Noi tutti
> Èramo senza parola
> Fissi alla gran maraviglia.
> Sospeso era il Giorno sul nostro
> Capo. Tutte le cose
> Tacevano con un aspetto
> Di eternità. L'occhio solo
> Era vivo e veggente.
> O tregua apollinea, Meriggio!
> . . . . Il silenzio
> Era come il silenzio
> Che segue o precede le voci
> Delle volontà sovrumane.
> Tutta la vita era a noi
> Quasi tempio lieve senz'ombra,
> Ch'entrammo non più morituri.[t18]

---

[t] The wind fell. All of us
Were speechless,
Intent on the great prodigy.
The Day was suspended above
Our heads. All things
Were silent with a look
Of eternity. Only our eyes
Were alive and perceiving.

This representation of a deathlike suspension of all things, including all human faculties and sensations save for the eye alone which is said to live, is strikingly similar to Nietzsche's characterization of a noontide ecstasy as "a death with waking eyes," a death in which "the heart stands still, and only the eye lives." In Nietzsche's experience, too, all things are said to have been stilled and bear the "expression" of a silent luminosity that is eternity. One thinks also of the ecstasy recorded in "Sils-Maria" or, better yet, of the poem "Nach neuen Meeren" where the images of boat, voyage, and sea are all present, and as midday "sleeps" over space and time, only the vast eye of infinity looks upon the poet (see my introduction). In D'Annunzio's verses the air of expectancy and infinite potency is an attribute of the all-pervading silence itself which is spiritually energized by the references to divine or suprahuman voices that may have preceded it or may follow it. The whole of the phenomenal world is transfigured, experienced as cosmos, and now appears as a shadowless, luminous temple of silent glory in which the poet and his companions move, feeling themselves shorn of mortality. Here too, then, the experience is clearly one in which there is a consciousness of *possession* of or participation in eternal life.

Although the last quoted passage gives an account of as mystical or spiritual a moment as one is likely to find in D'Annunzio, the highest poetic expression of his relationship with midday is connected with the naturalistic interpretation of existence that he unabashedly proclaimed. Three of his very best lyrics, *"Furit aestus,"* "Meriggio," and *Stabat nuda Aestas"* deal with the theme in this key. All three poems are from his finest volume of verse, *Alcyone*, which includes the sonnet "Il Vulture del Sole" referred to at the outset of this

> Oh Apollonian truce, Midday!
> .... The silence
> Was like the silence
> That follows or precedes the voices
> Of superhuman wills.
> All of life was for us
> Like the airy temple without shadows,
> Into which we entered no longer mortal.

chapter. And it is that poem's image of a feral sun that is here dithyrambically hailed over and over by the poet, the tawny lion/sun as a fiery libido symbol that burns into the poet its own insatiable thirst:

> O fulva fiera
> O infiammata leonessa dell'Etra,
> Grande Estate selvaggia,
> Libidinosa,
> Vertiginosa,
> Tu che affochi le reni,
> Che incrudisci la sete—[u]

It is a sun that is loved in its contrasting faces of Muse and Gorgon, an oxymoron or fusion of a Grace and a Bacchante, beautiful in its silent violence:

> Musa, Gorgòne,
> . . . .
> Grazia, Baccante,
> . . . .
> Bella nelle tue rabbie
> Silenziose, acre nei tuoi torpori.[v19]

The poem *"Furit aestus"* is a dramatic representation of the repressed energy and infinite potency that exist in a midsummer noontide and of the intense, almost wild state of expectancy in the poet:

[u] Oh tawny beast
Oh flaming lioness of the Ether,
Great untamed Summer,
Libidinous,
Dizzy,
You who set fire to our loins,
You who exacerbate our thirst.
[v] Muse, Gorgon,
. . . .
Grace, Bacchante,
. . . .
Beautiful in your silent
Fury, acrid in your languor.

Un falco stride nel color di perla:
Tutto il cielo si squarcia come un velo.
O brivido su i mari taciturni,
O soffio, indizio del sùbito nembo!
O sangue mio come i mari d'estate!
La forza annoda tutte le radici:
Sotto la terra sta, nascosta e immensa.
La pietra brilla più d'ogni altra inerzia.

La luce copre abissi di silenzio,
Simile ad occhio immobile che celi
Moltitudini folli di desiri.
L'Ignoto viene a me, l'Ignoto attendo!
Quel che mi fu da presso, ecco, è lontano.
Quel che vivo mi parve, ecco, ora è spento.
T'amo, o tagliente pietra che su l'erta
Brilli pronta a ferire il nudo piede.

Mia dira sete, tu mi sei più cara
Che tutte le dolci acque dei ruscelli.
Abita nella mia selvaggia pace
La febbre come dentro le paludi.
Pieno di grida è il riposato petto.
L'ora è giunta, o mia Mèsse, l'ora è giunta!
Terribile nel cuore del meriggio
Pesa, o Mèsse, la tua maturità.[w20]

[w]A hawk screeches in the color of pearl:
The whole sky is torn like a veil.
Oh shudder on the mute sea,
Oh breath, sign of the sudden storm.
Oh my blood, like the summer sea!
A force knots together all the roots:
It is under the ground, hidden and immense.
The rock gleams more than all other inert forms.

Light covers the abysses of silence,
Like a motionless eye that conceals
Wild multitudes of desires.
The Unknown comes to me, the Unknown I await!
That which was near me, behold, now it is far off.
That which seemed alive to me, behold, now it is dead.

From the opening image of the hawk's screech tearing the expanse of a bright yet hazy sky like the sudden tearing of a veil (and poetically here the sky *is* the pearl-colored veil), the highest pitch of tension is created. Though the sea is still, a tremor seems to course over it, caused by a breeze that announces a cloud. In an image that suggests a correspondence between the poet and nature that will be vital in the poem's conclusion, the blood coursing through the poet's veins is said to be like the waters of the sea that are apparently calm on the surface but are permeated with a mysterious current. It is the same energy, identified in lines 6-7, that pulsates secretly but with infinite potentiality beneath the surface of the earth. Line 8 identifies the mysterious force with light. All things appear inert in this charged stasis, yet that which would seem to be the most inert object of all, the mountain rock, glistens with more energy (reflected light) than anything else. The dazzling line (9) that follows—"La luce copre abissi di silenzio"—reveals that the midday light is master of all, filling heaven and earth and the space between with an absolute silence. Midday has imposed silence on all things. For the light *is* silence (or vice versa) in such a moment. The very substance of the universe is experienced as a luminous silence which is mysteriously (and paradoxically) pregnant with the desire and promise of life.[21] This is made clear in the succeeding lines (10-11) by the simile that equates the silent light with a motionless eye that conceals a restless host of desires, i.e., life in an inchoate state yearning to burst into form.

How different then is this absolute light and silence of midday from that recorded by Leopardi in the second stanza of

---

I love you, oh cutting rock that on the steep
Glisten ready to cut the naked foot.

My tremendous thirst, you are dearer to me
Than all the sweet waters of the streams.
In my wild peace there dwells
Fever as in the midst of swamps.
My stilled breast is full of cries.
The hour has arrived, oh my Harvest, the hour is here!
Terrifying in the heart of midday
Oh my Harvest, your ripeness weighs.

"La vita solitaria!" Where Leopardi sought and found insentience and a primordial stillness or void, which can only be thought of as a state of nonbeing, D'Annunzio finds the intimation of original energy. At this point of the poem (and of the experience) where the light and silence are experienced at the deepest level, D'Annunzio appears as a passionate devotee hovering between anxiety and ecstasy, caught in the timeless moment of absolute latency—"L'Ignoto viene a me, l'Ignoto attendo!" In such a moment all things prized in the past lose their value and give way to the expectancy of the future present (13-14). Thus the timeless moment being experienced, which is objectified in the jagged granite mountainside bathed in the light of midday (suggesting a "cruel" side to the encounter), is what the poet desires fiercely (15-16). The midday despot is met on his own terms by the poet, and the terrible thirst of desire—"dira sete"—which the sun has burned into the very body of the poet is dearer to him now than all the quenching sweet waters of the streams would be. The attitude that dismisses D'Annunzio as a theatrical wordmonger is itself superficial. His choice of the word *dira* is as precise as it is significant. It is a numinously charged word that Rudolf Otto in his study on the holy connects with the concept of *tremendus*. As such "it may mean evil or imposing, potent and strange, queer and daemonic, and a source of *energy*."[22] In the context of *"Furit aestus,"* the use of the term in the phrase *mia dira sete* expresses not merely the poet's subjective feeling but an awareness of and a positive response to original and infinite energy. The fierceness of midday's charged stasis, with its heat, light, and silence, pregnant with a repressed infinite potency, is matched by the poet in whom resides a violent peace ("selvaggia pace") vibrant with the fever of expectancy and potentiality. At this point, the expression *selvaggia pace* is followed by yet another oxymoron in which the midday silence is perceived as a wild howl. The poet's breast, apparently calm, barely represses a core of energy ready to explode into actualization. Now, in the very heart of noontide, is the eternally imminent moment of promise to be fulfilled, of latency on the verge of escaping into the infinite multiplicity of forms. In keeping with the poem's seasonal and diurnal context—a blazing summer midday—this repressed energy or latency is represented by the image of an awesome harvest heavy with ripeness (17-24). (And here we recall the "ripeness" and fullness that Nietzsche connected with the perfect hour of midday.) It is not too much to say that the poet has established an experiential equation between himself and the midday described by him in the first part of the poem, although the self has not been obliterated.[23]

D'Annunzio has written that force is the primary law of nature and can neither be abolished nor destroyed ("la forza è la prima legge della natura, indistruttibile, inabolibile"). His poem *"Furit aestus"* reveals this energy as original power at the highest possible level of tension, existing both in the heart of nature (midday) and in the human body.

On the other hand, the second great noon piece from *Alcyone*, entitled precisely "Meriggio," evokes a profound midday calm that seems almost devoid of tension. Here the complete identification between nature (i.e., midday = Pan) and the poet is realized via an interchange or fusion in which, while the poet's self is happily surrendered to nature, nature itself acquires something of a human identity. During a midsummer midday in which the poet lies on a sandy beach of the Mediterranean Sea near the mouth of the Arno, a sultry calm weighs heavily upon the waters: "A mezzo il giorno / Sul Mare etrusco / . . . grava / La bonaccia" (1-6).[x] A series of negatives (cf. Leopardi's second stanza of "La vita solitaria") describes the utter stillness of sky, sea, and land: "Non bava / Di vento intorno / Alita. Non trema canna / Su la solitaria / Spiaggia. . . . / Non suona voce" (6-12).[y] Once again, light and silence are apprehended as one and the same. Inasmuch as it belongs to the light, silence acquires a spatial dimension. All things are perceived as existing within this all-pervading luminous silence of midday ("Pel chiaro silen-

[x] At midday / On the Etruscan sea / . . . a dead calm lies heavily.
[y] Not even a light breeze whispers around. / No reeds waver / On the solitary shore . . . / No voice sounds.

zio"): the white sails fixed in a motionless sea, cape and islands in an indefinable distance, jagged mountains that stand majestically above the waters, the mouth of the Arno which in the morning rippled sparkingly and now has the appearance of a lifeless pond that suggests a Lethean oblivion, the distant meeting point of the banks of the river where the reeds seem to enclose the waters of forgetfulness ("l'oblio silente"). Everywhere there is nought but a vast stillness, sultriness, absolute light and silence; and yet, for all that, there is the sense that summer has ripened to fullness around the poet like a promise of rich fruit to be picked and enjoyed by him alone:

> Bonaccia, calura,
> Per ovunque silenzio.
> L'Estate si matura
> Sul mio capo come un pomo
> Che promesso mi sia,
> Che cogliere io debba
> Con la mia mano,
> Che suggere io debba
> Con le mie labbra solo.[z][24]
> (55-63)

As in "*Furit aestus*," so too in these verses there exists a relationship of desire between the poet and nature, but here the potential wildness suggested by the imagery is magically absorbed and nullified by the placid, lulling rhythm of the verses. The tension of expectancy and latency gives way to appeasement and fulfillment. First the human form of the poet is transfigured by the midday light:

[z] Dead calm, intense heat,
Everywhere silence.
Summer ripens
Over my head like a fruit
That is promised to me,
That I must pluck
With my hand,
That I must suck
With my lips only.

> .... Ogni duolo
> Umano m'abbandona.
> Non ho più nome.
> E sento che il mio volto
> S'indora dell'oro
> Meridiano.[aa]
>
> (66-71)

There follows the sense of a dissolving of the self into the various objects of the vast surrounding landscape which calls to mind Leopardi's *meriggio* from "La vita solitaria," a comparison between the two noonscapes that has already suggested itself because of the use in both poems of a series of negatives to indicate the absence of motion. But there is some question as to whether D'Annunzio means to describe a Leopardian passing into absolute insentience. Certainly there is a sense of the poet's own life force flowing into and becoming one with the multiplicity of nature's forms, even with those that are only apparently inanimate, and a sense of nature as being the very body of the poet himself: "E il fiume è la mia vena, / Il monte è la mia fronte, / La selva è la mia pube, / La nube è il mio sudore" (85-88).[bb] Even as the poet has been released from his human form and limitations, so too the multiplicity of nature's forms is experienced—or, we may say, experiences itself by way of the poet—as a transfigured whole (an anthropomorphized body), a single greater self that can be identified as the one-in-all. Between the poet and the whole of the phenomenal world there obtains a state of *coinherence*. And because midday with its stasis and absolute light is the experiential revelation of this miracle, the name of the poet, as of all things, is taken from the blazing hour of Pan:

[aa] ... All human
Suffering leaves me.
I have no name more.
And I feel that my face
Becomes gilded with the gold
Of midday.

[bb] And the river is my vein, / The mountain is my forehead, / The forest is my pubis, / The cloud is my sweat.

Ardo, riluco.
E non ho più nome.
E l'alpe e l'isole e i golfi
E i capi e i fari e i boschi
E le foci ch'io nomai
Non han più l'usato nome
Che suona in labbra umane.
Non ho più nome né sorte
Tra gli uomini; ma il mio nome
É Meriggio. In tutto io vivo
Tacito come la Morte.

E la mia vita è divina.[cc]

(99-109)

"Meriggio" records the serene but triumphant actualization of the miracle that is anxiously, even violently, intimated in "Panico," "L'Annunzio," and *Furit aestus*." It goes beyond these poems in giving expression to a sentiment which, if not pantheistic in the strictest theological sense of the word, is nonetheless "pamphysistic" and born of a genuine mystical experience of nature.[25] In it D'Annunzio describes the silent yet thrilling life of the self transcending human limitations ("Non ho più nome né sorte / Tra gli uomini") and realizing infinite identity. If this is so, then the last three lines of the poem are to be understood as proclaiming the abolition of all limits and of any division between life and death. While "Meriggio" is not in the dithyrambic mode common to much

---

[cc] I blaze, I glitter.
And I have no name more.
And mountains and islands and gulfs
And capes and lighthouses and forests
And the outlets I have named
No longer have their usual name
That sounds on human lips.
I have no name more or lot
Among men; but my name
Is Midday. In all I live
Silent like Death.

And my life is divine.

of *Alcyone*, it is not really far removed from the expansive manner in which the immanent glory of midday is sung by the poet on other occasions. D'Annunzio would seem to be all the more alive for being expanded into the calm "all" of nature where by virtue of possession (it is the poet who possesses and is all) the tension of desire is finally at rest. And yet a doubt or ambiguity remains, the suspicion that this divine quietude of fulfillment—the Nietzschean midday stasis of fullness—may somehow be the expression of still another desire, the secret desire for an absorption of the self into the silent light that is the night of nothingness. Nonetheless, the experience seems to me to remain on this side of the *antica quiete* of Leopardi's noonscape and the earlier poet's unambiguous absorption into nonbeing. The mood and "sensation" with which D'Annunzio concludes are perhaps nearer to what we found at the close of Swinburne's "A Nympholept."

There is no doubt that the principal direction of D'Annunzio's midday pamphysism or panism is toward a sensualistic identification of the self with the forms of nature, but this does not make his panism any less authentic.[26] It is for this reason that among the most successful of his poems are several dealing with metamorphosis or the mythological representation of the fusion of the human and the natural, although "Meriggio," which records the same experience, does without this device and supersedes all such poems. For D'Annunzio, to "know" nature does not mean to understand or to deduce an organizational principle in nature; rather it is to be immersed in a perception and sensation that is experienced not as annihilation but as an expansion of the self. This is the significance of his discovery and proclamation of joy and the abolition of sorrow in the concluding section of *Laus Vitae*:

> Ma il meridiano delirio
> Nel Deserto l'oblìo
> D'ogni cima più perigliosa
> Mi diede e d'ogni demenza
> Più lucida e d'ogni divieto
> Abbattuto.

. . . .
E l'anima mia dalla culla
Dell'eternità parve alzata
In quell'ora.
. . . .
Ed ella taceva, profonda
Del suo più profondo silenzio.
Ma parole erano dette
In lei, alla gran luce
Del mezzodì, chiare parole.
. . . .
Felicità, non ti cercai;
Ché soltanto cercai me stesso,
Me stesso e la terra lontana.
Ma nell'ora meridiana
Tu venisti a me d'improvviso.[dd][27]

Here *in nuce* is D'Annunzio's symbolic identification of midday with the epiphany of joy. Unsentimental, even cruel, joy is the fulfillment of the self. If one wishes, one may reverse the terms. In either case, joy or the unashamed realization of

[dd] But the midday delirium in the Desert
Brought me forgetfulness
Of all the most perilous peaks
And of all the most lucid
Follies and of every broken
Prohibition.
. . . .
And my soul seemed raised
From the cradle of Eternity
In that hour.
. . . .
And she [my soul] was silent, deep
With its deepest silence.
But words were spoken
In her, in the great light
Of midday, luminous words.
. . . .
Happiness, I did not seek you;
For I sought only myself,
Myself and the far away land.
But in the midday hour
You came to me suddenly.

the self is the means by which man truly "knows" (and one may rightly keep the sexual connotation of the word) life and nature, and by which he rises above the ordinary class of humans. In the final verses quoted above, the personification of joy suggests a woman whose appearance and surrender to the poet in the *ora meridiana* is yet another variation of the poet-as-faun myth. It is, in fact, one of the more extraordinary versions of the ancient theme of midday nympholepsy to be found in world literature. Hour of "ripeness" and fullness, and, because of that, hour of crisis, midday is the time for the revelation or the advent of joy as a value of self-realization and the immanental sense of original power which lies stored at the heart of existence.[28]

IV. Some Twentieth-Century Voices

> The motive for metaphor, shrinking from
> The weight of primary noon,
> The ABC of being.
> (*Wallace Stevens*)

Even more than writers in previous ages, writers of the twentieth century have made emblematic use of summer, noontide, and the midday sun—a fact that will not surprise anyone familiar with the great role modern art has allocated to the sun in general, and especially to its "intense utterances."[1] The explanation that this fact calls for will unfold throughout this chapter and the rest of the book, and it is only necessary at this point to say that it is connected with the sense of crisis that has been especially acute in Italy (as in all of Europe) since the outset of the century. Modern Italian authors of course have written of the sun and midday with a critical awareness of the presence of these images in the work of their predecessors, and, as one might expect, it is D'Annunzio's midday mythology that has exercised the greatest influence on them either by attraction or revulsion—attitudes, to be sure, that we have found to be prevalent in all ages in connection with the ambiguous solar phenomenon of noontide itself. But while the Dannunzian presence is massive, it is not the only one to be felt by the new century's writers, the best of whom reveal, in any case, an assimilation of the old into an unmistakable tonality and vision of their own.

This is clearly true of Clemente Rebora, a poet whose importance as one of the major voices expressing the general air of crisis in the decade before World War I from within the context of a personal "existentialist" drama is becoming more and more apparent.[2] Thus Rebora's own intense utterances in connection with our theme deserve close attention. We may begin with a look at the lyric entitled "Quassù" ("Up Here") which perhaps calls to mind Carducci's "Mezzogiorno alpino" even more than D'Annunzio or Leopardi's "L'infinito." Of the four quatrains that make up the poem, the last two are almost too abstractly or intellectually concerned with conveying the sense of a yearning for purity, for release from the crassness and mediocrity of the city and modern civilization. However, the first two quatrains (they are really self-sufficient) evoke an Alpine midday in which the joyous purity and pulsating harmony of the cosmos vibrate in the poet who thus "knows" them in a phenomenal or sensualistic way:

> Dentro il meriggio stanno alberi e scogli
> Vividi al sol che infiamma la sua ora
> Sopra le vette: e tu, aria, ne accogli
> Limpidamente la forma sonora.
>
> Tutta è mia casa la montagna, e sponda
> Al desiderio il cielo azzurro porge;
> Ineffabile palpita gioconda
> L'estasi delle cose, e in me si accorge.[a3]

There is expressed here the sense of the superior life of the cosmos, revealed in the absolute and vivifying light of midday glory to and through the poet. The trees and mountains are said to be *within* midday, partaking of its quality of absoluteness, while the midday sun itself emblazes its mastery from above and permeates all of space. Within the luminous meridian atmosphere the silence is so intense as to have its own sonority (3-4). In absorbed contemplation and yearning toward the infinite purity of the blue sky, the poet is invaded by

[a] Within midday trees and rocks stand
Vivid in the sun that emblazes its hour
Above the summits: and you, air, receive
From it, limpidly, its sonorous form.

The whole mountain is my abode, and
The blue sky offers a shore to my desire;
Ineffably, joyfully, the ecstasy of things
Throbs, and reaches awareness in me.

the thrill of the Absolute and experiences an intuition of the divine immensity. The experience is the more compelling because of the suggestion that the glorious life of the cosmos becomes known to itself by way of the poet. That is to say, the poet figures as the vehicle through which the absolute or the cosmic life acquires consciousness: "L'estasi delle cose . . . in me si accorge." It seems that what is meant here is not just communion but identification with the "all" in the hour of Pan. For what the poet feels is an identifying pantheistic ecstasy that involves the triumphant experience of self-expansion and self-realization. Yet this is not to be confused with D'Annunzio's mythology of the midday delirium (or panism) and the advent of joy. Because D'Annunzio's experience of self-realization and unity (the unity of all being) is grounded in a naturalistic pantheism, his root metaphor remains the "body" or "matter." In the case of Rebora's poem, the subjective center of experience, it somehow seems, is the core of being itself with which the poet has become identified in a way that transcends the body. Here the root metaphor is, as I have already suggested, "spirit" or, better yet, "consciousness." It is the consciousness not of the poet alone but of being itself. Thus this Alpine midday may remind us of D'Annunzio and certainly of Carducci's "Mezzogiorno alpino," but in its surge "upward" into a state of wonder and pure consciousness it is in fact closer to Pascoli's "Dall'argine." One thinks also of Emily Dickinson's vision of immortality where "The Centuries of June / And Centuries of August cease / And Consciousness—is Noon."[4]

In Rebora's poem *"Salve"* ("Hail!"), not the mountain in particular but the whole countryside is the setting for a vast midday calm in which the sun appears as a mighty, silent explosion of glory while all creatures are at rest. From this initial moment, which includes an awareness of cosmic expansion of life, the poem develops the motif of an interiorization of the quality of absoluteness felt in midday, the poet discovering in himself a corresponding inner immensity and infinite potency:

Per le deserte strade alla campagna
Il sol schioccando si spàmpana
Immane nel sovrano meriggio,
E dove è fronda intorno e ai casolari
S'acquietan nel torpor le creature.
Oh l'inseguirti, mio pensier, natanti
In un aperto libro gli occhi, mentre
Lo spazio ronzando scintilla
Fra i circostanti aspetti
Dove natura riposa tranquilla,
E risentir la quotidiana sorte
Come l'eterna verità che in noi
Dell'universo si fa vita e morte!
A me, che siete, o spregi insofferenti
Del comun senso, o dotti avvolgimenti,
O smanie ben pasciute,
Se nel cuore le forme conosciute
Degli uomini e del mondo
Mi rivelano il prodigio?
Salve, o ver di tutti i giorni!
Tu, per le case le patrie la terra,
Sei l'urto e l'impronta del ritmo seguito
Dai passi che leva e che sferra
Tra mete e ritorni
Il gigante che va per l'infinito.[b5]

[b] Through the deserted roads of the country
The sun cracklingly swells itself
Enormous in sovereign midday,
And where there are branches around and within farmhouses,
Creatures sink silently into the noon torpor.
Oh to follow you, my thought, with eyes
Swimming in an open book, while
Space, buzzing, sparkles
Among the surrounding aspects
Where nature rests calmly,
And to feel our everyday lot
To be the eternal truth which
Becomes in us the life and death of the universe!
What are you to me, oh fastidious refusals
Of common sense, oh learned convolutions,
Oh well-fed frenzies,

In the mysterious meridian hour of fullness and stasis where immensity quietly asserts itself, the poet's contemplation of the natural scene (the midday glory) leads him to intimations of the inner immensity and infinite potency that lie untapped and unsuspected at the heart of men and things. Here then is another midday revelation of the miracle or power latent in man. *Prodigio*, we note, is Rebora's word as it was D'Annunzio's in a similar context.[6] This is the sort of midday truth proclaimed earlier by Nietzsche and D'Annunzio, and in its light Rebora, no less than they, is scornful of the ordinary limits to which men too readily submit. The truth of everyday things that is rightfully man's is that of unbounded potentiality, the same that belongs to the deity adumbrated in the last line—"Il gigante che va per l'infinito." Thus Rebora, too, hails the possibility if not the advent of the superman, but again one must allow that his version is more spiritually charged than the earlier ones.

Both "Quassù" and *"Salve,"* in fact, are among those poems of *Frammenti lirici* (1913) that reveal in Rebora, even before his conversion to Catholicism (1929), the yearning for and the intuition of a divine presence or the Absolute. But other poems of the same period record also moments of anxiety, strife, and even a certain nausea with life—especially life in the city. The positive Alpine midday experience of "Quassù" and the rural noontide revelation of *"Salve"* have a negative counterpart in the urban midday of "Il sacrificio muto" ("The Mute Sacrifice"):

> Nell'avvampato sfasciume,
> Tra polvere e péste, al meriggio,
> La fusa scintilla

If in my heart the familiar forms
Reveal to me the miracle
Of men and the world?
Hail, o truth of every day!
You, throughout homes, countries, the earth,
Are the beat and the stamp of the rhythm followed
By the steps that the giant who walks through infinity
Raises and lands
In his going and coming.

> D'un dèmone bigio
> Atterga affronta assilla
> L'ignava sloia dei rari passanti,
> La schiavitù croia dei carri pesanti.[c7]
>
> (1-7)

The poem continues for a while in this mocking vein describing the city as a sort of Dantean *Malebolge* (the *bolgia* of the barrators in particular) peopled by a *perduta gente* moving in the destructive blaze of noon. The ashen-colored demon has obvious Dantean connections, but in this context he may also be taken as Rebora's version of the biblical *daemon meridianus*, the destruction that wasteth at noon. From this *bolgia*, however, the poet emerges untainted ("libero e terso"); he is not subject to the "arso dèmone bigio" because he has accepted the mute sacrifice of humble but pure service.

Equally sardonic is Rebora's ambiguous and somewhat blasphemous use of the sun as a symbol for his as yet uncertain concept of the Deity. In verses ("Notte," "Night") that have a suggestion of the cosmic eroticism and the meridian *atroce despota* found earlier in D'Annunzio, but now transposed into a skeptical key, Rebora evokes an image of the Deity as a fiercely reigning creative force that remains indifferent to individual suffering while it generates and perpetuates the multiple forms of existence:

> Ma sopra, Dio feroce nello spazio
> Guizza di luce e si sdraia
> Sul nostro patire, e lascivo non sazio
> Fra donne d'eternità gaia
> Rinnova le estasi libere
> Del suo piacere; e inconscio ricrea
> Del mondo le specie e l'idea.[d8]
>
> (10-16)

[c] In the blazing ruin,
  Betwixt dust and footsteps in midday,
  The melted spark
  Of a gray demon
  Assails from behind, and in front, goads
  The slothful tedium of the few passers-by,
  The vile bondage of the heavy wagons.

[d] But above, God in space fiercely

But in the poem "Sole," the sexually charged image of the midday sun as an *atroce despota* is put into the context of a more authentically human (and existentialist) drama wherein it figures as a positive rather than a negative value. The poem begins with an almost hallucinatory vision of the midday sun as a lover enacting a violent cosmic *hieros gamos* with a turgid earth that strains to respond:

>Da tutto l'orizzonte
>Il ciel fuso balenava
>Con slanci arcuati di luce
>Verso l'alta vertigine azzurra
>Che al sommo traboccando più vibrava;
>Giacevan sui confini
>Grembi di nuvole bianche,
>Ma il sol maschio sfuriava
>Sulla terra supina
>Nel grande amplesso caldo.
>E con turgidi muscoli
>Si sforzava ogni cosa violenta
>E si palpavan i sonori tonfi
>E s'incendiavan i colori secchi;
>E nel convulso spazio,
>Dalle coscie dei monti
>Al gran seno dei piani,
>Dalla testa dei borghi
>Ai nervi delle strade,
>Con àliti e gorghi
>Con guizzi e clangori
>Ebbra l'ora si stordiva.[e9]
>
>   (1-22)

---

[e] Quivers with light and stretches out
Upon our suffering, and lustful, never satiated,
Among women of joyous eternity
He renews the uninhibited ecstasies
Of his pleasure; and unaware recreates
Species and the idea of the world.

[e] From the entire horizon
The melted sky flashed
With arched leaps of light

From the very beginning of this cosmically dithyrambic noon piece, the verbs and images indicate a thrust or an aspiration of verticality as toward a superior realm. Thus the poem reveals the same yearning for a purer world of the spirit found in the Alpine noontide described in the poem "Quassù." But now what is suggested is a call to a higher life with unspecified Nietzschean overtones, a passionate invitation ("E scaturiva l'invito bramoso / D'intorno," 32-33) to a great noontide, as it were. And indeed it seems at first that the invitation will be realized by the young couple who have come under the spell of the intoxicating meridian hour: "Ebbra l'ora si smarriva / Nel senso delle voci / Di giovani a diporto / Di giovani cercanti / Dal pensiero la vita" (23-27).[f] The marvelous "truth" or superior state aspired to by the couple is analogically represented in terms of the dazzling vastness of noontide in whose luminosity the couple, in Dannunzian-like fashion, dreams of realizing new worlds and even, it seems, of attaining to the mystical two-in-one existence of lovers with a simultaneous reintegration (pantheistic) with nature: "Il compagno alla compagna / La compagna al compagno, / Volea ciascuno gridare / Ciò che non era mai

---

  Toward the high blue dizziness
  Which spilling over at the summit quivered the more;
  On the boundaries there lay
  Folds of white clouds,
  But the virile sun raged
  Over the supine earth
  In a great passionate embrace.
  And with turgid muscles
  All things strove violently
  And the resonant thuds were palpable
  And dried colors blazed;
  And in convulsed space,
  From the flanks of the mountains
  To the great bosom of the plains,
  From the head of the villages
  To the nerves of the roads,
  With gasps and gurgles
  With quivering and clanging,
  Drunken, the hour was dazed.

[f] Drunken the hour was dissolving into sensations of the voices / Of youths at play / Of youths seeking life / By their thoughts.

detto, / E passar da ogni varco / E popolare la reggia / E confondersi insieme / Nell'acciecante verità enorme" (42-49).[g] But Rebora's couple is not equal to the high intensity of midday; their first élan subsides, and they sink into a lesser, banal reality: "Ma rotolarono sillabe, / Ma ragionarono il mondo"(50-51).[h]

The poem has a diurnal time structure, and the downward plunge to ordinariness and separateness is emblematized first by the sky whose meridian glory has been extinguished, giving way to an ashen dullness: "S'annidò il cielo corto, / E si fece uno spento bracere" (55-56).[i] The violent joy of the earth in its upward surge to receive the embrace of the sun has subsided, and the earth itself takes on the aspect of a corpse: "Languì alla terra il piacere, / E si fece la spoglia di un morto" (57-58). Finally, as the culminating picture of desolation, night falls, and for nature is substituted the negative image of the city—a roaring abyss that swallows all—to which the couple has returned after a "day" (or, better, a rich noon) in the country:

> Strisciò la notte,
> Scivolò la partenza,
> S'aprì la voragine
> Della città rombante. Si lasciarono,
> E lasciarono la giovinezza.[j]
> (59-63)

Very likely the couple of this poem refers to Rebora and a female companion, but the poem's theme is not to be limited to that suggested by Daria Banfi Malaguzzi (a friend of the poet in the years of *Frammenti lirici*) who speaks of it as though

---

[g] He to her / She to him, / Each one wanted to shout / That which was never said, / And pass beyond every limit / And populate the court palace / And merge together / In the enormous dazzling truth.
[h] But they rolled out syllables, / But they reckoned the world.
[i] The sky quickly made its nest, / And turned into a spent brazier.
[j] Night crept,
The parting slid,
The abyss of the roaring
City opened. They left one another,
And they left youth.

it were no more than an account of an aborted sentimental adventure.[10] That there is an emblematic value in the couple and their experience can hardly escape one. What it is I have tried in part to suggest in the foregoing presentation of the poem. The sense of exacerbated frustration in not being able to sustain or fully realize the superior life is typical of Rebora's struggle before his conversion and is owing in part to the impossibility of specifying what the great noontide (if I may use the Nietzschean mythology) should be in practical terms if it was to be more than solipsistic idealism.[11] The couple's separation from one another, as the poet notes at the poem's end, is a renunciation of youth. If this is a statement of a moment of personal failure, it is certainly no less a picture of mankind falling away from the splendor and excitement of youthful vision—emblematized by nature's savagely joyous midday—and its submission to the confining, oppressive air of a mediocre reality. It is not nature in the season and hour of a summer noontide that is distressful and suffocating here but Rebora's version of the *city of dreadful night*.[12] The imagery of the poem is Dannunzian (perhaps with a suggestion of Nietzsche and Rimbaud), but its emblematical pessimism is Leopardian, not so far removed from the technique and the ecstatico-elegiac lament of "A Silvia" as one might think at first reading.[13]

With the gift of faith that was his by virtue of his conversion, Rebora's desire for the Absolute was no less "savage" than before, but now, of course, its focus was clear and its direction (still "upward" in terms of metaphorical space) unswerving. Thus many years after the period in which the poems discussed above were written, the image of the implacable sun burning cruelly over a parched, drought-stricken earth that yearns for life-saving rain becomes the emblematic representation of the soul's unquenchable thirst for mystical union with Christ:

> Inaridita la terra
> Protende la bocca:
> Implacabile il cielo di sopra.
> . . . .

> O Gesù, aver sete,
> Anelarti così![k][14]
> (1-3; 21-22)

The "rain," of course, will be God's succor to the burning soul; but in terms of the poet's imagery, God is also the spiritual force of the deity (the midday sun) that sears the soul.

Finally, the early poem "Quassù" has its counterpart in the three lines (from *Curriculum vitae* 1955) in which Rebora recounts a mystical experience that occurred in the brilliant blaze of the sun while he was gently rocking in a boat on a lake:

> Tutto era irraggiamento al solleone:
> Cullato in barca stavo in mezzo al lago:
> Svanì il creato e apparve il Creatore.[l][15]

In the midday splendor the world (and the self with it) falls away, and only Deity remains.

Yet another anguished voice of the tensive air of crisis in the pre-World War I period was that of Rebora's short-lived friend Giovanni Boine. In a piece that is somewhere between a Poesque prose poem and a philosophico-medical case history, the tubercular Boine, drawing upon his own physical and spiritual drama, created a powerful parable of the tormented human condition caught between idealism and an uninquiring, sensualistic immersion in life. Published in 1913, "Agonia" relates the case of one who has been forced by illness to undergo a cure in a sanatorium in the Swiss Alps. Throughout the story the word used to speak of this illness is not *malattia* but *male* which, although commonly used in Ital-

---

[k] The parched earth
  Extends its mouth;
  Implacable the sky above.
  . . . .
  Oh Jesus, to thirst,
  To yearn for you so!
[l] All was a radiance in the torrid light:
  Lulled in a boat I was in the middle of the lake:
  The world vanished and the Creator appeared.

ian to refer to certain illnessess (and especially to tuberculosis), in the present case persistently connotes the idea of an *evil* that impinges on the self. From the cold heights of the sanatorium, which becomes a symbol of his *male* and his enforced alienation from life, the protagonist yearns for his native town on the Ligurian coast. But at the same time that it represents a painful personal experience of physical suffering, the *male* also functions as an agent that provokes a crisis in the protagonist's belief in a life in which the spirit is triumphant and creative.[16] There is an existential ambiguity about this *male*. Just as it is the cause that spurs the protagonist, in his desire for health, to an instinctive and social communion with nature and with simple men of the earth (in the spring, in fact, he returns to his native Liguria) and to a recognition of what Boine calls the exteriority and heterogeneity of things— "eterogeneità dell'oggetto"—it appears also as a mysterious force smothering or denying the life of the spirit.[17] By plunging himself into the midst of life in a desperate reach for health, the protagonist arrives at an "indifferenza gioiosa" ("joyous indifference") in which the body—but the body alone—seems at first to triumph. But inasmuch as he is unable to surrender the "myth" of the spirit's paramountcy he soon feels that the true essence of reality is escaping him, as though life were being lived and the world perceived from the perspective of nothingness, and things, for all their corporeality, seem only an inchoate mass upon which the spirit, as a demiurge, has not acted. Thus, "things" seem to border on unreality: "E questo era il mondo veduto dal lato del nulla: percezion delle cose nei loro elementi, come non fatte ancora, non manipolate ancora di pensiero e di spirito" ("And this was the world seen from the perspective of nothingness: a perception of things in their elements, as though not yet formed, not yet concocted of thought and spirit," p. 513). Now corporeal joy yields to an anguish, which at first is of the spirit but almost immediately of the body as well, for the protagonist's illness (the *male*) has advanced until, hovering between life and death, between the sentiment of being and nonbeing, "between the vastness of night and the light" (p. 514), he passes into the final phase of his illness.

The last stages of the "agony" take place in the summer atmosphere of the hero's native Liguria, and the supreme crisis occurs, significantly, at midday, the hour of crisis par excellence. At this point of the story, the correspondence between the physical drama and the spiritual drama is so close as to obliterate the distinction. Exhaustion and feebleness have reduced the protagonist's relationship with the external world to naught. In the torpor of summer, the things surrounding him have become inert, a phenomenon that appears almost as an extension of his own inertia. Objects seem to have lost their remaining semblance of reality, and what is left is no more than shadow and annoyance—*ombra e fastidio*, a juxtaposition of terms suggesting metaphysical ennui and nothingness.[18] And indeed the immediately following words declare the nonexistence (or the nonreality) of things deprived of spirit or a thinking subject: "[Le cose] non erano più: il mondo non era" ("Things no longer were; the world was no more"). But just here—and it is Boine who introduces the motif with the strong adversative *Ma*—in the tense silence and shadowless clarity of midday, there occurs the critical and irrevocable revelation of the "hard" fact of otherness:

> Ma ad un tratto un meriggio, sollevatosi a pena, sudando come per respirare, e gli mancasse l'aria, gli occhi gli si smarrirono fuori nel gran vacuo innondato di sole.—Urto.—Le cose erano, sì. Senza ombra—nette, taglianti, diritte. Alberi, case, colline, due uomini fermi, le roccie ed il moto (nell'immobile mare). Spietate, immobili, dure sotto la perpendicolare diafanità del meriggio enorme-tacente. Corpose, tagliate, nettissime, quasi contro a lui a colpirlo, per dire che erano. Eternità, fissità, indissolubilità di tutte le cose del mondo nella lucida vampa di un estivo meriggio, viste dall'alto. E la terra salda dura amplissimo-stesa a portarle!—Serietà, veracità eternità delle cose e degli uomini: realtà della vita, realtà del pensiero, consustanzialità d'ogni cosa nel mondo col vivo pensiero.[m][19]

[m] But suddenly one day at noon, having raised himself with difficulty, sweating as though he were trying to breathe and he lacked air, his eyes wandered outside in the great emptiness flooded by the sun. —A jolt. —Things

This is a startling and dramatic passage in view of what we have come to expect in midday encounters, be they negative or positive. The absolute but ambiguous light and immobility of noontide have usually signified either a metaphysical nothingness (and we may note that the absence or the reduction of shadows to a minimum would normally suggest the ontological unreality of the world) or the sense of a superior, even divine, realm of eternity and true being (in which context the absence of shadows suggests glory and purity). But in the absolute intensity and pitiless clarity of Boine's midday, the world does not fall away into nothingness. Here the light and blazing heat of a southern midday do not rob things of their contours and identity.[20] Objects do not disintegrate as we will find they do in Ungaretti's noonscapes. Nor in the absence of shadows does the world seem to expand into a transcendental (or immanental) glory of the spirit. On the contrary, here the revelation is of the validity of the world's perceptible appearances—that is, of an objective reality other than and independent of the self. Thus things stand out in bold outline, cutting and hard, their fixity in the luminous silence of the noontide stasis giving them the absolute quality of eternity.

Without doubt, this appears as a hallucinatorylike vision, but that is the point of the passage. The terrible distinctness and hardness of things in the fatal clarity of midday—the hour of crisis and of menace—give to this revelation of the objectivity of reality its character of a hallucination.[21] And in connection with this revelation, the self experiences a "horrible ecstasy" of the kind Sartre's hero in *La Nausée* was later to know in his encounter—in the afternoon—with the viscosity

---

were, yes. With shadows—clear, sharp, erect. Trees, houses, hills, two men motionless, rocks and movement (in the motionless sea). They were relentless, immobile, hard under the perpendicular transparency of the enormous-silent midday. Corporeal, clear cut, sharply outlined, as though pressing against him to strike him in order to say that they existed. Eternity, immutability, indissolubility of all the things of the world in the bright blaze of a summer midday, seen from on high. And the earth—firm hard vast-outstretched—supporting them! —Actuality, veracity, eternity of things and of men: reality of life, reality of thought, consubstantiality of each thing in the world with living thought.

of reality. (We may note, in passing, that before his experience with the viscosity of reality, Sartre's hero also experiences the otherness of objective reality or thinghood in terms of the "hardness" of objects.) But Boine's hero undergoes this "horrible ecstasy" in the most literal and fullest sense, for he does in fact die—he is in his last agony during the revelation—and his death, we shall see, is described in a way that suggests a going outside of the self, a real but fatal *ekstasis*. With his acute awareness and "contemplation" of the otherness of reality, the struggle of the ego fearful of losing dominion over matter is recognized as false and meaningless. What is true is the consubstantiality of body and spirit; the struggle of the body is the struggle of the spirit, and not to yield to annihilation is the course he would follow. But this now is the struggle of the individual to survive, and what follows is an exact account of a man in the actual throes of death, wishing frantically but futilely to resist sinking into the "languor" of nothingness: "Gettarsi innanzi, gettarsi innanzi uscire, spogliarsi del torpore pesante, strapparsi dalla morte del corpo, dal nulla, uscire, uscire di colpo" (p. 516).[n]

To some extent, it may not matter, as far as the "lesson" of the falsity of the antagonism between matter and spirit (as of that between the individual and the universal) is concerned, that the protagonist is ultimately defeated by the *male*. The direction or the sense of the struggle has been determined: one must resist solipsism and passive nihilism. But the conclusion of the tale indicates that the personal case of the protagonist did matter to the author; and how could it be otherwise since it was his own *male*. In this respect, Boine was giving an anticipatory account of his own agony and death. And what matters still more to us is that the protagonist's death—narrated in such a way as to confirm the idea that the transcendence (or simply the independence) of the spirit is illusory—is connected with an experience of the self merging with the luminous vastness of noontide:

[n] To throw oneself forward, push ahead, go out, to shed the heavy torpor, tear oneself away from the death of the body, from the void, to go out, to go out suddenly.

Fuori per la finestra lo sconfinato barbaglio ed il ritmico senza fine stridore. Spalancò gli occhi, lento! Gli restarono così. Ed il bianchiccio meriggio gli colava dentro l'allargava vasto. Come a poco a poco gli si spegneva il respiro e gli moriva impercettibile il sussulto pel corpo, vagamente gli parve di farsi vacuo e leggero e di restare così come una trepida, irreale, vanente, inumana bolla, appena d'un lievissimo soffio appeso, sospeso alla colorata durezza dell'essere (p. 517).º

In this passage we meet again with the phenomenon of an audible impression of a relentless or suspended high-pitched stridor that seems to arise from the fierce meridian silence. One can reasonably assume that it is produced by the chirring of cicadas, but it is noteworthy that the ubiquitous insect of noontide is not mentioned, and the source of the sound is unspecified. For the sound, in fact, belongs to the midday silence, and this would be so even were its cause identified. It "bespeaks" the high tension of the absoluteness of the crisis hour. Now as the hero slowly opens his eyes wide, never to close them again, the spectral whiteness of midday "pours" into him, expanding or increasing him. But the Dannunzian suggestiveness (cf. "Meriggio") is quickly annulled when we realize that what is being poured into him is the great void. This filling of the self is really the emptying of the self, somewhat in the manner of the draining of personal sentiency and consciousness into the vast deadness of noontide that we found in Leopardi's *meriggio* from "La vita solitaria." Yet here too a difference is to be noted, for in Boine's account, where an actual death transpires, the final image is that of the self "inflated" into a fragile bubble of emptiness clinging perilously to the hardness of an objective reality that will perdure

---

º Outside the window the boundless glare and the rhythmic, endless stridulation. He opened his eyes wide, slowly! They remained like that. And the spectral noontide poured into him increased him immensely. As little by little his breathing subsided and the tremor of his body died down imperceptibly, he seemed vaguely to become empty and light and to remain thus like a trembling, unreal, vanishing, unhuman bubble, barely of the lightest breath, hanging on, suspended from the colored hardness of being.

after the bubble, as it must, has burst. Nonbeing has displaced the self's being, and that the bubble has in fact collapsed is indicated by the story's final brief annotation which is a reference to the loud cry emitted by someone (a relative?) who has entered the room: "Qualcuno entrò e gettò un grido." We can hardly doubt that this cry of a survivor after the death of the protagonist affirms (tragically or ironically) the heterogeneity, the exteriority or "otherness" of the universe. But if solipsistic idealism has been proved false as a philosophical and psychological attitude by the author-protagonist, one can hardly speak of a triumph. For, more than grief, there is utter despair in that cry. The protagonist's futile last hope at the moment of the midday revelation, we remember, was that he might, by struggling, recover his health and thereby liberate himself from a bodily death which is also the extinction of the self. And that he cannot do.

The "agony," we understand now, is indeed to be understood in its pregnant and etymological sense of *struggle*, no less so than in the case of Unamuno's *Agony of Christianity*.[22] It is, in the truest (and existentialist) sense, a death struggle. The theme of sickness, we know, is common among writers who express existential sentiments. Boine's "Agonia" is bound to call to mind Thomas Mann's *The Magic Mountain* because of the same situation of the protagonists in the two works, but we do better to think of Tolstoy's "The Death of Ivan Ilych." Boine's hero cannot overcome the crisis of the existential *cogito* in the face of the (arbitrary) absoluteness of an order of things for which, he now understands, he is not responsible and to which he is powerless to give value. Brought by illness to the realization that the self is inextricably involved with a physical body, the hero discovers the radical finitude of the individual's existence—his mortality. "Agonia," in short, is a piercing account of the experience of progressing toward death and nothingness. The choice of midday as the time of the final, irrevocable revelation and of the actual occurrence of death, it seems now, was as inevitable as it was uncanny. The crisis of the hero's physical illness was as one with the crisis of faith in the power of the spirit. Indeed

162 Some Twentieth-Century Voices

the physical illness appears at times almost as the symptom of the spiritual crisis. What could be more inevitable than that this twofold crisis should be symbolically and actually connected with the crisis of clarity that comes with midday?[23]

Boine's tormented struggle between idealistic subjectivism and a metaphysical realism recognizing the validity of the dualism of spirit and matter was a real one which, in the end, he was unable to resolve. The consequences of this struggle are to be found in the prose poems that make up the *Frantumi* (*Fragments*), once considered to be the author's most successful literary achievement. The *Frantumi* reveal a wavering between moments of unresolved doubt and moments of serenity.[24] But the serenity is connected not so much with a true resolution of the conflict as with a need to escape from the struggle, and this escapism takes the form not only of nostalgia for faraway places or of flight into a dream world, but also of a desire to dissolve sweetly. Noontide figures not as a space for the dramatic revelation of the hard objectivity of the world but as a time propitious for evading it. Thus, in one instance the idle passing of midday beneath the shade of a tree facing the sea releases the poet from the prison of present reality: "È così bello a volte meriggiare, all'ombra d'un carrubo in faccia al mare! L'arso deserto allor ci fa sognare dei viaggi dell'oriente."[p][25] This brief passage is more significant than might at first appear, for it emblematizes a condition of the spirit seeking respite from its travail. Moreover, the use of the word *meriggiare* and the setting in which the "activity" suggested by that verb takes place were to have a rich development, as we shall later see, in the poetry of Boine's fellow Ligurian, Eugenio Montale. An even more significant episode of midday escapism occurs in the *Frantumi* in the noon piece entitled, appropriately enough, "Deriva" ("Adrift") which is quoted here in its entirety:

> —Mi piaccion gl'indolenti meriggi ch'una lentissima nenia ti scande la siesta, e, scavi deserti sono le piazze in barbagli.

[p] It is so beautiful sometimes to laze at noon, in the shade of a carob tree in front of the sea. The burnt desolation then makes us dream of voyages in the Orient.

—La implacabile nebula assonna colli e marine, d'una bianchiccia malinconia: par che tutto si culli in una placida culla d'insensibilità.
—Armo allora piano la pendula vela e senza fiato di fiato, immobile scivolo nell'immobilità.
—Sciacquan sospiri di liquidità, fiottano l'ore dell'eternità, soffice lenta ogni cosa si sfa, e in lisci silenzi d'impassibilità si va non si va.
—Sono le spiagge di là dai pensieri, son gli orizzonti di là d'ogni meta (molli le scotte, lasci il timone, la vita abbandoni . . .) dove si sia nessuno sa più, cosa si voglia nessuno sa più, che il mondo sia nessuno vuol più.
  Alla deriva, senza memoria, senza respiro, sospesi in nulla si va non si va, per l'indolente insensibilità.^{q26}

The first three stanzas of this prose lyric are introductory and set the mood and scene. In them the poet declares his love for torpid noontides when a slow, monotonous rhythm (his word is *nenia*) measures out or "scans" the siesta hours, and the plazas under the dazzling light are like abandoned excavation ruins. The intense (*implacabile*) luminous haze invests all of nature (specified by the phrase "hills and seashores," which creates a sense of vast landscape) with drowsiness and a spectral whiteness of ennui—"una bianchiccia malinconia." Everything seems to be lulled in a calm cradle of insensibility or "indifference." In such moments the poet, surrendering to the mood, quietly sets sail into the "waters" of immobility.

q
—I like the lazy noontides when a slow monotonous rhythm scans your siesta, and the squares all aglare are [like] abandoned excavations.
—The relentless haze makes hills and seashore doze in a whitish ennui [melancholy]: it seems that everything is lulled in a peaceful cradle of insensibility.
—Then softly I raise the hanging sail and without the faintest breath, motionless, I glide into immobility.
—Sighs of liquidity lap, hours of eternity flow, softly, slowly all things dissolve, and in smooth silences of indifference we go we do not go.
—They are the shores beyond our thoughts, they are the horizons beyond all distances (you slacken the sails, you abandon the helm, you surrender life . . .), where we are no one now knows, what we want no one now knows, that the world be no one now cares.
  Adrift, without memory, without breath, suspended in nothingness we go we do not go, in a languid insensibility.

The last three stanzas have a calculated cadence (and rhymes) that could easily be indicated by breaking the "prose" up into actual verse lines. But this would lessen if not destroy the desired effect of the fluviatile rhythm that is created by having the lines run together. These stanzas reproduce the lulling rhythm of the boat that is allowed to drift, "carrying" the poet in revery to "shores" and "horizons" that lie beyond consciousness, beyond memory, to a condition that is nothing more (or less) than the sensation of a gentle rocking in a sea of nothingness—"sospesi in nulla si va non si va."

This being "adrift" (*deriva*) in a boat during the pervasive calm of noontide when the whole of existence seems to be lulled in a soothing cradle of insensibility ("par che tutto si culli in una placida culla d'insensibilità") must bring to mind the famous "Fifth Promenade" of the solitary rambler Jean-Jacques Rousseau who, during a stay on the Isle of Saint-Pierre (in the middle of the lake of Bienne), found it sweet to pass the midday hours in such fashion:

> Pendant qu'on était encore à table, je m'esquivais et j'allais me jeter seul dans un bateau que je conduisais au milieu du lac quand l'eau était calme, et là, m'étendant tout de mon long dans le bateau les yeux tournés vers le ciel, *je me laissais aller et dériver lentement au gré de l'eau*, quelquefois pendant plusieurs heures, plongé dans mille rêveries confuses mais délicieuses, et qui sans avoir aucun objet bien déterminé ni constant ne laissaient pas d'être à mon gré cent fois préférables à tout ce que j'avais trouvé de plus doux dans ce qu'on appelle les plaisirs de la vie.[r27]

Whether he is in the boat on the lake at noontide or seated on a bank looking at it in the evening, Rousseau's luxurious

---

[r] While they were still at table, I would steal away and go to throw myself all alone in a boat which I guided to the middle of the lake when the water was calm; and there, stretching out full-length in a boat, and with my eyes turned up to the sky, I would let myself go, drifting slowly whither the water willed, sometimes for several hours, sunk in a thousand vague but luxurious reveries which without having a precise or fixed object were nonetheless a hundred times more preferable to me than all that I had considered sweetest among what are called the pleasures of life.

(*délicieuses*) reveries are fed by the water's uniform motion—a rocking movement without strong jolts or pauses. Now it is significant that just this moderate amount of motion is considered essential by him. Indeed, he is careful to note in this context that an absolute stillness is an image of death: "Un silence absolu porte à la tristesse: il offre une image de la mort" (p. 72). We remember that this is precisely what characterizes Leopardi's *meriggio* of "La vita solitaria" and makes it unique even when compared to Rousseau's abandonment to a rhythm of flux and reflux sufficient only to keep the subject blissfully aware of a (prenatal) existence without obliging him to think. Thus even the reveries are without any clear object and are eventually reduced to emptiness.[28] Boine's "Deriva" clearly belongs to this Rousseauistic vein, and the final characterization of his mood or experience as an *indolente sensibilità* does not really approach Leopardi's meridian *antica quiete* any more than it approaches the mystical revelation of deity experienced by Rebora in his noontide boating (see above). Boine's repeated phrase, "si va non si va," is certainly the equivalent of Rousseau's "flux et reflux" in its evocation of a luxurious surrender, although it perhaps more effectively connotes that sense of suspension and ambiguity so often associated with midday. Here the ambiguity consists in the noontide paradox of motion in immobility (or vice versa), a theme that was to become obsessive in Eugenio Montale.

In the descriptions of Rousseau and Boine, although the sense of eternity is intimated and the impingement of immediate reality is erased ("soffice lenta ogni cosa si sfa"), the world does not fall away entirely into pure nothingness (or a full cancellation of *kinēsis*); nor is the self lost in an all-pervading deity. Both the world and the self (i.e., consciousness) remain suspended between motion and stasis, between nothingness and being. But it is worth noting the different rhythmic patterns by which this is effected in the two authors. Rousseau creates an endlessly rocking cradle "movement" to nowhere by means of long sentences with sinuous motions.[29] On the other hand, Boine's passage, in its second, slow tempo, proceeds as a series of short rhythmic phrases, each of which is terminated by an oxytonic word or a monosyllable repeating the accented vowel [à] in some ten cases and the accented diphthong *iù* in four: *liquidità, eternità, sfa, impassibilità, si va / non si va, di là, di là, più, più, più, più, si va / non si va, insensibilità.* The effect is to create a sense of movement that, without losing a fluviatile suggestiveness, is periodically suspended, resumed, and suspended again. It is a lapping to-and-fro rhythmic pattern beginning with the phrase "Sciacquan sospiri di liquidità," where the verb *sciacquare* is used intransitively (a rare and daring usage), and the washing waves are said to be liquid "sighs."[30] Even as it narcotizes, this rhythm creates the illusion of motion in immobility—precisely the motif and tempo indicated by the oxymoron that in closing the third stanza introduces the succeeding *nenia*: "immobile scivolo nell'immobilità." Real or imaginary, the poet's "boat" is the symbol of evasion (and of a cradle), of setting oneself adrift. The actual circumstance in which the poet finds himself, or so I think, is that of sinking into the siesta, of *meriggiando* beneath a carob tree on the coast of the Mediterranean as in the case of the previously cited *meriggio* from "I miei amici di qui" (see above). It is there, as he sees and listens to the lapping waters, that the motionless poet, without leaving his retreat, *glides* into the sea of immobility whose name is noontide.

More than any other Italian poet of the twentieth century, Arturo Onofri made a mystical or spiritual pantheism and a sense of arcane cosmic correspondences his subjects. As we shall see, however, the optimism that is basic to this vision was not without a perpetual tension of its own. Even before his resolution of the crisis of thirst for the Absolute in a view that is seeped in the theosophy and anthroposophy of Rudolf Steiner, Onofri's poetry reveals what Boine in 1918 referred to as a "nostalgic yearning" for a region of light beyond the earth.[31] Light and the sun are accordingly the most pervasive themes throughout his work. In the pre-theosophic period, despite a tendency toward the crepuscular mood of the first decade of the century, it is without doubt D'Annunzio who figures as the dominant influence. Thus at the core of his earliest volume of verse (*Liriche*, 1907) there is a dithyrambic hymn to life—"Il trionfo della vita" ("The Triumph of Life")—in which love and joy are celebrated as the supreme values, and the invitation to participate in them is made in terms of a paganizing noontide vision at the center of which the poet portrays himself as the last faun, anxious to create a new god from a yearning embrace with life:

> Deh, vieni! dònami
> La tua magnifica fiamma d'amore!
> Io sono l'ultimo fauno
> Bramoso che vuole creare
> Un nuovo dio dal nostro amplesso anelo.ˢ32
> (65-69)

The solar vitalism of both Carducci and D'Annunzio are felt in the poem "Canto Jemale a Febo Apolline" ("Hiemal Song to Phoebus Apollo") where the sun is hailed as a "nume cosmico," and the motif of an atavistic relationship between it and the poet is declared, perhaps too rhetorically, in the image that speaks of his blood yearning for the sun's rays:

> Sorridi, o Sole; risplendi, folgora
> Dell'Universo superbo principe,
> T'anela il mio sangue morente
> Un tuo raggio invocando; risplendi!ᵗ33
> (73-76)

A surpassing of the self or of limits by immersion in the life of nature is the basic motif here as it is in another early lyric, "Per confondersi con la natura" ("To Merge with Nature"), where the same image of blood/sun appears:

ˢ Oh, come, grant me
  Your magnificent flame of love!
  I am the last faun,
  Thirsting, who desires to create
  A new god from our yearning embrace.
ᵗ Smile, oh Sun; shine, dazzle,
  Proud prince of the Universe,
  My dying blood yearns for you,
  Invoking one of your rays; shine!

> Madre, ch'io mi dimentichi della mia forma umana
> Per confondermi in te, nella tua vita immensa;
> Ch'io rompa la strettoia della mia fosca tana,
> Ove sto nella triste obliquità che pensa:
>
> Per sentir nel mio sangue il brivido solare
> Della tua pura vita.[u][34]

The yearning and the tension in the context of solar symbolism find expression also in the Dannunzian motif of burning thirst and fever in a land where water is absent. In the second quatrain of the sonnet "*Salutis fons*" the poet speaks of his "pilgrimage" under the sun of May:

> Acqua non è nel mio pellegrinaggio,
> E, bruciato dall'afa e dall'arsura,
> Per la febbre che più m'arde e tortura,
> Già in me vien meno l'ultimo coraggio.[v][35]
>
> (5-8)

In this moment of dismay, upon taking a sudden turn, the poet seems to see a torrent rushing among the jagged rocks. But this water from which a parched flock drinks deeply, has all the marks of a mirage, and the variegated gushing of founts is said to be like the dream in the heart of a poet (9-14). Besides anticipating the mirage motif in Ungaretti and Montale, this development, significantly enough, seems almost a Pascolian or "crepuscular" reversal of D'Annunzio's midday mythology in which a cruel thirst is itself the preferred condition and is "nourished" by the sun. The same retreat, sugges-

---

[u] Mother, let me forget my human form
And merge with you, in your immense life;
Let me break the bonds of my gloomy hovel,
Where I remain in the wretched obliquity that thinks:

In order to feel in my blood the solar shiver
Of your pure life.

[v] There is no water in my pilgrimage,
And, scorched by the sultriness and the burning drought,
For the fever that burns and tortures me most,
Already my remaining courage fails me.

tive of uncertainty, is found in "Grido notturno" ("Night Cry") where a starry night offers a tremulous ocean of dreams toward which the poet from his cruel desert yearns: "A un tremulo ocèano di sogno, / Cui dolorando agogno / Dal mio deserto atroce." It is a sinking into the oblivion of the deep night/ocean that relieves one from the anguish of the boundless mystery, and this motif of relief or refuge is translated in images of rain or nocturnal dew that falls on the ruin of a world exhausted by the sun: "Ma piove . . . / Sul divorante sfacelo / Del mondo ch'è stanco di sole."

If the moments of doubt and crepuscular retreat do in fact alternate with exuberance and yearning in the young Onofri, the Dannunzian motif of a perpetual thirst that seeks the sun rather than water or the shade is the stronger of the poles.[36] Within this thematic structure, however, one can speak of a mystical or spiritual dimension in Onofri's solar thirst that already in this earliest period distinguishes it from D'Annunzio's more sensually grounded panism. In this respect, Onofri is closer to the early Rebora, both of them being examples of a spiritual impulse that has not yet defined itself specifically, and both of them, from our vantage point, too individualistic to be confused with the anonymous epigones of D'Annunzio who swarmed about in the first years of the century.[37] Rebora and Onofri are for this reason noteworthy representatives of an important feature of twentieth-century Italian poetry. The vital poetry of the century does not develop only by way of a sharp retreat from D'Annunzio into a crepuscular mode. It is also found in the expression of a new sensibility and vision that makes its own use of the solar mythology and imagery of the incomparable *artifex* himself. For what is said here of Rebora and Onofri will be equally true of Ungaretti and Montale. Like social revolutions, this poetic revolution was made from within.

The ambiguity or the uncertainty of the early Onofri is real enough, and it may be seen even in a lyric that borrows its title from an expression that belongs characteristically to D'Annunzio—"Delirio meridiano." And indeed, nothing could seem more Dannunzian than the first stanza:

> Nel solleone le cicale in coro
> Cantano ebbre tra gli olmi a gran distesa,
> E stupore di sole a piombo pesa
> Nel silenzio dell'arido pianoro
> Come l'angoscia d'un'immane attesa.[w,38]

Perhaps it is not only D'Annunzio who is an influence here. The sense of a light of ecstasy that has descended from directly above like a *weight* into the silence of the arid plain may owe something to Pascoli's "Dall'argine" where midday is said to rest or pause on the grasslands. Onofri's verb *pesa* seems to be an echo of the earlier poet's *posa*. In the one poet we have *posa/prateria*, in the other *pesa/pianoro*. But for the rest, the poet's mood is Dannunzian, and even the use of *pesa* suggests the sort of "splendid oppression" we associate with D'Annunzio. Again the wild chirring of the cicadas in the midday vastness is not so much absorbed by the light and silence as it is a component that bespeaks the tension of an infinite latency that is "repressed" but ready to burst. It is as though it were a suspended ecstasy not yet fully revealed and experienced; the moment of expectancy is an "anguish" because the poet is himself suspended or fixed in a state of limitless and, so, of cruel desire—"Come l'angoscia d'un'*immane* attesa."[39]

In the second stanza (not quoted here) the representation of an old woman who rests in the shade and is startled by the lizard that has darted by in the blazing sun is meant to set off the figure of the poet who returns in the final stanza:

> Sei, cicalìo, come un tremar di stelle
> In cielo d'alba, e scende, come suole,
> Fresca rugiada all'anima, cui duole
> L'eterno arsore del suo sogno imbelle.
> Ora, agli occhi accecati, è buio il sole.[x]

---

[w] In the fiery heat the cicadas in chorus
Sing drunkenly between the elms in the vast expanse,
And wonderment of sun vertically weighs
In the silence of the arid plateau
Like the anguish of an enormous suspense.

[x] You, oh chattering, are like the trembling of stars
At dawn, that descends, as is usual,

The imagery here may seem incongruous, but the sense is clear. In the heart of midday there is a truth or a reality not fully attainable by the poet, but the cicadas' intoxicated "song" is a guarantee for it and so is apprehended by him as the twinkling of stars in early morn and as a fresh dew that at least partially assuages the eternal thirst that torments his soul's unfulfillable and ineffectual dream ("L'eterno arsore del suo sogno imbelle"). The thirst remains because it can only be truly satisfied by the sun itself. But though he is driven by his thirst to seek the sun, the poet cannot sustain the encounter. He too is blinded by his thirst or, if one prefers, by the sun, which now appears dark at the moment of its most intense light: "Ora, agli occhi accecati, è buio il sole" ("Now, to my blinded eyes, the sun is dark"). Man overmastered by the midday sun is here the emblematic representation of the attraction to and the repulse by an absolute that is not clearly definable to the poet.

Both before and after his "conversion" to a semioccult Christian pantheism under the stimulus of reading Rudolf Steiner and Edouard Schuré and a current of German irrationalism, Onofri's poetry is marked by a yearning for liberation from the earthly and for infinity. But in the post-conversion period the motif of the upward surge is further accentuated, and the nocturnal and crepuscular moods give way almost entirely to the undisputed dominance of solar imagery and the fundamental optimism of a vision that sees the cosmos as a dithyrambic dance of light in which, under the impulse of the creator spirit, the things of the earth (of the lower world) seek to unite with the upper world (the world of spirit). As the *cosmos* is the ultimate image and idea of a luminous mystical unity toward which things aspire, so the sun figures as the object and symbol that serves as the *trait d'union* by which the world of physical things (nature) may attain to the spiritual union. Spiritual energy, the plasma that courses throughout the cosmos and which man knows as blood, pulsates from the sun, as though the sun were the heart

---

Like cool dew upon my soul pained
By the eternal feverish thirst of its faint-hearted dream.
Now, to my blinded eyes, the sun is dark.

of the cosmos. Thus while there is even an element of Angelo Conti's Schopenhaueran and aestheticizing mysticism (see the introduction) in Onofri, the latter is like D'Annunzio in vigorously brushing aside Conti's preference for half-light and the eschewal of unmediated (midday) light. For Onofri, as one of his poems puts it, "Il sol sa l'ombra, ma non l'ombra il sol."[y] At the same time, it is now that his solar thirst and surge can more clearly be differentiated from D'Annunzio's. The Panic impulse becomes truly cosmic and wholly mystical in its implications, though it is a mysticism in which sensuality is not denied but subsumed or transfigured. In the representation of this cosmic drama things move in a flaming vertical tension toward the sun, a whorling incendiary propulsion that leaves even D'Annunzio behind and can only be compared with the paintings of Vincent van Gogh, who even when he depicted nocturnal landscapes seemed to be expressing the solar delirium of which he was both victim and vessel. There is, to be sure, a tragic side to the drama of combustion as seen by the painter, but it is possible that the critics have overstressed it (transferring a personal tragedy to the vision revealed in the paintings) and have consequently tended to neglect or underplay the fact that the paintings are paeans to the sun (even the self-portraits are representations of the sun) and reveal, as do Onofri's poems, the aspiration of things toward a hierogamotic union with it. As we know, it was in the south (Provence) that van Gogh discovered what he called a "kingdom of light" in which the sun appears as a symbol of the creative force.

What has been said in the previous paragraph will help put into a meaningful perspective two short poems yet to be discussed, though it cannot supply all the clues to an understanding of their details. The poems, among the most unusual and fascinating accounts of the midday hour (or encounter) that we are likely to come across, are marked by an obscurity that is matched only by their significance. The first is a hallucinatory vision (the poet himself refers to the *manie del mez-*

---

[y] The sun knows the shadow, but the shadow knows not the sun.

zogiorno, which would be a good choice for its title) of the vitalistic force that pulsates throughout nature and in the poet in the very heart of the noontide stasis:

> Ecco il ritmo frenetico del sangue,
> Quando gli azzurri tuonano a distesa,
> E qualsiasi colore si fa fiamma
> Nell'urlo delle tempie.
> Ecco il cuor mio nella selvaggia ebbrezza
> Di svincolare in esseri le forme
> Disincantate a vortice di danza.
> Ecco i visi risolti in fiabe d'oro
> E in lievi organi d'ali.
> Ecco gli alberi in forsennate lingue
> Contorcersi, balzar fra scoppiettii
> Di verdi fiamme dalla terra urlante.
> E fra l'altre manie del mezzogiorno,
> Ecco me, congelato in stella fissa,
> Ch'esaspero l'antica aria di piaghe
> Metalliche, sull'erba di corallo.
> (Pulsa il fianco del mare sul granito
> Come un trotto infinito di cavallo.)[z40]

In a blazing midday the poet experiences an atavistic (and vitalistic) relationship with the sun which has energized his

[z] Behold the frenzied rhythm of my blood,
  When the blue thunders far and wide,
  And whatsoever color becomes a flame
  In the scream of my temples.
  Behold my heart in the wild intoxication
  Of liberating into beings forms
  Disenchanted in a dancing whirl.
  Behold faces resolved in golden fables
  And in wings resembling airy organs.
  Behold the trees twisting into frantic
  Tongues, leaping with the crackling
  Of green flames from the howling earth.
  And among the other obsessions of midday,
  Behold me, congealed into a fixed star,
  Exacerbating the ancient air with metallic
  Wounds, on grass of coral.
  (The flank of the sea throbs on the granite
  Like the infinite trot of a horse.)

blood to a wild rhythm perceived as a howl at his temples. The blue of the sky is so obsessive as to create an auditory impression of vast and continuous peals of thunder, and all colors of objects (things of whatever color) on the earth seem to be of the substance of flames. The driving intensity of the midday sun and sky is accentuated throughout the poem by the anaphoric repetition of the exclamation *Ecco* that introduces new images at the beginning of five different clauses. In the solar delirium that has seized his heart, the poet's vision liberates the forms of reality that had been immobilized as though by incantation (it is the midday "pause of being" according to Onofri's phrase in the second poem we shall be quoting) and sets them into a wild dance of being. Human faces are transfigured into golden fables with wings like organ pipes. And this is the motif of angels as a higher stage of spirituality which is a liberation from the earthly. It is a vision of an *umanità angelicata*, an angelicized humanity.[41] The trees are perceived as writhing tongues of crackling green flames soaring upward in a frenzied desire to be released from a "screaming" earth and to rejoin the sun (cf. Rebora's "Sole," and also van Gogh's painting "Wheat Fields and Cypress Trees"). The paradox here would seem to be that the earthly forms have been set in a dithyrambic rhythm in what is the hour of stasis. And indeed we do have here that mysterious midday phenomenon of motion (even combustive or explosive motion) in immobility.

At the same time, we note that it is not the midday hour that has fixed things in a state of inertia, caused them to be *incantate* as opposed to their now becoming *disincantate*. This is their condition as part of a fallen nature, for integral to Onofri's Christian pantheism is the doctrine of a Fall and the need for Redemption. In his midday delirium the poet sees things in their secret, anguished desire to return to their state of purity. The meaning of *disincantate* here is "freed from an incantation that has held them prisoner." In the poems of this period we can easily find many passages in which the motif appears:

> Mentre il verde in reclusa erba s'affanna
> Per salir su dal prato . . . .
> . . . .
>
> Odo il suolo bollir d'un fuoco eterno,
>   Nel sangue mio, che vuole
>   Già ringoiare il sole.[aa][42]

The anguish has a positive value because it is the "just suffering" that spurs things to overcome the imprisoning inertia that keeps them separated from the spiritual order of things. We read as much in the sonnet "L'anelito d'aprire ogni prigione" ("The Yearning to Open All Prisons"):

> Quest'angosica è la giusta sofferenza
> Ond'è vinta ogni inerzia in terra, e senza
> Di che niuna beltà nasce e s'adempie.[bb][43]

And the following terzina from yet another sonnet—"La densità dell'ossa va scemando" ("The Density of Bones Diminishes")—repeats the theme in imagery and words that are particularly relevant to our discussion:

> Or che un vortice angelico discioglie
> Le inerzie morte, e a sè le disincanta
> In fiamma alata, fuor di stolte voglie.[cc][44]

To be sure, we are dealing with that anguished oppression of imprisonment that was already acutely felt but only dimly understood by the poet in the early poem "Delirio meridiano." But now we are in a zone that is far removed

---

[aa] While the green in secluded grass struggles
  To rise from the meadow . . . .
   . . . .
  I hear the ground boil with an eternal fire,
   In my blood, that already
   Wants to swallow the sun again.
[bb] This anguish is the just suffering
  By which is conquered every earthly inertia, and without
  Which nothing of beauty is born and becomes fulfilled.
[cc] Now that an angelic vortex releases
  The dead inertias, and disenchants them unto itself
  In winged flame, away from foolish desires.

from the midday anguish of expectancy we found in D'Annunzio. We are, in fact, in the spiritually tense atmosphere of Michelangelo's anguished "Prisoners" seeking to extricate themselves from matter (be it the flesh or marble), and in this respect Onofri's use of the word *svincolare* in "Ecco il ritmo frenetico del sangue" is symptomatic. The word and synonymous terms for it return often in his writing, and already in the 1914 edition of *Liriche* we find the key verb in the opening line of the 1907 poem "Per confondersi con la natura" undergoing a change from a renunciatory *dimenticare* to the more aggressively dramatic *disvincolare*, as "Madre, ch'io mi *dimentichi* della mia forma umana" becomes "Madre, ch'io mi *disvincoli* dalla mia forma umana" (p. 90). Rather than to Mother Nature, however, the poet can now raise his prayer directly to the Creator Spirit as the force that provokes in things an urgency that may even be violent and apocalyptic in order to shake them out of the sterile rigidity of their "natural" (fallen) state.

> Meglio il grido e le lacrime e il martirio
> E il tremar della terra e il dislocarsi
> Dei monti, anziché sordi, orbi, riarsi
> Esasperarci in sterile delirio.[dd][45]

This last stanza from the poem beginning with the expressive line "In angosciose oppressioni, io sento" ("In anguished oppression I feel") helps us to resolve the perplexing image that is introduced by the final *Ecco* clause of "Ecco il ritmo frenetico del sangue." In this poem, too, we have heard and seen the cry and the martyrdom and the violent dislocation of the forms of the earth. We now understand the positive significance of it all. But just when one would think that the poet himself has been freed to join in the cosmic dance he seems almost to be directing, the final *Ecco*, which is itself introduced by an *E* (line 13) having the function of an adversative

---

[dd] Better the cry and the tears and the torment
And the trembling of the earth and the movement
Of mountains, than deaf, blind, parched
To exasperate ourselves in a sterile delirium.

conjunction, reveals a contrasting element in the midday delirium. In the midst of the fiery ascension of things the poet experiences himself as a congealed star fixed in immobility and "exasperating" the ancient air with metallic wounds. A further sign of this immobility is the attribute of coral applied to the grass on which he stands or reclines, suggesting another sharp-edged rigidity.

In Onofri's doctrine of spiritual evolution, metals, like minerals, belong to the lower, harder, and resisting order of things, and the word *antico* usually refers to a period in the "past" when man and things, "forgetting" their vertical impulse, seem to wish to remain fixed in their noncombustible and inferior condition as "prisoners." Man can resist or be cold to glory. For this reason the poet sometimes prays for the Creator Spirit to invade him fully. And at times we find such exhortations as that in which he calls for a release from the mineral element: "Alzati fuor del minerale!" ("Arise from the mineral element").[46] Metals and minerals are a condition of the fall from spirit and union. The poet may even recognize the urging of the Creator force within this lesser world that man carries inside himself, but he may not be at the stage necessary to respond to it:

> O spirito del sole, io ti ravviso
> Fra il nero delle selve minerali
> Ch'io trascino in me stesso. Tu mi chiami
> A schiudere al tuo Verbo di fanciullo
> Il decrepito me;
>
> . . . .
> . . . .   ma l'arcano
> Ch'io non ho vinto ancora è il mio morirne.[ee][47]
> (12-16; 19-20)

[ee] Oh spirit of the sun, I behold you
Midst the black of the mineral forests
That I drag within myself. You beckon me
To unlock the decrepit me unto
Your childlike Word;

. . . .
. . . . but the secret
That I have not yet vanquished is my death.

As with minerals and metals, so too rock is recalcitrant to the spirit though it may on occasion be vitalistically invaded by it:

> Un raggio della luce che tu scocchi
> Si configge, vibrando impeti e osanna,
> Nel granito ostinato e nei metalli.[ff][48]
>
> (16-18)

In sum, then, in "Ecco il ritmo frenetico del sangue" the poet has remained *incantato*, rigidly fixed, and, we may say, *incatenato*, a Michelangelo-like "prisoner" *enchained* by the lower, nonspiritual order of things. It is as though while everything around him is ablaze in a phantasmagorical solar turbulence and struggle for freedom, he alone has become midday's counteracting "pause of being." He remains among the "incatenate angosce della terra" ("the chained anguishes of the earth") spoken of in yet another poem, witnessing the fiery drama around him but unable (or unwilling) to whirl himself into it. The congealed star that the poet feels himself to be is fire that is spent and solidified into a mineral body, and in such a condition man is only an "unreal fetish."[49] Accordingly, the poet's anguish here is not of the fertile kind exemplified by the blazing whorl of the things surrounding him, but rather that of a "sterile delirium." The poem may therefore be taken as the representation of an *échec* in a dramatic midday encounter. But unlike what has occurred in other cases of recoil (such as, say, in Valéry), the *échec* results not from an overmastering of the subject by an annihilating absolute, but from a willful resistance within the subject. There is a violent tension between movement and immobility, but in this context immobility is the condition of spiritual death. Despite the battering of the blood/spirit at the heart and temples of the poet, he is stuck in the obduracy of the negative pole—the world (or man) dominated by the inferior elements of mineral and metal and imprisoned in lower desires.[50]

[ff] A ray of light that you dart forth,
 Vibrating impulses and hosannas, drives
 Into the stubborn granite and into metals.

This brings us to the poem's last two lines which are given in parentheses, as though to set them apart in a sphere of reality unaffected by the violent solar drama that unfolds in the previous verses. Yet there is a strong rhythmic beat here also, though of a more deliberate, less frenzied kind, corresponding to the new image. During the noontide delirium, the sea has been beating against the rocky coast, and this image, along with the accompanying simile that speaks of the infinite trot of a horse, conveys the impression of an endless succession of time. But rock, we have seen, is a negative element that is obdurate to the spirit. Water, on the other hand, is often a positive element or symbol in Onofri. In the present instance, I believe, there is a symbolic equivalence between spirit and water. Thus it would seem that this final, nonsurrealistic image really reiterates on a broader plane what has been described in the hallucinatory vision in connection with the poet. The horse's trot (in the simile) and the insistent beat of the sea correspond to the throbbing (of the blood/spirit) at the poet's temples. And as the poet remains unmoved by the spirit, so too the rocky shore resists, perhaps even "wounds" the waters that seek to engulf it in a unifying embrace.

The last of Onofri's poems to claim our attention is an evocation of an Alpine midday in which, unlike the previous poem, the dominant mood is one of vast calm. There is, however, an intimation of a mysterious and active force at the core of this calm:

> Simili a melodie rapprese in mondo,
> Quand'erano sull'orlo di sfatarsi
> Nei superni silenzi, ardono pace
> Nel mezzogiorno torrido le ondate
> Ferme dei pini, sul brillìo turchino
> Del mare che smiracola d'argento.
> E ancora dalle masse di smeraldo
> Divampa un concepirsi incandescenze;
> Ma un pensiero di su le incenerisce
> In quella pausa d'essere ch'è cielo:
> Azzurreggiar di tenebra, che intima

(Dal massiccio dell'alpe all'orizzonte)
Ai duri tronchi ergersi alati incensi
A un dio sonoro, addormentato, in forma
D'un paese celeste sulla terra.[gg][51]

In the stillness of a torrid noontide a forest of pine trees, seen from above, appears as a motionless undulation of green against the background of the distant sea's silvery glistening under the sun of high noon. The impression created by the motionless "waves" of the pines is that of music (a rhythmic pattern) that has become congealed just as it was about to dissolve into the uncanny silence of midday (*superni silenzi*; cf. the *sovrumani silenzi* of Leopardi's "L'infinito"). A calm glows intensely from the pines—"ardono pace"—an oxymoronic image suggesting that the "waves" are or would like to be flames, but that they are not under violent stress. Lines 7-8 nonetheless reveal the secret tension in the green waves/flames which seem to blaze with desire for a return to a life of fire, perhaps a primordial cosmic fire—"Divampa un concepirsi incandescenze." But the impulse is checked by the commanding midday demon as a force (the sun) that "incinerates" them and encloses all things in an absolute stasis ("in quella pausa d'essere ch'è cielo"). The intensity of the blue sky is such that it imposes upon the pines a religious stance of verticality in which, with their "incense" they pay homage to a musical

---

[gg] Like melodies congealed into a world
When they were on the verge of being dispelled
Into supernal silence, the still waves
Of the pines emanate a burning peace in the torrid
Noon, on the shimmering blue
Of the sea that glitters magically with silver.
And still from the mass of emerald
There flares a continual conceiving of incandescences;
But a thought from above incinerates them
In that pause of being that is the sky:
A blueing of darkness, that summons
(From the massif of the Alps to the horizon)
The hard trunks to rise up like winged incense
To a sonorous god, asleep, in the form
Of a heavenly land(scape) on the earth.

god ("dio sonoro") who, though asleep at this hour, yet pervades the noontide calm. This sleeping midday god to whom the pines exhale their incense is, I think, no other than universal Pan (a musical god) present here *in and as* the vast landscape (from mountain tops to the distant horizon, the whole expanse of which is occupied by the pines). As it lies in frozen motion in the midday stasis (it is, after all, the silent hour of Pan), the landscape takes on the appearance of an eternal, celestial land. If this interpretation is correct, we may speak of a religiously pantheistic sentiment wherein the landscape, i.e., nature, is indeed experienced as a deity—"in forma / D'un paese celeste sulla terra." Again we have a noontide encounter in which the impression of an antithetical motion in immobility is strong. Yet the suspension of motion, the *incantation*, in this case, is not experienced as oppressive, and there is no sense of imprisonment, of an *échec*, or of the "incatenate angosce" of things. The "god asleep" suggests a supernal calm that will be the condition of all things when they are finally reintegrated into a unified cosmic unity. For now, even as they were rhythmically moving upward in their "return," they have become entranced, halted in a state of ecstatic abeyance and participating in a midday pause that is not limbo, but a foretaste and an image of a "celestial" perfection.

In the vein of midday solar mysticism exemplified by Onofri, mention should be made of Girolamo Comi, another writer in whom light, the senses, and the sentiment of a deity combine in the creation of images that convey the impression of an intense cosmic panism. Midday has the greatest significance in what is perhaps his most important poem—"Cantico della luce" ("Canticle of the Light"). Here light is perceived as a warm, living "corporeal" substance of glory with which the poet feels an atavistic kinship; not only this, but, even more astonishing, he senses the possibility of participating in its life retroactively, from all time, by virtue of a cosmic memory that belongs to the light and that the light pours or burns into him: "Tu perchè io m'identifichi / In tutta la tua memoria / Rutili, ardi e prolifichi / Oh caldo corpo di gloria"

(11-14).^{hh} It is in this context that the light, still perceived sensually as the "radiant flesh of landscapes," is said to attain its apotheosis daily at midday, and noon becomes a cosmic hymn intoning a *Gloria* that heralds a divine becoming:

> Franta in smeraldi o condensata in raggi
> Di radiose carni di paesaggi
> In te contempli la tua fiamma agire
> Nell'inno sommo d'ogni mezzogiorno
> Che testimonia ed intòna il ritorno
> Di un soprannaturale divenire.ⁱⁱ52
>
> (19-24)

Perhaps here, even more than in Rebora's "Quassù" or in Onofri's poems, being, consciousness, and noon are one.

It is a less cosmically intoned midday ecstatic suspension that is recorded in Adriano Grande's poem "La tomba verde" ("The Green Tomb," 1927-1929):

> Dentro una tomba verde ho riposato
> In un silenzio non protetto d'ombra.
> Il cielo la chiudeva d'ogni lato,
> Fermo più che il coperchio d'una tomba.
> In quel silenzio il cuore, impreparato,
> Tonfò come una pietra quando affonda.
> Nel torpor vegetale dell'Estate
> Tosto la pace delle cose inconscie,
> Delle terre sommerse e abbandonate,
> M'invase come una marea che sale.
> Eternità, inutile certezza,
> Per un momento intorno a me t'ho avuta:
> E mi parevi tutta quanta verde.

---

^{hh} So that I may identify myself / In all your memory / You glow, burn and beget / Oh warm body of glory.

ⁱⁱ Shattered in emeralds or condensed in rays
   Of radiant flesh of landscapes
   Within yourself you contemplate your flame operating
   In the supreme hymn of each noon
   That testifies to and intones the return
   Of a supernatural becoming.

Ma il vento, a un tratto, scosse un poco l'erbe
E ti perdetti, trasalendo come
La volpe che ode trepestar la muta.[jj][53]

At the very outset the rhythm and imagery suggest an account of an enchantment or a dream. Concerning the descriptive elements, we note that once more light is so much a part of the silence (and vice versa) that the latter word (*silenzio*), used twice, suffices to signify both elements. The second line—"In un silenzio non protetto d'ombra"—by its reference to the absence of all shade makes it clear that this is the hour of midday's incandescent silence. The "green tomb" in which the subject "reposes" is the countryside (perhaps a grassy meadow as the reference to *l'erbe* in line 14 would suggest) where at noon the green color of the vegetation has become most intense. The "cover" of the tomb is the immensity of sky which presses down and round the "tomb," sealing it on all sides. Into this tombal midday silence the poet's heart has suddenly plummeted like a stone in water, an image that suggests total submersion and which brings to mind the ending of Leopardi's "L'infinito."[54]

Indeed, on the whole, the poem would seem to be somewhere between the midday experiences recorded by Leopardi in "L'infinito" and "La vita solitaria." But the next seven verses (7-13) are characterized also by a Dannunzian strain. In the heavy summer midday torpor Grande is *invaded* by the ab-

---

[jj] Within a green tomb I reposed
In a silence unprotected by shade.
The sky closed it on all sides,
Tighter yet than the cover of a tomb.
In that silence my heart, caught by surprise,
Plunged like a stone that sinks.
In the vegetal torpor of Summer
At once the peace of unconscious things,
Of submerged and deserted lands,
Invaded me like a rising tide.
Eternity, useless certitude,
For a moment I felt you around me:
And you seemed wholly green to me.
But the wind, on a sudden, rippled the grass
And I lost you, starting like
The fox that hears the tread of hounds.

solute *peace* of inert, unconscious things and of "submerged and abandoned lands" (this latter expression being an echo of the *morte stagioni* of "L'infinito"). It is the undisturbed peace of thinghood or of inanimate things, a peace without the dynamic ambiguity that an intellectual confrontation (such as in "L'infinito" or Valéry's "Le cimetière marin") would bring. On the other hand, this peace is not quite the *antica quiete* (the absolute of nothingness) experienced in the *meriggio* of "La vita solitaria," but more of a tensionless pantheistic peace of unity. That it is said to invade or swell up in the poet like a swiftly rising tide (*marea*) reveals another echo (in sound and image) of the sea (*mare*) of infinite silence in which Leopardi sweetly drowns at the end of "L'infinito." But what happens to Grande befalls him without the momentary panic or awe that gripped Leopardi—"ove per poco / Il cor non si spaura." He has simply been surprised by the moment on an almost wholly instinctual or sensual level.

Grande's attribution of the color *green* to the eternity he experienced (lines 11-13) deserves a brief commentary. In a poem called "What We See is What We Think," Wallace Stevens noticed that "The trees stood green, / At twelve, as green as ever they would be,"[55] suggesting a sense of the Absolute which is most deeply present—antiquest felt—at noon. A falling away from that absolute begins immediately upon the passing of noon sharp. And in the last line of his famous sonnet in celebration of the ox ("Il bove"), Carducci spoke of the presence of something divine (of an absolute) in the vast silence (at noon?) of the green plain in such a way as to permit reading the line as *the divine green silence of the plain*—"Il divino del pian silenzio verde." *Green* is the last word or image we are left with in Carducci's poem, and in the context of a vigorous line it creates a vivid impression that is connected with a concrete reality and, at the same time, with the quality of divinity that the poet senses in that reality. Carducci's pantheism is as intellectual as it is experiential. One senses that Grande's attribution of green to eternity—in a rather languid line—is without intellectual conviction or real intuition, and that it is the result of an aestheticizing impressionism tacked on to an experience whose core was perhaps real enough. As to the appositive phrase *inutile certezza* (useless certitude), it is clearly a rational interpolation, now that the "moment" is over, stating the poet's awareness (or skeptical view) that the idea of eternity is a fiction. But this, too, is said almost nonchalantly, without creating tension. This skepticism, however, does not invalidate the core of the experience itself; as he says, he felt eternity around him; indeed, he *possessed* it for a brief moment: "Per un momento intorno a me t'ho avuta."

The enchantment is broken by a sudden wind strong enough to disturb the grass around the poet. The parallel with the wind in "L'infinito" is obvious enough, but it is the difference between the two poems in this regard that is truly significant. "E come il vento / Odo stormir tra queste piante," says Leopardi, and from there he goes on to tell how he is led by that sound of the wind rustling through the foliage to thoughts of eternity, the ages and seasons now "dead," and the present "season," which is also passing, until his thoughts drown in the immensity. The wind, itself an image of time, nonetheless is an agent that stimulates him to an intellectual (and imaginative) activity that leads to a triumph over the limits of time and reality. In the same way, in the first part of the lyric, Leopardi succeeds in going beyond the limits of enclosed space by using the particular arrangement of the landscape—his position atop the hill, the "hedge" with sky above and below it, a partial view of the distant horizon (a view obstructed in great part by the hedge)—as a springboard. It necessitates the participation of the mind and the imagination in an act of *feigning*—"io nel pensier mi fingo"—which supplies the creative half to what is only "half perceived." Thus Leopardi comes wakefully and lucidly to the illusory experience of a temporal and spatial infinity in which he ultimately finds it sweet to sink. Grande, on the other hand, is engulfed by his "tide" not as a result of a Leopardian meditation on the *ubi sunt* theme (which nonetheless seems to be behind his almost gratuitous and undeveloped reference to "submerged and abandoned lands"), but somewhat in the manner of a Dannunzian experience of Panic union with nature such as we find in "Meriggio." But while Grande may be said to begin where Leopardi ends, that is, in an "ecstasy," it is also true that he ends where Leopardi begins. For in his case the wind of reality blows away the midday fiction, and he is startled out of "eternity" like a fox startled out of its repose at the sound of approaching hounds. We can say that the wind functions here in much the same way as does the wind that breaks the midday spell (but how different a spell from Grande's midday enchantment!) in Valéry's "Le cimetière marin"; but unlike the French poet who responds positively to it in an acceptance of change and reality, Grande is left in a state of disillusionment at finding himself back in the world of time and reality. There is however, no profound anguish here. The fox image is elegant, but it is precisely this that instead of redeeming only further betrays the lack of depth in the experience and the poem. In the final analysis, this green tomb of eternity seems a bit too cosy, and the poem, which is cerebral in its construction, is, like the experience itself, without intellectual fiber. For all its borrowings from "L'infinito," it is quite un-Leopardian, and even its aestheticizing impressionism has little of the intensity that often lends to D'Annunzio's similar experiences a mark of authenticity and the sense of something deeper behind them.

In the case of the Sicilian poet Giuseppe Villaroel, midday has a rich suggestiveness of southern erotic luxury in the context of an amatory poetry that develops analogic correspondences between the female figure and a sensually impressionistic representation of nature. One of Italy's most authentic modern poets of love, his particular use of the midday topos has more to it than first meets the eye.

The tradition of a classicizing and Mallarméan-Dannunzian evocation of a trepid midday voluptuousness is continued in Villaroel's poem "Meriggio" with its faunesque vision—suspended between dream and reality—of sprightly modern-day nymphs whose luminous nudity is fleetingly glimpsed as they laughingly speed by on their bicycles under a torrid noonday sun. They are hastening home from work for lunch, the noon sirens having sounded:

Some Twentieth-Century Voices

> Filtra nell'aria un senso di vaga lussuria,
> E al grido delle sirene dileguano, appena intraviste,
> Le nudità balenanti di tutte le allegre cicliste
> Che si offrono a volo con mosse di perfida incuria.
> Preme l'arsura sui bianchi stradali sfiniti
> E il riso delle femmine squilla di fresca follia.[kk][56]
>
> (1-6)

An even earlier poem, "Meriggio estivo" ("Summer Midday," 1923), after an initial description of the sultry midday of a city, closes with a reference to the erotic reveries induced by the vast midday languor that pervades all things:

> . . . e la città sembra sfinita
> Dal sole, sembra che un languore enorme
> Snervi la terra; e gli uomini, in un blando
> Assopimento, sognino adorando
> La splendente bellezza delle forme.[ll][57]
>
> (16-20)

The forms dreamed of are female bodies which for Villaroel acquire the attributes of nature and are ideally "possessed" at midday. The sensualistic apprehension of nature is either concomitant with or equated with the possession of the beloved. One recognizes this at once as a Dannunzian motif, and just as the earlier poet's embodiment of the joyous essence of life (*Felicità*) appeared at midday, so too in the case of Villaroel the erotic epiphany of the *donna/natura* occurs in the hour that is supremely and absolutely nature's own, as at the close of the poem "Arrivo" ("Arrival"):

[kk] A sense of vague sensuality pervades the air,
And at the cry of the sirens, there disappears, barely
Glimpsed, of all the happy cyclists the flashing nudity
That is offered glancingly with moves of seductive nonchalance.
The scorching heat weighs upon the prostrated white roads
And the women's laughter peals with fresh abandon.
[ll]   . . . . and the city seems prostrated
By the sun, it seems that an enormous languor
Enervates the earth; and that the men, in a soft
Drowsiness, dream adoringly of
The radiant beauty of forms.

> Arrivi accanto a me, nel torpore meridiano
> Tiepida e profumata dal respiro dei tigli.[mm58]

In the short lyric entitled "Estate," the identification of the woman with nature is revealed to the poet in the luminous stasis of a summer midday. The force that "burns" secretly in the vegetative life of the earth is sensed as belonging in the very same way to the life of the woman's body:

> Chiaro il meriggio. Le carnose curve
> Posano al sonno dell'està. Dal mare
> Insiste il tenue risciacquio dell'onda.
> Vègeta calma la tua vita come
> La fronda dei palmizi. Nel tuo corpo
> Arde un segreto stimolo di pianta
> Che nutre il vento di sue linfe e fiori.[nn59]

This same principle of identity or equivalence obtains in the poem "Vuoi ch'io t'immerga nella limpida acqua" ("Do you want me to plunge you into the clear water") where the "avid languor" of the beloved is at one with the midday hour, so that the erotic dissolution of the lover is experienced as a merging into the sultry noontide stasis:

> . . . E l'avido languore
> Della tua bocca mi disvena in questa
> Canicolare calma del meriggio.[oo60]
> (8-10)

And in the lyric "Baciarti è come vivere il meriggio" ("To kiss you is to live the noontide") the fusion of the beloved and

[mm] You arrive beside me, in the midday torpor,
   Warm and scented by the breath of lindens.
[nn] Bright the midday. The fleshy curves
   Lie quietly in the sleep of summer. From the sea
   The mild lapping of the waves persists.
   Your life vegetates quietly like
   The leaves of palms. In your body
   Burns a secret urge of plants
   That the wind nourishes with its lymph and flowers.
[oo] . . . . And the avid languor
   Of your mouth enervates me in this
   Canicular calm of noontide.

nature in the hour of mystery and fullness is so complete that the beloved's kiss is described in terms of a voluptuous transport into the luxurious heart of a late summer noontide. Here the poet is suspended in regions of a perfumed brightness that seems the more intense by virtue of the shrill singing of the cicadas and the sound of the rushing luminous river:

> Baciarti è come vivere il meriggio
> In una landa molle di profumi
> Al vivo lume dell'està morente.
> L'aroma dei tuoi denti e il tuo respiro
> Mi sospendono in lucide regioni,
> Ove, al sopore blando degli ulivi,
> Cantano le cicale e il chiaro fiume.[pp61]

The attribution to the beloved of the quality of absoluteness and the sense of timelessness experienced in the midday stasis were anticipated in the poem "Origini" ("Origins," 1938) where a sense of the mystery that resides in woman and her primordial connection with the origins of existence are suggested by a comparison with the vast silence that reigns in the country at noon:

> Hai nel profumo la grazia primaverile del vento
> E il senso meridiano della campagna se taci.[qq62]
>
> (7-8)

Surely, Villaroel's poems of midday eroticism refer to much more than mindless sexual deliquescence. One may rightly see in them accounts of the mystical experience of carnal love. In this respect, we are helped to a greater appreciation of the pregnant value given to the role of midday

---

[pp] To kiss you is to live the noontide
In a soft heath of perfumes
In the vivid light of the dying summer.
The aroma of your teeth and your breath
Suspend me in bright regions,
Where, in the soothing drowsiness of olive trees,
The cicadas and the bright river sing.

[qq] You have the springtime grace of the breeze in your scent
And the noontime sense of the country when you are silent.

(whether it be the actual setting for the experience or a term of comparison as in the last two examples cited) by a highly suggestive page of prose-poetry that evokes the noontide of a Sicilian village. Interspersed amid the details that tell of the diminished signs of life at that hour—the deserted streets, the inhabitants retiring to the cool shade of their houses, the field hands who sink into the torpor of the siesta—are observations that refer to the noontide silence being perceived as a living substance, the sun reigning supremely over all (over time itself), and the all-enveloping languor gravid with a secret ferment. Most remarkable of all are the references to the scorched earth that seems to rediscover a sense of its cosmic origins during its very disintegration in the light that has vanquished it, and, finally, the image of the incandescent pause in which, while life and time are suspended, all things are transfigured into a *stationary mobility* of fiery air.[63]

In a more traditional vein of midday eroticism Ada Negri's poem "Cicale" ("Cicadas") must be given here because it is perhaps the finest modern example of the parallel between the implacable heat of midday and the relentless torment of unrequited passion, a motif, as we have seen, that goes back to Virgil. The persistent shrill of the cicadas that pervades the parched, sun-baked country is at one with the inner cry that in the time of her passion repeated endlessly a name in her soul and veins. Like the earth fiercely scorched by the midday sun, she was burned by the violent flame of her love:

> Stridere senza fine
> Nel torrido silenzio. Altro non s'ode
> Per la campagna tutta sole e sete.
> Sempre lo stesso grido
> Che scoppia dal midollo
> Dei tronchi, dalle spire
> Delle radici, dalla terra gialla
> Che al sol si spacca—ed io non so se goda
> O soffra. E in esso a me ritorni, folle
> Eco del tempo innamorato, quando
> Anima e sangue non avean che un solo

Grido, quel grido, sempre uguale—ed era
Un nome—: ed io non ero se non terra,
Cieca terra mortale,
Bruciata dalla vampa del mio male.[rr][64]

The poem is interesting also for the fact that the cicadas' maddening chirr and the fiery heat of the hour are perceived as the same phenomenon (within the heart of midday's *torrid silence*, we may also note). That is, the two components, especially in the interiorization of the experience where the cry seems the explosive crackling of the amatory flame, are so closely fused as to produce a single image that the contemporary poet Andrea Zanzotto has actually verbalized in a nonerotic midday context. It is that of the flame of the cicadas, *la fiamma delle cicale*, a compelling emblem of midday.[65]

Another writer to be remembered for a modern variation on a traditional theme of midday eroticism—the faun-in-waiting motif in this case—is Aldo Palazzeschi and his novella entitled "Meriggio d'estate" ("Summer Midday"). This is a poignant version of the themes of yearning and spying on nudity in the burning stillness of noontide. Written in a manner that combines poetic prose with narrative exposition, it recounts the outing in a boat of a group of adolescent boys in bathing trunks seen by an observer (the author) who, hidden behind vegetation on the shore (oh Actaeon!), longs to be among them but is all too aware that he is in the role of an avid but powerless faun.[66]

[rr] Stridor without end
 In the torrid silence. Nothing else is heard
 Throughout the countryside all sun and thirst.
 Ever the same cry
 That explodes from the marrow
 Of tree trunks, from the coils
 Of roots, from the yellow earth
 That cracks in the sun—and I know not whether
 It rejoices or suffers. And in it you return
 To me, mad echo of the time of my enamorment,
 When my soul and blood had but one
 Cry, that cry, always the same—and it was
 A name—: and I was nothing but earth,
 Blind mortal earth,
 Scorched by the blaze of my torment.

192   Some Twentieth-Century Voices

Umberto Saba's early poem "Meriggio" takes us into still another area of twentieth-century treatment of the theme of midday. A cursory reading might lead one to judge it as no more than an unremarkable variation on earlier genre descriptions of the midday stasis and the retreat. But there is something in its language and tone that makes it more than that. As the relentless light inundates the earth, shutters and doors of houses are closed in order to keep out the invading sun (1-5). The stillness is so intense that humankind seems to have become extinct. "Sembrano estinti / Gli uomini, tanta è ora pace" (11-12). Here too the silence is not the less deep for being filled with the shrill "whistle" of the cicadas (13-16). Completing the scene is the figure of an old man (perhaps a beggar) lying asleep on the stone (bench or pavement?) of a tree-lined road, indifferent to the fiery noonday sun in which the surrounding foliage "burns" without motion (17-24). Of particular interest is the irony or ambiguity that attaches to the triumphant midday sun whose effulgence is connected with a sense of glory from which people must protect themselves. Thus the poet has chosen a most significant verb—*volere*—used in the negative in order to indicate man's avoidance of the midday encounter, and by repeating it he suggests a polemical thrust at a force that, while it seems admirable, is actually pernicious.

> Silenzio! Hanno chiuso le verdi
> Persiane e gli usci le case.
> Non vogliono essere invase
> Dalla tua gloria, o Sole!
>
> Non vogliono.[ss67]
>
> (1-5)

Because Saba was much influenced by Pascoli's use of a humbler subject matter, we are not wrong to think that he has

[ss] Silence! The houses have closed up their green
Shutters and their doors.
They do not wish to be invaded
By your glory, Oh Sun!

They do not wish it.

here continued the polemic of the earlier poet's "Gloria." Now, however, it is more clearly D'Annunzio that is rejected. *Meriggio, gloria, Sole* are immediately recognizable as bywords in D'Annunzio's solar poetry and much proclaimed meridian "vivere inimitabile."[68] Like Pascoli's Belacqua, Saba's humanity prefers, even demands, to have its noontide siesta, the proper place for which is in the shade inside the unheroic interiors of ordinary houses. It is in this sense too that we are to understand the poem's final image depicting the figure of an old man, an example of a humble reality, sleeping in the shade undisturbed by the wild singing of the sun-drunk cicadas and indifferent to the blaze of noon:

> E un uomo, c'è un uomo nell'arsa
>   Solitudine del viale,
>   Un vecchio, che ha fatto guanciale
>   Delle sue grucce, che dorme
> Là sulla pietra, e non cura
>   L'incendio meridiano,
>   L'incendio onde presso e lontano
>   Immobili sono le foglie.[tt]
>   (17-24)

The poet Elpidio Jenco has developed this Pascolian antimeridian mode still more programmatically in a poem entitled, interestingly enough, "Umiltà" ("Humility"). Finding the dazzling light of midday too strong to withstand, Jenco would withdraw from it in favor of the twilight hour in whose obscurity he might live his portion of suffering:

> Fa, Signore, ch'io viva umile e scuro
> Nel mio bozzolo d'ombra . . . . .
> . . . .

[tt] And a man, there is a man in the scorched
  Solitude of the road,
  An old man, who has made a pillow
  Of his crutches, who sleeps
 There on the stone, and pays no heed to
  The midday blaze,
  The blaze wherewith near and far
  The leaves are motionless.

> Questa luce m'abbàcina . . . . . .
> . . . .
> Dammi mezzombra a carezzarmi gli occhi
> Labili . . . .
> . . . .
> Non la gloria, ch'è un'ora di meriggio,
> E schianta nelle sue piene di lume.
> Dammi il buio che addicasi al mio pianto.[uu][69]

One can hardly fail to see in these verses a restatement of Pascoli's "Gloria." The blinding meridian glory that wounds Jenco and from which he retires is, as in the case of Saba's poem, the Dannunzian solar mythology of the superman. At the very least it refers to an active life of high ambitions and the fame attendant on such a life. Though the term *twilight poetry* (*poesia crepuscolare*) in critical usage refers to a body of poetry that arose in the early years of the present century, precisely as a conscious rejection of the solar poetry of Carducci and D'Annunzio, I can think of no poem that more deserves to be so characterized than this by Jenco, unless, of course, it be Pascoli's own "Gloria."

When Jenco later gave expression to this same psychological and moral state, he again had recourse to those images of nature specifically connected with the diurnal and seasonal cycles. Indeed, now the evening twilight that follows the violence of the canicular season comes as a sweet foretaste of death—the only lasting relief:

> Conforto all'ardente strazio dei solleoni
> A me giunge il crepuscolo, aurora delle notti assorte:

[uu] Lord, let me live humbly and obscure
In my cocoon of shade . . . . . .
. . . .
This light dazzles me . . . .
. . . .
Give me half-light to caress my weak eyes.
. . . .
Not glory, which is a noontide hour,
And shatters in its floods of light.
Grant me the darkness that is suited to my tears.

Cola in cuore una pace siderea, una calma bianca di
   costellazioni,
Assaggio furtivo d'una quasi dolcezza di morte.^{vv}[70]
                                            (13-16)

The fact that the diurnal image of twilight is used in conjunction with and in opposition to the season of summer (*solleone* = dog days, i.e., July and August) is yet another example of the symbolic equivalence of midsummer and high noon in the language of poets. Indeed, the word *solleone* is often employed by poets to refer precisely to the rabid midday sun of high summer.

Seasons (even months) and the diurnal cycle are felt and sung by twentieth-century poets no less than they were by those of earlier times. And of the modern Italian poets who have expressed the "seasons and hours" of their own lives in terms of those of nature, Jenco is, along with Vincenzo Cardarelli and Giuseppe Ungaretti, among the most persistent and consistent. It is interesting to note, then, that summer and midday could on occasion strike a responsive chord in him, an example being the short lyric "Estate" where the poet experiences a feeling of increase and inner transfiguration, as if he were nature itself overflowing with the boundless luminosity of midday.[71] On the other hand, "Ora torrida" ("Torrid Hour") evokes the torpor of an immense stasis where not even the cicada is heard; and as the midday sun of July consumes the grass and pulverizes the clods of earth, the poet dreams of restorative waters and the caress of a beloved that might descend like the cool moonlight of a summer night.[72]

Closely connected with the motif of midday are a number of poems on the theme of summer that, without specific reference to noontide, clearly evoke that hour. We have already met with examples of this kind in baroque and Arcadian poets. And such a poem is Vincenzo Cardarelli's well-known anthology piece "Estiva" ("Summer Piece") whose first

---

^{vv} Like comfort to the burning torment of the canicular season
Twilight comes to me, the dawn of pensive nights:
A sidereal peace filters into my heart, a white calm of constellations,
Furtive foretaste of a quasi-sweetness of death.

line—"Distesa estate" ("Widespread Summer")—immediately creates in that one adjective and one noun the image of a vast, almost corporeal reality of light and immobility. The poem's last lines evoke the sense of a limitless stasis that is metaphysically intuited as a pause of eternity in the flow of time:

> Stagione estrema, che cadi
> Prostrata in riposi enormi,
> . . . .
> E sembri mettere a volte
> Nell'ordine che procede
> Qualche cadenza dell'indugio eterno.[ww][73]
> (14-15; 20-22)

The seasons, which are at the core of Cardarelli's poetry, are emblematic of the seasons of the human life cycle. The analogy is so close that in the poem "Saluto di stagione" ("Season Salutation") he could say "L'uomo è stagione" ("Man is season"). Within this equation, summer of course is the time of fullness or maturity, and it is significant that Cardarelli experiences it as a time of serenity and even of some ecstasy. It is for him the season that offers, as no other season can, the "certezza di sole" ("guarantee of the sun," "Estiva," 12), and, with its long hours of light, the illusion of an endless moment of peace. Yet to be conscious of the succession of the seasons (or of the parts of the day), is to be aware of the passing of time, and behind Cardarelli's dream of endless summer is the anguished sense of time fleeing—the *sentimento del tempo* as Ungaretti was to call the collection of poems of his own summer season. It was the same sentiment that caused D'Annunzio to plead anxiously that his summer not abandon him.[74] Cardarelli too would have that season linger on, and,

---

[ww] Ultimate season, you that fall
Prostrate in vast repose,
. . . .
And seem at times to put
Cadences of an eternal lingering
Into the order that proceeds.

as we have seen, summer to him is even an image of a pause in the passage of time. That this pause or illusion of timelessness is ideally connected with midday is implicit in the imagery of "Estiva." It is even clearer in the earlier lyric—"Saluto di stagione":

> [Io] che amo i tempi fermi e le superfici chiare,
>   E ad ogni transizione di meriggio,
>   Rotta l'astrale identità del mattino,
>   Avverto gli spazi irritarsi,
>   E sento il limite e il male
>   Che incrinano ogni cambio d'ora,
>   Saluto nel sol d'estate
>   La forza dei giorni più eguali.[xx][75]
>   (27-34)

Bidding a serene farewell to spring (i.e., his youth), and welcoming the advent of summer, the poet declares his love for the immobility and luminosity that reign in nature at midday. Each day, with the passing of noontide, the poet becomes aware of the irregularity, the loss of serenity, that comes into the atmosphere; the perception of the changes in the quality of the light causes him to feel the limit and evil that undermine and "crack" each hour. That is, he is disquieted by the sense of the "flaw" (i.e., time) inherent in existence. Summer, with its succession of long days of light, is hailed by him because it promises the illusion of an extended season of what is experienced diurnally at midday—"i tempi fermi e le superfici chiare."[76]

The serene, luminous immobility envisioned by Cardarelli as the ideal characteristic of his desired summer (i.e., the season of a long, untroubled maturity in the human life cycle) is

---

[xx] [I] who love unmoving times and bright surfaces,
    And with each passing of noon,
    When the astral identity of morning is broken,
    Perceive space becoming troubled,
    And feel the limit and the evil
    That crack each change of hour,
    I hail in the summer sun
    The strength of the most equal days.

an element of midday and implies the immensity of silence. The experience of silence as the dominant quality of midday was expressed by him in a single isolated line of unusual imaginative force when, in the midst of a prose description of the countryside where he passed his childhood, Cardarelli noted: "Il silenzio a mezzogiorno fa marea."[yy][77] Silence has here acquired the character of an ocean that has swelled and extended itself like a tide. One thinks of the infinite sea of silence of Leopardi's "L'infinito" and perhaps of the tidal silence that engulfs Grande in "La tomba verde." But there is no sweet drowning in the case of Cardarelli's evocation. For he too knew the ambiguity of the midday hour and the Gorgon aspect of the summer sun, and the reference to midday's oceanic silence is followed by a brief notation on the condition of his native region in the summer as a parched, forbidding place rendered even more melancholy by the cicadas' song. "Terra stoppiosa e bruciata in estate, caldissima e indolente, sbavata dal vento di mare, lambita dal canto dei bifolchi, immelanconita dal canto delle cicale."[zz][78]

This is the real summer without metaphorical or allegorical allusions. But the same negative side of the summer midday sun is present in the anxious metaphysical inquiry made by Cardarelli's version of Zarathustra who complains that the sun in its midday splendor has incinerated all his former hopes and ideas and has replaced them with unsubstantial appearances and colors. He even suspects that the function of the sun, from the heights of its meridian glory ("al sommo dei tuoi splendori meridiani"), is to spread its effulgence over, and thereby conceal, the nothingness of reality: "Dimmi se la tua funzione è di creare o di distruggere, oppure, come dubito, di diffondare bagliori sul nulla. È questo il mistero mediterraneo?"[aaa][79] That is a question and an anguish that

[yy] At midday, silence swells like a tide.
[zz] A land that is stubbly and scorched in summer, hot and inert, slobbered by the sea winds, lapped by the ploughman's song, made melancholy by the song of the cicadas.
[aaa] Tell me if your function is to create or destroy, or, as I suspect, to spread flashing radiance over nothingness. Is this the mystery of the Mediterranean?

had been asked and experienced in various modes by earlier poets during encounters with the midday sun, most notably Leopardi, Leconte de Lisle, and Paul Valéry.[80] And among Cardarelli's own Italian contemporaries, Giuseppe Ungaretti and Eugenio Montale in particular were more profoundly affected than he by the question and the anguish.

Indeed, it is a fact of the utmost significance to this study that in the work of Italy's two chief poets since World War I the images of summer and midday have figured centrally in the representation of the metaphysical and, in part, historical and political anguish of modern man. We have seen that a sense of crisis permeated the Italian scene from the beginning of the century. Its expression in terms of the theme of spiritual aridity and thirst—with the concomitant natural setting in images of drought, desert, and an implacable summer midday sun—is in evidence even before the Great War, and in addition to the poets we have cited, others could be called on to bear witness to it.[81] But crisis has been the hallmark of all Europe throughout the century. That the theme of aridity and the reality of the crisis behind it (despite the variations in some of the underlying specific national political and cultural characteristics) are far from being peculiar to Italy need hardly be argued here. Suffice it to say that for the Western world in general, the best-known emblematic poem of the twentieth century is still T. S. Eliot's *The Waste Land* (1922). Without doubt, the modern metaphysical anguish is closely connected with the bitter historical disillusionment of our century, although a similar disillusionment was known to many spirits of Europe during and after the Napoleonic wars. It was deeply felt, for example, not only by Foscolo and Manzoni but also by Leopardi, a poet whose presence is fundamental in Ungaretti and Montale. But it would be foolhardy to deny that the bestial events of our own century have made both the metaphysical anguish and the bitter taste of history more pervasive, with the result, so frequently commented on, that the great temptation of our time is the temptation of despair and nihilism. And yet, the experience and the representation of that despair do not always signify a resignation to it; indeed, a declaration of it may at times contain, implicitly or explicitly, a protest against nihilism. This is as true of Ungaretti and Montale as it is of Leopardi.

However, I believe that it would be a mistake to connect the "negativity" and the sense of anguish found in our two remaining poets too closely with fascism. Though Montale's poetry was to become a protest against that politico-cultural phenomenon for those who would listen, the dates of the poems discussed here suggest he would have written them (or poems very much like them) in any case. The earliest and most famous of them, in fact, was written in 1916. But that, after all, was when World War I was raging! As for Ungaretti, he was an early friend of Mussolini's and he even supported the political regime, though, when policies of racial persecution began to be enforced in Italy, not without misgivings. If there is something mythical in the relationship that he, the Italian born abroad, establishes between himself and Italy in such a poem as "Italia" (1916), it has to do with his need of finding his "origins," and his poetry was never linked with the fascist creed. Indeed, it is remarkably alien to it. More than in the case of Montale, his anguished vision was nurtured in great part by direct contact with the tragic madness of the First World War. And even when he recovered a traditional religious faith, he remained a tormented spirit. This is to say that for Italian poets, too, the theme of spiritual sterility and the vision of fiery annihilation transcend specific historical and political events even when they have been touched and partially determined by them. Finally, the same point is to be made about the personal events in these poets' lives that may have served as the occasions for specific poems. No less than Leopardi, Ungaretti and Montale (but of what true lyric poet may this not be said?) are poets in whose work the biographical element, while it is unusually strong, is rarely diaristic but, on the contrary, is inevitably made to express an existential sense of the plight of man.[82]

V. Giuseppe Ungaretti

Ci vendemmia il sole
(*"Fase d'oriente"*)

When he left Alexandria, where he had lived the first twenty-odd years of his life at the edge of the real desert, Ungaretti carried with him the memory of a city flooded in the dazzling glory of noon. The event is commemorated in the poem "Silenzio" (1916):

> Conosco una città
> Che ogni giorno s'empie di sole
> E tutto è rapito in quel momento
>
> Me ne sono andato una sera
>
> Nel cuore durava il limio
> Delle cicale.[a1]
>
> (1-6)

The memory arises in the depth of a *silence* (the poem's title) that is characteristic also of the experience of the meridian light evoked in the vision. Following a pause, the poet recalls that his departure took place in the evening (by ship, as the last part of the poem, unquoted here, makes plain), and after yet another pause we are told that the shrill of the cicadas continued in his heart. One would not be wrong in referring the cicadas' shrill back also to the vision evoked (for the poet says clearly that it *continued*), in which case we could speak of another example of a noontide silence charged with a high

[a] I know a city
That fills with the sun every day
And all is enraptured in that moment

I departed one evening

In my heart there remained
The cicadas' rasping.

tension. But this tension is retrospective insofar as the vision itself is concerned, because the most significant thing about Ungaretti's choice of the word *limio* (rasping, gnawing, from *limare* = to file) is that it totally internalizes the cicadas' persistent shrill into a negative affective (subjective) quality and conveys the idea of a consuming action that recurs in many of his midday evocations. In "Silenzio" it is a consuming homesickness. The poet left his city in the evening, and the relentless stridulation and gnawing of the cicadas that he says continued in his heart tells us that he bore within him not only the vision of a city wrapped in light but also an intense torment at leaving it.

The first three lines of "Silenzio" evoke an ecstatic vision having the quality of a luminous miragelike memory ever before the poet, but when the same descriptive elements reappear in the short lyric "Ricordo d'Affrica" ("Memory of Africa," published first in 1919 under the revealing title "Meriggio di agosto," "August Midday") they record an apocalyptic vision of a desert sun in the guise of a destroyer Gorgon:

> Il sole rapisce la città
>
> Non si vede più
>
> Neanche le tombe resistono molto[b2]

Rather than being enraptured in the glory of a meridian luminosity as in "Silenzio," the city is now a prey to the devouring sun within which it seems to dissolve. The shift to a sense of violence is seen in the fact that the three lines of the ecstatic vision of "Silenzio" are here condensed into one line—the first—with the sun now having become the subject

---

[b] The sun abducts the city

  It can no longer be seen

  Even the tombs soon yield

and the verb *rapire* used in the active voice. In "Silenzio," moreover, the line "E *tutto è rapito* in quel momento" refers not only to the city, but to *everything* (all of nature, including the poet himself) as being rapt, i.e., enraptured. Wrenched into the first verse of the new context where the semantic value of the verb undergoes a drastic change, the line gives way to the stark but fearful assertion that nothing (in the blinding and devouring blaze) can be seen: "Non si vede più." Finally, the reference to the tombs—traditional symbol of the continuation (the *resistance*) of life after death—that also succumb to the sun's vehemence evokes, ironically but awesomely, the image of a universal disintegration into nothingness. Ungaretti's device of spacing the poem's three verses between two blank lines of whiteness effectively renders the impression of awful silence in which the relentless work of annihilation goes on.[3]

This sentiment of a metaphysical nothingness experienced in and emblematized by the blazing and blinding hour of midday in the desert is fully documented by Ungaretti in a page from an account of a return trip he made to Egypt in 1931. With the sun's rays streaming down perpendicularly, the desert world is suspended in a stasis charged with foreboding; all objects seem to merge in the undifferentiated, yellow grayish light diffused by the sun. It is an ambiguous luminosity that removes one's sight and makes this hour the real night of the desert. Within it one feels engulfed in nothingness:

Il sole già cade a piombo; tutto ora è sospeso e turbato; ogni moto è coperto, ogni rumore soffocato. *Non è un'ora d'ombra, né un'ora di luce.* È l'ora della monotonia estrema. *Questa è l'ora cieca; questa è l'ora di notte del deserto.* Non si distinguono più le rocce tarlate, tigna biancastra fra la sabbia. Le fine ondulazioni della sabbia anch'esse sono naufragate nella *fitta trama dei raggi che battono uguali da tutte le parti*. Non c'è più né cielo, né terra. *Tutto ha un rovente ed eguale colore giallo grigio*, nel quale vi muovete a stento, ma come dentro a una nube. Ah! se non fosse quella frustata che dalla pianta dei piedi vi scioglie il sangue in una canzone, rauca, malinconica, maledetta, *direste che questo è il nulla.*[c4]

This phenomenon of an ambiguous midday light experienced as neither darkness nor clarity but as a paradoxical fusion of both (with the emphasis perhaps on the darkness) seems particularly true of desert noonscapes. The same impression was recorded in a remarkable page of the diary of the French painter and writer Eugène Fromentin during a stay in the Sahara in the summer of 1853. Because the similarities of detail (and almost of language) between Ungaretti's account and Fromentin's are so striking, it is not amiss to consider the latter here. I italicize those phrases of most immediate interest to our discussion:

> C'est aussi l'heure, je l'avais remarqué dès le jour de mon arrivée, où *le désert se transforme en une plaine obscure*. Le soleil, suspendu à son centre, l'inscrit dans un cercle de lumière dont *les rayons égaux le frappent en plein, dans tous les sens et partout à la fois. Ce n'est plus ni de la clarté, ni de l'ombre; la perspective indiquée par les couleurs fuyantes cesse à peu près de mesurer les distances; tout se couvre d'un ton brun, prolongé sans rayure, sans mélange*; ce sont quinze ou vingt lieues d'un pays uniforme et plat comme un plancher. Il semble que le plus petit objet saillant y devrait apparaître, pourtant on n'y découvre rien; même, on ne saurait plus dire où il y a du sable, de la terre, ou des parties pierreuses, et l'immobilité de cette mer solide devient alors plus frappante que jamais. On se demande, en le voyant commencer à ses pieds, puis s'étendre, s'enfoncer vers le sud, vers l'est,

[c] The sun already falls vertically; now everything is suspended and troubled; every motion is blanketed, every sound suffocated. It is neither an hour of shadow nor an hour of light. It is the hour of utter monotony. This is the blind hour, this is the hour of the night of the desert. The eroded rocks, no longer distinguishable, are but a whitish mange in the sand. Even the subtle undulations of the sand are submerged in the dense weft of rays that beats down evenly from all sides. There is neither sky nor earth anymore. Everything has a burning and uniform yellow gray color in which you move with difficulty, as though enveloped within a cloud. Ah! if it were not for the scourge that from the soles of the feet loosens your blood into a song—raucous, melancholy, damned—you would say that this is nothingness.

ver l'ouest, sans route tracée, sans inflexion, *quel peut être ce pays silencieux, revêtu d'un ton douteux qui semble la couleur du vide*; d'où personne ne vient, où personne ne s'en va, et qui se termine par une raie si droite et si nette sur le ciel. L'ignorât-on, on sent qu'il ne finit pas là et que ce n'est, pour ainsi dire, que l'entrée de la haute mer.[d5]

Fromentin's account reveals the careful eye of the painter, but if, on the whole, it appears less dramatic in its metaphysical suggestiveness than Ungaretti's, it is not without such implications. The passage does in fact communicate an authentic *frisson* by its evocation of the mysterious suspension of things at midday in a world where the uniformity of dark yellow has abolished the sense of distance between things. And especially noteworthy is the characterization of the light (and the silence with it) as being the "color of nothingness."[6]

Returning to Ungaretti's desert noonscape, we find that its internalization is concomitant with its external representation. Noon is experienced as a physiological reality according to the image in which the poet notes that the scourging heat that penetrates through the soles of the feet into the blood is like the absolute light that consumes itself on the sterility of the sands: "Essa entra nel sangue come l'esperienza di questa luce assoluta che si logora sull'aridità."[7] The idea of absolute

---

[d] As I noticed from the day of my arrival, it is also the hour when the desert is transformed into a dark plain. The sun, suspended at its center, envelopes it in a circle of light whose uniform rays beat fully on it, in all directions and everywhere at the same time. It is neither brightness nor shadow; the perspective marked by departing colors ceases little by little to measure distances; everything is shrouded by a dark tawny tone, extended without streaks, without nuance; fifteen or twenty leagues of a monotonous land flat as a board. It seems that the smallest protruding object ought to be noticed, and yet one discovers nothing there. In fact, one would be unable to say anymore where there is sand, solid land, or rocky sections; and the immobility of this solid sea then becomes more astonishing than ever. In seeing it begin at one's feet, then stretch out, plunging south, east, and west, without any delineated track, without variation, one wonders what this silent land may be that is covered by an indistinct tone that seems the color of emptiness; a land from which no one comes, where no one moves, and which ends in so straight and precise a line in the sky. If one did not know otherwise, one would think that it does not end there and that it is, so to speak, but the entrance into the deep sea.

stillness and total barrenness is further emphasized by the continuation of the midday description in terms of a series of negatives indicating the muting or absence of those signs of life one might normally expect to find. The procedure is the same as that used in Leopardi's noonscape in "La vita solitaria," although the specific elements of (absent) life are, of course, those proper to the desert: "Non c'è una locusta a quest'ora, non un camaleonte, non un porcospino, non una lucertola, non uno scorpione; non c'è una quaglia, né uno sciacallo, né uno scarabeo, né una vipera cornuta" (p. 81).[e] It is at this point that the emblematic importance of the poet's presence as a solitary figure walking on that broiling desert becomes clear. In this empty land of sightlessness, there is one object, after all, upon which the poet stumbles: "Ma inciampo nello scheletro d'un mehari che farà musica stanotte quando il vento marino gli passerà tra le costole" (p. 81).[f] The dromedary's skeleton partly buried in the burning sands and bleached by the sun is the ultimate revelation of nothingness.

Of some importance is the fact that the original title of this piece (as it was given in the *Gazzetta del Popolo*, September 12, 1931), "La risata dello Dginn Rull" ("The Laughter of the Jinni Rull"), was changed in 1949 when the author replaced it with a separate title page carrying the words "Il demonio meridiano" ("The Midday Demon").[8] This is significant for two reasons. In signaling a more obviously dramatic and emblematic value (accentuated by having the title appear on a separate title page), the expression almost surely is intended to suggest erotic energy which, as we have seen, is one of the two most common notions associated with the idea of the "demon of noontide," the other being precisely that of a destructive and annihilating force in nature. These two concepts tend to fuse in Ungaretti's midday summer mythology. Nothing, for example, could better suit the 1949 title—"Il

---

[e] There is not a locust at this hour, not a chameleon, not a porcupine, not a lizard, not a scorpion, not a quail, nor a jackal, nor a scarab, nor a horned viper.

[f] But I stumble upon a mehari's skeleton that will make music tonight when the sea wind blows through its ribs.

demonio meridiano"—than the essay's ending. In answer to Ungaretti's query about the fatalities caused by the desert wind, the wise Arab laughs and says that on the desert one does not die because of the wind but because of thirst—"Di vento non si muore. Si muore di sete." There follows the poet's closing meditation:

> Se l'Arabo ritorna dal deserto, ah! nelle vene gli latrano i mastini. Ecco perché il nomade è inguaribile: il deserto è un vino, ed è una droga, e accende un'ira che non si sfoga se non nel sangue, o in lentissimi amori.
>
> Fra tanti sensi di morte che la sua vita millenaria gli ha impastato nelle vene, l'Egiziano ha ricevuto dall'Arabo il senso più triste: che il desiderio del piacere sia una sete estrema, la sofferenza che non si calma se non nella pazzia. Questo senso: che la pazzia sia come un accrescimento dell'anima, che il premio per l'anima sia la liberazione nel piacere mortale dei sensi (p. 84).[g]

In view of this passage (and the 1949 title), it is not hazardous to assume that erotic heat is connoted in that part of the essay (really a prose poem) where the poet speaks of the scourging heat that comes from the desert's burning sands through the feet and into the blood. If it were not for that sensation, Ungaretti observed, one would be left only with the sentiment of nothingness![9]

While Ungaretti recognized night as one of the magic moments of the desert, the desert obviously has its deepest relationship with the sun, particularly with midday, even as the prose poem under consideration indicates. In this respect the second main point to be made regarding the title "Il demonio

---

[g] If the Arab returns from the desert, ah! in his veins the mastifs bark. This is why the nomad is incurable: the desert is a wine, and it is a drug; it kindles a rage that vents itself only in blood, or in long-savored loves.

Among so many intimations of death that his millenary life has kneaded into his veins, the Egyptian has received from the Arab the most desolate one: that the desire for pleasure is an extreme thirst, a suffering that is appeased only in madness. This intimation: that madness is a sort of expansion of the soul, that the reward for the soul is release in the deadly pleasure of the senses.

meridiano" is that although the account itself goes on, after the initial passage quoted above, to describe the phenomenon of desert light beyond the period of high noon as such—perhaps until just before sunset or thereabouts—the entire description is meant to be understood as a noontide encounter. With a painter's eye not inferior to Fromentin's, Ungaretti describes the subtle changes in the light as the sun's rays become slightly oblique. The paradoxical impression continues. The hour is not less "dark," but it dazzles differently: "Quando i raggi incominciano ad obliquare, l'ora non è meno *nera*; ma abbaglia diversamente" (p. 81). The burning sand is "tawny" ("e la sabbia fulva"), the color of Mallarmé's fiercely burning midday hour—"Inerte, tout brûle dans l'heure fauve"—which Ungaretti translated in 1946 with the same term: "Inerte, tutto brucia / Nell'ora fulva."[10] And just as in French the word actually refers to a savage beast as well as to the color, so too in Italian, in D'Annunzio especially, it is the color of both the lion and the sun. (The same color is specified in a Montalean noonscape that we shall later consider.) Now everything appears as a blondish undulation speckled here and there for a moment with a darker hue, and all objects that can be seen at all appear bordered with a burnt yellow darkening into violet. But if things now begin to be distinguished, distances are still not determinable ("è l'ora degli errori della distanza"), a feature noted also by Fromentin. Finally, even when the sun's rays are more obviously oblique, the light cannot be sustained, though the sky cannot be said to be clear. As the blue palès, it becomes granulated with red, and still there are the burnt outlines of things with the yellow deepening into violet. Soon one will be able to make out figures, but then the desert noontide will have passed. Meanwhile it is in this hallucinatory atmosphere that water appears, cruel water, however, which can never quench a thirst because it is only a sadistic joke played by the light (p. 82).

Within this context of midday on the desert the recurrent and interrelated Ungarettian themes of thirst, nothingness, the oasis, and the mirage receive their most intense utterances and their richest emblematic value. While the obsessive motif of the mirage is occasionally connected by the poet with other moments or different climatic conditions, it most readily and most persistently (most naturally, we may even say) appears in relation to midday with which it comes close to forming a dyad. In a late commentary on his penchant for "indulging" in mirages, Ungaretti made clear both its existential implications and its close tie with his early experience with the desert noon.[11] As a dyad, midday/mirage is particularly suggestive in Italian because the mere sound of the one word is enough, especially in allusive contexts, for both words to be understood. Although one cannot quite say that in Ungaretti's work there is always present a paronomastic play in the word *miraggio* intending to evoke *meriggio*, or vice versa, this is without doubt the case in one of the most famous poetic openings in his entire body of verse, that of the early lyric "Agonia" where the poet expresses the wish "to die as skylarks athirst in the presence of (or, actually, *on* or *in*) a mirage":

> Morire come le allodole assetate
> Sul miraggio[12]

Granting the richness that often results from the meaningful liberties taken by true poets, the oddity (or such it would be in prose) of the use of the preposition *su* with the noun *miraggio* would nonetheless be the more noticeable, if not jarring, were it not for the fact that it is sustained precisely by the paronomastic recall of *sul meriggio*. Though it is not itself among the most common phrases in the language, the latter expression could not but be familiar to the reader of poetry. If nothing else, one could hardly fail to think of the miragelike enchantment invoked by Foscolo's "sul meriggio" in the famous passage from *Le Grazie*. It is also a fact that "sul meriggio" is legitimized (and actually used) in ordinary speech by virtue of the currency of analogous expressions concerning the parts of the day such as *sul mattino* and *sulla sera*. One can say that Ungaretti's use of the preposition *su* here is a device intended precisely to call up the image of midday while keeping the idea of the mirage to the fore.[13] The death-by-thirst motif would seem to leave no doubt about the matter. It was years later that the Bedouin of "Il demonio meridiano" ("La risata dello Dginn Rull") reminded the poet that, indeed, on the desert at noon "si muore di sete." But as the poem "Agonia" indicates, death from the torment of thirst could be a heroic preference to the sorry alternative of a whining existence deprived of ("blind to") the possibility of illusions and desire or hope, a condition exemplified by the image of the lamenting finch that has been blinded and confined to a cage:

> Morire come le allodole assetate
> Sul miraggio
>
> . . . .
>
> Ma non vivere di lamento
> Come un cardellino accecato.[h]
>
> (1-2; 8-9)

Again, however, it is hard to avoid the thought that even in this existentially emblematic imagery there is a strong erotic undercurrent. The adjective *assetato* has a well-known figurative meaning of sensual desire, and the mirage motif in Ungaretti is often connected with the figure of a woman. The title of the poem is "Agony," but there is something ecstatic in the opening image and its rhythm, particularly in the initial word *Morire (To die)* which seems almost like an exclamation and may have its well-known sexual sense here too. This agony is also an ecstasy and so is to be preferred to the *other* agony in the poem, that of the blinded and caged finch unable to go out in pursuit of a desire.

Of course there may even be a sort of *voluptas dolendi* associated with the "thirst." It is here, especially in connection with Ungaretti's desert mythology, that one remembers the poet of *"Furit aestus."* We need not essay too long a comparison between the Italo-African's vehement noontide eroticism,

---

[h] To die like skylarks athirst
Upon a mirage

. . . .

But not to live in anguish
Like a blinded finch.

with its emblematic dyad thirst/mirage, and the *dira sete* (demonic thirst) of D'Annunzio's savagely sensual midday, with its tense air of expectancy, but we may at least suggest that for Ungaretti no less than for his predecessor the thirst, fierce as it is, sometimes seems to be dearer than any water having the potential to quench it. Ungaretti's desert midday in which everything is suspended and at the same time *uneasy* or *agitated* ("tutto ora è sospeso e turbato") speaks of a stasis charged with a restless erotic energy (the adjective *turbato* is pregnant in this respect) that recalls D'Annunzio's noontide stasis throbbing with repressed force. And what can be more Dannunzian than the solar atavism professed in Ungaretti's evocation of the Sudanese nurse who suckled him and the ambiguous nostalgia or thirst for his torrid native land expressed in the image of an erotic symbiosis of death (the destroyer sun) and life (the lithesome Sudanese nurse):

Balia sudanese che m'ha allevato
Il sole che l'aveva bruciata le ho succhiato

O mio paese caldo ho avuto stanotte nostalgia del tuo sole
O sudanese snella tutta evanescente in grigio azzurro[i14]

The ambiguity here is reinforced by the fact that the sun can, indeed must, be understood as an attribute of both the poet's homeland and the nurse.

One thinks also of Ungaretti's "Godimento" ("Enjoyment," 1917), a poem that was once included in a group of lyrics under the heading *Il ciclo delle 24 ore* where it clearly signified an emblematic midday in the sense of a libido symbol:

        Mi sento la febbre
        Di questa
        Piena di luce

---

[i] Sudanese nurse who suckled me
I have sucked from her the sun that had burned her

Oh my torrid land tonight I have longed for your sun
Oh lithesome Sudanese all evanescent in blue gray

> Accolgo questa
> Giornata come
> Il frutto che si addolcisce.[j15]
>
> (1-6)

The feverish desire that burns the poet at summer midday (in the fullness of life, if one likes) and the poet's ready embrace of this fullness of time and life (and of love, of course, as is suggested by the sensual image of welcoming the "day" as one does a fruit ripened into sweetness) is like the noontide eroticism expressed by D'Annunzio in the last verses of *"Furit aestus"* or in lines 57-63 of "Meriggio." But Ungaretti's "Godimento" ends with the anticipation of remorse, a sentiment that is as characteristic of him as it is foreign to the earlier poet:

> Avrò
> Stanotte
> Un rimorso come un
> Latrato
> Perso nel
> Deserto[k]
>
> (7-11)

It is a sentiment that distinguishes him not only from D'Annunzio, but also from the Arabs of the desert with whom he otherwise felt a deep affinity. The howl lost in the desert that is an image of the poet's remorse is also a cry of despair and existential aloneness.[16]

---

[j] I feel the fever
Of this
Fullness of light

I welcome this
Day like
A fruit that ripens into sweetness.

[k] Tonight
I will feel
A remorse like a
Barking
Lost in
The desert

Ungaretti's cruel midday despot has its reality in nature, but it is also an inner midday demon of the void that accompanied him throughout the years, particularly during the first extended period he lived in Rome. Speaking of that time, he later noted that he was unable then to feel nature except when it was in the grip of the sun: "In quegli anni non arrivavo ad afferrare la natura che quando era in preda al sole."[17] Hence he could say of the volume *Sentimento del Tempo*, whose poems belong to those years, that it represents the implacable fullness of the sun, the season of violence and, at the same time, in the second part of the volume, the seclusion of man within his own frailty. This sounds like what he wrote in the prose-poetry of his Egyptian "diary" which falls within the same period and of which certain images help us to elucidate significant references to midday in the verse of *Sentimento del Tempo* where, according to Ungaretti himself, one of the three dominant themes or obsessions is "il tema della morte, del nulla"—the theme of death, of nothingness.[18]

Thus in the poem "Le stagioni" ("The Seasons," 1920) noontide is a "notturno meriggio," an oxymoron that is readily understandable in the light of the passage we have read where Ungaretti speaks of midday as "l'ora cieca . . . l'ora di notte del deserto." In the poem, the "dark" midday hour of summer disheartens the poet and brings him thoughts of death:

> È già oscura e fonda
> L'ora d'estate che disanima.
>
> Già verso un'alta, lucida
> Sepoltura, si salpa.[1]9
> (17-20)

The seasons the poem's title speaks of are those of the four ages of man, but these are described in terms of the changing

---

[1] Already dark and deep
Is the summer hour that disheartens [us].

Already we set out
Toward a high gleaming sepulcher.

seasons of the annual cycle. This of course is in keeping with a long tradition. Of further interest is the fact that summer itself figures here as the midday "hour," the part of the diurnal cycle, as we also know, that corresponds symbolically to summer in the seasonal cycle and to fullness or maturity in the cycle of human life. In this pattern of symbolical equivalences the basic term is taken from the diurnal cycle when the sun is at its zenith. The fullness of life is experienced by Ungaretti as the cruelest and most dramatic season and hour, like the vehemence of the midday hour when absolute light is the revelation of darkness and nothingness. For the sense of time is not suspended then. Thus in the season of fullness, which is for this poet a "notturno meriggio" in which life is violently consumed, the poet seeks in memories the dream of an Edenic dawn:

> Dal notturno meriggio,
> Ormai soli, oscillando stanchi,
> Invocano i ricordi.[m][20]
>
> (21-23)

The variants of "Le stagioni" include expresssions that insist still more forcefully on the violent face of this summer midday. Here we find "Già si consuma / l'ora d'estate che disanima" ("the summer hour that dismays us already is wasting"). Now it is the "ora voraginosa" ("Abysmal hour"), the "ora di luce nera nelle vene" ("the hour of black light in our veins"), the fierce, "dark" hour that haunts the poet with the thought of death and a surrealistic vision of tombs suspended:

> È l'ora truce e persa
> Dei sospesi sepolcri.[21]

Some of these variants find a place in the lyric "Ti svelerà" ("Unveiling," 1931) where they emblematize the tormented meridian of the poet's life. Again Ungaretti portrays himself in that season and hour as seeking to recover in memory the time of youth and a dream of a restorative dawn:

[m] From the nocturnal noontide,
  Henceforth alone, wavering wearily,
  Our memories invoke.

Bel momento, ritornami vicino.

Gioventù, parlami
In quest'ora voraginosa.

O bel ricordo, siediti un momento.

Ora di luce nera nelle vene
E degli stridi muti degli specchi,
Dei precipizi falsi della sete . . .ⁿ²²
(1-7)

In the same year (1920) as "Le stagioni," Ungaretti wrote a companion piece entitled "Paesaggio" ("Landscape")—an inner landscape of the self and of the four ages of man, described, significantly, in terms of the four parts of the day, and so, like "Le stagioni" (with its four seasons), an expression of the anguished sentiment of time passing. For the purpose of defining the value of this prose lyric in relation to our theme it will be useful to refer to it in its several variants. In the last version (1943), the brief evocation of morning's fresh moment of serene happiness—"Ha una corona di freschi pensieri, / Splende nell'acqua fiorita"ᵒ²³—is followed by a "midday" in which a troubled atmosphere descends upon the landscape (i.e., the poet's life):

Le montagne si sono ridotte a deboli fumi e l'invadente deserto formicola d'impazienze e anche il sonno turba e anche le statue si turbano.ᵖ²⁴

In this inner landscape of the poet's heart and mind, the light of noon has begun its work of consuming or devouring; the

---

ⁿ Fair moment, come close to me again.

Youth, speak to me
In this abysmal hour.

Oh beautiful memory, sit here a moment.

Hour of black light in the veins
And of mute stridulations of mirrors,
Of treacherous precipices of thirst . . .

ᵒ [It] has a crown of fresh thoughts, / [It] shines in the flowering water.

ᵖ The mountains have faded into pale mist and the invading desert swarms with restlessness and even sleep troubles and even the statues become uneasy.

sharp features of the mountains have been lost in a nebulous haze. The desert (i.e., place of heat and light) has invaded more and more of the "landscape," bringing with it not torpor but uneasiness and importunate desires. There can be no siesta, for sleep itself brings anxiety. In an image that will seem the more significant to the reader familiar with Montale's ironically saving grace presented as the "divine indifference" of a statue that stands in the blazing noontide torpor (in a poem to be discussed later), even statues, which one would think cold and insensible in any case, appear surrealistically agitated. Here too, we note, the key word is the erotically connotative verb *turbare* (cf. especially *conturbare*). It should be noted also that the text quoted here appeared first in 1933, whereas in the first version of the prose lyric (1920) the statues succumb to sleep in the deep of summer, and the desert becomes enveloped in a mystery of desolation.[25]

An important feature of Ungaretti's "day" in "Paesaggio" is the fact that evening is not envisioned as bringing peace. On the contrary, the awareness of the destructive force of time is even more acute. Although this is clear enough in the final edition of the piece, the 1933 version is more relevant to our discussion because it more overtly couples erotic significance with the revelation of the nothingness that is inherent in the flesh, in beauty, and, indeed, in everything:

> Mentre una bella ragazza nuda si vergogna in un mare verde bottiglia, ella non è più che fiamma, brace, nulla e un'ambra. Per un momento, in lei è palese il consumarsi senza fine di tutto.[q][26]

The erotic suggestiveness of the girl's nakedness has an ambiguous and, perhaps, ironic value. Her shame on account of this nakedness may in one sense signify her awakening to sexual desire or her remorse for it. Ungaretti's final version is perhaps more explicit on this particular point, for we read there "Mentre infiammandosi s'avvede ch'è nuda" ("While

---

[q] While a beautiful, naked maiden becomes ashamed in a bottle-green sea, she is no more than a flame, an ember, nothing and an amber. For a moment, there is revealed in her the endless consuming of everything.

becoming inflamed she realizes she is naked"), where *infiammandosi* suggests, on one level (the figurative) being aroused to erotic passion and, on the other level (the literal) the color acquired by the naked girl's body in the light of the sun's rays. (Her flesh is iridescent—*madreperla*—in the definitive text of the poem; she is *ambra* or reddish yellow in the 1933 version.) But the nakedness and the shame refer also to the vulnerability and essential nothingness of life. Surely the biblical figure of Eve is present in this female image evoked by Ungaretti. At the same time, however, he has transferred his own state of awareness to her as well as to the "landscape" in general of which she is here an integral part. The awareness of being consumed by erotic desire—*fiamma*, emphasized by the immediately following *brace*—is accompanied by the sense of being consumed by time (the sun, which is a symbol of time in the diurnal cycle on which the prose lyric is structured) and by the knowledge of death.

In summary then, the figure of the naked girl is phantasmagorically transformed into a flame that is soon a glowing ember (*brace*) and, finally, an amber nothing—*nulla e un'ambra*. In this last expression there is clearly a paronomastic play by which *ambra* = *ombra*; and just as the dark yellow color itself suggests a shadow so too there is at work the equation *ombra* = *nulla*. That this association is not accidental is indicated by the very first published version (1921) of the piece where the girl (more exactly her body) is referred to as a rosy shadow (*ombra rosata*) "modulated" to an infinite melancholy in the impassive emerald of the sea: "L'ombra rosata del corpo gentile si modula d'un'infinita malinconia nello smeraldo impassibile del mare."[27] The same passage occurs in the 1923 printing of the piece with the significant exception that *ombra* is replaced by *ambra*. The "infinite melancholy" of course is Ungaretti's own awareness of the "infinite vanity" (biblical and Leopardian) of all things.[28] In the 1933 text this melancholy awareness becomes the "shame" of the "bella ragazza nuda" in whose flaming nakedness (her nude body which is "inflamed" by the rays of the sun and seems in the process of being consumed into nothingness) Ungaretti sees revealed the relentless destruction of all things. A further shift is made in the final draft of the vision where the shame of Eve (let us call her so) has become a sentiment of "shame" at mortality which is now shared by the whole of creation. It is this universal shame/awareness, analogized by or made visible in the hue that the (setting) sun's rays give to all things, that betrays the implacable disintegration of everything and, at the same time, justifies man's melancholy:

> Quel moto di vergogna delle cose svela per un momento, dando ragione dell'umana malinconia, il consumarsi senza fine di tutto.[r][29]

In "Paesaggio" the revelation of the destructive force of the sun and time and the awareness of the essential vanity of all things—the progression is *fiamma-brace-nulla e un ambra* (= *ombra*)—occur in the light of a sunset that really has something of the annihilating force of the sun at midday. And, indeed, it can be said that for Ungaretti, light, or the sun, at any moment from the midday fullness on has a "corrosive" function, a feature that is true to some degree of his American contemporary Wallace Stevens. In Ungarettian terms noontide and evening merge into one experiental perception of time and nothingness that he often refers to as the *demon of noontide*. The naked girl of "Paesaggio" is inflamed and consumed in the same way as the poet's native city of Alexandria in the poem "Ricordo d'Affrica" ("Meriggio d'agosto"). The amber/shadow that is her color as she is transformed into flame and ember and finally into nothing has the same character of the desert under the high-noon sun in "Il demonio meridiano" ("La risata dello Dginn Rull") where everything has a fiery (*rovente*) and uniform yellow gray color which is perceived as nothingness: "Tutto ha un rovente ed eguale colore giallo grigio. . . . Direste che questo è il nulla."[30]

Ungaretti, we know, had a strong interest in painting and a keen painter's eye. In his writings, so far as I know, there is only one reference to van Gogh, a fleeting but significant one

---

[r] That impulse of shame of things reveals, for a moment, the endless consuming of everything, thereby justifying human melancholy.

made in 1960 in the context of a discussion of the painter Jean Fautrier. There the Dutch painter is mentioned as a predecessor of Fautrier in attaining a tragic height in the representation of an annihilating absolute.[31] Yet Ungaretti's apocalyptic noonscapes may be said to have an affinity not so much with the tragic midday delirium of van Gogh's whorling landscapes as with certain canvases of J.M.W. Turner, that other painter from the north who also found his true self in the sun of the south. No less than the Italian poet, Turner, in the words of Kenneth Clark, "is penetrated by a sense of nature's unsubduable, destructive force."[32] A number of his paintings match Ungaretti's noontide visions in having as their true subject the disappearance or annihilation of things in a deluge of light that has invaded the universe (the sea and the desert), leaving the impression of a fiery (even, at times, an amber) nothingness. Several poems of the one and several paintings of the other could bear as an inscription Ungaretti's words to the effect that everything was rendered vain (void space) because of the excess of light: "Tutto era vano per la troppa luce."

The most dramatic of Ungaretti's representations of the fierce summer midday of life is found in "Di luglio" ("In July," 1931). Although in the poem the grammatical subject *lei* refers to summer (*estate*, specified in line 8) the implied subject wreaking destruction on the earth is of course the summer sun with all the characteristics of its midday fury. (We have seen that there is a perfect symbolic equivalence between midsummer and midday and between these and the meridian of life):

> Quando su ci si butta lei,
> Si fa d'un triste colore di rosa
> Il bel fogliame.
>
> Strugge forre, beve fiumi,
> Macina scogli, splende,
> È furia che s'ostina, è l'implacabile,
> Sparge spazio, acceca mete,
> È l'estate e nei secoli

Con i suoi occhi calcinanti
Va della terra spogliando lo scheletro.[s33]

The bestial nature of this sun is announced immediately in the violence of the image of the very first line and in the harshness of its rhythm. The picture is one of the sun as an implacable fury—the merciless Gorgon—ravaging the earth and reducing it to a sterile wasteland: it sears the leaves, consumes gorges, drinks up the rivers, and disintegrates rocks. Like the sun in the desert midday of "Il demonio meridiano" (in *Quaderno egiziano*), here too the light is absolute and possesses everything; space seems to be expanded while at the same time the excess of light prevents the eye from distinguishing the distant horizon or from recognizing the distance between things. The poem's final image is that of the earth as a skeleton progressively ravaged and exposed through the centuries by an eternal calcinating summer midday sun, as though there were no other season and no other hour. We recall that the Egyptian account of midday culminates in the figure of the poet blinded by the violent light and stumbling upon a skeleton in the desert sands. Both that account and the poem belong to the same year (1931). Moreover, in commenting on his state of mind during the period of writing *Sentimento del Tempo* Ungaretti himself cites the influence on him of his discovery of the Roman baroque, which brought with it the sentiment and horror of emptiness of the void, an emotion he says one can experience more profoundly in Rome than in any other part of the world, including the desert. The specific image symbolizing this sentiment is that of a skeleton, such as even the Colosseum is in his eyes: "Quando si è

---

[s] When she pounces upon it,
The beautiful foliage
Takes on a sad color of rose.

She consumes gullies, drinks rivers,
Grinds rocks, she gleams,
A fury that persists, she is the relentless one,
She expands space, blinds limits,
She is summer, and through the centuries
With her calcinating eyes
She goes on ravaging the earth's skeleton.

in presenza del Colosseo, enorme tamburo con orbite senz'occhi, si ha il sentimento del vuoto. . . . Quando dicevo che il barocco provoca il sentimento del vuoto, che l'estetica del barocco romano era stata mossa dall'orrore del vuoto, citavo il Colosseo. Temo di non essere stato chiaro. L'orrore nel barocco proviene dall'idea insopportabile d'un corpo privo d'anima. Uno scheletro provoca orrore del vuoto."[t34]

The earth is such a skeleton in the final baroque image of "Di luglio." Surely, it cannot be sufficient to read this poem solely as an emblematic representation of a season in the cycle of a human life, the summer or meridian of the poet, which, even as it explodes, consumes itself violently.[35] Nor is it merely a symbolic statement of the aridity of modern civilization. While these interpretations are not to be discarded, the poem's deeper meaning lies in its being a representation of the ontological ambiguity of reality by way of a description of nature which, precisely at the moment of its apparent "fullness" (summer's midday sun), consumes itself and reveals its nonbeing. It is, in short, an apocalyptic vision of the metaphysical nothingness that resides at the core of existence. In this sense the poem may be placed alongside the similar midday revelation of Leconte de Lisle's "Midi."[36]

Another page of poetic prose (this too written in connection with impressions received during a journey to a "land of the sun") can be seen as an even more striking parallel to "Di luglio" than the desert passage of the *Quaderno egiziano* ("Il demonio meridiano"). It is especially revealing for the way in which the erotic impulse and the agonizing sense of the void appear together. The sun-bathed region of Apulia seen on a mild February day evokes the idea of the earth as the beloved of the sun, but Ungaretti is nonetheless invaded by the thought of the fiercer face of the Gorgon sun:

[t] When in the presence of the Colosseum, that enormous drum with eyeless sockets, one experiences the sentiment of the void. . . . When earlier I said that the baroque arouses the sentiment of the void, that the aesthetic of the Roman baroque originated in the horror of the void, I referred to the Colosseum. I fear I was not clear. The emotion of horror in the baroque derives from the intolerable idea of a body without a soul. A skeleton arouses the sentiment of horror of the void.

L'amante del sole, l'hanno chiamata [La Puglia] i poeti. Egli, il sole, la copre di gioie. Non solo, e subito mi viene incontro l'altro suo simbolo: il fulgore d'uno scheletro, nell'infinito. Quale merito ci sarebbe altrimenti ad addomesticarlo? Sarà perché sono mezzo Affricano, e perché le immagini rimaste impresse da ragazzo sono sempre le più vive, *non so immaginarlo se non furente e trionfante su qualche cosa d'annullato.* Mi commuoverebbe altrimenti così a fondo, un sole reso gentile? *Voglio dire che anche qui ha regno il sole autentico, il sole belva.* Si sente dal polverone, fatti appena due passi fuori. Penso con nostalgia che dev'essere uno spettacolo inaudito qui vederlo d'estate, quand'è la sua ora, e va, nel colmo della forza, tramutando il sasso nel guizzare di lacerti.

Non c'è un rigagnolo, non c'è un albero. La pianura s'apre come un mare.

Vorrei qui vederlo nel suo sfogo immenso, ondeggiare coll'alito tormentoso del favonio sopra il grano impazzito.

È il mio sole, creatore di solitudine.[u37]

Here the poet has substituted his own vision of a bestial summer midday sun for the gentle lover-sun that is actually before him. And now, in this vision, it is not only the earth that is ravaged, as in "Di luglio." I have already remarked that encounters with midday call forth the most extravagant

---

[u] The poets have called her [Apulia] the mistress of the sun. It, the sun, bedecks her with brilliant gems. But there is more, and at once its other symbol comes before me—the effulgence of a skeleton, in the infinite. Otherwise, what merit would there be in taming it? Perhaps because I am half African, and because the images of our childhood are always the most vivid, I am unable to conceive of the sun as other than raging and triumphing over something that has been annihilated. Otherwise would I be so deeply moved by a sun that has become so gentle? I mean to say that even here it is the true sun that reigns, the sun-beast. You smell it in the dust after only a few steps outside. With yearning I think of what an extraordinary spectacle it must be to see it here in the summer, in its own hour when at the height of vigor it transmutes stone into quivering muscles.

There isn't a rivulet, not a tree. The plain spreads out like a sea.

I long to see it here in its vast erupting blaze, swaying with the tormenting breath of the west wind over the crazed wheat.

This is my sun, the creator of solitude.

and hyperbolic imagery. Perhaps nothing is more intensely and dramatically baroque than Ungaretti's sun appearing as a fulgurating skeleton in infinity—the refulgent symbol of the midday demon of destruction and death. The gentle sun of February is referred to as a "tamed" sun which, however pleasing it may be, is considered to be out of character. The real sun is the sun-beast—*il sole autentico, il sole belva*—which can even be smelled in the surrounding dust as soon as one ventures forth from a refuge. It is this terrifying sun in its supreme hour (the sun's midday "hour" is summer) reigning over a land of desolation (the desert image) that Ungaretti, and we are almost startled by the word, evokes *with nostalgia*, a sentiment of yearning that one would not normally associate with a violent scene. One must go to D'Annunzio, in particular (and significantly) to *Il trionfo della morte* where the sun is symbolically master in more than one scene of death, to find anything like this paean to the sun's triumphant vehemence and the secret but savage (should we fear to say sadomasochistic in the case of the often tender Ungaretti?) desire for self-destruction in a blaze that is the night of oblivion.

But if this is, as the poet himself calls it, *his* sun—the maker of solitude—the ambiguity of Ungaretti's attitude toward it in its emblematic sense of the annihilating force in life was to give way, a few years later, to an almost blasphemous protest on the occasion of the death of his child. In the last three lines of the poignant elegy "Tu ti spezzasti" ("You were shattered"), the blasting Gorgon appears as the symbol of the cruel, consuming force against which the poet now cries out in pain. The child Antonietto has died because he was too human and fragile a light (i.e., *lampo*: a flash or ray) to withstand the ravenous fury of a sun whose naked (obscene) ferocity is felt so acutely that negative acoustic values are evoked to bespeak its profaning bestiality. It will be well to have all of the final stanza here:

> Grazia, felice,
> Non avresti potuto non spezzarti

> In una cecità tanto indurita
> Tu semplice soffio e cristallo,
>
> Troppo umano lampo per l'empio,
> Selvoso, accanito, ronzante
> Ruggito d'un sole ignudo.[v38]

There is a fierce and tragic irony in the suffering that has been visited on the poet. The child was a pause of serenity, a "grace" and a happiness that was an anomaly in the real world, and as such he was bound to be destroyed. In the elegy there is no room for the suspicion the previously quoted texts may have aroused in us that the poet was secretly attracted by the annihilating force at the core of existence (emblematized by the vehemence of the midday summer sun). By means of the rich ambiguity of poetry, the savage roar of the sun-beast is also the poet's accusing cry of grief and anger.[39]

"Tu ti spezzasti" has taken us beyond the period of *Sentimento del Tempo*. In returning to this earlier (and central) volume we may consider Ungaretti's meditation on death in a cycle of six poems entitled "La morte meditata" (1931-1932), that is, "Death Meditated." In the earliest editions of *Sentimento del Tempo* (Florence, 1931 and Rome, 1936) the first three poems (or *canti*) of the cycle appear as a tryptich under the title "Sentimento della memoria" ("Sentiment of Memory"), and it is only this group that is relevant to our theme. Leaving aside other factors that suggest that the three cantos are a unit, we can say that they are interconnected by the presence (not overtly stated, but metaphorically alluded to) of the image of midday and the association of this "hour" with death. The idea of midday appears as a "submerged" metaphor in the opening of the first canto:

> [v] Grace, joyous,
>   You were bound to shatter
>   In so unrelenting a blindness
>   You, simple breath and crystal,
>
>   Too human a flash [ray] for the cruel,
>   Wild, ruthless, droning
>   Roar of a naked sun.

> O sorella dell'ombra,
> Notturna quanto più la luce ha forza,
> M'insegui, morte.[w,40]

Death, the sister of the shade, is said to be as deeply nocturnal as the light's greatest intensity. That is, the absence of light is equated with the hour of maximum light but also, as the phrase "quanto più la luce ha *forza*" suggests, the hour of most power. That hour, of course, is midday which phenomenologically is the equivalent of midnight but is even more "primary." Put simply, it seems that the second line is a paraphrase of the oxymoron *notturno meriggio* used in the poem "Le stagioni." The shade (*ombra*) surely connotes nothingness, and we have seen how obsessedly Ungaretti dwells on the idea of midday as the encounter with the real night that is nothingness.

The third line, in which death is said to *pursue* the poet, implies the sense of the passing of time, and this might seem to militate against the image of midday. The sequence of light and darkness in the diurnal solar cycle and the progression of the seasons from birth to death have sharpened man's awareness of the passage of time, and few poets have been so centrally concerned with these images as has Ungaretti in a volume whose very title announces this preoccupation. But if, as we have observed in the case of so many other poets, midday is often the image of a stasis that even creates the impression or experience of eternity, we are brought back to a special feature in Ungaretti's perception of midday and summer. For him these "spots of time" are experienced not so much as a pure stasis but as a "time" of the most intense "burning" and "consuming." That is, the sense of time somehow remains and is even felt more acutely than at other moments. Thus we have noted that in the prose lyric "Paesaggio" and in the emblematic account of "Il demonio meridiano," along with a careful attention to the slightest change in the color of light

---

[w] Oh sister of the shade,
  As deeply nocturnal as the light at its greatest strength,
  You pursue me, death.

there is a sense of merging of noontide with evening, an awareness of a relentless destructive force in the light which remains the constant or the common denominator. In the present context Ungaretti is also saying that he is most aware of death in the very hour that is the "time" of fullness, the hour of greatest intensity: the midday of both the diurnal and the human life cycles.

This persistence of death (or of time's pursuit) is suggested in the succeeding verses (lines 4-12) of the first canto where the poet, as though with a memory that is as much humanity's as his own (but the memory, like death, belongs to both), says that since the time of the Fall he has "heard" death in the *flow* (an image of time) of his mind: "Ti odo nel fluire della mente." The line and the motifs of death's persistence and the poet's ever more acute awareness of its overtaking him are dominant in the closing verses of the second and third cantos of the tryptich:

>   *Canto Secondo*
> Morte, muta parola,
>
> . . . .
> Ti odo cantare come una cicala
> Nella rosa abbrunata dei riflessi.
>   (6; 9-10)
>
>   *Canto Terzo*
> Tu, nella luce fonda,
> O confuso silenzio,
> Insisti come le cicale irose.[x][41]
>   (4-6)

[x]   *Second Canto*
Death, mute word,

. . . .
I hear you singing like a cicada
In the darkened (widowed) rose of the reflections.

   Third Canto
Within the deep light,
Oh confused silence,
You insist like the rabid cicadas.

Death, a "mute word" (another quasi-oxymoron) because it is (existentially) nothingness (and also because it renders us mute), is nonetheless "heard," just as the silence of midday is "heard" in or as the corrosive chirr of the cicada. In *Canto Secondo* death is (like) the implacable cicada that is heard singing (cf. the *limio delle cicale* of "Silenzio") in the "rose" that is darkened into "mourning" by the reverberations of its own (midday) light and heat. The *rosa abbrunata* is also analogically the color of the light of things in general at midday. We think of *ambra/ombra* and *ombra rosata* (connected with "the endless wasting of all things" in "Paesaggio"), of the burnt, tawny color darkening—but "dying" is the poet's word—into violet in the desert noontide of "Il demonio meridiano," and of the *triste color di rosa* of "Di luglio." *Abbrunata*, the word used to indicate the darkened color of the "rose," in ordinary speech is used exclusively to indicate the color or condition of mourning, and so is appropriate to the poet's subjective sentiment here. As I have already suggested, the "rose" is not of course a real flower but what is seen when looking into the heart of midday, into a light (i.e., the sun) which is the equivalent of night. The metaphor is more readily apprehended in Italian where *rosa* often is used in the sense of *irraggiamento*. In English we may think of *rosette* or rose window. In other words, the rose is the midday sun's irradiation which by virtue of its excessive intensity blinds the onlooker or causes him to see a brilliance that is the color of mourning, or, we may say, the color of that very death which in the first canto is figured in the meridian oxymoron "Notturna quanto più la luce ha forza."

Critics have spoken of *Canto Terzo* as a variant of *Canto Secondo*.[42] Indeed the first three cantos of "La morte meditata" proceed by a series of poetic "tautologies" that build up an increasing tension. The oxymoron of line 2 in the first canto becomes "la rosa abbrunata dei riflessi" of the second canto, and this becomes nothing less than what the third canto calls "la luce fonda," an expression that has such related Ungarettian referents to midday and summer as "l'ora nera," "l'ora di notte," "l'ora cieca" (in "Il demonio meridiano"), "ora di luce nera" (in "Ti svelerà"), "È già oscura e fonda / l'ora d'estate che disanima," and, of course, "notturno meriggio" (in "Le stagioni"), not to mention the "Notturna quanto più la luce ha forza" of *Canto Primo* in the tryptich itself. Death, the "muta parola" that sings like a cicada, becomes in *Canto Terzo* the "confuso silenzio" that now insists like the rabid cicadas in the deep (the dark) light of noontide. Leaving aside the acoustical note of the cicadas, we can see in the references that the three cantos make to death and darkness in the heart of the most intense light something like what occurs in Pascoli's "Morte e sole." In Pascoli's poem, death is ironically said to be a "brief word" which, like the sun, reveals to the eye that dares look into it an empty vortex, the infinite blackness (nothingness) that resides in both the word and the sun. Ungaretti, a poet who is particularly rich in synesthetic imagery, "hears" and "sees" the "mute word."

Insofar as he hears the mute word or the "confused" (indistinct) silence that is death, it is in connection with the image of the cicada. One of the most interesting things to happen in the "elaboration" of the second canto into the third canto is the anagrammatical passage of "come una cicala / Nella rosa" into the concluding emblematic line "Insisti come le cicale irose." The poet has insisted on the sound *rosa / irose* in a way that seems to make it a phonetic symbol for the idea of an eroding, a consuming, or a gnawing away—*(e)rodere* with its past participle *(e)roso*. Again we think of the *limio delle cicale* in "Silenzio." Again it is a chirr that scans the tension of midday's absolute and fierce silence (the consciousness of death), becoming ever more agressive and rasping in its relentless aim of overtaking the poet. It is the same cicada / death whose piercing shrill accentuated the luminous but blank silence of midday at the moment of death for the protagonist of Boine's "Agonia."[43]

There is another side to Ungaretti's midday mythology, connected with what we have seen so far and to some degree with the Arcadian tradition, but more closely connected with the nympholeptic reveries of Foscolo's Jacopo Ortis,

Chenier's lovely fragment, Leopardi's "Alla primavera," Mallarmé's "Après-midi d'un faune," and, again, with D'Annunzio's midday eroticism. The beautiful poem "L'isola" ("The Island," 1925) has all the signs of a midsummer's midday dream:

> A una proda ove sera era perenne
> Di anziane selve assorte, scese,
> E s'inoltrò
> E lo richiamò rumore di penne
> Ch'erasi sciolto dallo stridulo
> Batticuore dell'acqua torrida,
> E una larva (languiva
> E rifioriva) vide;
> Ritornato a salire vide
> Ch'era una ninfa e dormiva
> Ritta abbracciata a un olmo.
>
> In sé da simulacro a fiamma vera
> Errando, giunse a un prato ove
> L'ombra negli occhi s'addensava
> Delle vergini come
> Sera appiè degli ulivi;
> Distillavano i rami
> Una pioggia pigra di dardi,
> Qua pecore s'erano appisolate
> Sotto il liscio tepore,
> Altre brucavano
> La coltre luminosa;
> Le mani del pastore erano un vetro
> Levigato da fioca febbre.[y,44]

[y] At a shore where evening was perennial
With ancient rapt forests, he descended,
And penetrated
And a sound of wings called him back
That was released from the piercing
Heartbeat of the torrid water,
And he saw (it was languishing
And reflowering) a phantom;
Having returned to climb again he saw that

In a dream an unidentified figure arrives at the shore of an island where a forest of trees standing motionless in the midday hour ("anziane selve assorte") offers a refuge of shade which seems like a perpetual evening. The adjective *anziane* (ancient) immediately lends a fablelike atmosphere to the scene, as does the word *assorte* (absorbed) which, with its suggestion of profound contemplation or enchantment, evokes the deepest silence imaginable. After entering into this retreat, the visitor is momentarily startled by the sound of water agitated by the flapping wings of a bird suddenly taking flight from the sea near the shore of the island. Inasmuch as this "island" is almost surely metaphorical (the image of a midday retreat in general), the waters referred to may not in fact be the sea, but a smaller body—a pond or a spring. In any case, that the water is said to be "torrid" suggests that it is indeed exposed to a blazing midday sun. That its agitation is suddenly heard suggests that it was calm before the bird's action. Though he looks back quickly, in the steady succession of events of this dreamlike world the visitor's attention is now caught by the presence of a phantom or apparition (*larva*) said to be palpitating ("languiva e rifioriva") but not immediately definable. This contributes to the sense of suspension which in fact permeates the whole atmosphere of the poem. The reference to the "languishing and reflowering" of the apparition introduces a sensual note which is soon accentuated. As he

> It was a nymph and she was sleeping
> Upright embracing an elm.
>
> Within himself from illusion to true flame
> Wandering, he came to a meadow where
> Shade thickened in the eyes
> Of the virgins like
> Evening at the base of olive trees;
> The branches distilled
> An indolent rain of arrows,
> Here some sheep had dozed off
> Under the caressing warmth,
> Others nibbled
> On the luminous coverlet;
> The shepherd's hands were glass
> Levigated by a subtle fever.

continues his climb and his penetration into the island's enchanted forest, the visitor discovers the apparition to be a nymph sleeping upright with her arms around an elm. Thus it would seem that the "languishing and reflowering" is the erotically perceived breathing of the sleeping nymph, the rhythmic subsiding and swell of her torso in a position that suggests a coital embrace.[45]

Proceeding still deeper into this magic and erotic island refuge, the distinction between dream fantasy (or uncertainty) and reality is obliterated: "In sé da simulacro a fiamma vera / Errando." The meaning in the Italian text is obscure here, but we may note with certainty one thing: the word and the image of *fiamma* (flame) has enormous significance in Ungaretti's poetry. That ancient metaphor for erotic desire is unabashedly taken over and revitalized by him as perhaps by no other modern poet. Placed in a complex context where it does double duty with overlapping or interrelated connotative meanings, it serves as a libido symbol and as an image of the disintegration (the burning and consuming) of things—of life and the world. In the context of "L'isola," at this point the breakdown of the distinction between reality and the midday mirage or dream may represent a momentary triumph or wish fulfillment in which the *fiamma vera*, erotic fire, is kept pure or free from the awareness of death. For all this takes place in the depths of the poet—"In sé"—or in the dream where the poet-visitor lives his truer and deeper reality, his life of secret desire.

Picking up the thread of the poem, we see that the visitor has now come to a clearing, a meadow, where he sees a number of maidens—the poet's erotically charged word is *virgins*. In their eyes, the shade has gathered like evening concentrated beneath the foliage of olive trees. We may recall that olive trees are present in the idealized noonscape of Boccaccio's *Decameron* where they supply the shade that protects the blithe band of storytellers from the midday sun. They are, in any case, another image of an ancient and southern Edenic refuge. The shade they offer in Ungaretti's poem is both real (within the dream's reality) and metaphorical. It refers, I believe, to the somnolence of midday that has come upon the virgins, who may be conceived of as sitting or reclining at the edge of the meadow and thus still within the actual shade of the forest's foliage. This seems to be the case inasmuch as the next detail noted is sunlight being filtered through the branches (the image occurs at least twice in evocations of midday eroticism by D'Annunzio) and falling like a slow intermittent rain of weak darts (i.e., scattered thin rays).

In this area ("Qua") where the warmth is gentle and caressing (*liscio tepore* suggests an inviting sensual torpor) sheep have fallen into a doze. And here the choice of the verb *appisolare* (doze) clearly bespeaks the noontide siesta. Some sheep, however, continue to browse in the open sun-flooded meadow ("la coltre luminosa") which stands in contrast to the crepuscularlike shade created by the thick and ancient forest. This final image is completed by the presence of the shepherd whose hands (and the poet speaks precisely of those hands rather than of the shepherd, just as he speaks of the shade or torpor in the eyes of the virgins rather than of the virgins as such) have a vitreous luster indicative of a subtle fever (the "fioca febbre") that burns and consumes. Indeed, the analogical technique of the poet allows him to say that those hands *are* levigated by that insidious fever, suggesting an action of wasting or emaciating that also "polishes." The *fioca febbre* is the culminating erotic image of the lyric and as such is connected with the theme of the enervating, wasting heat of midday. In this sense the poem belongs to a tradition of midday eroticism that goes back to Virgil's second eclogue. But its most immediate tie is with the midday nympholepsy in Leopardi's "Alla primavera," a poem enormously admired by Ungaretti who went so far as to consider it an anticipation if not the fount of modern ("hermetic") poetry.[46] The *vergini* of "L'isola" have their precedent in Leopardi's *candide ninfe*, though we may also recall the nymphs of Boccaccio's *Ameto* and those of Mallarmé. And Ungaretti's shepherd and flock of sheep also have their counterparts in the earlier poem. But in "L'isola" the erotic impression is marked by a more sultry atmosphere.

In his observations on "Alla primavera," Ungaretti states that the biblical and classical allusions to midday listed in Leopardi's own notes to the poem are meant by the poet (or by the sources he gives) to indicate that certain ancient fables had their origin in the mirages and the delirium connected with that hour in hot southern lands. He then goes on to assert that in reviving that tradition in his own midday evocation Leopardi (and later Mallarmé) was not indulging in a neoclassicizing nostalgia for the fables of antiquity but was intent rather on expressing an indeterminate psychic state that lies between dream and memory.[47] That Ungaretti seeks to do the same thing in "L'isola" can hardly be doubted. Its evocation of an enchanted isle peopled by nymphs seems indeed to partake of the character of both a dream and a mirage. The theme of the mirage and the oasis, we know, has a significant place in the work of Ungaretti, man of the desert, and in this respect the very title of the poem "L'isola" is revealing.[48]

The idea of a noontide delirium (i.e., a real nympholepsy) referred to by Ungaretti in his comments on Leopardi's poem is hinted at in his own poem by the *fioca febbre* that consumes the shepherd's hands during the dream. This brings us to the connection between the visitor to the island (i.e., the dreamer) and the shepherd who, it seems to me, are one and the same. That is to say, the visit to this prelapsarian land is the shepherd's dream as he takes his siesta (or as he sinks into the midday torpor). The line separating the dream from the "reality" of the presence of the shepherd and his flock is not indicated precisely because the one has merged with the other. The meadow in which the virgins with shade (i.e., the midday somnolence) in their eyes are seen (but seen in the dream) seems almost to be the meadow in which the dreaming shepherd and his flock are in fact. The shepherd dreams of the erectly sleeping nymph and the virgins just as Leopardi's shepherd at midday expects to see Diana and the *candide ninfe*. (Compare the uncertainty of Mallarmé's faun: "Aimai-je un rêve?") It is a dream of troubled desire as the expression *fioca febbre* tells us. One may speak here of a *somnium Veneris*. In this case, of course, we must go one step further and identify the shepherd with Ungaretti (the "dreamer" of the vision) himself. The same kind of identity obtains between Leopardi and his shepherd.

Besides the element of dream/mirage, there is the matter of memory—the erotic memories of the poet. We have earlier taken note of other poems by Ungaretti in which an urgent sensuality is present. And anyone who has read the lyrics "Fase" ("Phase"), and the poet's note to it, and "Giunone" ("Juno") knows how deep-rooted such memories were in him. Written in June 1916, "Fase" (from the collection *Allegria*) has a special relevance here because in its evocation (in memory) the erotic encounter is situated in an atmosphere of sultry noontide deliquescence:

> Agli abbandonati giardini
> Ella *approdava*
> Come una colomba
>
> Fra l'aria
> Del meriggio
> Ch'era uno svenimento
> Le ho colto
> Arance e gelsumini[z][49]
>
> (7-14)

Ungaretti's late note to the poem tells us that his native city of Alexandria was the place and that the pronoun *Ella* refers to a woman with whom he was involved in an "experience of wild sensuality." He also says that he was to return to the motif in *Sentimento del Tempo*.[50] The memory of that experience may have been the inspiration for the poem "Giunone" (1931) in *Sentimento*:

[z] At abandoned gardens
She landed
Like a dove

In the air
Of midday
Which was a swoon
I gathered for her
Oranges and jasmine

> Tonda quel tanto che mi dà tormento,
> La tua coscia distacca di sull'altra . . .
>
> Dilati la tua *furia* un'acre notte.[aa][51]

It seems highly significant to me that this poem of three lines invoking the "fury" of erotic passion should, in the ordering of the poems of *Sentimento*, be placed precisely between "Di luglio" with its evocation of the implacable destructive fury of the midsummer midday sun ("È *furia* che s'ostina, è l'implacabile") and "D'agosto," another hallucinatory vision of the devouring sun. And the thought suggests itself now that "Di luglio" also may be read as a statement of the poet's tormented erotic life. At any rate, it is such experiences as are evoked in "Fase" and "Giunone" that make up the dimension of memory in "L'isola." The erotic memories are not specified, because they have merged with the dream and feed it, lending to the poem its tremulous atmosphere of a secret life of desire.[52]

"L'isola" illustrates the theme that Ungaretti referred to (in connection with the volume *Sentimento del Tempo*) as the desire for a return to an Edenic state. Thus it is interesting to note here one or two elements that have an astonishing similarity to the Eden recovered by Dante at the top of Mount Purgatory. Ungaretti's prelapsarian *isola* is thick with ancient (i.e., primordial) woods that create a perpetual shade: "A una proda ove *sera* era *perenne* / Di *anziane selve* assorte." Dante's steps into Eden took him into the depth of just such a *selva antica* which in keeping out the light of sun and moon creates precisely an *ombra perpetua* (*Purgatorio* XXVIII, 23, 32-33). Moreover, whatever allegorical interpretation one may wish to give to Dante's encounter with Matelda in that setting, the event is given in terms of a highly erotic encounter. In narrating it, Dante even makes use of the tradition of the medieval amatory *pastourelle*, mingling it with erotic reminiscences

---

[aa] Round just enough to cause me torment
  Your thigh stands out upon the other . . .

  Let your fury expand an acrid night.

from classical literature.[53] Thus not only the "sieste *antique* de midi" to which Mallarmé's faun voluptuously succumbs (in the "Monologue d'un faune") and Leopardi's "*ombre meridiane*" are present in "L'isola." The themes of memory and innocence are at the heart of Ungaretti's poetry. The mirage/dream or oasis of "L'isola" is the garden-island image of an Eden that is indeed the recovery of innocence, not, however, associated with justice, as in Dante, but rather with sensual or natural desire.[54] Even as the figure of the shepherd would indicate, Ungaretti's poem is yet another version of twentieth-century pastoral.

"L'isola" reveals two series of alliterations that seem not to be casual but, on the contrary, appear to be entrusted with a functional role in creating the poem's mood. The first three lines have a concentration of dental fricatives (the sibilants *s* and *z*) which, coming as they do at the poem's outset, contribute to the suggestion of silence (or of sleep itself) in which the opening sequence of the dream unfolds. More conspicuous are the labiodental fricatives (voiced and unvoiced) *f* and *v* which occur twenty-two times in the not very long poem and in all but nine of the twenty-four lines. The greatest cluster of these comes in the four lines (7-10) that speak of the apparition "languishing and reflowering" that is soon discovered to be a sleeping nymph. The lips, we know, are one of the most erogenous parts of the body, and the phonosymbolic value of these sounds within the thematic context referred to seems indeed to be one of erotic suggestiveness. We can now appreciate fully the presence in the poem's last scene of a detail we would not normally expect in a "pastoral" noontide retreat. Traditionally, in such a setting, one finds the sheep lying down "ruminating," or, at most, drinking from a stream or fount. But here some sheep still browse. That is, they continue to "nibble," an activity that, even as it is given all its erogenous value by the Italian word *brucavano* which carries its own labiodental elements (as does English *nibble*), also suggests that the meadow is slowly being wasted or consumed. Thus just as it carries forward the sensually tactile (caressing) value of the immediately preceding expression—"liscio tepore"—the image also anticipates the final component of the scene. It is here, significantly, that we have the second highest concentration of labiodental fricatives which occur four times in the last five words of the poem. And they speak precisely of the covert fever ("*fioca febbre*") of desire that "polishes" (i.e., levigates, consumes) the shepherd's vitreous hands. Finally, we now can recognize in this "*fioca febbre*" that closes the poem a phonosymbolic recall of the "*fiamma vera*" with which the second and concluding part of the poem opens.

Perhaps the best commentary on the verses we have been discussing (which also applies to much of the rest of this chapter) is the observation Ungaretti made about one of Rembrandt's representations of *Susanna and the Elders* (1637). We recall that the biblical episode was a noontide occurrence. First, in commenting on the 1668 canvas depicting *Ruth and Boaz*, the poet (for such he remains even when discussing painters) has Rembrandt explain to the characters of the painting his vision of the flesh destined to be consumed by the corrosive element of light:

> "Ho voluto," direbbe Rembrandt per tramite suo [i.e., the painting], "fare il mondo come mi è chiaro dopo averlo scontato. Non è altro che materia. Non sentite che anche i vostri cari visi, le vostre mani che amo, non sono altro; e nuotano, come ho imparato con tanta fatica, nella corrosione letale della luce?"[bb][55]

Rembrandt knew that the "truth" of forms was not in their decay but in their perennial renewal:

> È la *Susanna*, ed è del 1637. Il carnato è fiamma restituita amorosamente da acque. Fiamma di disfacimento? Fiamma

[bb] Through its medium [i.e., the painting] Rembrandt would seem to say: "I wanted to reveal the world as it is clear to me after having paid dearly for a full experience of it. It is nothing other than matter. Don't you feel that your dear faces, too, your hands that I love, are nothing else; and that they swim, as I have learned with great anguish, in the lethal corrosion of the light?"

fatua? È fiamma. C'è sapeva, il crepuscolo dell'aurora e il crepuscolo del tramonto, e il delirio meridiano, notte della luce."[cc56]

The flesh is flame; the waters in which Susanna has bathed have restored it, but it remains a flame. Flame of decay or *ignis fatuus*? As a flame it is destined to be consumed and eventually reduced to nothingness, as was the "bella ragazza nuda" (also a *flame*) of "Paesaggio." The elders are not mentioned by Ungaretti, but they are as important here as the presence of Actaeon contemplating Diana or that of Petrarch looking on the ablutions of Laura. Rembrandt's awareness of the *delirio meridiano* is his understanding of the impulse that drove the elders to their undignified voyeurism. They too are victims of the fiery noontide rage—the midday demon—that is both a blind (uncontrollable) desire and the sentiment of impending annihilation—*notte della luce*.

Earlier we saw how the summer midday sun figures in Ungaretti's "Di luglio" as a savage force that consumes and reduces (*levigates*) the earth to a skeleton. It is also the emblem of the meridian of life experienced by the poet as a cruel hour and season: "la pienezza implacabile del sole, la stagione di violenza." This is the atmosphere of *Sentimento del Tempo* to which "L'isola" also belongs. It is the season in which the poet was tormented not only by the specter of a metaphysical nothingness but also by a delirium of sensuality. I have already suggested that it would not be at all awry to read even "Di luglio" in an erotic key, though to limit it to such an interpretation without keeping in mind the complexity of the author's erotic vision would be to minimize the significance of the poem. Ungaretti's thirst of the flesh is no less existential an anguish than is, say, Rebora's thirst of the soul. Both are savage or desperate, and each perhaps includes something of the other. To an unprecedented degree midday eroticism and

---

[cc] It is the *Susanna* of 1637. The texture [of her flesh] is a flame restored lovingly by waters. Flame of decomposition? *Ignis fatuus*? It is flame. There is, he knew, the twilight of dawn and the twilight of evening, and the midday delirium, the night of light.

noontide as the hour of the revelation of nothingness have a relationship of reciprocal exacerbation in Ungaretti. Others before him knew and expressed the one theme or the other, but perhaps in no other poet are the two strains so intimately and so dramatically united.

VI. Eugenio Montale

> Tu sola sapevi che il moto
> Non è diverso dalla stasi,
> Che il vuoto è il pieno e il sereno
> È la più diffusa delle nubi.
> (Xenia I, 14)

Eugenio Montale is the twentieth-century poet whose name is most readily associated with the topos of midday. His first collection of verse, *Ossi di seppia* (*Cuttlefish Bones*, 1925), one of the most important landmarks of modern Italian poetry, has noontide and the sea as its most significant and pervasive images.[1] In this respect, it is no accident that this basically anti-Dannunzian book (which has, of course, both deliberate and unconscious debts to the earlier poet) necessarily recalls D'Annunzio's *Alcyone*.[2] The book's earliest dated poem, "Meriggiare pallido e assorto" (1916), may well be the most famous Italian lyric of our time. Written when Montale was but twenty years old—though the last stanza was refashioned later—this noonscape has come to emblematize, almost as universally as *The Waste Land*, the spiritual aridity of modern life and a sense of the negativity, even the frustrating absurdity of existence:

> Meriggiare pallido e assorto
> Presso un rovente muro d'orto,
> Ascoltare tra i pruni e gli sterpi
> Schiocchi di merli, frusci di serpi.
>
> Nelle crepe del suolo o su la veccia
> Spiar le file di rosse formiche
> Ch'ora si rompono ed ora s'intrecciano
> A sommo di minuscole biche.
>
> Osservare tra frondi il palpitare
> Lontano di scaglie di mare

Mentre si levano tremuli scricchi
Di cicale dai calvi picchi.

E andando nel sole che abbaglia
Sentire con triste meraviglia
Com'è tutta la vita e il suo travaglio
In questo seguitare una muraglia
Che ha in cima cocci aguzzi di bottiglia.[a][3]

The verb *meriggiare*, as we know, normally indicates a retreat to the shade during noontide. But what is described by the poet is anything but a siesta of the usual sort, and there is scant relief suggested in his experience. There would be little shade from the garden wall at midday, and the focus, in any case, is on the searing heat of the wall itself beneath the merciless sun. The poet, moreover, is "pallido e assorto," a pallor that, while it results from the enervating heat, also suggests that his "absorption" in the elements of nature that surround him is a condition somewhere between wakeful anguish and semistupor.[4] With a marked intensity (*spiar*) his eyes fix upon the coming and going of rows of red ants in the cracks of the dry ground or on weeds. Lifting his gaze, he notes, through the branches of the trees, the distant sea. But beneath the glare of the sun the glistening waves appear as heaving "scales,"

[a] To laze in the shade at noon pale and absorbed
  Next to a searing garden wall,
  To listen in the thorn bushes and the underbrush to
  The cracking call of blackbird, the rustling of the snake.

  In the dry cracks of the earth or in the vetch
  To watch intently the rows of red ants
  That now break ranks and now intersect
  At the crest of miniscule mounds.

  To observe through branches the distant
  Heaving of the scales of the sea
  While the tremulous squeaks of cicadas
  Rise from the bald hills.

  And going into the sun that dazzles
  To feel with sad surprise
  That all of life with its travail
  Is in this moving along a wall
  That has jagged bits of bottle glass along its top.

sharp-edged fragments of some hard and dry substance.[5] The poem's acoustic impressions corroborate this sense of hardness, dryness, and harshness. The cracking calls of the blackbirds and the rustling of serpents among the thorn bushes and dry undergrowth are listened to intently. And here too the ubiquitous cicadas are present as an irritant; the sound they make descends from barren hilltops and is perceived as a dry, shrill creaking or quiver. No reader can fail to note the large number of words (perhaps even too programmatically chosen) whose very sounds, for the Italian ear, produce grating or stridulous effects: *pruni*, *sterpi*, *schiocchi*, *frusci*, *veccia*, *formiche*, *s'intrecciano*, *minuscole*, *biche*, *scaglie*, *scricchi*, *cicale*, *calvi*, *picchi*.

The negativity and cutting hardness of the poem's imagery culminate in the final stanza where we find that the poet leaves whatever shade he may have been in and now walks directly in the cruel glare of the midday sun. The trigrammatic *gli*, corresponding to the palatal liquid, is a cumbersome group that creates something forbidding to the very eye of the reader who sees it repeated on the printed page almost in a vertical column as it occurs in a series of assonances in the end words of the stanza's verses: *agguaglia*, *meraviglia*, *travaglio*, *muraglia*, *bottiglia*. So too its phonosymbolic effect is to create a sense of being fettered. This sense is consonant with (and contributes to) the final image in which with pained stupor the poet recognizes that human existence has the character of an oppressive noontide lived on this side of an impassable wall whose top is covered with jagged pieces of broken bottle glass.

In another poem, "Spesso il male di vivere ho incontrato," the negativity of life (the law of an existential suffering of all things in nature) is mirrored in a series of three images that includes a vision of a drought-stricken season in which sun-seared leaves shrivel up as in a painful spasm—"Era l'incartocciarsi della foglia / Riarsa." But it is significant that the dominant image chosen to emblematize the indifference (disengagement, retreat from life) proclaimed as the only possible "salvation" or antidote is that of a stone statue standing immobile (i.e., without sentiency or consciousness) in the torrid midday sun that seems to envelop it in its perfect torpor:

> Spesso il male di vivere ho incontrato:
> Era il rivo strozzato che gorgoglia,
> Era l'incartocciarsi della foglia
> Riarsa, era il cavallo stramazzato.
>
> Bene non seppi, fuori del prodigio
> Che schiude la divina Indifferenza:
> Era la statua nella sonnolenza
> Del meriggio, e la nuvola, e il falco alto levato.[b6]

The cloud and the hawk high above also are symbols of detachment from the earth, the pure indifference that is ignorance of or removal from the sphere of earth's evil and harm. One notes that the word *prodigio* in the first line of the second stanza is verbally echoed in a quasi-rhyme by *meriggio* at the opening of the last line. *Prodigio* and *divina* are words used first by D'Annunzio in his experience of noontide as the time of imminent revelation and infinite potency in the one case and of reciprocal fusion or coinherence with nature in the other. In Montale's poem, the same two words acquire an ambivalent and somewhat ironic (and anti-Dannunzian) value. Here the miracle (*prodigio*) experienced at midday is not any sense of expectancy or of repressed cosmic energy on the verge of exploding; much less is it an epiphany of joy. On the contrary, it is a sense of escape from life; and what is divine is not, as in D'Annunzio's "Meriggio," nature or the man-nature coinherence experienced at midday, but rather the saving indifference that results from absorption into noon's stasis, into the insensibility and the nonconsciousness of

[b] Often I have met the evil of existence:
It was the strangled brook gurgling,
It was the shriveling up of the seared
Leaf, it was the prostrated horse.

No good have I ever known, save for the miracle
That divine Indifference unlocks:
It was the stone statue in the torpor
Of noon, and the cloud, and the hawk on high.

thinghood. This meridian divine indifference is therefore closer to the nirvanalike noontide of Leopardi's "Vita solitaria" (though it is not quite the same thing) than to any of D'Annunzio's *meriggi*. It is of course also far removed from Carducci's throbbing noontide nirvana, but it can be said to have a kinship with Pascoli's antimeridian "Gloria," a connection to which we shall soon return. The paradoxical feature in Montale's poem is that midday (or its equivalent, the consuming, destroying summer sun) figures at once as an image of the suffering or evil of life (in the first stanza) and as a zone of refuge.[7]

Yet it is precisely this midday retreat or escapism that Montale urges us to reject in the poem "Non rifugiarti nell'ombra." Here he reminds us of Leopardi, the supreme poet of negativity, who oscillated between nostalgia for those illusions—now forever lost—that once preserved man from an awareness of his nothingness and a Promethean need to unmask truth (or reality) and so lay bare that very nothingness. Thus Montale would have us shake off the divine (i.e., liberating) indifference (noontide somnolence) and come out from the shade in the very hour—the hour of bewilderment and dismay: "quest'ora di disagio" (14)—that more than any other reveals the aridity and the disintegration of existence:

> Non rifugiarti nell'ombra
> Di quel folto di verzura
> Come il falchetto che strapiomba
> Fulmineo nella caldura.
>
> È ora di lasciare il canneto
> Stento che pare s'addorma
> E di guardare le forme
> Della vita che si sgretola.[c]
>
> (1-8)

[c] Do not retreat to the shade
  Of that thicket of greenery
  Like the hawk that plummets
  With lightning swiftness in the hottest hour.

In the cruel light of midday which even as it envelops all things seems also to dissolve them, mankind moves unsteadily and exhausted:

> Ci muoviamo in un pulviscolo
> Madreperlaceo che vibra,
> In un barbaglio che invischia
> Gli occhi e un poco ci sfibra.[d]
> (9-12)

Nonetheless, just here Montale, like a latter-day Dantean Ulysses, makes an *orazion picciola* in which the appeal is to the dignity of man. To stay in the shady retreat is unworthy of man, and the poet's way of saying so now is to exhort us not to surrender to the lulling rhythm of the "arid" waves, and not to abandon our wandering lives in a bottomless whirlpool, which is to say, an abyss of unawareness or ignorance:

> Pure, lo senti, nel gioco d'aride onde
> Che impigra in quest'ora di disagio
> Non buttiamo già in un gorgo senza fondo
> Le nostre vite randage.[e][8]
> (13-16)

There is an ironical but positive reversal in this echo (as I think it is) of Dante's figure of Ulysses who, after all, did suffer a shipwreck and was sucked into a whirlpool precisely because of an inordinate (from Dante's perspective) desire to know.[9] To some degree, then, Montale's "message" in this

---

It is time to leave the stunted canebrake
That seems as if it were falling asleep
And to look at the forms
Of life that crumbles.
[d] We move in a haze
Of iridescent dust that quivers,
In a glare of light that
Limes our eyes and somewhat unnerves us.
[e] And yet, you sense it, in the play of arid waves
That enervates [us] in this uneasy hour,
Let us not so soon cast into a bottomless vortex
Our wandering lives.

poem must be considered as vitalistic though not necessarily optimistic, especially in view of the final verses which proclaim that our scorched souls lose themselves in the calm (but also the clarity, as the word *sereno* may suggest) of a certainty which is light: "Tali i nostri animi arsi // . . . / Si perdono nel sereno / Di una certezza: la luce" (20-24). It is true that there seems to be an ambiguity if not a paradox here. For the light that is said to represent the serenity (the calm and clarity) of a certainty is of course that same annihilating midday light that reveals the stark truth of man's condition and in the dazzling blaze of which the weary figures of the poet and his ideal interlocutor were seen groping (9-12). Even in the context of negativity, however, the dignity of man consists in knowing, no matter how much anguish that entails. Thus there is no joyous impulse toward a light that is the revelation of a basically harsh truth. How could there be? At most, perhaps, the reference to finding in it the calm of a certainty hints at resignation.[10] But it ought to be read as a heroic resignation. The exhortation not to surrender to the bottomless whirlpool is firm. Whatever the denotative value of this *gorgo*, it is a negative symbol of the attraction of midday's enticement to oblivion and unawareness. In some way it is symbolically equivalent to the shady retreat that the poet urges us to eschew. Valéry, we recall, following a repulse in the face-to-face confrontation with midday, shook off the noontide paralysis or torpor (i.e., nothingness) and exhorted himself and others to mobility and immersion in life's activity:

> Non, non! . . . Debout! Dans l'ère successive!
> Brisez, mon corps, cette forme pensive!
> Buvez, mon sein, la naissance du vent!
> . . . .
> Le vent se lève! . . . il faut tenter de vivre![f]
>   ("Le cimetière marin," 127-129, 139)

[f] No, no! . . . Arise! Into the succeeding phase!
Break, oh my body, this pensive mode!
Drink, my breast, the birth of the wind!
. . . .
The wind rises! . . . . We must seek to live!

So, too, Montale would shake off the torpor, contrary to the lesson of "Spesso il male di vivere." But though he stands boldly in the light of midday, he seems unable to do aught but declare the negativity of existence.

An equally ambiguous treatment of the absolute light of midday occurs in the lyric "Gloria del disteso mezzogiorno":

> Gloria del disteso mezzogiorno
> Quand'ombra non rendono gli alberi,
> E più e più si mostrano d'attorno
> Per troppa luce, le parvenze, falbe.
>
> Il sole, in alto,—e un secco greto.
> Il mio giorno non è dunque passato:
> L'ora più bella è di là dal muretto
> Che rinchiude in un occaso scialbato.
>
> L'arsura, in giro; un martin pescatore
> Volteggia s'una reliquia di vita.
> La buona pioggia è di là dallo squallore,
> Ma in attendere è gioia più compita.[g][11]

With its opening image of the "glory" of the sun inundating a limitless expanse (*disteso mezzogiorno*; cf. Cardarelli's *Distesa estate*) in the shadowless hour of high noon, the poem ostensibly begins (and we note the emphatic effect of the heavily accented initial word *Glòria*) as an exultant hymn of joy to the absolute light of midday. One might have expected it to develop in the manner of a Dannunzian meridian

---

[g] Glory of widespread noon
When trees cast no shadows
And more and more all around appearances,
Because of too much light, show themselves tawny.

The sun, on high,—and a desiccated riverbed.
My day, then, is not yet over:
The fairest hour is beyond the little wall
That encloses us in a whitewashed sunset.

The burning drought, all around; a kingfisher
Circles above a relic of life.
The good rain is beyond the barrenness,
But in waiting is joy more complete.

dithyramb or perhaps in the vein of the more serenely ecstatic apostrophe to summer (and midday) of a Cardarelli. In fact, however, already in the first quatrain there is an opposition between the sun's dazzling light of glory and the condition of the earth (and the poet in particular). For here too, the light is really excessive ("troppa luce"); and its effect is to cause objects to seem to dissolve into unreality or unsubstantiality—they are said to be *parvenze*—as they are reduced to a uniform dark yellowish color (*falbe*).[12] Contributing to this sense of dissolution or unreality, moreover, is the fact that there are no shadows. And here is a matter of the greatest importance for understanding the perception of midday as an ambiguous or negative value. It is not just that the absence of shadows (or shade) deprives us of a refuge from the heat or blinding light. In much primitive thinking and, to a degree, even in Greek antiquity the shadow (of persons) is associated with the soul, so that the midday hour is feared because of the shortness or absence of shadows.[13] In a place of true glory, such as Dante's Paradise, shadows would indeed be out of place. On earth, however, the absence of shadows, even for inanimate objects, can suggest the ontological ambiguity of reality. Even D'Annunzio, as we saw, had a moment of mystic rapture that he expressed in the image of entering into a cosmic temple of shadowless midday splendor. But in the full context of Montale's poem, the reference to the lack of shadows has an ambiguous and tragically ironic sense.[14]

The first line of the poem's second quatrain states the opposition starkly: above is the overmastering sun at its zenith; beneath it lies a desolate, dry riverbed symbolic of the aridity of existence. It is true that at this point what appears to be a note of hope is introduced as the poet symbolically juxtaposes the solar diurnal cycle to the cycle of human life (his own).[15] Like the sun at the meridian, so too, he is almost surprised to note, the poet's own "day" has not yet run its course. But there is no optimistic or aggressive impulse to fuse with nature or the noon hour as in D'Annunzio. Nor is there a desire to rest in the apparently timeless hour and season of a serene unchanging meridian light such as we found in Cardarelli. Not even in this poem is midday a cause for rejoicing. Thus one does better, I think, to read the opening reference to the "glory" of noon's presence not as an affirmative assertion but rather as a declaration of a disturbing meteorological and spiritual condition. The sun at its zenith burns implacably on the waterless riverbed which is the poet's life.

There is a skeptical attitude toward the "hope," if indeed it be a hope, enunciated by the poet. In point of fact, the "better" hour is forever beyond the reach of the poet who is imprisoned within that wall (*muretto*; cf. the *muraglia* of "Meriggiare . . .") and condemned thereby to a bleak existence defined as an "occaso scialbato"—a colorless or wan sunset. (The *occaso scialbato* may denote the color and the powdery, flaky condition of the calcined wall.) Is there here perhaps a mixing of metaphors or a lyrical coalescence by which the overmastering, desiccating high noon and the pale sunset are equated? Montale, at any rate, seems to deny the possibility of the "ora più bella" at the very moment he wistfully and vaguely evokes it. Like the first two stanzas, the third stanza opens with an obsessive reference, made more explicit now, to the withering drought that possesses, indeed, *encircles* all of existence: "L'arsura *in giro*." The image that follows this statement confirms it by means of a dramatic pictorialization of a cruel and suffering nature that has the law of self-destruction built into it and within which we are enclosed. A bird (a kingfisher) circles (*volteggia*) above a "relic of life," that is, something that once was alive but is now a desiccated remains, something, say, like the calcified internal shell of a cuttlefish that gives the title—*Ossi di seppia*—to the volume of poems and, within it, specifically to the group of lyrics in which "Gloria del disteso mezzogiorno" is included.

The image of a bird in flight could be thought of as a sign of life and freedom, or, like the hawk aloft in "Spesso il male di vivere ho incontrato," a symbol of detachment or divine indifference vis-à-vis the confining negativity of life. But in "Gloria" the kingfisher's persistent or monotonous motion does not break but rather accentuates the impression of the burning stasis. Its *encircling* movement, moreover, is bound to or determined by the "relic of life" with which it combines to form yet another image of the *male di vivere*; it is therefore to be equated with that of the fiercely "glorious" midday sun that reduces the earth to a dried-up riverbed. The vision is not unlike that in Ungaretti's "Di luglio" where a never-ending midsummer's high-noon sun dries up rivers and reduces the earth to an ever starker skeleton.[16]

An end to the drought and the midday oppression is announced in the next line. But the rain—"La buona pioggia"—that would bring relief is not given as a certainty. Rather, like the "ora più bella" to which it corresponds, it is said only to lie beyond (*di là da*, in lines 7 and 11) the present bleakness, i.e., the "muretto / Che rinchiude in un occaso scialbato." Just this much "feigning" is carried over from Leopardi's "L'infinito."[17] Not enough, that is, for Montale to take the leap *beyond* in a full surrender where release from contingency is a triumph. The meteorological conditions in the two poems (I would say in the two noonscapes, for, as I have suggested more than once in this study, I believe that "L'infinito" does, in fact, reflect a noontide experience) are different, of course, being ambiguous but ultimately hostile in the case of "Gloria del disteso mezzogiorno," and serene, even subjectively benign, in the case of "L'infinito." But if, for the radically skeptical Montale, the *muretto* and the *squallore*, unlike Leopardi's *siepe* (hedge), remain impassable, he nonetheless finds it necessary (perhaps *expedient* is the proper word) to *feign* a belief in a better hour, a hope for an end to the drought. And this, interestingly enough, allows him a solution which, though it is still Leopardian, derives not from "L'infinito" but from the concluding gnomic verses of "Il sabato del villaggio" ("The Village Saturday").[18] In Montale's hedging references to "L'ora più bella" and "La buona pioggia" there is a Leopardian anticipation or forestalling of the disillusionment that would ensue even with the arrival of sunset (i.e., with the evening of one's life when one might expect to find serenity) or with the advent of rain (would the rain really be restorative?). Thus his conclusion, borrowed from Leopardi, is that true or perfect happiness is really in the act of hoping and waiting for the better hour: "Ma in attendere è gioia più compita."

And yet, as a poem on midday, Montale's lyric is perhaps closer to Pascoli than to Leopardi. In it, we have seen, the poet's "hope" is not for a disclosure of a miracle at noon, but for a more serene or better hour which, if it is to be, will come at sunset. To this extent the poem betrays a "crepuscular" or renunciatory attitude, and whatever echo from D'Annunzio there may be in the word *Gloria* of the first verse is rendered ambiguous by a mood and attitude that, however contradictory of "Non rifugiarti nell'ombra," are in a direct line with Pascoli's "Gloria."[19] Indeed, there is as much of the antimeridian Pascoli-Belacqua (who is content to wait in the shade) as there is of Leopardi in the concluding statement that the greater joy (actually the *only* joy) is in the waiting. But the Montalean situation (as his poem) is more complex and more tragic. Again there is no Valéry-like resistance to the midday immobility ("Il faut tenter de vivre"), but neither is there shade in which to sit while waiting. Consequently, there is less satisfaction and more ambiguity in the renunciation. Though Pascoli's poem also includes an invocation for rain (made by the croaking frogs which may be said to correspond, vaguely at least, to Montale's kingfisher) there is not, as there is in "Gloria del disteso mezzogiorno," a description of the destruction that wasteth at noon.

As I have already suggested, Montale's poem has a close affinity with Ungaretti's "Di luglio." And like "Di luglio" it descends, in an ideal sense surely, and, perhaps, in an actual sense as well, from Leconte de Lisle's "Midi." Montale's opening *Gloria* intonation may even owe something to the French poem's first line: "Midi, *roi* des étés, *épandu* sur la plaine."[h] So too one finds specific references to the absence of shadows and to dried-up founts where formerly there was life-giving water:

---

[h] Midday, sovereign of summers, spread out on the plain.

> L'étendue est immense, et les champs n'ont point d'ombre,
> Et la source est tarie où buvaient les troupeaux.[1]
>
> (5-6)

The torrid sun of "Midi" is an all-consuming force through which the metaphysical nothingness at the heart of nature operates. There is neither sadness nor joy in the immobility of a country noontide, only a sense of a deathlike void. Hence, the man attached to life by reason of joy or bitterness is advised to flee the midday encounter:

> Fuis! la nature est vide et le soleil consume:
> Rien n'est vivant ici, rien n'est triste ou joyeux.
>
> (23-24)

Such features, we know, are not unique to Leconte de Lisle's midday, there being many precedents for them. But the metaphysical implications and the technique of using the negative descriptive elements of the noonscape to objectify them are his own. In this sense, "Midi" anticipates such physical-to-metaphysical noonscapes as we find in Ungaretti's "Di luglio" and Montale's "Gloria del disteso mezzogiorno."

The solution offered by Leconte de Lisle, however, was of the kind that the two Italian poets could not be satisfied with, though each in his way was characteristically ambivalent about it. For the totally disillusioned man seeking refuge from the cold indifference of the world, the French poet suggests, the contemplation of the forbidding noonscape may offer a supreme if saturnine pleasure. If such a man surrenders himself "infinitely" to the contemplation of the consuming fire of the midday stasis, he will discover in it the revelation of divine nothingness (*le néant divin*). But paradoxically he will find himself fortified thereby and able to return to the dismal world of men (*les cités infimes*) armed, we may say, in a superior Stoic (or Hindu) indifference:

---

[1] The expanse is immense, and the fields are without shade,
And the fount is dried up where the flocks once drank.

Viens! Le soleil te parle en paroles sublimes;
Dans sa flamme implacable *absorbe-toi* sans fin;
Et retourne à pas lents vers les cités infimes,
Le coeur trempé sept fois dans le néant divin.

(29-32)

One would not be wrong, I believe, to see in the saving grace of indifference that is suggested here an anticipation, even a literary source, of the "divine indifference" of Montale's statue infinitely *absorbed* in the burning noontide stasis ("Spesso il male di vivere ho incontrato"). However, we should note that the indifference spoken of by Montale derives from a rare moment of ignorance or forgetfulness and that he alternates "indifference" with a wakeful acceptance of anguish. Ungaretti, we saw, reveals a particular ambiguity of his own. It is not the "indifference" or the quiet of the midday stasis that sometimes attracts him, but the vehemence of the consuming flame itself which he felt to be both his natural element and an implacable enemy. But it was that most heroically anguished and most unrhetorical of poets, Leopardi, who, by as total an absorption in noontide as is possible (and unmatched, in the second stanza of "La vita solitaria"), anticipated the midday revelation to which "Midi" invites us.[20]

The poems of Montale discussed hitherto are from the section of *Ossi di seppia* that gives the title to the whole volume. Though they offer what are perhaps the book's most important emblematical representations of midday, they are by no means the only cases of significant use of the theme. "Il canneto rispunta i suoi cimelli" ("The canebrake puts forth its spires") also evokes a landscape in which an oppressive noontide engulfs all things in immobility. "Debole sistro al vento" ("Feeble sistrum on the wind") tells of a cicada, lost in a torrid noontide stasis, weakly emitting its shrill sound; this particular cicada thus becomes an image of the isolation of man and the existential *male di vivere* inherent in all nature where things are threatened or surrounded by a metaphysical void.[21] Even the cycle of nine poems that comprises Montale's rhapsodic dialogue with the sea—*Mediterraneo*—has a summer noontide as its initial symbolical season and hour. The first poem of the cycle, "A vortice s'abbatte" ("Like a vortex, there smashes"), is set in the Montalean atmosphere of a scorched, cracked earth and a sultriness that veils the poet's view of the nearby sea. The torrid midday has imprisoned him in its torpor, and his condition is one of immobility as with head reclined he listens to the voice of the monotonous yet vigorous pulsation of the sea. And the final poem of the group, "Dissipa tu se lo vuoi" ("Dissolve it, if you wish"), finds the poet recognizing the incommensurability that obtains between the sea and himself. The lesson that he has learned comes not from the sea's majestic fury and glorious might, which he cannot match in himself, but rather from the subdued panting of the sea during the calm of a desolate noontide:

> Presa la mia lezione
> Più che dalla tua gloria
> Aperta, dall'ansare
> Che quasi non dà suono
> Di qualche tuo meriggio desolato,
> A te mi rendo in umiltà.[j22]
>
> (16-21)

It is a lesson of humility and resignation. Like the glory of the midday sun itself, the glory of the sea belongs to a realm to which the poet cannot aspire. Here then is the antithesis of D'Annunzio's *Alcyone*.

The volume *Ossi di seppia* even includes a section (the second largest in number of titles and the largest in number of verses) that bears the title *Meriggi e ombre* (*Noontides and Shadows*), suggestive of the drama of being caught between the cruel glare of a nature that consumes and the desire for evasion. To this section belongs "Egloga" ("Eclogue") with its further insistence on the theme of the solitude of man suf-

---

[j] Having learned my lesson
More than from your
Open glory, from the almost silent panting
Of some desolate noontides of yours,
I humbly yield to you.

fering in a disintegrative noon where only the "solemn" cicadas can prevail: "Non durano che le solenni cicale / In questi saturnali del caldo" (34-35), and one senses that here again it is the cicada/death that endures. Here too we find "Crisalide" ("Chrysalis"), in which creatures and nature in general are discovered to belong, like man, to the bleak limbo of defective (mutilated) existences ("nel limbo squallido / Delle monche esistenze"). The oft-recurring Montalean illusory hope for a way out of existential despair is figured first by the image of the midday sun becoming veiled by clouds that seem to promise a restorative rain (cf. "La buona pioggia" of "Gloria . . .") that will cool our fever and, second, by the mirage of a ship of grace approaching in the midst of the suffocating noontide. In the anticipation of being rescued by the lifeboat launched by the ship, man's anguish itself is celebrated as "glorious," a quasi-religious oxymoron of a Dannunzian kind, except that in the negative context of Montale's poem it has, again, an ironic (but not sarcastic) quality:

> . . . Il sole s'immerge nelle nubi,
> L'ora di febbre, trepida, si chiude.
> Un glorioso affanno senza strepiti
> Ci batte in gola: nel meriggio afoso
> Spunta la barca di salvezza, è giunta:
> Vedila che sciaborda tra le secche,
> Esprime un suo burchiello che si volge
> Al docile frangente—e là ci attende.[k]
> (50-57)

The phantom lifeboat will never reach man. The irony, tragic now, is that the boat waits for man who has no way of reaching what he knows to be a mirage. Thus there is no Dannun-

[k] . . . The sun plunges into the clouds,
The fever hour, tremulous, is over.
A glorious anguish without clamor
Throbs in our throats: in the oppressive noon
The boat of salvation comes into view, it has arrived:
Look how it sways between the shoals,
It sends forth a small boat that turns
In the mild breakers—and waits for us there.

zian sense of a promise of an inimitable life to be fulfilled in the midday hour, no sense of repressed energy or infinite latency in the heart of this immobility to give a positive value to its oppressiveness. On the contrary, here and elsewhere in Montale's verse, D'Annunzio's drama of meridian expectancy, of the vibrant, optimistic wait for the miracle to be revealed at noon—

> *L'attesa del prodigio* gonfiava questo mio
> Cuore come il cuor del mondo
>   ("L'annunzio," 107-108)
>
> L'Ignoto viene a me, *l'Ignoto attendo!*
>   (*"Furit aestus,"* 12)

—has been transformed into the existentialist drama of waiting for a deliverance in which one perhaps does not really believe.[23]

Yet precisely the immobility of noontide offered an almost morbid attraction to Montale. Alongside the theme of the torment of immobility, the poems of *Ossi* repeatedly express a renunciatory mood that seems to exalt immobility. The formulation of this latter motif often reveals characteristic elements of noontide even when the time of day is not specified. Such is the case, for example, with the poem "Arremba su la strinata proda" ("Beach your paper boats on the scorched shore," from the section *Ossi*) where Montale seems to go very far indeed in advocating renunciation, the hour of crisis here suggesting a corrosive and hostile midday atmosphere from which we are asked to retire in favor of a haven in a state of inertia.[24] It is in the poem "Marezzo" ("Waves," from the group *Meriggi e ombre*), however, that noontide appears most unequivocally in its aspect of a stasis that attracts. In a rowboat the poet and his female companion have come out from the crepuscular world of a grotto into the open sea which lies under the blazing light of a sun that has come to its midday pause. The sky has the appearance of a hollow dome of pure luminous glass (and the image of glass emphasizes the impression of immobility):

> Fuori è il sole: s'arresta
> Nel suo giro e fiammeggia.
> Il cavo cielo se ne illustra ed estua,
> Vetro che non si scheggia.[1]
>
> (9-12)

Ceasing to row, the poet invites his companion to surrender totally to the lulling motion (*sciaborda*) of the boat and the noontide calm. Not even memory (which in Montale is often a disturbing element associated with the sense of time and remorse) must be allowed to intrude upon the forgetfulness of this moment:

> Nel guscio esiguo che sciaborda,
> Abbandonati i remi agli scalmi,
> Fa che ricordo non ti rimorda
> Che torbi questi meriggi calmi.[m]
>
> (17-20)

The situation, mood, and invitation expressed in these verses recall the noontide evasion of Montale's fellow Ligurian, Giovanni Boine. Not only the imagery but the connotative value of the lexicon of "Deriva" seems to be reproduced. Where the boat for Boine is a *culla*, for Montale it is a *guscio*, both of which suggest a protective element and a return to a state of "divine indifference" and comfort, the womb if one likes. The lulling or rocking motion which Boine expressed with the word *sciacquare* is echoed in "Marezzo" by *sciabordare*, a word for which Montale shows a certain predilection. (The intransitive use of the two words in their respective contexts is very literary.)

As in other cases of Montalean noontides, "Marezzo" is

[1] Outside is the sun: it stops
In its course and blazes.
The hollow sky is lustered by it and burns,
Glass that does not splinter.

[m] In the small boat [shell] that sways,
With the oars abandoned in the rowlocks,
Let no memory trouble you
That might muddle these calm noons.

characterized by an excess of light that "beclouds" the couple's sight, preventing them from distinguishing the elements of reality. But the disintegrative action is welcome. Even the thoughts of our isolation are dissolved in the annihilating midday atmosphere: "la troppa luce intorbida. / Si struggono i pensieri troppo soli" (23-24). Like Ungaretti, however, this anxious poet, too, is never long without the sense of time's threat. The sea (*l'onda*), which is almost still, will become troubled and its hue darker as a feeling of a harsher reality returns. Now, before the end of the suspended hour, the water is calm beneath the flood of sunlight whose fiery heat produces a torpor in which things are extenuated:

>Tutto fra poco si farà più ruvido,
>Fiorirà l'onda di più cupe strisce.
>Ora resta così, sotto il diluvio
>Del sole che finisce.[n]
>
>(25-28)

As my explication suggests, I read *finisce* as a transitive verb in the sense of *extenuates* or *prostrates* and not in the sense of *about to end*. This interpretation seems to be more in keeping with the situation of suspension and surrender. We may compare this meaning and image with something similar in the poem "Non rifugiarti nell'ombra" where, as we saw earlier, the blazing light of midday is said to have just such an effect: "Ci muoviamo in . . . *un barbaglio* che invischia gli occhi e un poco *ci sfibra*" (9-12). I also consider the verb *resta* to be an indicative with *l'onda* as its subject, and not, therefore, an imperative addressed to the poet's companion.

However, imperatives soon follow, and with them the poet invites his companion to surrender or "drown" personal identity like ballast sinking into water, the image of ballast suggesting ironically the negative value of the self or life, of one's "name":

[n] Soon everything will become rough,
The water will flower with darker streaks.
Now it is still thus, under the flood
Of the sun that extenuates [us].

> Disciogli il cuore gonfio
> Nell'aprirsi dell'onda;
> Come una pietra di zavorra affonda
> Il tuo nome nell'acque con un tonfo!⁰
>
> (37-40)

Montale, too, resorts to an oxymoron in order to describe the strange or ambiguous impression of noontide and its effects. The midday stasis is said to be an "astral delirium" that invades the atmosphere, a luminous and calm evil or fever. Precisely in this captive noontide space, the poet suggests, the hour that restores serenity (again the meteorological image refers to a human drama of hope) may come to them, there on the sea that seems to be ablaze as it reflects the sun:

> Un astrale delirio si disfrena,
> Un male calmo e lucente.
> Forse vedremo l'ora che rasserena
> Venirci incontro sulla spera ardente.ᵖ
>
> (41-44)

But this rage for immobility—"delirio d'immobilità" as Montale refers to it in "Arsenio"—is frustrated. Signs of life appear as a disturbing factor, and soon the charm is broken. After a period during which she had sunk into oblivion, the poet's companion has again become aware of her "weight," that is, her personal identity: "tu riprovi il peso / Di te" (57-58), and all things which during the magic spell seemed to be in a benedictional state of undulation are felt to exist in all their heavy reality. The final stanza is a plea to resist the reentry into mobility and time, not to shake themselves from the present state of inertia ("Non siamo diversi"), but to remain

---

⁰ Release your swollen heart
  Into the opening of the waves;
  Like ballast drop
  Your name into the waters with a splash!
ᵖ An astral delirium breaks loose,
  A calm and shining ill.
  Perhaps we shall see the brightening hour
  Come to meet us on the burning sphere.

in the possession of the noontide stasis, submerged in a vortex of blue of ever-increasing density. The blue is perhaps that of the sky; it is, at any rate, the color symbolizing the Absolute or the purity of nothingness:

> Ah qui restiamo, non siamo diversi.
> Immobili così. Nessuno ascolta
> La nostra voce più. Così sommersi
> In un gorgo d'azzurro che s'infolta.[q]

Once again, Montale does not follow in the wake of Valéry.[25] Nor, despite apparent similarities, is "Marezzo" an invitation to noontide pantheistic fusion or interpenetration with nature in the manner of D'Annunzio's "Meriggio." The poem expresses instead an aspiration to the condition of midday's divine indifference proclaimed by Montale as a saving grace in "Spesso il male di vivere ho incontrato." The last image of the poem indicates a willingness to drown the self in the kind of vortex—*gorgo*—of indifference or oblivion that the poet of "Non rifugiarti nell'ombra" had urged us, Ulysses-like, to avoid. Accordingly, the truest affiliation of "Marezzo," too, would seem to be with the midday experience of surrendering to nonbeing or of release into nirvana, such as we found in Leopardi's "Vita solitaria." Or we may think again, and perhaps more appropriately, of that intermediate state of pure ambiguity and suspension between being and nonbeing suggested by Boine's "Deriva" where *si va non si va*.

In connection with this theme of pure suspension or the paradox of motion in immobility, one of Montale's most original and significant uses of the midday topos (or so it seems to me) occurs in the first poem of the group *Sarcofaghi*. Here the image of immobility is the sculptured and so forever frozen scene on a bronze sarcophagus (with its suggestion of the immobility of death) depicting young maidens bearing amphoras who "walk" (a frequent image of time in Montale)

---

[q] Ah, let us remain here, let us not change.
Motionless, thus. No one hears
Our voices any more. Like this, submerged
In a vortex of blue which thickens.

lightly toward a valley they will never reach. A sun is also represented and is said to be approaching its zenith: "Il sole che va in alto" (8). The choice of the verb *va* (from *andare*) rather than the verb *sta* that one might expect in speaking of this sculptured sun was made, I suspect, because *va* as a verb of motion (which signifies the flow of time) in reference to an object forever fixed (like those "walking" maidens whose own frozen movement is rendered by the same verb: "Dove se ne *vanno*") contributes to the illusion of movement in immobility or vice versa. But that the sun is already at the meridian and in its moment of apparent or "actual" pause (and for this reason more than anything else one expects the verb *sta*) is indicated by the next details of the scene. The sculptured hill slopes are said to reveal no tints: "Le intraviste pendici / Non han tinte" (9-10). That is because the bronze sarcophagus on which they are represented is of a uniform color. But it is also true that at midday there are no shadows, and at that hour, moreover, all things are reduced to a single color which, as Montale's adjective *falbe* (in "Gloria del disteso mezzogiorno") indicates, is not unlike the color of bronze. Thus the central question that Montale asks in the poem follows upon the evocation of a suggestive midday scene and is as revelatory of the ambiguity of the noontide stasis in general as it is of the scene depicted on the sarcophagus with its ambiguous interplay between motion and immobility, between life and death:

> Mondo che dorme o mondo che si gloria
> D'immutata esistenza, chi può dire?[r]
>
> (15-16)

The question, as it develops from its unusual but cogent context, suggests the peculiar midday impression of a simultaneous revelation of an absolute nothingness and an absolute fullness, and one wonders whether the extremes have not in fact met. For here indeed we are left with a paradoxical and ironic identity between being and nonbeing.[26]

[r] A world that sleeps or a world that glories
In an unchanging existence, who can say?

The critics have long been divided in their assessment of this poet's vision of life. *Ossi di seppia* has been judged by some to express a totally negative and despairing point of view, while others insist that its pessimistic pronouncements are punctuated by affirmative statements of hope and even by a heroic if unflamboyant attitude. Whatever one's opinion on the matter, it is hardly possible to deny that the volume betrays an unresolved (perhaps deliberate) tension between negation and illusion, between hope in a salvation (*varco*, *prodigio*, etc.) from the aridity of existence and a desire to evade the *male di vivere* by sinking into the heart of the nothingness that is on some occasions felt as a threat. Certainly it is symptomatic that in one of the volume's most emblematic (even allegorical) and celebrated poems—"Arsenio"—when the stifling midday stasis is broken (in a noontide that is itself of an uncertain character—"or piovorno ora acceso"), it is not by "la buona pioggia" or by a life-giving wind, but by an apocalyptic wind-and-rain storm that turns noon into night—

> Discendi in mezzo al buio che precipita
> E muta il mezzogiorno in una notte[s]—

—and, without the promise of a new life to follow, engulfs all things in its own destructive fury. *Ossi di seppia*, in short, reveals a marked ambivalence that is perfectly mirrored by Montale's choice of the most ambiguous and most critical of hours—midday—as its dominant atmosphere and by the different attitudes the poet displays toward it.

[s] Go down into the midst of darkness that suddenly falls
And changes midday into night.

Conclusion

Morning, evening, and night, we know, are themselves symbolically rich literary themes, yet besides often giving rise to banal or conventional considerations they are also often used by writers in indiscriminate or casual ways. This is not often the case with midday which is evoked less frequently than the other main parts of the diurnal solar cycle but whose presence in literary texts is almost always fraught with special meaning. The common opinion associates noontide with indolence or the languishing of both nature and mankind in stifling heat. Although this is a very real connection—and the motif occupies a large place in literature—our enquiry shows that it is really secondary to and often subsumed under a more dramatic context of an archetypal encounter with midday as a moment of existential crisis.

The blaze of noon is variously experienced as a timeless tide of glory or as a bewildering moment of demonic dread or panic; the occasion for reaching out to the Absolute or for retreat from oppression and an undefined hostile force threatening destruction; a suspended "moment" of fullness and limitless original energy or of stasis and nothingness; a release (or evasion) into a divine torpor (or indifference) that may even arrive at the cancellation of sentiency, or a thrilling sense of expansion of the self into the all of nature. The ambiguity of midday is such that any one of these pairs of contraries (and others like them) may be felt not only in one or the other of the terms but as an experiential reality in which the contrasting terms coexist and are even fused into a single, paradoxical affective quality or tonality. Thus it is not surprising that oxymoronic expressions are common in evocations of midday, for they are in keeping with the perception of midday as a moment of perfect but precarious balance between opposite values. But it is not, strictly speaking, a resolution of extremes or a case of *concordia discors* that is to be understood here. An air of tension is seldom if ever wholly absent from the pregnant but uneasy unity of noontide. In the heart of the most absolute midday stasis where all emotions may seem muted—such as in Leopardi's *meriggio* of "La vita solitaria"—there is a store of (original) energy to be reckoned with even if it is only negatively perceived or suggested. Even the most blissful and seemingly untroubled midday nympholepsy, as in the cases of Foscolo, Leopardi, and Ungaretti, not to mention D'Annunzio, depends upon an (erotic) energy that is, as Ungaretti knew, correctly diagnosed as a delirium. Even the most religiously permeated vision of the lure of midday glory and peace may contain a wild vibrancy. The hour of most intense brightness may, by its very excess of light, be perceived as a dazzling darkness. It is no wonder, then, that the preeminent character of midday is its atmosphere of crisis, even when the encounter seems weighted on the positive side.

The preceding chapters give ample evidence for the claim advanced in the preface that the presence of the image of midday in Italian literature amounts to a richly variegated psychological and aesthetic experience. There are of course many other examples of the topos that could be included in this essay if my intention were merely to make an encyclopedic compilation. My aim, however, has not been to give a complete record (a task as impossible as it is unnecessary), but rather to present both a general view and a particularized analysis of some of the more meaningful cases of the theme's occurrence. The use of the image of noontide in widely different contexts (and in key situations) by Dante, Petrarch, and Boccaccio shows us that the image had a special value virtually from the beginning of Italian literature. But if it is true that midday has never been absent from any particular literary period, so to speak, it is nonetheless clear that allusions to the theme have increased significantly since the eighteenth century. In part this can be explained by the fact that there developed at that time a strong philosophical and literary interest in the description of nature and in the relationship between man and nature, nature being understood in the dual sense of landscape and the force responsible for the maintenance, if not the creation, of life and things. Yet the intensity of man's experience of midday and the awareness of crisis in connection with it have been characteristic of the topos since the earliest times, so that in the final analysis the impression that the most intense utterances have come in the last century or so is perhaps more a quantitative than a qualitative or affective matter.

Nonetheless, although we must emphasize that from the beginning midday has, in literary texts, almost always been put to use in an emblematic or symbolic way in order to represent a crisis, it is equally certain that for historical and social reasons the sense of crisis has become progressively more widespread and acute over the last hundred years or so. The use of the image of midday in its several variations has increased as writers have become more and more conscious of moral and metaphysical crises experienced on both the personal and the public level. Surely it is not farfetched to see in the concrete reality of an age of such crisis consciousness as the twentieth century a chief cause for the extraordinarily frequent use of the topos, especially in a land of the sun such as Italy. In this respect, it is noteworthy that French literature of the modern period reveals an equally obsessive preoccupation with the themes of the sun and midday. The sense of crisis that so often characterizes man's experience of noontide assures us that the theme will always find a significant place in literature, even if it takes a turn for the grotesque as, say, in the irreverently parodistic and satiric treatment accorded it in the final pages of Witold Gombrowicz's novel *Ferdydurke*. It is, as we have said, an archetypal encounter, and we have seen that even men of the north have been fascinated by the uncanny experience. But whatever the literary future of the topos may be, it can be said to have peaked in the present century with Ungaretti and the early Montale, the two writers who more than all others in the long history of the emblematization of the image, have expressed the lure and the revulsion, the ambiguity and the crisis that are "antíquest felt at noon."

Notes

INTRODUCTION

[1] The correspondence between the various parts of the day and the four seasons is clearly suggested by what James Thomson wrote in the preface to the second edition of *Winter*: "I know no subject more elevating, . . . more ready to awake the poetical enthusiasm, the philosophical reflection, and the moral sentiment, than the works of Nature. . . . In every dress nature is greatly charming—whether she puts on the crimson robes of the morning, *the strong effulgence of noon*, and sober suit of the evening, or the deep sables of blackness and tempest! How gay looks the Spring! *how glorious the Summer!* how pleasing the Autumn! and how venerable the Winter!" *The Complete Poetical Works of James Thomson*, ed. J. Logie Robertson (London, 1908), pp. 240-241. I have emphasized the references to noon and summer because they are of most interest to this study. I think it safe to say that in this passage the closest correspondence—one amounting almost to a direct equation—is that which obtains between the "effulgent" hour and the "glorious" season. Also to be noted is the strong assertion that the various parts of the day and the different seasons are an invitation to philosophical meditation and poetry, in itself not a new thought but one that allowed Thomson to look intently at the different faces and moods of nature and to contribute to the formation of a "new" feeling for it in his age.

[2] From the poem "Extracts from Addresses to the Academy of Fine Ideas." In *The Collected Poems of Wallace Stevens* (New York, 1969), p. 258.

[3] "Si l'on nous objectait que l'introversion et l'extroversion doivent être désignées en partant du *sujet*, nous répondrions que l'imagination n'est rien autre que le sujet transporté dans les choses. Les images portent alors la marque du sujet. Et cette marque est si claire que finalement c'est par les images qu'on peut avoir le plus sûr diagnostic des tempéraments." *La terre et les rêveries du repos* (Paris, 1948, 1969), p. 3.

[4] *Biographia Literaria* by S. T. Coleridge, edited with his Aesthetical Essays by J. Shawcross (London, 1907), II, p. 258. A little earlier in the essay Coleridge wrote: "Art itself might be defined as

of a middle quality between a thought and a thing, or, as I said before, the union and reconciliation of that which is nature with that which is exclusively human. It is the figured language of thought" (pp. 254-255).

⁵ *The Collected Poems of Wallace Stevens*, p. 532.

⁶ In Albert Camus' essay "L'été" (1939), we read: "Il est midi, le jour lui-même est en balance." *Noces; L'été* (Paris, 1959), p. 111. So too Boccaccio indicated midday by noting that "il sole tiene ancora il dì librato" (in *Ameto*). It is, paradoxically, a point of perfect yet precarious balance.

⁷ I have quoted from the translation by Anthony Holden in his anthology, *Greek Pastoral Poetry* (Middlesex and Baltimore, 1974), p. 45. The reflection of the dread of noon in Theocritus's idyll does not necessarily mean that the sophisticated poet himself shared in it. Thomas G. Rosenmeyer writes: "In the pastoral uses of the motif, notably the vision of Pan in Theocritus' *Idyll* I (15 ff.), it would be wrong to read more than a slight tremor into the equanimity of the herdsman. He is not afraid of Pan, much less mysteriously touched. Theocritus merely uses the ancient motif, not without humor, to indicate that *even this almost perfect stillness has a core of suspended energy to be reckoned with*, and that the herdsmen-poets must be careful to do the right thing by the opportunity given to them." *The Green Cabinet: Theocritus and the European Pastoral Lyric* (Berkeley and Los Angeles, 1969), p. 89. While I agree with this judgment, I would emphasize those words (italicized by me) in it that suggest the special pregnancy of the noontide motif, in particular as we shall find it developed in some of the authors discussed in the present study. Other interesting observations on the theme of noon in antiquity occur in Rosenmeyer's book at pp. 67, 76, 88-89, and 91. Of course, his words on Theocritus's use of the motif are not meant to minimize the importance of ancient Greece's association of midday with a sacred terror.

⁸ "Il n'y a pas de doute que l'heure de midi ait été, en Grèce, l'heure religieuse par excellence." So writes Roger Caillois in his enormously erudite and perceptive study on the midday motif in antiquity. It is no part of the present book to go over ground that has already been so brilliantly covered. Caillois' concern is with the theme of noon as the time of day when malevolent spirits or influences visit, tempt, and afflict man, a theme he traces primarily in antiquity but also, to a significant degree, in the early centuries of the Christian era and in a number of medieval legends. Though his

study is made from the point of view of a historian of religion, his observations are far-reaching. See "Les démons de midi," in *Revue de l'histoire des religions*, 115 (1937), pp. 142-173, and 116 (1937), pp. 54-83 and 143-186.

Caillois adduces evidence to indicate that even to sleep at midday was dangerous, for then Pan or nymphs might aggressively instill nightmarish terrors and disorders. An erotic element is also often present. Indeed, the so-called "hour of Pan" was just as much the "hour of nymphs" or the "hour of Diana."

[9] Caillois, "Les démons de midi," Vol. 116, p. 163. See also pp. 83, 146, and, for midday eroticism with Pan, p. 151.

[10] See in *Patrologia Latina*, ed. Migne, Vol. 171, col. 1291.

[11] The new Latin translation refers to the "pernicies quae vastat meridie." Saint Jerome's revision of the Vetus Latina according to the Septuagint gives the passage as: "Non timebis a ruina et daemonio meridiano" (*PL* 29, 290). His second revision of the Latin text (the text of the Vulgate) reads: "ab incursu et daemonio meridiano" (*PL* 29, 289). In his final revision, translating from the Hebrew, Saint Jerome rendered the passage as "a morsu insidiantis meridie." For discussions of the questions raised by the biblical text, see: S. Landersdorfer, "Das *daemonium meridianum* (Ps. 91 [90] 6)," in *Biblische Zeitschrift*, 18 (1929), pp. 294-300; P. de Labriolle, "Le démon de midi," in *Bulletin Du Cange*, 9 (1934), pp. 46-54; Caillois, "Les démons de midi," Vol. 116, pp. 156-162. For the allegorical and moral interpretations in the exegetical writings of Saint Augustine, Saint Jerome, and Theodoret of Cyrus, see the article by Rudolph Arbesmann, "The *Daemonium Meridianum* and the Greek and Latin Patristic Exegesis," in *Traditio*, 14 (1958), pp. 17-31.

[12] Nonetheless, the idea of a demonic agency may not be totally absent here. In Babylonian mythology, *Nergal* is a solar deity of midsummer and midday who visits men with death and pestilence. See M. Jastrow, *Aspects of Religious Belief and Practice in Babylonia and Assyria* (New York and London, 1911), pp. 107, 134. In Hindu mythology, the destroyer god *Siva* sometimes figures as the midday solar deity, and for the ancient Egyptians, who developed the most complete cult of sun worship, the supreme solar deity *Ra* (or *Re*) was above all the omnipotent god of the glorious midday sun, but a positive one. See William Tyler Olcott, *Myths of the Sun* (New York, 1967), pp. 163, 152-153.

[13] For discussions see the studies by Caillois and Labriolle mentioned in notes 8 and 11. For a full treatment of the question of

acedia, see Siegfried Wenzel's *The Sin of Sloth: Acedia in Medieval Thought and Literature* (Chapel Hill, N.C., 1960, 1967).

[14] The description occurs in Book X ("de spiritu acediae") of Cassian's treatise on the monastic life and the eight chief vices: *De institutis coenobiorum et de octo principalium vitiorum remediis*. The most reliable edition is that printed in the series *Sources chrétiennes* (no. 109): Jean Cassien, *Institutions cénobitiques*, revised Latin text, introduction, translation, and notes by Jean-Claude Guy (Paris, 1965). For the passage referred to above in the text, see p. 384.

[15] One need not complain that Reinhard Kuhn has monopolized the concept of the *daemonium meridianum* in entitling his recent fine study on ennui *The Demon of Noontide* (Princeton, N.J., 1976). Though Kuhn has little to say about midday save for some references to the clerical tradition, the phrase is a good metaphor for the book's true subject which is indicated by the subtitle: *Ennui in Western Literature*. However, he is aware that the early Christian writers on noontide acedia do not write as profoundly about the true demonic quality of midday as some modern poets. "Modern poets have been acutely sensitive to the demonic quality of the noon hour, and, by comparison, the noontide demon of Evagrius seems to be an almost abstract figure" (p. 43). Kuhn would extend this lack of psychological profundity to Christian writers in general, a view that can be accepted only if we have in mind the whole picture of midday. Cassian's description of the midday acedia that overtakes monks is remarkable for its psychological characterization.

An earlier appropriation of the expression was made by Paul Bourget in the title of his novel *Le démon de midi* (1914). Bourget has one of his characters, a cleric, make a deliberate transferral of the biblical expression from the acedia of the anchorites to the ambition that tempts a man in the middle age of life: "L'*acedia* monte, ce dégoût, cette tristesse des choses de Dieu qui donne au cénobite la nostalgie du siècle quitté, le désir d'une autre existence, un révolte intime et profonde, et c'est le *Demon de midi*. Je donne, moi, le même nom à une autre tentation, et je ne crois pas manquer de respect à la Sainte Ecriture, toujours chargée de plus de sens que n'en comporte la lettre nue. Cette tentation, c'est celle qui assiège l'homme au midi, non pas d'un jour, mais de ses jours, dans la plénitude de sa force. Il a conduit sa destinée jusque-là, de vertus en vertus, de réussite en réussite. Voici que l'esprit de destruction s'empare de lui,—entendez bien: de sa propre destruction." *Le démon de midi*, as published in *La petite illustration*, 16 Mai 1914, p. 5. Here too we note the symbolic equation between the diurnal solar cycle and the human life cycle and the idea in both cases that midday represents the fullness of strength. But there is also the idea, again applicable to either cycle, that midday as a time of crisis is above all a time of self-consuming passion, a thought we shall find expressed in different ways in writers as far apart, chronologically, as Petrarch and Ungaretti.

If the expression "the demon of noontide" were to be used to characterize solely, or chiefly, the association (symbolic and real) between midday and indolence or lethargy, then perhaps no book would more deserve to have it for its title than Ivan Goncharov's novel *Oblomov* (1858). Henry Gifford writes that "Goncharov's novel is the history of an hallucination in which time appears immobilized; hence the prominence of its static images, and its slow meditative course, and the paucity of action." *The Novel in Russia* (New York, 1965), p. 56. Chief among these static images, and emblematic of the immobility and torpor—moral and social—that characterize the hero and his world, is the noontide stasis: "The day was burning hot, not a cloud in the sky. The sun stood right overhead, scorching the grass. There was not the faintest stir in the motionless air, not a rustle in the trees, nor a ripple on the water; unbroken stillness reigned over the fields and the village, as though everything were dead. The human voice echoed far in the empty air. A cockchafer could be heard flying and buzzing a hundred feet away, and there was a sound of snoring in the thick grass as though someone were fast asleep there." Ivan Goncharov, *Oblomov*, trans. Natalie A. Duddington (London, 1929), p. 116. It is this mood that permeates the novel.

[16] Cornelis Verhoeven, *The Philosophy of Wonder*, trans. Mary Foran (New York, 1972), pp. 47-48. So far as I know, Verhoeven's pages on the "noontide devil" and Panic terror constitute the most insightful inquiry into the peculiar quality of midday and its implications of any modern philosopher. (See pp. 44-58.) Another modern philosopher willing to give serious attention to man's experience with midday is Otto Friedrich Bollnow who has looked at the question in connection with an inquiry into the consciousness of time and the affective quality of the different parts of the day. "Der Mittag: Ein Beitrag zur Metaphysik der Tageszeiten," in *Unruhe und Geborgenheit im Weltbild neuerer Dichter* (Stuttgart, 1953), pp. 143-177. As a philosopher who takes poets seriously (as most serious philosophers have always done), Bollnow considers the midday motif in writings of J. P. Eichendorff, Leconte de Lisle, Nietzsche, D'An-

nunzio, and Mallarmé. Bollnow also notes the resemblance between the midday stillness and the idea of death, between noontide and the sentiment of eternity, noontide as both a time of blessed release from limits and a time of fear in the presence of the uncanny, in short, the ambiguous face of midday: "Das Erlebnis des Mittags ist ein seltsames, schweres und dunkles Glück. Die Erhebung über die Schranken des individuellen Daseins wirkt befreiend und beglückend. Aber da die vollendete Reife dieses Daseins zugleich das Ende des einzelnen Daseins bedeutet, ist mit der leuchtenden Erfahrung der Ewigkeit zugleich der Mitgeschmack des Todes verbunden. Das gibt der beseligenden Erfahrung des Mittags zugleich einen Zug beängstigender Unheimlichkeit. Das Erlebnis ist eigentümlich doppelseitig" (p. 176). Bollnow has also dealt with the midday motif in Nietzsche in his volume *Das Wesen der Stimmungen* (Frankfurt am Main, 1943), pp. 195-212. But before either of these philosophers, Caillois, even while stressing the attraction of midday because of its power of inducing a mood of supreme indolence, concluded his study on the theme in antiquity by commenting on the peculiar ambiguity of noontide: "A midi, la vie, semble-t-il, s'accorde un temps d'arrêt, l'organique retourne à l'organique, tout brûle inutilement et sans ardeur pour un vain contentement de luxe et de théâtre. . . . Toute pulsation s'est arrêtée au point mort. Le triomphe suprême des forces positives se résout en renoncement, leur jaillissement en sommeil, leur plénitude en faiblesse. Elles aussi, montées sur le faîte, aspirent à descendre. . . . La vie et la conscience sont, au dire des biologistes, des conquêtes pesantes pour la matière inorganisée qui tend toujours pour des raisons internes à retourner à l'état inanimé primitif. Le complexe de Nirvana, le désir essentiel d'atteindre une façon d'être qui soit à la fois un paroxysme et une démission n'aurait pas d'autre origine: on ne saurait en trouver de plus irréductible, de plus primaire. Si c'est à une telle nécessité que l'heure de midi offre un support sensible, ses prestiges sont assurés de toujours éveiller un écho complice dans le coeur humain." "Les démons de midi," Vol. 116, pp. 175-176.

[17] "The tendency to seek out optimum environmental conditions and to avoid dangerous and injurious ones is found in almost all animals and may be called shelter-seeking." J. P. Scott, *Animal Behavior* (Chicago, 1958), p. 59.

[18] Max Picard, *The World of Silence*, trans. Stanley Godman (London, 1948), p. 141.

[19] *Versi d'amore e di gloria*, 9th ed. (Milan, 1964), II, p. 972.

[20] Zanzotto's phrase occurs at the end of the second poem of "Altrui e mia," an evocation of the poet's native land in summer and of his mother who was born in that season. The first two and the last two verses are as follows:

> É luglio, la cicala
> Ha miriadi di petali; sei nata.
>
> . . . .
>
> Eri bambina, giacevi nella culla
> Nella fiamma delle cicale.

From *Vocativo* (Milan, 1957), pp. 19-20. The seasons, summer, and midday are an important part of the thematic content of Zanzotto's poetry.

[21] Vitaliano Brancati, *Paolo il Caldo* (Milan, 1955), p. 11.

[22] See Bachelard, *La terre et les rêveries du repos*, p. 3.

[23] I have here summarized the thoughts of Robert Mauzi who has dealt at length with this dichotomous relationship in relation to the idea of happiness in eighteenth-century French writers. He proposes the following definition for that age's concept of happiness: "l'état d'une âme ayant résolu l'antagonisme fondamental entre la tentation du vertige et le rêve du repos, entre le mouvement et l'immobilité." *L'idée du bonheur dans la littérature et la pensée françaises au XVIIIe siècle* (Paris, 1960), pp. 126-127. For his exhaustive treatment of the question see pp. 125-135 and 330-431. It is worth noting that midday does not appear to figure in eighteenth-century speculation on happiness.

[24] Angelo Conti, *La beata riva: trattato dell'oblìo* (Milan, 1900), pp. 242-243. My translation. Conti's reputation was very high at one time in Italy, so high that he was taken to be no less important a thinker than Henri Bergson. More interesting for us is the fact that he was the respected friend of D'Annunzio who, besides figuring as an interlocutor-antagonist in a part of Conti's book, wrote a long preface to it. In view of what we shall later see was the poet's quite different stance before midday, Conti's attitude takes on added interest.

[25] *The Collected Poems of Wallace Stevens*, p. 288.

[26] In a profounder way than is found in Conti, the rejection of the midday sun of unshadowed clarity in favor of half-lights, moonlight, or uncertain lights is found in Coleridge. The *locus classicus* for this poetic principle is the beginning of chapter XIV of *Biographia Literaria*, in the account of his early association with Wordsworth

and the discussions the two poets held on the nature of poetry: "During the first year that Mr. Wordsworth and I were neighbours, our conversations turned frequently on the two cardinal points of poetry, the power of exciting the sympathy of the reader by a faithful adherence to the truth of nature, and the power of giving the interest of novelty by the modifying colors of imagination. The sudden charm, which accidents of light and shade, which moonlight or sun-set diffused over a known and familiar landscape, appeared to represent the practicability of combining both. These are the poetry of nature." *Biographia Literaria*, ed. Shawcross, II, p. 5. Coleridge connected such images with the creative imagination, but also, as Humphrey House has noted, "with the subtler processes of the mind and the more delicate modes of feeling. They were used especially for the mysteries and uncertainties of mental life which Coleridge was beginning to explore more fully as he became more dissatisfied with the crude associationism represented by Hartley and its 'inanimate cold world.' " See House's essay on "The Ancient Mariner" in *English Romantic Poets: Modern Essays in Criticism*, ed. M. H. Abrams (New York, 1960), pp. 192-193. The essay was first published in House's *Coleridge: The Clark Lectures* (London, 1953), pp. 84-113. The use of moonlight to symbolize the imagination and its projection of a subjective element into external reality is a theme found also in Wallace Stevens. See, for example, his poem "Note on Moonlight" in *The Collected Poems*, pp. 531-532, or even "The Motive for Metaphor" (p. 288).

[27] In a lecture entitled "Inspirations méditerranéennes" given in 1933, Valéry says: "Mais avez-vous jamais regardé le soleil? Je ne vous le conseille pas. Je m'y suis risqué quelquefois dans mes temps héroiques, et j'ai pensé perdre la vue." But from there Valéry goes on to note the importance of the sun as a physical and symbolic phenomenon in the development of man's psyche. See Paul Valéry, *Conférences* (Paris, 1939), pp. 41-42.

[28] For the image of the breeze that signals the end of the midday stasis (experienced as a condition of "heavy beatitude") and a return to life (a state of movement, of change, etc.) see the paragraph "At Noontide" from Nietzsche's *Human, All Too Human*, quoted below, and note 37.

[29] Marghanita Laski, *Ecstasy: A Study of some Secular and Religious Experiences* (London, 1961), pp. 189-190. My italics.

[30] Mircea Eliade, *Images and Symbols: Studies in Religious Symbolism*, trans. Philip Mairet (New York, 1952), pp. 74-75.

[31] Ibid., p. 75.

Notes to Pages 22-26   275

³² Nietzsche, *Götzendämmerung, Der AntiChrist, Ecce Homo, Gedichte* (Stuttgart, 1964), p. 495. Sils-Maria is the name of the village in the Upper Engadine where Nietzsche passed the summers from 1881 to 1888 save for 1882. It should be noted that the poem also commemorates an ecstatic midday vision experienced by Nietzsche while on the Ligurian coast, a region he much favored. In some manuscripts of the poem, the title is given as "Portofino." See Charles Andler, *Nietzsche, sa vie, et sa pensée*, II (Paris, 1958), p. 472. If one uses "Portofino" as the title, then the word *See* is to be understood not as *lake* but *sea*.

³³ *The Philosophy of Nietzsche* (New York, 1927, 1954), p. xxv.

³⁴ I quote from the well-known translation by Thomas Common, printed in *The Philosophy of Nietzsche* (see preceding note). The words cited occur at pp. 308-309 and are from the chapter entitled "Noontide" in *Thus Spake Zarathustra* (part IV, 70). The next three brief quotations are from this same chapter, at pp. 309-310.

³⁵ In *Ecce Homo*, Nietzsche wrote: "My life-task is to prepare for humanity a moment of supreme self-consciousness, a great Noontide when it will gaze both backwards and forwards, when it will emerge from the tyranny of accident and the priesthood, and for the first time pose the question of the Why and Wherefore of humanity as a whole." Ibid., p. 887. The announcement of the great midday is the promise of the actualization of potentiality, a call to a cultural "resurrection" for Western man. The great midday signifies the time when man will have overcome the merely human and so step onto the plane of the superman. Philosophically and historically, such a midday presupposes the "death of God," the destruction of the traditional Western metaphysics and ethics that have prevented the realization of the potential. In *Thus Spake Zarathustra* (part IV, 73, 2), we read: "Before God!—Now however this God hath died! Ye higher men, this God was your greatest danger. Only since he lay in the grave have ye again arisen. Now only cometh the great noontide, now only doth the higher man become—master!" Ibid., p. 320.

³⁶ In the *Nachgelassene Werke von Friedrich Nietzsche*, published in *Werke* (Leipzig, 1901), XII, pp. 63, 362.

³⁷ Bollnow noted that the difference between this passage from *Human, All Too Human* and the employment of the midday topos in *Zarathustra* lies in the fact that in the first case it is a matter of midday as a simple pause followed by the return of life's habitual course, whereas in the second the great noontide refers to a fundamental turning point in history whereby a new phase or "another history" is to begin. As to the doctrine of eternal return, Bollnow too holds that

it is to be understood as a conceptual interpretation of the sentiment of eternity experienced in the supreme beatitude of midday. See *Das Wesen der Stimmungen*, pp. 208-210.

[38] Nietzsche, *Götzendämmerung, Der AntiChrist, Ecce Homo, Gedichte*, p. 495.

[39] In his work on the concept of the holy, Rudolf Otto discusses the German word *ungeheuer*: "The German *ungeheuer* is not by derivation simply 'huge,' in quantity or quality;—this, its common meaning, is in fact a rationalizing interpretation of the real idea; it is that which is not *geheuer*, i.e., approximately, the *uncanny*—in a word, the numinous. If this, its fundamental meaning, be really and thoroughly felt in consciousness, then the word could be taken as a fairly exact expression for the numinous in its aspects of mystery, awefulness, majesty, augustness, and 'energy'; nay even the aspect of fascination is dimly felt in it." *The Idea of the Holy*, trans. John W. Harvey (New York, 1958), p. 40. The term *weird* which is given by Otto as the best English equivalent for the concept in question would perhaps not be a good choice to translate *ungeheuer* as used in Nietzsche's poem.

[40] Henry Daniel-Rops, *Jesus and His Times*, trans. Ruby Millar (New York, 1956), p. 409.

[41] Hugo Rahner, *Greek Myths and Christian Mystery* (New York, 1963), p. 93.

[42] See J. M. Neale, *Medieval Hymns and Sequences* (London, 1867), pp. 93, 97. For the place of prayer at the hour of none see *The Catholic Encyclopaedia*, XIII (New York, 1910), p. 947. And for a brief historical survey of *noon* in English see the entry in *A New English Dictionary*, VI, part II (Oxford, 1908), pp. 204-205. Eventually *none* became our English *noon* under the influence of the advancing of the prayers of the canonical hours. In the Florence of Dante's time the *ora nona* no longer referred to three o'clock in the afternoon, but to midday or noon, according to the testimony of the chronicler G. Villani: "essendo il sole al meriggio, che noi volgarmente diciamo ora di nona." *Cronica di Giovanni Villani* (Florence, 1845), III, p. 333. Dante notes that the church bells must ring at the beginning of the seventh hour of the day (i.e., just after noon), because they gave the signal of the beginning of the liturgical *nona*.

[43] See the excellent treatment of this subject in Jackson I. Cope, *The Metaphoric Structure of Paradise Lost* (Baltimore, 1962), pp. 134-146 and in Albert R. Cirillo, "Noon-Midnight and the Temporal Structure of *Paradise Lost*," *ELH*, 29 (December 1962), no. 4, pp. 372-395.

⁴⁴ Obviously, there are various ways of reading Coleridge's poem, but just as obviously this is not the place for a treatment of the matter. I would, however, mention Robert Penn Warren's rich essay *The Rime of the Ancient Mariner by S. T. Coleridge, with an Essay by Robert Penn Warren* (New York, 1946), which in part interprets the poem in terms of the beneficent life of the imagination, symbolized by the moon under whose light the favorable and saving events of the Mariner's story occur, and the hostile clarity of reason (and conscience?), symbolized by the sun. At one point Warren writes of the sun that "it is the light which shows the familiar, it is the light of practical convenience, it is the light in which pride preens itself, it is, to adopt Coleridge's later terminology, the light of the 'understanding,' it is the light of that 'mere reflective faculty' that 'partook of Death' " (p. 93). One must also turn to Humphrey House's pages on the poem and the correctives he supplies to Warren's essay, much admired as it is by him, in *Coleridge: The Clark Lectures 1951-1952*, reprinted in *English Romantic Poets*, ed. Abrams, pp. 170-195.

⁴⁵ Vaughan's poem "The Night" begins with the following stanza:

> Through that pure virgin shrine,
>   That sacred veil drawn o'er Thy glorious noon,
> That men might look and live, as glow-worms shine,
>   And face the moon:
> Wise Nicodemus saw such light
> As made him know his God by night.

The first and the last stanzas of the poem by Herman Melville, entitled "In the Desert" (a manuscript variation has "The Egyptian Noon"), may be quoted for the image of an immense midday light that the poet hails as the glorious "effluence" of God's essence:

> Never Pharoh's Night
> Whereof the Hebrew wizards croon,
> Did so the Theban flamens try
> As me this veritable Noon
>
> . . . .
> Holy, holy, holy Light!
> Immaterial incandescence,
> Of God the effluence of the essence,
> Shekinah intolerably bright!

In *Collected Poems of Herman Melville*, ed. H. P. Vincent (Chicago, 1947), pp. 253-254. In Alexander Pope's *Messiah* (which he called a "sacred eclogue") the vision of a new glorious age that is to come upon the advent of the Messiah is given by way of imagery that speaks of the rising sun and the evening moon as being superseded and absorbed into a midday that is "One Tyde of Glory, one unclouded Blaze."

[46] *A Philosophical Enquiry into the Origin of our Ideas of the Sublime and Beautiful*, ed. J. T. Boulton (London and New York, 1958), p. 80. Burke's observation is made in commenting on a line by Milton in which the poet "describes the light and glory which flows from the divine presence." He comments further on the matter thus: "Here is an idea not only poetical in an high degree, but strictly and philosophically just. Extreme light, by overcoming the organs of sight, obliterates all objects, so as in its effect exactly to resemble darkness. After looking for some time at the sun, two black spots, the impression which it leaves, seem to dance before our eyes. Thus are two ideas as opposite as can be imagined reconciled in the extremes of both; and both in spite of their opposite nature brought to concur in producing the sublime" (pp. 80-81).

[47] Romano Guardini, *Sacred Signs*, trans. Grace Branham (St. Louis, 1965), p. 93.

CHAPTER I

[1] *Convivio*, II, xiii, 15-16.

[2] Most commentators on the *Divine Comedy* agree that the time in question is midday. Charles S. Singleton's annotation deserves to be quoted here: "Now it is noon in Eden, midnight in Jerusalem, the hemisphere of water is all light, the hemisphere of land all dark. It should be recalled that the entrance into Inferno took place in the evening and that the journey through Purgatory began at dawn. Now the upward journey of Paradise will begin at high noon. The symbolic value of this arrangement is rich in meaning and is, of course, deliberately calculated. . . . The sun is in full glory, and the *Paradiso* has begun with an invocation to Apollo, god of the Sun." *The Divine Comedy*, translated with a commentary, by C. S. Singleton; *Paradiso*: 2 *Commentary* (Princeton, N.J., 1975), p. 15.

[3] *Convivio*, IV, xxiii, 10-11. In point of fact, Luke (who is referred to by Dante) does not say that Christ died at the *ora sexta* (noon sharp) but that it was about noon when the darkness came over the

earth and, with Christ on the cross, lasted for three hours. At the end of this period Christ died (Luke 23:24).

⁴ *Expositio in Psalmum* CXVIII, in *Patrologia Latina*, ed. Migne, vol. 15, col. 1,385.

⁵ In journeying into the after-world, and especially into Paradise, Dante was conscious of a parallel between himself and St. Paul who was raised to the third heaven in a rapture (*Inferno*, II, 28-32; *Paradiso*, I, 73-75; 2 Cor. 12: 2-3). Thus it is well to recall here that Paul's mystic encounter with Christ on the road to Damascus occurred at midday.

In the last canto of the *Paradiso*, during the great prayer to the Virgin in which Bernard implores that Blessed Lady's mediation for Dante so that the pilgrim can take the last step of his journey to God, the saint addresses these extraordinary words to her:

> Qui se' a noi meridiana face
> Di caritate, e giuso, intra i mortali
> Se' di speranza fontana verace. (XXXIII, 10-12)

Exalted praise, indeed, for the Virgin is here said to be the midday sun (or a burning torch like the midday sun) that kindles love in the blessed souls residing in Paradise. One would have thought such a role to be exclusively God's. The Christian tradition, at any rate, has long been familiar with the expression "noonday blaze of charity."

⁶ It is significant that Dante felt the need to include the figure of the goatherd in the scene although there is no corresponding figure in the narration of the poem. Virgil and Statius have their term of comparison not in the simile given above but in the immediately succeeding image which speaks of the shepherd who spends the night in the open alongside his flock in order to protect it from wild beasts: "E quale il mandrian che fòro alberga, / Lungo il peculio suo quieto pernotta, / Guardando perchè fiera non lo sperga" (82-84).

⁷ "*Non era di molto spazio sonata nona*, che la reina [Pampinea, selected "queen" for the group], levatasi, tutte l'altre fece levare, e similmente i giovani, affermando esser nocivo il troppo dormire il giorno; e così se n'andarono in uno pratello, nel quale l'erba era verde e grande, *né vi poteva d'alcuna parte il sole*; e, quivi, sentendo un soave venticello venire, sì come volle la lor reina, tutti sopra la verde erba si puosero in cerchio a sedere." *Decameron, Filocolo, Ameto, Fiammetta*, ed. E. Bianchi, C. Salinari, N. Sapegno (Milan and Naples, 1952), p. 24. (My italics.) The olive trees are mentioned immediately after this passage.

If, as we have seen, the liturgical *ora nona* in Florence corresponded to the solar hour of midday, the time reference in this passage is not clear, for the activities of the *lieta brigata* begin with a nap. The *ora nona* may refer to three o'clock (or, possibly, to one o'clock). In any case the overall period in question is noontide, and whatever solar hour is intended here by the liturgical reference *ora nona*, no prayers in accordance with the Divine Office will be said by this group.

[8] Ibid. The discussion and the discussants are different in Plato's *Phaedrus*, but the principle of pausing in the shade to talk rather than venturing into the midday sun is the same. Socrates has invited Phaedrus to sit and talk. After a while, Socrates is ready to leave, but Phaedrus detains him thus: "Not yet, Socrates: not until the heat of the day has passed; do you not see that the hour is almost noon? There is the midday sun standing still, as people say, in the meridian. Let us rather stay and talk over what has been said, and then return in the cool." *The Dialogues of Plato*, trans. B. Jowett (New York, 1937), I, p. 246. The dialogue, in fact, takes place under a shady plane tree on a grassy bank by a stream. The spot was sought out by Socrates and Phaedrus, and the latter observes that they may even cool their feet in the water. And this "at midday and in the summer is far from being unpleasant" (I, p. 235).

[9] It is worth remembering that Boccaccio cites as the most commonly held opinion the idea that the plague was a chastizing visitation of God brought on by the wickedness of man. *Decameron* . . . , pp. 18-19.

[10] "Lia così cominciò con le donne: —Giovani, il sole tiene ancora il dì librato [i.e., it is still noontide]: per che la sua calda luce ne vieta di qui partirci; i pastori dormono, le cui sampogne poco avanti ne ficiono festa, e ogni maniera di diletto infino alla bassa ora c'è tolta, fuori solamente quello che i nostri ragionamenti ne posson dare; i quali di niuna cosa conosco così convenevoli, considerata l'odierna solennità, come li nostri amori narrare." *Commedia delle ninfe fiorentine (Ameto)*, ed. A. E. Quaglio (Florence, 1963), pp. 65-66.

[11] Ibid., p. 27.

[12] Another classical source for the theme of midday eroticism as we find it in Boccaccio's passage and even more so as it was to be developed later, is to be found in Ovid's *Amores*, I, 5, referred to in my introduction.

[13] Boccaccio's "profanation" of midday occurs in his earliest literary work of any consequence, the *Caccia di Diana*. Beautiful damsels who have joined Diana's troupe and hunted all morning are called by

the chaste but cold goddess at noon, the hour of respite, for Diana wishes to offer a sacrifice to Jove. But in the heat of midday, the maids, whose breasts burn with erotic desire, revolt against her and reject her invitation to become full-fledged members of her train. The indignant (but here evidently powerless) Diana leaves, returning to heaven whence she descended. (It is likely that Diana adumbrates the Holy Virgin in this work.) The maids then invoke another goddess who is more in keeping with their inclinations. Venus, in fact, in the shape of an "ignuda giovinetta" descends from the heavens and immediately succors them.

[14] As one commentator's terse annotation on the verb *Stetti* puts it: "Voluttuosa lunga contemplazione." Petrarca, *Rime sparse*, ed. Ezio Chiorboli (Milan, 1924), p. 48. Concerning hunters as fauns and vice versa, we may point out that Boccaccio shows himself (or one of his characters) to be a true midday faun considerably beyond the voyeurism stage of Actaeon, Ameto, or Petrarch in the *Ninfale fiesolano* (stanzas 209-245), where Africo succeeds in ravishing the nymph Mensola. Significantly, this episode has another Ovidian source: the tale of amorous Jove's rape of the nymph Callisto at the height of a fiercely hot noontide (*Metamorphoses*, II, 417 ff.).

[15] It is also less tremulous or "religious" than the attitude of wonder or ecstasy (or "bewilderment") of the *dolce stil nuovo* poets whose verse Boccaccio is also echoing in his own lyric poetry. But in the two sonnets referred to above, Boccaccio seems closer to Petrarch precisely because of the common Ovidian source that also informs their respective pieces and makes them landmarks in what I have called a new or modern (secular) midday nympholepsy. Boccaccio's allusions to the meridian position of the sun are clearly derivative from the tale of Actaeon. It is, however, characteristic of his idealization of the noontide retreat that in both sonnets, a mild breeze is present. For the sonnets I have used V. Branca's indispensable edition, G. Boccaccio, *Rime, Caccia di Diana* (Padua, 1958).

[16] Lest I be misunderstood in my reading, I would repeat that in no way do I consider the first, the "grammatical," reading to be undercut by the second (or "other") meaning even though this other meaning may be the real reason for the poem. Nonetheless, one may make the following observation without being bound by it in order to see the double meaning. Even grammatically one can argue that the initial *Che* of line 6—"Ch'a l'aura il vago e biondo capel chiuda"—can *also* be considered a direct object having an antecedent in the immediately preceding *velo* (in the sense of body or an even

more specifically erogenous zone). The subject then becomes the beautiful blonde hair that "encloses" Laura (*l'aura* = *Laura*), that is, keeps her nakedness (partly) concealed, or it could even be the pubic hair that conceals Laura's hymen. None of this is a *necessary* reading, because Petrarch has concealed it all behind the propriety of the first reading. As to the subjunctive *chiuda*, it is needed for the rhyme with *ignuda* and *cruda*, but it does not offer any more of a problem in this second semantic context than in the more straightforwardly grammatical one. By the same token the initial *Tal* of line 7 that introduces the motif of the poet's erotic chill may refer not only to the whole scene and the action of the "shepherdess" but also and more specifically to the *velo*. Again, however, this is not crucial to an acceptance of a generic double meaning in the poem.

[17] "Contra autem hic noster nil prepropere, sed fugientis temporis cursum videns et cupiens illic esse ubi sine fluxu temporum ac sine metu mortis degitur, iterum versus in preces, non unius tantum lucis, sed totius evi claram vesperam et nunquam occidentis vite gloriam—eamque non suo merito, sed sacre Cristi mortis—poscit in praemium." In Francesco Petrarca, *Prose*, ed. G. Martellotti et al. (Milan and Naples, 1955), p. 312.

[18] This noontide drama takes up five stanzas in all, although in typical Ariostesque fashion it is interrupted only to be picked up after a considerable space. The stanzas occur in *Orlando Furioso*, VIII, 19-21 and X, 35-36.

[19] Peter V. Marinelli, *Pastoral* (London, 1971), p. 47.

[20] In his annotated edition to the work, Enrico Carrara sees the "shepherdesses" of both Petrarch and Sannazaro as *washerwomen*. "L'invenzione deriva dal madrigale del Petrarca, *Non al suo amante*: ove si tratta parimenti d'una lavandaina." *Opere di Iacopo Sannazaro* (Turin, 1952), p. 55. (I have used this edition for my quotations from the *Arcadia*.)

In his English translation ("literal beyond the usual") of the work, Ralph Nash has opted for a rendering that leaves no room for a doubling meaning. He sees the shepherdess with her skirts raised to her knees washing out a garment while standing in midstream under the hot sky. For Nash's rendering, see Jacopo Sannazaro, *Arcadia and Piscatorial Eclogues*, translated with an introduction by Ralph Nash (Detroit, 1966), p. 30. The work also includes a good introduction.

[21] "Qui dove alta in sul lido elce verdeggia, / Le braccia aprendo in spazïosi giri, / E del suo crin ne' liquidi zaffiri / Gli smeraldi vaghissimi vagheggia; // Qui, qui, Lilla, ricorra, ove l'arena / Fresca in

ogni stagion copre e circonda / Folta di verdi rami ombrosa scena. // Godrai qui meco in un l'acque e la sponda; / Vedrai scherzar su per la riva amena / Il pesce con l'augel, l'ombra con l'onda." In *Marino e i Maristi*, ed. G. G. Ferrero (Milan and Naples, 1954), p. 343.

[22] Ibid., p. 920.

[23] "Ferve il ciel, bolle il suol, langue ogni fronda, / E qual tomba di foco, urna d'ardore, / Assetata la terra arde infeconda" (9-11). In *Opere scelte di G. B. Marino e dei Maristi*, ed. G. Getto (Turin, 1962), II (*I Maristi*), p. 352.

[24] See Paul Van Tieghem, *Le sentiment de la Nature dans le Préromantisme Européen* (Paris, 1960), p. 36. An important essay on the philosophical and aesthetic implications in eighteenth-century poetry of the seasons is Rosario Assunto's "Arte e natura nella poesia stagionale settecentesca," in the author's *Stagioni e ragioni nell'estetica del Settecento* (Milan, 1967), pp. 11-59. (The essay appeared first in 1965 in the *Rivista di Estetica*.) For the motif of the seasons in medieval literature, with pertinent references to ancient Latin sources, a study that remains of much value is Rosemond Tuve's *Seasons and Months: Studies in a Tradition of Middle English Poetry* (Paris, 1933).

[25] *Le sentiment de la nature*, p. 131.

[26] Quoted in Elizabeth Wheeler Manning's *Italian Landscape in Eighteenth Century England* (New York and London, 1925), p. 14.

[27] Dwight L. Durling, *Georgic Tradition in English Poetry* (New York, 1935), p. 54.

[28] Saint-Lambert consciously structures his themes on the element of contrast. See his "Discours préliminaire" in *Les Saisons* (Amsterdam, 1769), p. xvii. For the text of the poem I have used the excellent edition prepared by Luigi de Nardis in his *Saint-Lambert: Scienza e paesaggio nella poesia del Settecento* (Rome, 1961). The verses cited appear on p. xxvii.

[29] *Poesie di Ossian*, rendered into Italian verse by the abbot M. Cesarotti (Pisa, 1801), p. 108. Cesarotti's version of Ossian appeared first between 1762 and 1772. The original of the passage quoted above reads as follows: "O sun! Terrible is thy beauty, son of heaven, when death is descending on thy locks; when thou rollest thy vapours before thee, over the blasted host." *The Poems of Ossian, etc., containing the Poetical Works of James Macpherson, Esq. in Prose and Rhyme* (Edinburgh, 1805), II, p. 78.

[30] See Assunto, *Stagioni e ragioni nell'estetica del Settecento*, p. 22.

[31] "Pur l'estate tormentosa / S'io rimiro, amata Fille, / Le tue placide pupille, / Sì penosa a me non è. / . . . Un ombrosa opaca

valle / Cela il monte al caldo sol: // . . . Là del sol dubbia è la luce / Come suol notturna luna; / Né pastor greggia importuna / Vi conduce a pascolar." *Tutte le opere di Pietro Metastasio*, ed. B. Brunelli, II (Milan, 1947), p. 773. Similar features, with the same aristocratic disdain for proletarian reapers and rusticity in the real, are to be found in the brief cantata, *L'estate*, of 1759. Ibid., p. 749.

On the other hand, Alexander Pope's pastoral, "Summer," presents the topos in a manner more in keeping with the Virgilian mode:

> But see, the shepherds shun the noonday heat;
> The lowering herds to murmuring brooks retreat;
> To closer shades the panting flocks remove;
> Ye Gods! and is there no relief for love?
> But soon the sun with milder rays descends
> To the cool ocean, where his journey ends:
> On me love's fiercer flames for ever pray,
> By night he scorches, as he burns by day. (85-92)

[32] *Poesie dell'Abate Carlo Innocenzo Frugoni* (Lucca, 1779), III, pp. 335 and 338. There is a second poem on summer ("La state") by Frugoni in which the nymph (Clori) is more directly invited to escape from midday's broiling heat into Love's shady bower. Ibid., IX, pp. 106-108.

[33] See G. Santangelo's introduction to G. Meli, *Opere* (Milan, 1965), I, p. 68. It is from this edition (pp. 191-202) that I quote Meli's poem.

[34] *Operette in verso e in prosa dell'Abate De' Giorgi-Bertola* (Bassano, 1785), I, p. 63. I also quote the poem from this edition.

[35] For Socrates' invitation to pause to talk in the shade at midday, see above at note 8.

[36] *Operette in verso e in prosa*, I, pp. 155-156; 172-173.

[37] Ibid., pp. 243-244.

[38] *Saggio di Prose e Poesie Campestri* (Verona, 1795), p. 50.

[39] Ibid., p. 61.

[40] There is an indirect but significant confession of recoil from the blaze of the midday sun in Pindemonte's verse epistle "To Homer." In this poem the translator of the *Odyssey* admits to an inability to translate the *Iliad*. For in the *Iliad*, he says, Homer is like the overmastering sun at noon that Pindemonte's gaze cannot sustain. In the *Odyssey*, however, the Greek poet is like the sun at its setting, having still a grandeur of its own yet with its rays tempered so that the Italian poet can reach toward it: "È ver, che quando il sì fatale ai Greci / Sdegno tu canti del Pelìde Achille, / Sole sei tu, che raggi a

denti e forti / Scocca in furia dall'alto, e audace troppo, / Mirando allora in te, fôra il mio sguardo. / Ma se racconti del ramingo Ulisse / Il difficile ad Itaca ritorno, / Come sole che piega in vêr l'Occaso, / Benchè grande non men, pur della luce / Così ritieni i più pungenti dardi, / Che vagheggiarti io posso, e di te spero / Con pennello toscan trar qualche imago." *Opere di Ippolito Pindemonte* (Naples, 1854), p. 459. Perhaps mention should be made here of Giuseppe Barbieri, author of a poetic seasonal cycle, *Le stagioni*, for which he felt he deserved the title of Italian successor to Thomson and Saint-Lambert. His "Estate" contains a brief (eight lines) description of a midday countryside, parched and languishing, and filled with the endless din of the cicadas. It is relieved by a rainstorm. *Opere* (Padua, 1823), pp. 9, 72.

Charles Baudelaire evinces the same negative attitude and uneasiness in connection with midday which is significantly absent as an attribute of Beauty in his "Hymne à la Beauté" whereas sunset and sunrise are in evidence: "Tu contiens dans ton oeil le couchant et l'aurore." Baudelaire's preference for sunrise and even more for sunset has been studied by Marc Eigeldinger in "La symbolique solaire dans la poésie de Baudelaire," *Revue d'histoire littéraire de la France*, 67 (April-June 1967), pp. 357-374. Eigeldinger notes the French poet's aversion to the violence of the midday sun: "il hait l'intensité du feu solaire qui brûle dessèche et dévore, qui exerce une action destructrice sur le monde et l'humanité" (p. 361). In Milton's *Paradise Lost*, Eve celebrates the beauty of the world by twice referring to the rising sun of morn, the advent of evening, and the silent moonlit night. From this "hymn to beauty," too, midday is absent. See *Paradise Lost*, IV, 639-658.

CHAPTER II

[1] *Le ultime lettere di Jocopo Ortis,* letter of May 15, 1798.

[2] For the *Ameto* reference, see the previous chapter. Usually noontide is represented as the hour of such total immobility that even the wind is at rest. Indeed, we have seen that the end of noontide is signaled by the rising of the wind in the case of Valéry and Nietzsche (see the introduction). Thus the presence of the breezes in Foscolo's passage may cause one to question whether midday is intended. But aside from the fact that Foscolo (in some ways more Greek than Italian) was writing with knowledge of the ancients' representation of nympholepsy as a midday phenomenon, his own evocation is a highly idealized depiction. We have to do not with a wind in the

usual sense, but with soft caressing breezes that cause just the amount of stirring in nature (rippling of the waves and slight undulation in grass and flowers) needed to convey an intimation of voluptuousness and to complete the suggestion of a *locus amoenus*. In this sense, the presence of a breeze is not an uncommon feature in noonscapes. We may recall that Zephyr is present both in the verses evoking midday in Boccaccio's *Ameto* and in the idealized noonscape of the *Decameron*. We have also noted its presence in Pindemonte's "Mezzogiorno."

[3] In this respect one may compare it with the charming eight-line fragment of midday eroticism (tensionless even if more overtly faunesque) of the French neoclassical poet André Chenier:

> Je sais, quand le midi leur fait désirer l'ombre,
> Entrer à pas muets sous le roc frais et sombre
> D'où, parmi le cresson et l'humide gravier,
> Une source se fraie un oblique sentier.
> Là j'épie à loisir la Nymphe blanche et nue
> Sur un banc de gazon mollement étendu,
> Qui dort, et sur sa main, au murmure des eaux,
> Laisse tomber son front couronné de roseaux.

In *Les Bucoliques*, ed. José-Maria De Hérédia (Paris, 1907), p. 134. Most editions give the fourth line as "La naïde se fraye un oblique sentier"; the words *Une source*, in fact, are a variant.

[4] In a famous discourse (in the form of a letter to the Marchese Cesare D'Azeglio) on the question of romanticism in Italy, Manzoni condemns the use of classical mythology in modern literature because of its basis in a morality that is limited to earthly values to the point of idolatry. This "idolatry" survives even though the belief in the existence of the supernatural beings of mythology is dead.

[5] " . . . Così // Dalle squarciate nuvole / Si svolge il sol cadente, / E, dietro il monte, imporpora / Il trepido occidente: / Al pio colono augurio / Di più sereno dì" (114-120).

[6] In *Tutti gli scritti inediti, rari e editi 1809-1810 di Giacomo Leopardi*, ed. Maria Corti (Milan, 1972), pp. 51-52. The poem may be read under the title "La campagna" in the well-known editions of the complete poems of Leopardi by F. Flora and W. Binni.

[7] *Tutti gli scritti di Leopardi*, ed. Corti, pp. 30-31.

[8] *Tutte le opere di Giacomo Leopardi*, ed. Francesco Flora (Milan, 1953), *Le poesie e le prose*, II, pp. 280-281.

[9] Ibid., p. 281.

[10] Ibid., p. 290.

[11] That the whole passage I have quoted, and not just that part of it that introduces the shepherd, is connected with the midday hour is made clear even by Leopardi's own annotation: "Anticamente correvano parecchie false immaginazioni appartenenti all'ora del mezzogiorno, e fra l'altre, che gli Dei, le ninfe, i silvani, i fauni e simili, aggiunto le anime de' morti, si lasciassero vedere o sentire particolarmente su quell'ora." From the *Annotazioni* to the ten *canzoni* published at Bologna in 1824. In *Tutte le opere di Leopardi*, ed. Flora, *Le poesie e le prose*, I, p. 174. In this annotation Leopardi cites a number of the secondary sources that he had already used in his *Saggio sopra gli errori popolari degli antichi*.

[12] In his *Annotazioni*, Leopardi himself calls attention to the episode and, incidentally, again refers it specifically to midday: "Circa all'opinione che le ninfe e le Dee sull'ora del mezzogiorno si scendessero a lavare ne' fiumi o ne' fonti, dà un'occhiata all'Elegia di Callimaco *Sopra i lavacri di Pallade*, e in particolare quanto a Diana, vedi il terzo libro delle *Metamorfosi*." Ibid., p. 175.

[13] I believe that a sort of noontide nympholepsy is fleetingly suggested in the opening verses of the poem "Alla sua donna": "Cara beltà che amore / Lunge m'inspiri o nascondendo il viso; / Fuor se nel sonno il core / Ombra diva mi scuoti, / O ne' campi ove splenda / Più vago il giorno e di natura il riso." The point of these lines, as of the rest of the poem, is that the poet's "lady"—an abstract concept of loveliness with affective value (*Cara beltà*) and, so, a poignant projection of the desire for happiness—is an ideal with no possibility of an incarnation in a real creature. The only time that this divine incorporeal creature (*Ombra diva*) appears to the poet with her countenance disclosed (suggesting an ecstatic vision) is when she appears to the poet in a nocturnal dream or in the open country when the sun shines most brilliantly and nature is accordingly most radiant. This latter moment refers, it seems to me, to the luminosity of midday in which the poet is thrilled by a *vision fugitive*.

[14] The words *Nè farfalla ronzar* evidently are meant to suggest the presence, or rather the absence, not only of butterflies that flutter (but do not of course buzz or drone) but also of bees or mosquitos (which do buzz).

[15] It seems to me that Emilio Peruzzi misses the point when, after noting that the still sultriness and blinding glare of the midday sun are absent in Leopardi, he goes on to complain that even when the poet attempts to convey such impressions, as in "La vita solitaria," he succeeds only in describing the opposite: "In Leopardi non si trova mai l'accecante fulgore del sole meridiano, l'aria che fiammeg-

gia senza respiro. . . . Leopardi non riesce a sentire l'immobile calura meridiana ed anche quando si prova ad esprimerla finisce per descrivere proprio l'opposto come nella *Vita solitaria* 28-32 (nè gli vale servirsi della negazione perchè questa, come tutti i morfemi, non ha valore poetico)." "Saggio di lettura leopardiana," *Vox Romanica*, 15 (July-December 1956), pp. 148-149. The truth is, of course, that Leopardi succeeded amazingly well in creating the impression of midday's stillness which is what he was writing about, but not of hot sultriness, which is what Peruzzi evidently thinks the poet *ought* to have been trying to express. Moreover, he has succeeded precisely by way of a use of negatives which Peruzzi curiously prejudges as being ipso facto without poetic value.

The vision of a lifeless world lying beneath a midday sun is evoked by Leopardi also in the "Cantico del gallo silvestre," the most apocalyptic of his *Operette morali*: "Se sotto l'astro diurno [i.e., the sun], languendo per la terra in profondissima quiete tutti i viventi, non apparisse opera alcuna; non muggito di buoi per li prati, nè strepito di fiere per le foreste, nè canto di uccelli per l'aria, nè sussurro d'api o di farfalle scorresse per la campagna; non voce, non moto alcuno, se non delle acque, del vento e delle tempeste, sorgesse in alcuna banda; certo l'universo sarebbe inutile; ma forse che vi si troverebbe o copia minore di felicità, o più di miseria, che oggi non vi si trova?"

[16] Such as in Richard Jeffries from whom the phrases in quotation marks are taken. See *The Story of My Heart* (London, 1968), p. 140.

[17] Thomas G. Rosenmeyer, *The Green Cabinet* (Berkeley and Los Angeles, 1969), pp. 89-90.

[18] In Friedrich Heiler's study on prayer, there is a distinction made between ecstasy and nirvana that can serve to define the character of the Italian poet's *meriggio*: "Ecstasy is boiling point, Nirvana is freezing point, ecstasy is a positive height, Nirvana is a negative height (and yet as 'height' something positive); ecstasy is infinite fulness, Nirvana is infinite emptiness. . . . [Ecstasy] is generally pictured as a being 'seized,' 'overmastered,' 'submerged,' 'swallowed up,' 'possessed,' 'filled full.' Nirvana, on the contrary, is complete disappearance of emotion, a continuous permanent state of profound quiet and perfect solitariness, a blessedness without excitement, transport, or storm, not a being possessed, but a being utterly self-absorbed." *Prayer: A Study in the History and Psychology of Religion*, trans. and ed. Samuel McComb (New York, 1958), p. 140.

[19] There are other passages in Leconte de Lisle's poetry where the

midday moment appears as a burning, consuming stasis with metaphysical implications. In particular I think of "La mort de Valimki" where as "Tout se tait" and "L'univers embrasé se consume," the sage goes to his voluntary death. But it is a moment of contemplation of a sunset on the sea that brings Leconte de Lisle even closer to Leopardi's self-absorbed midday of "La vita solitaria" than does "Midi." It occurs in the poem "L'orbe d'or" which concludes with the following quatrain: "Et l'âme, qui contemple, et soi-même s'oublie / Dans la splendide paix du silence divin, / Sans regret ni désirs, sachant que tout est vain, / En un rêve éternel s'abîme ensevelie."

[20] I do not mean to imply that only poems about midday reveal this relationship with Leopardi's lyric. One could make a small anthology of poems in which subsequent authors have situated their versions of "L'infinito" in one of the other three parts of the day.

[21] In *Poeti minori dell'Ottocento*, ed. Luigi Baldacci (Milan and Naples, 1958), I, p. 356.

[22] Ibid., pp. 827-828.

[23] In *Poeti minori dell'Ottocento italiano*, ed. Ferruccio Ulivi (Milan, 1963), p. 565.

[24] Ibid., p. 751. In a more traditional religious vein, Niccolò Tommaseo's "Preghiera a Mezzodì" recognizes in the radiance of the midday sun the image of the glory of God: "Diciamo alle valli ed ai monti illuminati dal sole meridiano: Ripeteteci la parola del Signore. Tutto l'universo è ripieno dello splendore della gloria di Dio. Un giorno, un'ora che Dio ci dà, può essere mille secoli di benedizione." *Poesie e prose di Niccolò Tommaseo*, ed. P. P. Trompeo and P. Ciureanu (Turin, 1966), I, p. 220.

[25] In *Poeti minori dell'Ottocento*, ed. Baldacci, I, p. 747.

[26] Zanella may also have been aware of the figure of "la bionda Maria" of Carducci's "Idillio maremmano" which was published first. And how different is this meridian Ruth from the tragic noontide protagonist of Verga's "La lupa" which we are presently to consider.

[27] Giovanni Verga, *Opere*, ed. L. Russo (Milan and Naples, 1955), p. 126. The novella was first published in 1880 in the volume *Vita dei campi*. In a note to the text, Russo has explained the inversion of the sequence of terms in the expression *fra vespero e nona* as the result of Verga's desire to emphasize the rhyme between *buona* and *nona*. At any rate, the hours intended are not three to six, but the midday hours, which according to Sicilian beliefs are ruled over by malefic

spirits. In short, we have another example of the liturgical terms (*nona* and *vespero*) being used to refer to the diurnal hours of noon to three.

[28] That *la Lupa* is seen as the midday demon especially by her son-in-law (her victim) is indicated by the fact that after he has surrendered to her for the first time in the noontide hour, in despair and remorse he explicitly addresses to her the expression used first by the narrator in describing her midday sally: "—No! non ne va in volta femmina buona nell'ora fra vespero e nona!—singhiozzava Nanni, ricacciando la faccia contro l'erba secca del fossato, in fondo in fondo, colle unghie nei capelli." Yet another indication occurs in the play Verga adapted from the novella. Here when Nanni finally raises the ax to slay *la Lupa* (as one might do to a real wolf), he shouts wildly at her in the last words of the play: "Ah! . . . ah! . . . Il diavolo siete?"—whereupon the curtain falls.

One may compare the figure of *la Lupa* with Baudelaire's *belle Dorothée*. The latter too is portrayed as the only living creature who dares to walk under the immense blue sky during noontide when the sun rains its brutal light and heat upon the city: "Le soleil accable la ville de sa lumière droite et terrible. . . . Cependant Dorothée, forte et fière comme le soleil, s'avance dans la rue déserte, seule vivante à cette heure sous l'immense azur, et faisant sur la lumière une tache éclatante et noire." "La Belle Dorothée," from *Le spleen de Paris*, in *Oeuvres complètes* (Paris, 1961), p. 266. As striking as this passage is, Dorothée is neither a haunting midday demon nor a haunted solar victim. She is as strong and as proud as the sun, but though this creature who dares to walk at the hour when even dogs moan with suffering beneath the scorching sun is beautiful, she is also as cold as bronze (p. 267). She is, after all, a coquette (and a prodigious one, at that) and thoroughly uncomplicated. As a solar victim, Verga's "she wolf" is closer to the protagonist of Albert Camus' *L'Etranger*; in her defense too one can plead "que c'était à cause du soleil."

[29] *Opere*, ed. Russo, p. 549.

[30] As fascinating as the preceding cases of midday symbolism are, perhaps the most tragic of Verga's emblematic noontides is to be found in the page that opens the novella "Malaria." Here the Sicilian countryside has as its protagonist the killing fever of malaria, described as though it were a malefic force that literally permeates the landscape, weighing with a heavy stillness upon all things while implacably destroying human life in the midst of vegetative fertility. It

is the perfect picture of the malefic noontide demon, or if one prefers, the pestilence that wasteth at noon of which the Psalmist spoke.

[31] *Poesie di Giosue Carducci 1850-1900*, 24th ed. (Bologna, 1957), p. 678. The peacock, we may recall, was sacred to Juno.

[32] Ibid., p. 659.

[33] Ibid., p. 688.

[34] Ibid., p. 709. In the poem the image of the midday sun already occurs at lines 26-27: "e de gli eletti / In su le fronti il sol grande feriva." The poem opens with references to the Alpine landscape seen in the morning and in the setting sun, the place being dear to the poet at both moments. But the evocation of the commune itself and of its inhabitants is set in the brilliant light of noon.

[35] *Prose di Giosue Carducci 1859-1903* (Bologna, 1957), pp. 943-945.

[36] Ibid., p. 945.

[37] Ibid.

[38] *Poesie di Carducci*, p. 640.

[39] Ibid., p. 1,045.

[40] This sensation will be readily recognized as true by the reader, but I offer another poetic testimony to it in the following lines from Wordsworth's "Airey-Force Valley":

                           —————————— Not a breath of air
Ruffles the bosom of this leafy glen.
From the brook's margin, wide around, the trees
Are steadfast as the rocks; the brook itself,
Old as the hills that feed it from afar,
Doth rather deepen than disturb the calm
Where all things else are still and motionless. (1-7)

[41] This too must necessarily bring to mind Leopardi's "L'infinito" where the wind's rustling is an image of the flow of time, of the present "age" that is "flowing" into the infinite "sea" of silence. Lines 3-4 of Carducci's poem also recall Leopardi's poem. The flow of water as an archetypal image of the flow of time, passing and "disappearing" amid rocks and stones, recurs in the poem "Crisalide" by E. Montale, a poet who will receive much attention later in this study: ". . . ecco precipita / Il tempo, spare con risucchi rapidi / Tra i sassi, ogni ricordo è spento." Also in Montale we find the phrase: "il gocciare / Del tempo inesorabile" ("Mediterraneo," 3, in *Ossi di seppia*) and, in a late poem by the poet, there occurs the clear statement

that "I grandi fiumi sono l'immagine del tempo / Crudele e inesorabile" ("L'Arno a Rovezzano," in the volume *Satura*). This is existential time, that is time experienced as *Angst*—the awareness of one's finitude and the dread of being swept along into nonbeing.

[42] There is a fine commentary on Carducci's poem by Cesare Federico Goffis. Concerning the last line of the first stanza he writes: "Il quarto verso con la tronca segna un distacco vivace nel ritmo, una sincope che pare sospendere indeterminatamente l'impressione." So too on the poem's second stanza he notes: "È colto un istante di pace che il verbo al passato dell'ultimo verso sembra sospendere, dissolvendolo in armonia musicale." In *La poesia di Giosue Carducci* (Genoa, 1972), II, p. 120. And on the use of the past definite *fluì* he has the following excellent observation: "L'uso del perfetto con valore continuativo che indica il fluire dell'acqua ('*fluì*') sembra proprio voler rimuovere ogni senso di tempo dall'animo del poeta, che si stacca dalla vita e s'immerge non nella gioia panica del meriggio di *Davanti San Guido*, ma nel regno immutabile ('sereno intenso ed infinito') dell'ora solare." Ibid., p. 119.

[43] Giovanni Pascoli, *Poesie*, 14th ed. (Milan, 1958), I, p. 25.

[44] Ibid., p. 92.

[45] Cf. Leopardi's image from "La sera del dì di festa" (2-3): "E queta sovra i tetti e in mezzo agli orti / Posa la luna."

[46] I read *ala orma ombra* as three nouns, all dependent upon the initial negative. It is possible to read *orma* as a verb signifying *casts* or *imprints*. The line would then be understood as speaking of the absence of any bird seen as a "shadow" against the sky or on the meadow (or casting a shadow on the meadow as it flies above?). The effect, in any case, is still that of an absence of any motion or of any nuances in the light.

[47] The wood lark is associated with yet another midday evocation in Pascoli. In "La calandra" the bird is again on high, "immobile nel sole / Meridïano," effusively and virtuosically pouring out a variety of familiar and benign sounds while all other creatures—including the usually perpetual cicadas—are silent and still. The atmosphere is somewhere between serene and joyous.

[48] *Poesie*, I, p. 67.

[49] Ibid., p. 38.

[50] Midday as the time of sacred terror and epiphany, in classical terms, is at the center of Pascoli's evocation of the figure of Homer in "Il cieco di Chio" (one of the *Poemi conviviali*). To Delias, a young priestess of Apollo, Homer reveals the origin of his gift of poetry. It

was on a summer noon of dazzling sunlight, when the sun-drunk cicadas filled the air with their song, that he sought refuge in a deep forest:

> . . . . . Era un meriggio estivo:
> Io sentivo negli occhi arsi il barbaglio
> Della via bianca, e nell'orecchio un vasto
> Tintinnìo di cicale ebbre di sole.

In *Poesie*, II, p. 927. Entering with sacred dread and sensing the unseen presence of nymphs, he came to a magic singing fountain with which he was tempted to vie by playing on his lyre. The musical duel filled the tremulous noon ("tremulo meriggio") until the Muse herself appeared. Punishing him with physical blindness for his temerity, she yet converted the penalty into a grace by the gift of poetry as a power of inner illumination and penetration into matters inscrutable to men of ordinary vision. This episode recalls the blinding of Tiresias as recorded by Callimachus in his hymn to Athena bathing. But there, though it is midday, no musical contest is involved.

CHAPTER III

[1] From the poem "Lucertole" (1880), in *Primo vere*. I quote from the Mondadori complete edition of the poems under the general title *Versi d'amore e di gloria*, 9th ed. (Milan, 1964), I, pp. 108-109. All quotations from D'Annunzio's poetry are from this edition.

[2] From the sonnet "Il Vulture del Sole," in the volume *Alcyone* (1903), *Versi d'amore e di gloria*, II, p. 759.

[3] In *Versi d'amore e di gloria*, I, p. 94.

[4] Ibid., p. 840.

[5] Ibid.

[6] Ibid., pp. 844-845. The poem goes on to describe the brutalization of peasants forced to work throughout these torrid hours of the day. It may be compared with "Palude" (1879) from *Primo vere*: "Pigra, limosa, fetente, coperta di dense gramigne, / La vasta palude sogghigna in faccia a 'l sole," etc., in *Versi d'amore e di gloria*, I, p. 17.

[7] *Versi d'amore e di gloria*, I, p. 180.

[8] Ibid., pp. 201-202.

[9] In *Prose di romanzi*, II (Milan, 1949), p. 36.

[10] *Versi d'amore e di gloria*, I, p. 221.

¹¹ *Il trionfo della morte*, 3rd ed. (Milan, 1967), p. 275.

¹² It would be unfair to attribute this intent to D'Annunzio as author. However much D'Annunzio himself may have shared these thoughts, in the context of the novel they belong to his hero. The concluding chapter, following on the meditation, thoroughly demystifies the hero, his mistress, and his aims. It is a scene in which the vulgarity of the couple's behavior is clearly in contrast (and meant to be so) to the deaths of Tristan and Isolde. (Giorgio deliberately gets his mistress drunk, and she struggles furiously.) It is Giorgio who wishes to see a parallel between the Tristan story and his own tale which, as the last chapter shows, is basically a sordid one. But the motif of the sun is what concerns us here.

¹³ In *Versi d'amore e di gloria*, II, p. 4. D'Annunzio intended the *Laudi* to consist of seven books bearing the names of the seven Pleiades. Only five books actually materialized, the first being *Maia* (1903). *Elettra* and *Alcyone* appeared in 1904. *Merope* and *Asterope*, which were published much later as volumes, contain poems written in connection with the Italian campaign in Libya (1911-1912) and the First World War (1914-1918). Strictly speaking, the poem "L'Annunzio" belongs to the volume *Maia* as does the dedicatory poem "Alle Pleiadi e ai Fati," since both pieces were printed in that volume. However, *Maia* is really made up of one long paean to life, entitled *Laus Vitae*, in the form of a celebration of the poet as a modern day Ulysses and superman.

¹⁴ Ibid., p. 8.

¹⁵ In this respect, it is not without interest here to note that Carducci had earlier announced the resurrection of Pan to earth, sky, and sea in a cry that deliberately echoes and polemically "corrects" the Christian Easter announcement that Christ is risen: "O terra, o ciel, o mar, *Pan è risorto*." The reader familiar with Italian poetry will immediately think of Manzoni's sacred hymn "La Risurrezione" with its opening words "È risorto!" Carducci's line concludes the last of a series of four sonnets written in 1893 to celebrate the art of Nicola Pisano as an expression of the rising new spirit of life of the Renaissance in opposition to the renunciatory spirit of the Middle Ages.

¹⁶ *Prose scelte* (Milan, 1920), p. 17. The same thought appears, again in connection with Venice, in the novel *Il fuoco*. "L'anima vera non si discopre se non nel silenzio e più terribilmente—siatene certa—nella piena estate, di mezzogiorno, come il gran Pan." *Il fuoco* (Milan, 1967), p. 81.

[17] Dissi: 'Canterò i tuoi mille nomi e le tue membra
Innumerevoli, perocché la fiamma e la semenza,
L'alveare, ed il gregge,
L'oceano e la luna, la montagna ed il pomo
Son le tue membra, Signore; e l'opera dell'uomo
È retta dalla tua legge.' (137-142)

[18] In *Versi d'amore e di gloria*, II, pp. 138-139.

[19] From "Ditirambo," III, 64-70, 72, 76, 84-85. In *Versi d'amore e di gloria*, II, pp. 719-720. It may be pointed out that, on the whole, *Alcyone* remains a work within the inspiration of the Dannunzian superman's ideal of possession. The introductory poem entitled "La tregua" has too frequently been interpreted as an announcement of a desire for respite from that ideal. But there is little pause or respite in the book. Arcangelo Leone de Castris describes the true state of affairs, pointing to the fact that what is involved is not a pause in the superman's desire for possession, but rather a shift in direction from the oratorical and political sphere to the Panic urge for the conquest of nature. "In verità, per chi legga senza pregiudizi, neppure nelle intenzioni quell'annunzio ["La tregua"] voleva riferirsi a una tregua *dal* Superuomo, bensí a una tregua *del* Superuomo, al suo trascorrere e trasferirsi da una all'altra delle proprie funzioni, dall'avventura oratoria e 'politica' dell'esperienza parlamentare . . . all'avventura panica della poesia ('il lauro'). O semmai, all'interno di questa nuova misura di azione (la poesia), dal canto dell'incitamento eroico al canto delle metamorfosi naturali, dalla ardenza estiva: in sostanza, dall'uno all'altro dei suoi oggetti di conquista, delle sue brame di possesso estetistico del mondo, da un gesto all'altro del suo programma di sonante esibizione." *Il decadentismo italiano* (Bari, 1974), pp. 230-231. This is generally true, but it is perhaps more a question of degree. The Panic urge for the conquest of nature, we have seen, is a constant in D'Annunzio from the earliest stages of his career. In this respect, and in accordance with Leone de Castris's opinion, the final image of "La tregua" is logical and significant:

> Dèspota, or tu concedigli che allenti
> Il nervo ed abbandoni gli ebri spirti
> Alle voraci melodìe dei venti!

> Assai si travagliò per obbedirti.
> Scorse gli Eroi su i prati d'asfodelo.
> Or ode i Fauni ridere tra i mirti,

> L'Estate ignuda ardendo a mezzo il cielo.

The fauns, and especially the poet-faun, are no less energetic and aggressive than the heroes. See the last note to this chapter. We will see that there is a pause of a special sort in the poem "Meriggio," but even then the motif of possession will be present.

[20] In *Versi d'amore e di gloria*, II, p. 591.

[21] This sense of the total identification of light and silence occurs in the most explicit terms in two lines from the poem "Undulna" (in *Alcyone*): "In ogni sostanza si tace / La luce e il silenzio risplende." (See the introduction.)

[22] Rudolf Otto, *The Idea of the Holy* (New York, 1958), p. 39.

[23] The interaction between the noonscape and the poet begins in the first stanza of the poem, but there the "description" of noonday is foremost. The second stanza further develops the theme of the interrelationship between midday and the poet. In the final stanza the poet appears alone with all the characteristics of the summer noontide itself as it was evoked in the poem's first eleven lines.

[24] In *Versi d'amore e di gloria*, II, p. 642.

[25] I use the term *pamphysism* in the sense given to it by R. C. Zaehner who speaks of the "pamphysistic" (or "pan-enhenic") experience as "an experience of Nature in all things or of all things being one." Although there is no mention of God in such an experience (and it is this that distinguishes it from pantheism), "the person who has the experience seems to be convinced that what he experiences, so far from being illusory, is on the contrary something far more real than what he experiences normally through his five senses or what he thinks with his finite mind. It is, at its highest, a transcending of time and space in which an infinite mode of existence is actually experienced." *Mysticism Sacred and Profane* (London, Oxford, and New York, 1961, 1967), p. 50.

[26] The term *Panismo* is not, strictly speaking, a philosophical term. It is used widely in modern Italian literary criticism to refer to a paganizing or pantheistic sense of nature in which the poet feels himself immersed and by which he feels exalted. D'Annunzio is the writer to whom the term is most often applied, although he is not the only one. Because he has almost nothing to say about God or spirit, D'Annunzio's panism has often come under severe attack or has even been declared to be inauthentic. One of the earliest and most effective of such attacks was made by Alfredo Gargiulo who insisted that the true Panic intuition fosters a high moral sense and brings one in touch with the ultimate source of all that is *spirit*. "L'intuizione pànica riposa, sempre, su di un ricco patrimonio concettuale

convergente alla convinzione che l'universo è uno ed è spirito . . . L'intuizione pànica porta con sé una grande elevazione morale, un disinteresse assoluto per ogni aspetto allettatore dell'universo. Il poeta pànico è un poeta religioso. Ma allora, un sensuale e un visivo come il D'Annunzio è proprio l'opposto del poeta pànico. Il poeta visivo-sensuale ama i singoli aspetti dell'universo e non risale alla fonte unica: indugia su ciascuno di essi, vi si profonda, lo vive nella sua singolarità, ne trae diletto, lo loda (le *Laudi*!), non ha alcuna elevazione morale e religiosa, vale a dire non affisa un principio nel quale egli e il suo oggetto particolare debbano dissolversi. Quand'egli si tramuta in un mare, in una montagna, in una selva, quand'egli vive la vita di questi oggetti naturali, non fa altro, in sostanza, che affermare la vita particolare e indipendente degli oggetti stessi." *Gabriele D'Annunzio* (Florence, 1941), pp. 331-332. This view, however, besides begging the question, shows no comprehension of the fact that there is such a thing as natural mystical experience (or nature mysticism). Gargiulo was referring to the poem "Meriggio" in particular when he made the preceding indictment, and one can only conclude that his narrow view of panism (or, as we would say with Zaehner, *pamphysism*) kept him from appreciating the sense of coinherence between nature and the poet that that poem does in fact communicate. So too his judgment that in "Meriggio" D'Annunzio, after celebrating a moment of nature, coldly and intellectually tacked on (in the last line) the idea of a divinity betrays a misunderstanding of the poem. It is more than a moment of nature alone that D'Annunzio has celebrated, and the last line refers not to a divinity or a god in a theological sense but to the sensation experienced by the poet, the sensation of having passed into a state in which the concepts of death, life, and time have no place.

[27] Near the very end of *Laus Vitae* D'Annunzio announces boldly, even brazenly: "Più ragione v'è nel mio corpo / Valido che in ogni dottrina." In *Versi d'amore e di gloria*, II, pp. 317-319.

[28] D'Annunzio's midday erotic panism or nympholepsy receives its highest poetic expression in "*Stabat nuda Aestas.*" In this poem nature, in the guise of a midsummer noonscape, is personified or, better, is sensually metamorphosed into the naked body of a nymph (or goddess) pursued and ultimately possessed by the poet-faun. The nudity of this midday nature goddess is as luminous as it is sensuous. The poem is, needless to say, a more satisfying representation of the motif that was dealt with early in D'Annunzio's career in such poems as "Canto del Sole" VII, and "Canto dell'ospite" XIII. We

have already noted that this Panic urge to possess nature is a constant feature in D'Annunzio from his earliest work and that it often takes the form of the faun myth. The faun, of course, is symbolic of the return to and the participation in the life force of nature; the nymph, with her connotation of a female arboreal divinity, represents or suggests the immanental character of nature.

CHAPTER IV

[1] See the brief but suggestive account by Reinhold D. Hohl, "The Sun in Contemporary Painting and Sculpture," in *The Sun in Art*, ed. Walter Herdeg (Zurich, 1962, 1963), pp. 128-130. The phrase "intense utterances" is Hohl's.

[2] Rebora's "existentialist" drama, his tense yearning for a concrete absolute, and his coming just short of embracing it (until the time—1928-1929—of his full conversion to Catholicism) is treated lucidly by Artal Mazzotti in "Clemente Rebora," in the series published by Marzorati, *Letteratura italiana: I contemporanei* (Milan, 1963), pp. 595-601. On Rebora's first volume of verse—*Frammenti lirici* (1913)—Mazzotti writes: "I *Frammenti* vanno forse letti in chiave di una scelta proposta e non attuata. Ciò che per primo balza da essi, è il senso vivido dell'esistenziale, dell'intero sperimentabile quotidiano nelle sue allusioni sottintesi e rimandi; la duplice faccia dell'essere e quindi la sua ambiguità essenziale, che ha il contraccolpo nel modo interno d'essere del poeta, nell'alterne vicende del suo sentimento esistenziale" (p. 597).

[3] The rest of the poem is as follows: "Quassù quassù, fra il suonar dei campani / E il canto lungo di un prono bifolco, / L'uman destino vincola le mani / Con lacci che non han peso né solco; // Quanto misero mal vita perdoni, / Quanta bontà ci volle a crear noi, / Quassù quassù non è chi non l'intoni / Mentre vorrebbe far puri i dì suoi." The poem is from the collection *Frammenti lirici* which was first published in 1913. I quote from Clemente Rebora, *Le poesie* (Florence, 1947), p. 27.

[4] From the poem "There is a Zone whose even years." Apart from the question of any influence (unlikely) of the American writer on the Italian, there is, it seems to me, an almost Dickinson-like quality in the imagery and tone of Rebora's second quatrain. It should not be forgotten, however, that the experience in question was, in fact, not unknown to D'Annunzio who recorded his own version of it in *Laus Vitae* (see the discussion in the previous chapter),

Notes to Pages 148-154

and Carducci's "Mezzogiorno alpino" itself is to be interpreted in the same key.
[5] From *Frammenti lirici*. In *Le poesie*, pp. 60-61.
[6] In D'Annunzio's "L'Annunzio," where we read of "l'annunzio del prodigio meridiano" (14) and "L'attesa del prodigio" (107). See the preceding chapter.
[7] In *Le poesie*, p. 71.
[8] Ibid., p. 62.
[9] Ibid., pp. 39-40.
[10] "Il tema è assai semplice: una gita in campagna, a conclusione di una fine d'anno di studio; la possibilità di una confidenza, forse del primo fiorire dell'amore tra due giovani: un compagno e una compagna; e poi tutto torna a ׳ chiudersi nell'estraneità del rapporto banale, tutto rimane inespresso." Daria Banfi Malaguzzi, *Il primo Rebora* (Milan, 1964), pp. 109-110.
[11] The volume *Frammenti lirci* was dedicated by Rebora to the first ten years of the new century. Its poems are as dramatic a statement of the hopes and uncertainties—suggestive of a time of transition or crisis—as one can find in Italian literature of the pre–World War I period. The anxious reaching out or the supine passivity (the poles between which Rebora moved in that period) and the sense of the loss or insecurity of the wild desire to possess a superior life that we have found in "Sole" were expressed by the tormented poet in these words from an early letter (to Daria Banfi Malaguzzi) that can help to explicate the poem: "L'ellenica armonia di equilibrio? Io non la conosco. O balzo o giaccio; altro non so. Tendo perennemente verso qualche cosa che non sarà mai; esulto talvolta di creature che si agitano in me e che io non potrò mai scorgere nella realtà degli uomini. Ecco, la fonte regina della mia angoscia perenne; il mio tormento lusingatore e vano! Tutto mi scivola via; anche il volere, che pure mi domina talvolta selvaggio." In Malaguzzi, *Il primo Rebora*, p. 20. See also in the preface of the same volume the remarks by Luciano Anceschi: "Un uomo così perplesso, umbratile, sempre diviso tra slanci, e angosce . . . un uomo che, così umiliato, è il suo tempo in modo tanto più vero di tutti gli olimpici, sicuri e falsificati che ne apparvero i dominatori" (p. 10).
[12] The expression of course is from the nineteenth-century poet James Thomson, admirer and translator of Leopardi, whose narrative poem *The City of Dreadful Night* also pits the negativity of the city against nature.
[13] Cf. also the verses from Leopardi's *Le ricordanze*: "E qual mor-

tale ignaro / Di sventura esser può, se a lui già scorsa / Quella vaga stagion, se il suo buon tempo, / Se giovanezza, ahi giovanezza, è spenta?" (132-135). Echoes from Rimbaud in "Sole" have been noted by Diego Valeri who suggests that the depiction of the couple in the Italian poem may owe something to the French poet's prose lyrics "Royauté" and "Aube" from the *Illuminations*. In "Royauté" we read: "Un beau matin, chez un peuple fort doux, un homme et une femme superbes criaient sur la place publique: 'Mes amis, je veux qu'elle soit reine!' 'Je veux être reine!' Elle riait et tremblait. Il parlait aux amis de révélation, d'épreuve terminée. Ils se pâmaient l'un contre l'autre. En effet ils furent rois toute une matinée, où les tentures carminées se relevèrent sur les maisons, et toute l'après-midi, où ils s'avancèrent du côté des jardins de palmes." Valeri notes the different endings in the two episodes. In "Royauté" the couple are joyous together throughout the day; in "Sole," on the other hand, "c'è la delusione che fatalmente segue al confidente immaginare; c'è l'inevitable fine." In "La poesia di Clemente Rebora," *Quaderni Reboriani* (1960), no. 1, p. 109. Valeri does not speculate further on the poem. Another Rimbaudian echo suggested by Maura Del Serra in connection with the opening of "Sole" is from the poem "Soleil et chair": "Le Soleil, le foyer de tendresse et de vie, / Verse l'amour brûlant à la terre ravie, / Et, quand on est couché sur la vallée, on sent / Que la terre est nubile et déborde de sang; / Que son immense sein, soulevé par une âme, / Est d'amour comme Dieu, de chair comme la femme, / Et qu'il renferme, gros de sève et des rayons, / Le grand fourmillement de tous les embryons! // Et tout croit, et tout monte!" (1-9). Obviously these "sources" (which may have been mediated by D'Annunzio) and any others from any number of authors have passed through the crucible of Rebora's own existential anguish and have become his own. Concerning the poem "Sole," Del Serra speaks of a "vera apoteosi di panismo simbiotico fra coppia umana e natura . . . che . . . si spegne col precipizio di un'allucinazione mitologica nella caduta alienante dell'uomo e della donna nel tempo (la ragione come solitudine della maturità)." *Clemente Rebora: Lo specchio e il fuoco* (Milan, 1976), pp. 73-74. The view expressed by Marziano Guglielminetti that "il *Sole* è chiamato quasi a rendere più spasmodica la prostrazione in cui vive immersa la città, formicolante di umane esistenze in cerca della loro libertà spirituale" seems to me to misjudge the poem. If I read him right, Guglielminetti interprets the sun in Rebora's poem as a suffocating force against which the "giovani cercanti" revolt in the search for spiritual freedom. See his *Clemente Rebora* (Milan, 1961), pp. 30-31. This is curious in light of the fact that in connection with the same poem the critic makes judicious remarks on the theme of the antagonism between city and country (nature) in Rebora's work. On this last topic, see also Margherita Marchione, *L'imagine tesa: La vita e l'opera di Clemente Rebora* (Rome, 1960), pp. 118-120.

[14] In *Le poesie 1913-1957* (Milan, 1961), p. 324.

[15] Ibid., p. 282.

[16] This is the view (with which I concur) of Giancarlo Bertoncini whose book on Boine is a major contribution to the study of our author. See his *Giovanni Boine nella civiltà letteraria del primo Novecento* (Padua, 1973), p. 121. Concerning a series of five of Boine's writings composed between January 1912 and February 1913, the latter being the date of "Agonia," Bertoncini notes that the fundamental motif central to all of them is the multiple question of what rules the world, how it is ruled, and what the possibilities are for man to live harmoniously with it (p. 105). The problem and any solution suggested for it vary from piece to piece without a strict linear development.

[17] "E gli pareva d'esser sceso in sé come alle radici embrionali, nell'incerto umidore di un plasma di carne e di spirito, d'esser sceso giù alla scaturigine buia dell'essere suo, e d'avervi nel viscidume del male, di là dal male come sentito toccata l'eterogeneità dell'oggetto. Come se il male, la originaria inimicizia del male fosse il palpabile segno, il visibile indice di un sostanziale mondo di là dal nostro, non nostro. . . . Onde il male non alternativamente sforzo verso la vita o diminuzione di vita (diminuzion di realtà) ma invasione era, ma sopraffazione allagante di una sconosciuta realtà come una gran ombra stendentesi, un gran buiore opaco. . . . Vinceva ogni suo sforzo." Giovanni Boine, *Il peccato e le altre opere*, ed., G. Vigorelli (Parma, 1971), pp. 508-509.

[18] "Le cose si facevano inerti d'intorno; (inerte lui stesso senza forze senza soffio, opaco, disteso); atone, afone, imbottite ed inutili. Senza sapore né moto. Come se avesser perduta l'ultima loro realtà e non fossero più che ombra e fastidio. Non erano più: il mondo non era." Ibid., p. 515.

[19] Ibid.

[20] In his meditation on the character of midday in southern lands, the philosopher Cornelis Verhoeven noted what is, in fact, a frequent feature: "In this paradox of light which is the southern noon, things lose their contours which only a tempering of light can give

them. . . . Light is fatal; it robs things of their identity." *The Philosophy of Wonder*, trans. Mary Foran (new York, 1972), p. 47. Boine's experience, we see, is contrary to this "norm." Both types of vision have a "hallucinatory" quality in their different revelations of the heart of existence. For Verhoeven, see the introduction to this study.

[21] In discussing the organic and plastic character of the visions in Rimbaud's *Illuminations*, Marcel Raymond notes that "a hallucination often takes on a distinctness and relief that one would seek in vain in a landscape normally perceived." *From Baudelaire to Surrealism* (New York, 1950), p. 34.

[22] Although *The Agony of Christianity* (1925) was written after Boine's death, and "Agonia" was finished before the publication of *The Tragic Sense of Life*, the Italian writer was, from a very young age, a reader of Unamuno's earlier works. Indeed, his first published work was a review of Unamuno's *Vida de D. Quijote y Sancho*, published in *Rinnovamento*, 1 (February 1907), no. 2, p. 248. A second review on Unamuno (*Inteligencia y bondad*) appeared in the same journal, 1 (November-December 1907), nos. 11-12, pp. 640-642. *Rinnovamento* was a journal of the Catholic Modernism movement.

[23] In connection with Boine's "Agonia" we may think also of Nietzsche who idealized his own struggle for health in *Zarathustra*. But in Nietzsche's work the hero successfully passes through the midday crisis and is then able to proclaim the advent of a great noontide. Another case of the presence of midday in Boine that should be mentioned here occurs in *Il peccato*, a narrative monologue built on the story of the love of a young man and a nun. The origins of the adventure are in a "spectral midday" of June in whose immense whitish glare the shadowless objects appear cruelly distinct, as in "Agonia." Walking in this crisis atmosphere, the man is attracted to the chapel of the convent of the Carmelites by the sound of a harmonium whose music comes to him like a restorative fountain in the vast burning thirst of the hour, as though it were undaunted by the brazenly triumphant blaze of the midday sun. In this noontide the shrill of the cicadas is specifically mentioned as filling the surroundings. Again it is the acoustical note that bespeaks the high tension of the crisis hour. "La lontana origine . . . era stata l'anno innanzi in uno spettrale meriggio del giugno ch'egli vagabondava fuori solo nell'enorme barbaglio. Frinire di cicale per tutto, barbaglio accecante bianchiccio, cose nette, sfacciate senz'ombra. . . . Profonda, lenta, come non curante della sfacciata trionfale arsura del sole al di fuori, musica come una sicura anima giù in un immobile corpo nascosta a

meditare quiete-canora. Veniva a lui come di lontano . . . ; buon gorgoglio come di fontana fluente in questo bruciare vasto di sete." *Il peccato*, p. 11. One notices here some of the same characteristics connected with the noontide of crisis in "Agonia": the "enorme barbaglio," the "barbaglio accecante bianchiccio" in which things nonetheless appear in sharp contour, brazen without shadows— "cose nette, sfacciate senz'ombra," etc.

[24] See Bertoncini, *Boine*, p. 143.

[25] From "I miei amici di qui" (*Frantumi*), in Boine, *Il peccato*, p. 157.

[26] Boine, *Il peccato*, pp. 147-148.

[27] *Les rêveries du promeneur solitaire*, ed. H. Roddier (Paris, 1960), p. 67.

[28] "Là le bruit des vagues et l'agitation de l'eau fixant mes sens et chassant de mon âme toute autre agitation la plongeaient dans une rêverie délicieuse où la nuit me suprenait souvent sans que je m'en fusse aperçu. Le flux et reflux de cette eau, son bruit continu mais renflé par intervalles frappant sans relâche mon oreille et mes yeux, suppléaient aux mouvements internes que la rêverie éteignait en moi et suffisaient pour me faire sentir avec plaisir mon existence, sans prendre la peine de penser. De temps à autre naissait quelque faible et courte réflexion sur l'instabilité des choses de ce monde dont la surface des eaux m'offrait l'image: mais bientôt ces impressions légères s'effaçaient dans l'uniformité du mouvement continu qui me berçait, et qui sans aucun concours actif de mon âme ne laissait pas de m'attacher au point qu'appelé par l'heure et par le signal convenu je ne pouvais m'arracher de là sans effort." Ibid., pp. 68-69.

[29] There are excellent remarks on Rousseau's "Fifth Promenade" in Reinhard Kuhn's *The Demon of Noontide: Ennui in Western Literature* (Princeton, N.J., 1976). Concerning the important passage quoted in the preceding note, Kuhn writes: "The rhythmic sound of the waters (echoed by the slow rhythmic text) is hypnotic ('immobilizing my senses') and empties the soul of all other motions and emotions. Everything is effaced, even internal movements. . . . All activity is annulled. . . . The sinuous motions of the long sentences, which reproduce the roll of a slow-breaking set of waves, lull by their harmony and create a quietistic void within which, between the world of sensation and the world of dream, is suspended a beatific consciousness forever on the verge of passing into pure unconsciousness" (p. 158). Kuhn's concern is with ennui in literature, and it is from this perspective that he has studied this and other passages

from Rousseau. In this respect, his conclusions on the "Fifth Promenade" are highly suggestive and (to me) convincing. The uninterrupted to and fro of the rocking motion which is natural to the waters of a lake can only be induced artifically in a human being. "To maintain such a state, a person must ceaselessly pay attention, and constant vigilance is hardly consonant with true ecstasy. Rousseau wants to be conscious of existence without feeling its pains or joys, to taste the nothingness of ennui without partaking of it" (p. 162). For the use of the title *The Demon of Noontide* in Kuhn's book, see note 15 of my introduction.

[30] Very likely, Boine's use of *sciacquare* owes something to D'Annunzio's noun *sciacquío* in the poem "I pastori." As the shepherds from the Abruzzan mountains have finally reached the shores of the Adriatic with their flocks, seeking the lower plains for the winter, the poet, who has evoked the scene, hears the vast slow washing of the waves and the trampling of the sheep: "Isciacquìo, calpestìo, dolci romori" (20). *Versi d'amore e di gloria*, II, p. 816. Even more suggestive is D'Annunzio's use of the verb itself in the poem "L'onda," where it serves as one of a series of words meant to create both visual and acoustic impressons of waves:

> O sua favella!
> *Sciacqua, sciaborda,*
> Scroscia, schiocca, schianta,
> Romba, ride, canta. (62-65)

Ibid., p. 707. It is pertinent to note that *sciacqua* is followed immediately by *sciaborda*, for the latter verb, as we shall see, is used by Montale in a context that also suggests a familiarity with Boine's prose lyric.

[31] Boine's remark was made in a brief review of Onofri's 1914 volume *Liriche*. It appears in his *Plausi e botte*, reprinted in *Il peccato*, pp. 233-235.

[32] I quote from the Garzanti reprint of *Liriche* (Milan, 1948), p. 92.

[33] Ibid., p. 50.

[34] From the volume *Canti delle oasi* (Rome, 1909). Reprinted in the Onofri anthology *Poesie*, ed. A. Bocelli and G. Comi (Rome, 1949), p. 5.

[35] *Liriche* (Naples, 1914), p. 17.

[36] The point has been well made by Anna Dolfi: "La tensione, quale si esplicherà, in modo paradigmatico, nei volumi del *Nuovo rinascimento* è alla luce, all'aurora, alla fonte solare della rivelazione.

La palingenesi onofriana, nella sua dimensione titanica, si presenta già come scelta possibile del sole/sangue/fuoco. La sete si ciba di fuoco; per questo la tensione all'acqua potrà risolversi nella solarità, nello svanire dell'ombra e del canto, nell'abbandono degli erronei inganni, delle terrestri fole. La sete immensa si alimenta al sole che si trasforma in 'vivida fiamma di sangue,' segnale e speranza della nuova aurora, auspicio della rinascita, della resurrezione collettiva destinata, tramite il poeta all'umanità." In *Arturo Onofri, Il Castoro*, nos. 115-116, July-August 1976 (Florence, 1976), p. 37.

[37] The presence of D'Annunzio in Onofri's work has been noted by more than one critic. Donato Valli writes of "quell'immagine tutta dannunziana della gola riarsa e sempre voluttuosa di nuovi sapori; il placido sogno nell'arsura estiva cui segue l'esaltato, panico risveglio della mente e dei sensi, e così via: tutto un furoreggiare di sensazioni e di sentimenti, di quelle più che di questi, che riportano il giovane Onofri nell'area ben circoscritta degli imitatori dannunziani del primo Novecento. Eppure, anche qui, c'è qualcosa di genuino, non tanto nella resa poetica, quanto nel sentimento: ed è la ricerca d'una dimensione nuova, non più superficiale e sensitiva, delle proprie radici paniche e universali: rari accenni, ed ancora troppo immaturi, ma che lasciano intravedere nell'inesperto discepolo una profondità sconosciuta alla grazia lieve e magistrale, alla orgogliosa efflorescenza impetuosa del maestro. Sicché l'influsso dannunziano, che persisterà per lungo tempo ancora nella poetica dell'Onofri, comincia ad assumere sin d'ora i caratteri di una reinvenzione personale e di un'ambiguità letteraria della quale il poeta romano [Onofri] si libererà per gradi con l'avanzare della sua meditazione filosofica e col progredire delle sue interiori certezze." From the essay "Il misticismo della forma: il primo Onofri," in the author's *Anarchia e misticismo nella poesia italiana del primo Novecento* (Lecce, 1973), pp. 163-164. The same idea is stated by Franco Lanza in discussing Onofri's early production: "Eppure anche le espressioni del dannunzianesimo più autolatrico . . . sono percosse da un'ansia segreta di conoscenza, che nel giovane Onofri tentava ancora confusamente il mistero delle origini, lo sdoppiamento dionisiaco dell'Apollo dannunziano. . . . L'ansia morale dell'epigono [Onofri] sgretola e oltrepassa la splendida ma inerte solarità del modello." in *Arturo Onofri* (Milan, 1973), p. 22. These are excellent statements, but I also quote them because in the effort to indicate the "difference" in Onofri both critics run the risk of reducing D'Annunzio's sun mythology to something less vital than it is. D'Annunzio's panism is without doubt grounded in

the senses, but it is not so "superficial" or "inert" as is suggested by Valli and Lanza.

[38] In *Liriche* (Naples, 1914), p. 59.

[39] It is possible that Onofri's use of the adjective *immane* is meant to express something in the nature of the word *ungeheuer* in Nietzche's poem on midday ecstasy, "Nach neuen Meeren" (see the introduction). That is, besides its suggestion of a limitless and cruel desire, the word may also indicate something of the *uncanny* or the *tremendous*.

[40] *Terrestrità del sole* (Florence, 1927), p. 24.

[41] I use the phrase advisedly, for this is indeed what it is. The term *angelicato* is used by Onofri in "Dove le Voci? E il sangue ineloquente," a poem that includes the phrase "terrestrità del sole" which in turn gives the title to the richest of Onofri's volumes of verse. The word refers to the blood (*sangue*) of man when it will have been fully redeemed. Moreover, Onofri makes deliberate use of the manner of the *dolce stil nuovo* poets on more than one occasion to speak of this renewal or higher (angelic) condition.

[42] *Terrestrità del sole*, p. 86.

[43] In the volume of verse *Vincere il drago* (Turin, 1928), p. 38.

[44] Ibid., p. 41.

[45] *Terrestrità del sole*, p. 155.

[46] Ibid., p. 230.

[47] From "Chi parla il suono della terra in doglia?" in *Terrestrità del sole*, pp. 173-174.

[48] From "Nel sollievo dei monti incisi d'aria," in *Terrestrità del sole*, p. 42.

[49] The term "unreal fetish" and the imagery of spent fire congealed into mineral substance representing man's resistance to the urging of the spirit that courses through every stasis occur in the following initial stanzas of the first poem in the volume *Vincere il drago*, p. 9:

> L'alto movente, ch'eccita ogni stasi
> Del passato a riprendere contatto
> Col volere che intìma nuove fasi
> In avanti alla terra, urta di scatto
> Le resistenze nere
> Illuse di volere.
>
> Volontà d'uomo è solo movimento
> Verso il proprio rinascere immortale;

Notes to Pages 178-183 307

E il desisterne è morte, è il fuoco spento
D'antichi dèi, nel corpo minerale
Ove l'uomo è feticcio
Irreale, e terriccio.

⁵⁰ Compare the *stolte voglie* referred to in one of the excerpts quoted above. And in another of the poems that express the liberation motif we find the phrase *sorde voglie* along with the typical Onofri lexicon of such words as *svincola, imprigionato, mutismo, incantesimo*:

Nel suo gesto, che svincola il mutismo
D'essere imprigionato in sorde voglie,
Si rompe l'incantesimo del limbo
Dove il volersi mondi brancolava.

From *Vincere il drago*, p. 118. The very title of this volume is indicative of the motif.

Just as there is a vertical impulse from the natural to the spiritual there is also a corresponding (and vertical) impulse from the spiritual to the natural for the purpose of activating or energizing the latter. In considering this matter as the guiding motif of the imagery in Onofri's cycle of six volumes of verse having a theosophic and anthroposophic content, Franco Lanza makes the following remark that is pertinent to our discussion: "L'anelito segreto delle cose, secondo l'ipotesi teosofica, è tale non già come poetica e romantica partecipazione della vita naturale alla spirituale, ma come cosciente trasvalutazione dell'Io che ne scioglie in cieli le stregate apparenze. È questo l'altro grande vettore fantastico, dallo spirito alla natura, che dà origine a tutta una serie parallela di motivi lirici. . . . Se il mondo è preistoria dell'Io, la sua presenza è avvertita come necessità di trasformazione dall'inorganico all'organico al cosciente, in una dialettica tensione: dramma cosmico di paurosa vastità, in cui il polo negativo è dato sì dall'ovvia sordità del mondo 'impoverito a minerale,' dei 'mostri' e dalle 'incatenate angosce della terra,' oppure dalla 'memoria oscure d'altri corpi / che già patimmo inconsapevolmente,' ma anche e soprattutto dalla fisica resistenza del soggetto stesso, dalla sua scarsità d'amore." In *Arturo Onofri*, p. 158.

⁵¹ In the posthumous volume of verse that takes its title from the first line of this poem, *Simili a melodie rapprese in mondo* (Rome, 1929).

⁵² Girolamo Comi, *Poesia, 1918-1938* (Rome, 1939), p. 48.

⁵³ In *La tomba verde e Avventure: Liriche e prose 1916-1929* (Milan, 1966), pp. 67-68.

[54] There may also be an echo from Montale's poem "Marezzo" (lines 37-40) which is discussed in the last chapter.

[55] *The Collected Poems of Wallace Stevens* (New York, 1969), p. 459.

[56] In *Ombre sullo schermo* (Milan, 1929), pp. 75-76.

[57] In *La bellezza intravista*, ed. G. Spagnoletti and L. Curci (Florence, 1959), pp. 13-14.

[58] In *Stelle sugli abissi* (Milan, 1938), p. 57.

[59] In *Poesie d'amore* (Siena, 1948), p. 48.

[60] Ibid., p. 52.

[61] Ibid., p. 50.

[62] In *Stelle sugli abissi*. Reprinted in *La bellezza intravista*, p. 85.

[63] "Sole. . . . A poco a poco tutti gli usci si accostano, le persiane si socchiudono, le vie si svuotano. C'è un'ora in cui comincia la paura del sole, in cui sovrasta l'inerzia e il silenzio diventa vivo e sensibile. . . . Allora veramente il sole è il dominatore assoluto del tempo. Bruciata in tutta la sua crosta, la terra ritrova il senso della sua origine, un senso mitologico di sovrannaturale innesto; il raggio la pervade, la satura, la scompone chimicamente, la rinnova, la possiede, l'esalta. Un languore, colmo di fermenti, è in quella sua pace discinta. Le piante soffrono, i rami pesano, le foglie si accortocciano. . . . Una pausa incandescente è nella vita, il cielo, le campagne, i monti si trasfigurano in una ferma mobilità d'aria combusta." In *Gli occhi dei figli* (Milan, 1943), pp. 182-183.

[64] Ada Negri, *Poesie* (Milan, 1948), p. 963.

[65] For the use of the expression by Zanzotto, see note 20 of the introduction.

[66] See Aldo Palazzeschi, *Tutte le novelle* (Milan, 1957), pp. 188-193.

[67] The poem belongs to the years 1905-1907. Published in the earliest edition of Saba's *Canzoniere* (Trieste, 1920), pp. 46-47, the poet excluded it from the later editions of his poems. The poem may now be read in Umberto Saba, *L'adolescenza del 'Canzoniere' e undici lettere*, introduction by S. Miniussi (Turin, 1975), p. 52.

[68] "Ora meridiana / D'inimitabile vita!" as D'Annunzio exults in *Maia*.

[69] From *Cenere azzurra* (1933). Now in the volume *Marsilvana* (Siena, 1959), p. 105.

[70] "Betelgeuse," from *La vigna rossa* (1955). Now in *Marsilvana*, p. 188.

[71] "Tu mi liquefi dentro, come un oro, / Profumo d'orti

maturi / E in me coli una luce di frutteti. // Tra lucenti verdezze / Di melagrani, fulgidi racconti / S'aprono in me meriggi, / E straripo di sole agli orizzonti." In *Marsilvana*, p. 128.

[72] "Torpido dorme il gregge / Nel magro tondo dell'ombra, / Nè più il limío delle cicale, // Alta noia, / Spietata ristagna. / E il meriggio di luglio / Divora l'erbe e spacca / In cenere le zolle. // Sogno acquatili limbi, / Redole erbose / Tra campi di rugiada: / E la carezza d'Una / Che cali da freschi cieli / Come in estiva notte / Raggio di luna." Ibid., p. 185.

[73] Vincenzo Cardarelli, *Opere complete*, ed. G. Raimondi (Milan, 1962), p. 364.

[74] "Estate, Estate mia, non declinare! / . . . / Estate, Estate, indugia a maturare." From "Madrigali dell'Estate," in *Alcyone*. But Cardarelli's vision of summer is not Dannunzian.

[75] *Opere complete*, p. 356.

[76] There is something obscure or uncertain in the expression of the lines "E ad ogni transizione di meriggio / Rotta l'astrale identità del mattino." It would seem that Cardarelli has here fused morning with midday to make of them one long calm space of time.

[77] From "Memorie della mia infanzia," written in 1922-1923; in *Opere complete*, p. 156.

[78] *Opere complete*, p. 157.

[79] From "Un'uscita di Zarathustra," written in 1916-1917; in *Opere complete*, p. 83.

[80] In Valéry's "Ébauche d'un serpent," the sun both conceals from man the truth of the evil of existence and is itself a symbol of the flaw that stains the purity of nonbeing:

> Soleil, soleil! . . . Faute éclatante!
> Toi qui masques la mort, Soleil,
> . . . .
> Tu gardes les coeurs de connaître
> Que l'univers n'est qu'un défaut
> Dans la pureté du Non-être! (21-22; 28-30)

[81] Above all, Camillo Sbarbaro should be remembered in this connection. In his slim volume of verse *Pianissimo* (Florence, 1914) this poet from Liguria expressed the crisis of modern man in the representation of himself as a figure fixed in a sterile estrangement, unable to participate in life and able only to observe it in a daze. The lyric "Talora nell'arsura della via" portrays the poet as he walks the city streets, suddenly surprised by the song of cicadas in the noontide

heat. He is transported in memory to a vision of a vast countryside "prostrated" by the blazing light of midday, perhaps in the time of his childhood. But though he is "amazed" to think that the beautiful and good things of nature still exist, they no longer suffice to "entrance" him. His amazement now is like the daze of a drunkard who suddenly feels the rush of fresh air against his face when he steps into the night. The poet is imprisoned by the city, attached to its stones, image of a spiritual desert. So too in the poem "Talor, mentre cammino solo al sole," as he walks alone under the sun, even as he seems to recognize a sense of something "fraternal" (beckoning to him) in the life of nature, the poet is suddenly seized with a "chill" of fear that prevents him from seeking to embrace life. The desert of existence and, more particularly, of his own inner life is represented emblematically in the very first poem of *Pianissimo*. Seeking to ausculate his soul, the poet can hear nothing, for his soul is enveloped in the most absolute apathy, indifferent to joy and suffering alike— "Taci, anima stanca di godere / E di soffrire." The "siren of the world" (the attractions of life) has been muted, and the world is now a vast desert. Into this desert (the world and the inner landscape of the poet) the poet gazes with *dry* (indifferent, apathetic) eyes: "Nel deserto / Io guardo con asciutti occhi me stesso."

Finally, in another early poem, "Afa di luglio," which describes the absorption of the poet into the torpor of a sultry July noonscape, occur these verses: "E sento come divenute enormi / Le membra. Nel torpore che lo lega, / Mi pare che il mio corpo si trasformi. / Forse in macigno. Rido. Poi mi butto / Bocconi. Nell'immensa afa s'annega / Con me la miseria, il mondo, tutto." Here, it seems obvious to me, Sbarbaro has borrowed something from Leopardi's "L'infinito," although the presence of D'Annunzio's "Meriggio" can also be detected.

[82] The image of a violent destroyer sun used to emblematize specifically the basic aridity and negativity of the fascist nightmare occurs in Romano Bilenchi's allegorical tale "La siccità" (1941), which describes a drought that wastes the countryside and threatens all of mankind. In the same year appeared Alberto Moravia's "L'epidemia" which also allegorizes the sociopolitical calamity. See the interesting remarks on this subject by Walter Moretti in his *Dalla negazione all'attesa* (Bologna, 1974), pp. 99-101. In connection with the description of a suffering or forbidding nature meant to evoke the oppressiveness of the fascist experience, we may mention Carlo Levi's description of a brutal midday in the desolate, poverty-

Notes to Pages 201-204   311

stricken southern village to which he was confined during 1935-1936. *Cristo si è fermato a Eboli* was written in 1945, some years after the event, and the passage in question is not, strictly speaking, allegorical. Its style, moreover, is realistic, and as a "document" its depiction of an almost dehumanized world is not limited to the particular historical moment.

CHAPTER V

[1] Giuseppe Ungaretti, *Vita d'un uomo: Tutte le poesie*, ed. Leone Piccioni (Milan, 1969, 1970), p. 33. All quotations from the poetry will be made from this edition which will be referred to henceforth as *Tutte le poesie*. "Silenzio" was published first in the slim volume of verse *Il Porto Sepolto* (Udine, 1916) and subsequently placed definitively in the volume *L'Allegria* (Milan, 1942, 1943). The problem of the various volumes of Ungaretti's verse and the different versions of the poems is a complicated one which, fortunately, need not concern us too much. However, it will be necessary to refer to it on a few occasions. In the case of "Silenzio," the first three lines have remained unchanged since the first printing of the poem.

[2] *Tutte le poesie*, p. 11. The title "Ricordo d'Affrica" appears first in the 1942 edition of *L'Allegria*, after the appearance of another poem by that title published in 1924 and included in the volume *Sentimento del Tempo* (1933 and thereafter). The earlier printed versions of "Meriggio di agosto" included a fourth line (as verse 3)—"Gli uomini hanno sonno"—that represents the vanquishing of mankind by the midday sun. But while the line fits the theme of the poem, it is almost too intrusive as a realistic annotation. Without it the poem retains all the force of a surrealistic or hallucinatory vision.

[3] A fine comment on the poem by Renata Lollo deserves to be quoted here: "L'uso del presente *(rapisce* [*è rapito* in "Silenzio"], *vede, resistono)* stacca le immagini da un preciso riferimento temporale immobilizzandole nella pienezza dell'ora in cui si compie silenziosa e implacabile l'aggressione-distruzione del sole, della luce che acceca con la stessa forza del suo abbagliare. La compresenza di vita e morte in un medesimo atto, di luce e oscurità nella stessa *ora* voraginosa genera insieme attrazione e orrore davanti a un dissolversi che, continuamente iterato, conduce oltre la morte fisica e la tomba, secondo quanto suggerisce la lettura dell'ultimo verso." From "Il deserto nella poesia di Ungaretti," in *Studi in onore di A. Chiari* (Brescia, 1973), II, p. 736.

[4] From *Quaderno egiziano* (1931); now in *Il deserto e dopo* (Milan, 1961, 1969), p. 80. My italics. The account was first published in one of a series of lyrical essays in the *Gazzetta del Popolo*, September 12, 1931.

[5] *Un été dans le Sahara*, ed. Maxime Revon (Paris, 1938), pp. 184-185.

[6] Concerning the impression of the "darkness" that derives from the intensity of midday's excessive (or absolute) light, see the last part of the introduction to this study. The testimony of two other modern writers—men of the south and the desert—is also pertinent here. The first is from a passage in a novel by the Sicilian author Vitaliano Brancati. In recalling the August noontides of his native island, he seeks to give an almost "scientific" explanation of the phenomenon: "E tuttavia, nonostante la sua intensità, o forse a causa di questa, la luce del sud rivela nella memoria una profonda natura di tenebra. Nella sua esorbitanza, varca continuamente i confini del regno opposto, e quando si dice ch'è accecante, si vuole forse alludere, senz'averne esatta coscienza, a certi guizzi di buio che vengono dal suo interno, a certi squarci sulla notte cupa come può farli un'eclissi nel cielo di mezzogiorno, salvo che questi sono lenti e progressivi e, a volta chiusi, non si riaprono più, e quelli invece rapidi e continui, sicché la sensazione della luce per chi, insospettito della propria malinconia o tetraggine, voglia esaminarla, risulta composta di due sensazioni contrarie, di chiaro e di scuro, alternate fulmineamente, in modo che l'impressione totale è di chiaro." *Paolo il Caldo* (Milan, 1955), p. 12.

In considering how he could at one time have felt so sure of the "absurdity" or "non-sense" of the world, Albert Camus makes use of the image of the ambiguous light of the high-noon sun which envelops things in a "dark brilliance" to suggest that what we are faced with is not the absurd (or nothingness?) but an enigma: "Avec tant de soleil dans la mémoire, comment ai-je pu parier sur le non-sens? On s'en étonne, autour de moi; je m'en étonne aussi, parfois. Je pourrais répondre, et me répondre, que le soleil justement m'y aidait et que sa lumière, à force d'épaisseur, coagule l'univers et ses formes dans un éblouissement obscur." From "L'énigme" (1950), in *L'été*. See *Noces*; *L'été* (Paris, 1959), p. 149. The point made in this passage is that the world is an enigma, that is, the sense that it contains is poorly perceived because it "dazzles" us just as the sun's excessive light dazzles and causes us to see darkly. The reader need hardly be reminded of the importance of the sun and the desert in the works of Camus. Of major importance in this connection is the author's novel

Notes to Pages 205-209   313

L'Étranger on which one may consult the interesting study by René Andrianne, "Soleil, Ciel et Lumière dans *L'Étranger* de Camus," *Revue Romane*, 7 (1972), pp. 161-176.

[7] *Il deserto e dopo*, p. 80.

[8] In the slim volume *Il povero nella città* (Milan, 1949), p. 69. The volume includes some of the pieces first published between 1931 and 1932 in the *Gazzetta del Popolo*. In his prefatory note Ungaretti observes: "Sono paesaggi e persone e epoche visti a lume di fantasia e di proposito sottratti quindi ad ogni precisa informazione obiettiva. Rispecchiano solo miei stati d'animo, attimi fuggenti del mio sentimento" (p. 9). Concerning the piece of interest to us, the original title was restored in *Il deserto e dopo*, perhaps as being more in keeping with the general title of this volume.

[9] Elsewhere Ungaretti has used similar imagery in speaking more explicitly of the raging sensuality that the desert burns into its children, one of whom he remained throughout his long life. The sands that burn fiercely into the desert dweller are said to be aphrodisiac: "Sabbie afrodisiache, che luccicano come brillanti: sabbie che ti prendono dalla pianta del piede e poi arrivano su, su, su, e vi sconvolgono tutto." The connection between desert (the real desert, but with it the sentiment of desolation and nothingness) and fierce erotic desire is made unequivocally in the following words: "Uno degli stimoli del mio sentirmi staccato da tutto e uomo solo, in assoluto uomo solo, proviene anche dalla prossimità, durante i miei primi vent'anni, del deserto e dal conseguente privilegio che avevo di avventurarmi senza difficoltà nella sua desolazione. Anche solo nei pochi passi che vi potevo fare, l'entrata nel deserto, nel nulla sterminato, mi sconvolgeva a fondo. Chi può averne idea del deserto se non lo ha frequentato almeno appena? L'effetto più tremendo orrendo stupendo del deserto è il suo effetto erotico. . . . Quindi due almeno degli elementi che contribuiscono a formare la mia ispirazione mi vengono dal deserto e sono il sentimento della solitudine irriducibile [= the existential aloneness or nothingness of man] e il sentimento della schiavitù carnale." Quoted by Leone Piccioni in his book *Vita di un poeta: Giuseppe Ungaretti* (Milan, 1970), pp. 41-42.

[10] Though Mallarmé was an early and persistent influence on Ungaretti, the Italian poet's translation of "L'Après-midi d'un faune" was made relatively late in his life. See Giuseppe Ungaretti, *Traduzioni: da Gongora e da Mallarmé* (Milan, 1948), II, pp. 80-81.

[11] These interconnections and their dependence upon the poet's early years in Alexandria and his acquaintance with the desert were

lucidly and eloquently stated by him late in life in a commentary on his collected verse: "Si tratta della mia prima infanzia, di quel momento della vita che rimane nella mente tuffato nella notte o nel solleone del miraggio. Il miraggio. Nel Sahara, i beduini, l'occhio esorbitato, la lingua di fuori secca, non sapevano come salvarsi dalla loro condizione di rantolanti. Da laggiù, laggiù, allora, dalla scalea di strati di compatta luce contagiati sul suolo percosso da solleone martoriato di rabbia, mentre la sua luce rarefatta rimbalzava attraversa da strati più densi: nel cuore di quegli abbagli sovrapposti brusca eleggeva luce sospesa capovolta una sembianza di dimore felici, attorniate da giardini, specchiantesi in un lago con zampilli impazienti, . . . *La più allettante illusione, la più crudele delusione*. . . . Nacque a quel modo il gusto e la passione di slanciarmi, di tuffarmi, di imbozzolarmi in miraggi. Era un puerile scoprimento del proprio esistere interiore; insieme, l'abbaglio d'un'immagine, e quasi il nulla, dentro di me, d'una realtà, di quella realtà che più tardi m'occorrerà afferrare, domarla ed avvincermela, di quella realtà rugosa familiare a Rimbaud." In *Tutte le poesie*, pp. 502-503.

[12] In ibid., p. 10. The poem, first published in 1919, belongs to the collection *L'Allegria*.

[13] In one of the most important studies to appear on Ungaretti in recent years, a critic remarks acutely that the final metaphor (*miraggio*) in these two lines would hardly have all its tension and bitterness if the image did not presuppose the concrete reality of being athirst at noon (*meriggio*). From this literal and, according to Carlo Ossola, somewhat banal precision the figure (the mirage) anagrammatically separates itself. See Ossola, *Giuseppe Ungaretti* (Milan, 1975), p. 106.

[14] From the poem "Nebbia," published first in 1919; now in *Tutte le poesie*, p. 390. The lines quoted are the last verses of the poem.

[15] *Tutte le poesie*, p. 70.

[16] In a recent book Glauco Cambon speaks of Ungaretti's sense that all things of positive value are at bottom a mirage (cf. Leopardi's theory of illusions) and points to the tyranny of the sexual drive in the poet as deriving from his sense of death and the void: "Se tutto è miraggio, ben tuonerà a suo tempo la risata dello Dginn Rull. Il deserto è sete infinita. La sensualità è l'altra faccia della coscienza del vuoto, contro la quale l'Oriente egizio eresse montagne di pietra, e l'Oriente musulmano, trine di pietra." *La poesia di Ungaretti* (Turin, 1976), p. 75.

[17] In Ungaretti's note to *Sentimento del Tempo*, in *Tutte le poesie*, p. 531.

[18] "Il *Sentimento* è dunque la pienezza implacabile del sole, la

stagione di violenza, e nello stesso tempo, la clausura dell'uomo, nella seconda parte del libro, dentro la propria fralezza." In *Tutte le poesie*, p. 535. "Se prendete il *Sentimento del Tempo*, vi trovate tre temi principali: il tema dell'aurora—un'aurora non edenica, non di perfetta felicità, in qualche modo contaminata dalla storia; il tema del desiderio a un ritorno dello stato edenico; e il tema della morte, del nulla." In ibid., p. 551.

[19] Ibid., p. 283.
[20] Ibid., pp. 105-106.
[21] Ibid., p. 680.
[22] Ibid., p. 127.
[23] Ibid., p. 104.
[24] Ibid.
[25] "Oggi che s'illuminano di ombre flebili le distanti montagne / E s'empie il deserto di desolante mistero / Prendono sonno le statue nella folta estate." In ibid., p. 676.
[26] Ibid., p. 677.
[27] Ibid. In the earliest version of the piece, morning itself has a greater erotic suggestiveness, for it is described in connection with the image of the fresh young flesh of bathing nymphs: "Ondeggia sull'acqua flessuosa il carnato primaverile delle ninfe rinate."
[28] For this sense of vanity (the nothingness) of man and the awareness of being a fragile shadow, see lines 7-16 of the poem "Vanità": "E l'uomo / Curvato / Sull'acqua / Sorpresa / Dal sole / Si rinviene / Un'ombra // Cullata e / Piano / Franta." In ibid., p. 78. The short poem entitled "Ombra" (1927, 1943) expresses the theme of man as a shadow that will soon become *indistinct*: "Uomo che speri senza pace, / Stanca ombra nella luce polverosa, / L'ultimo caldo se ne andrà a momenti / E vagherai indistinto . . ." (p. 140). In "La pietà," Ungaretti writes "È nei vivi la strada dei defunti, // *Siamo noi la fiumana d'ombre*" (p. 170) where the idea of the "vanity" (i.e., nothingness) of man is determined by man's being subject to time imaged in the rushing stream. In fact, the poet says, "We are the stream of shadows." Concerning "Paesaggio," we may also note that the 1933 passage we are considering reappears in the 1936 version except that the word *nulla* is omitted, perhaps as being too obvious.
[29] In *Tutte le poesie*, pp. 104.
[30] There are times in the poetry of Ungaretti when night offers a respite in which the poet experiences calm or even the return of illusions. But in "Paesaggio" night concludes the cycles of life and the day with the most complete sense of dismay and disillusionment:

Tutto si è esteso, si è attenuato, si è confuso.
Fischi di treni partiti.
Ecco appare, non essendoci più testimoni,
Anche il mio vero viso, stanco e deluso.

The nocturnal "astrali nidi d'*illusione*" of a poem such as "O notte" here give way to the "true visage" of the poet, "stanco e *deluso*."

[31] The observation is made in a preface Ungaretti wrote to Palma Bucarelli's *Jean Fautrier* (Milan, 1960). It is reprinted in *Saggi e Interventi* (Milan, 1974), pp. 671-672.

[32] Kenneth Clark, *Landscape into Art* (London, 1949), p. 108. On p. 97 Clark writes: "Turner and van Gogh. Both are fundamentally northern artists—painters of the midnight sun and the aurora borealis. Yet both were inspired by the landscape of Mediterranean countries, because only in these could they find the delirium of light which was the release of their emotions."

[33] In *Tutte le poesie*, p. 122. The poem underwent a minimum of change through the years, the only difference being in line 9 which originally was "Con indiscrete, schiette seduzioni" rather than "Con i suoi occhi calcinanti."

[34] Ibid., p. 533.

[35] G. Getto and F. Portinari, *Dal Carducci ai contemporanei: Antologia della lirica moderna* (Bologna, 1956), p. 235.

[36] I have spoken of Leconte de Lisle's "Midi" in connection with Leopardi, but the poem will be considered in greater detail in the discussion of Montale. Concerning the vision of a merciless midday sun that symbolizes the negative force by which nature consumes itself, we may quote from one of Italy's major modern novelists, Cesare Pavese, a passage that has essentially the same concept: "Non c'è niente che sappia di morte più del sole d'estate, della gran luce, della natura esuberante. Tu fiuti l'aria e senti il bosco, e ti accorgi che piante e bestie se ne infischiano di te. Tutto vive e si macera in se stesso. La natura è la morte." From *Il diavolo sulle colline*. In the volume *Romanzi* (Turin, 1961), II, p. 163. Perhaps reference should also be made here to D'Annunzio's short poem "Nella belletta" (from *Alcyone*) and its evocation of an August sun burning its consuming rays on a marsh (as on a miry flower) causing it to exhale a sickly sweet, pestilential sultriness. But one of the most remarkable visions of the corruption and death that lie at the very heart of an apparently beautiful and luxuriant nature is the prose passage on nature's "garden hospital" in Leopardi's *Zibaldone*, pp. 4,175-4,177. In *Zibaldone*

Notes to Pages 222-224 317

di pensieri, ed. Francesco Flora (Milan, 1937, 1961), II, pp. 1,005-1,006.

[37] The paragraph quoted is given as an independent unit, in the form of a prose lyric, in the section entitled "Il tavoliere" from *Le Puglie*; in *Il deserto e dopo*, pp. 314-315. It was published first as "Foggia: Fontane e Chiese," in the *Gazzetta del Popolo*, February 20, 1934.

[38] "Tu ti spezzasti" is from the volume *Il dolore 1940-1945*. I quote from *Tutte le poesie*, p. 216.

[39] In connection with this bestial "roar" of the sun, we may recall what was said earlier about the subjective nature of the auditory impressions of midday's silence, whether the sounds be actual sensory perceptions or not. (See especially the introduction.) Such violent acoustical images (suggesting aggressiveness or hostility) associated with the implacable sun of summer or midday are, as we have seen, not uncommon. Camus gives us an example when he writes: "A midi, sous un soleil assourdissant, la mer se soulève à peine, extenuée." And another, more suggestive yet: "Tombés de la cime du ciel, *des flots de soleil rebondissent brutalement* sur la campagne autour de nous. *Tout se tait devant ce fracas* et le Lubéron, là-bas, n'est qu'un énorme bloc de silence que j'écoute sans répit." From *L'été*, in *Noces*; *L'été*, pp. 180, 149. In the latter passage the sun is the *fracas*. Also worth quoting here is the brief poem "Estate" by Ardengo Soffici, an evocation of a summer that suggests the overmastering midday sun vanquishing the earth in its white-hot "liquid" fire and imposing a silence so absolute that it produces a violent sonority. The poem's second stanza impressionistically depicts air, rooftops, gardens, and orchards broiling under the sun while deserted fields extend endlessly in an immense torpor: "Estate, disco bianco, bianca / Vampa, / Liquefazione d'oro, / *Cembalo di silenzio sonoro* / Sulla terra stanca. // Respiro infiammato, bollore / Di tetti, di giardini e d'orti; / Stupore di campi smorti / Abbandonati nell'immensità." Ungaretti's vision in "Di luglio," of course, is both more dramatic and more tragic.

The *nakedness* attributed by Ungaretti to the sun ("sole ignudo") in the last verse of "Tu ti spezzasti" has been well explicated by Glauco Cambon who speaks of it as "la nudità fisica e metafiscia, la negazione estrema, la verità-scheletro." In *La poesia di Ungaretti*, p. 160. I do not know whether Cambon, in speaking of this sun as the "truth-skeleton," had in mind the vision of the sun as a fulgurating skeleton that we have found in Ungaretti's page on Apulia. My guess is that he was thinking of the sun-bleached dromedary skeleton of the *Quaderno egiziano*. In any case, there is truth enough in that skeleton, and the connection between the two images is also clear enough. Pages 158-169 of Cambon's study should be read for a rich if dense analysis of the whole of Ungaretti's elegy.

[40] *Tutte le poesie*, p. 181.

[41] Ibid., pp. 182-183.

[42] There are important pages by Glauco Cambon on "La morte meditata," especially concerning the way in which the cycle, rather than proceeding in a linear progression, develops as a "concentric radiation" of autonomous moments from the first canto. On the question of the relationship between death and the poet in the cycle, he writes: "L'ambiguità centrale sta nel fatto che la morte viene di lontano ('insegue'), è un Altro esistenziale, l'antitesi della luce, eppure si annida nell'intimo della coscienza e della carne, in certo senso anzi è la coscienza e la persona, il loro fermento buio ('notturna quanto più la luce ha forza')." See "Appunti per *La morte meditata* di Ungaretti," in *Forum Italicum*, 6 (June 1972), pp. 232-243. The essay is also incorporated in Cambon's volume *La poesia di Ungaretti*, pp. 125-137.

[43] The question of the relationship between the second and third cantos has been discussed by Carmine Anthony Mezzacappa who notes that in the second canto "la morte è venuta a questo punto a fare tutt'uno sia col tempo che con la noia, mediante l'analogia della 'cicala' che svolge il suo canto monotono e opprimente nell'afosa ora meridiana annunziatrice del tramonto." And on the repetition in the third canto of the motifs of *Canto Secondo*, he writes: "Non si tratta, però, di una semplice variante in cui il poeta miri soltanto a raggiungere una maggiore purezza e robustezza delle parole; si tratta piuttosto di un vero Canto nuovo che ripetendo quello precedente vuole farci sentire tutto il peso e la durata della sofferenza che di continuo si rinnova e sempre più si acuisce nello spirito umano. . . . Mercé la ripetizione, essendo ogni cosa vista e sentita sempre più da vicino, ecco infine quel 'Ti odo cantare come una cicala' mutarsi in 'Insisti come le cicale irose,' e il canto muto ad una voce diventa lo stridio confuso d'un coro ossessionato, che penetra, penetra, fino al midollo, fino ai più intimi recessi dell'anima." *Noia e inquietudine nella 'Vita d'un uomo' di Giuseppe Ungaretti* (Padua, 1970), pp. 210-211.

Carlo Ossola has the following comment on the matter: "Le esigenze di maggiore sinteticità che fanno del *Canto terzo* un emblematico compendio del *Secondo*, riducono il paragone finale a un solo intenso verso, tra i più belli del *Sentimento del Tempo*; ma esso, ancora una volta, pur nella divergenza della semantica, è ottenuto per concentrazione dei significanti, per l'isomorfismo che si stabilisce tra 'una *cicala / Nella rosa*' e le '*cicale irose.*' Nell'economia del testo la sintesi figurale avviene per calcolo anagrammatico che lascia inalterata la curva melodica, 'rubandone,' riducendone i tempi: l'*enjambement* 'cicala / Nella rosa' con la pausa di senso che il 'bianco' di fine verso determina, viene coagulato in un solo verso; e quel tempo di 'vuoto,' bruciato dall'anagramma, si trasforma però in nuova metafora, di suono e di senso, nell'ossessivo urgere del tempo metrico e metafisico ('*Insisti* come le cicale irose'): cicala / Nella rosa → [cicale in rose] cicale i[n] rose → *cicale irose.*" In *Giuseppe Ungaretti*, pp. 101-102.

[44] *Tutte le poesie*, p. 114.

[45] Compare André Chenier's midday sleeping nymph who is espied in a reclining position on the grass. But see especially the sestet of Stecchetti's sonnet "*Dies*" and Villaroel's "Meriggio estivo."

[46] "Secondo discorso su Leopardi," in *Paragone*, 1 (October 1950), p. 28. In addition to his remarks on "Alla primavera" in his "Discorso," Ungaretti contemplated writing a documentary treatise which would connect Leopardi's poem to previous treatments of the midday demon and compare it with other poets' treatment of ancient fables. The sketchy manuscript, which was never put into a final form, remains unedited. A brief description of its contents and proposed plan is given by the editors of the volume *Saggi e interventi* (Milan, 1974), pp. 966-967. It is a curious and even (to me) astonishing fact that Ungaretti nowhere seems to have mentioned (in writing) the *meriggio* from Leopardi's "La vita solitaria."

[47] "I testi greci e latini, e anche il San Girolamo della vita di *San Paolo, primo eremita*, dei quali il Leopardi si servirà per ottenere l'atmosfera della Canzone ["Alla primavera"], sono citati . . . a spiegare il significato di 'demonio meridiano,' e come certe favole antiche fossero nate dai miraggi e dal delirio di quell'ora di clima caldo. . . . Più che rimpiangere come avrebbe fatto un Neoclassico, le favole antiche, il Leopardi si proponeva dunque di esprimere quello stato incerto tra sogno e ricordo, proprio come più tardi anche Mallarmé vorrà fare nell'*Après-midi d'un faune.*" In "Secondo discorso su Leopardi," *Paragone*, 1 (October 1950), p. 29.

For the significance of Leopardi in Ungaretti see the fine pages in Luciano Rebay's *Le origini della poesia di Giuseppe Ungaretti* (Rome, 1962), pp. 113-132. There are also excellent remarks on the relationship between Ungaretti and Mallarmé in Rebay's volume and, from a different perspective, in Olga Ragusa's *Mallarmé in Italy* (New

York, 1957). For Leopardi and Ungaretti, one may also consult Mezzacappa's *Noia e inquietudine nella 'Vita d'un uomo' di Giuseppe Ungaretti*, pp. 46-58 and 130-138. Unfortunately, Rebay does not touch on Ungaretti's "L'isola," and Mezzacappa, who does discuss it, makes no connection between it and Leopardi. Untenable in my view is Mezzacappa's reading of "L'isola" as a nocturne. (See his book at p. 141.) On the other hand, a recent critic who makes acute remarks on "L'isola" as a poem under the influence of Leopardi's "Alla primavera" is Gilberto Lonardi, in " 'Leopardismi' tra ideologia, mito e linguaggio," in *Studi novecenteschi*, 1 (March 1972), pp. 43-45, now also in the author's *Leopardismo: saggio sugli usi di Leopardi dall'Otto al Novecento* (Florence, 1974), pp. 51-53. However, Lonardi does not discuss "L'isola" as an erotic vision. Without noting the connection with Leopardi's "Alla primavera," the American critic Joseph Cary has caught in Ungaretti's poem "its evocation of the erotic atmosphere enveloping this land of heart's desire, close and sultry." Cary has fine things to say in this light about "L'isola," although I am not sure he sees the poem as situated in the midday hour. See his *Three Modern Italian Poets: Saba, Ungaretti, Montale* (New York and London, 1969), pp. 185-187.

[48] Ungaretti's note to the poem says: "Il paesaggio è quello di Tivoli. Perchè l'*isola*? Perchè è il punto dove io mi isolo, dove sono solo: è un punto separato dal resto del mondo, non perchè lo sia in realtà, ma perchè nel mio stato d'animo posso separarmene." In *Tutte le poesie*, p. 537. On the theme of the oasis (in relation also to the theme of nothingness) there are good remarks in Renata Lollo's article "Il deserto nella poesia di Ungaretti," in *Studi in onore di A. Chiari*, II, pp. 735-739. Although she does not deal with "L'isola," an observation on the psychology of the oasis motif is pertinent here: "oasi può essere appagamento ma può essere anche desiderio" (p. 739). For other significant remarks on the oasis motif in Ungaretti see the essay by Luciana Stegagno Picchio, "*Semantica* di Ungaretti: Varianti, testo e contesto," in *Studi in onore di Natalino Sapegno* (Rome, 1975), II, pp. 1,010-1,016 and 1,019. But see also the books already mentioned by Ossola, Cambon, Mezzacappa, and Piccioni.

[49] *Tutte le poesie*, p. 32. I have italicized the word *approdava* which has an echo in the opening line of "L'isola": "A una *proda* . . . scese."

[50] "Allusione a una presenza femminile con la quale feci esperienza di forsennata lussuria, alla quale tornerò anche in *Sentimento del Tempo*." In ibid., p. 524.

[51] Ibid., p. 123.

Notes to Pages 235-240

[52] This dream of the shepherd-Ungaretti of "L'isola" may be compared to the more explicit midday erotic fantasy in Jenco's poem "L'ora di Pan." As his flock reposes during noontide, a shepherd, leaning in the shade of an olive tree, dreams of passionate sexual conquests under the blazing sun:

> Il branco rumina il sonno del meriggio,
> E il pastore, poggiata all'ombra,
> Sogna una canicola di amplessi sull'erba.

From *La vigna rossa* (1955), now in the volume *Marsilvana* (Siena, 1959), p. 175. Of the modern poets he read with devotion, Jenco admired Ungaretti perhaps second only to Pascoli. It is not unlikely that he read "L'isola" as an erotic dream fantasy and was influenced by it here. Even the olive tree and its shade (present metaphorically in Ungaretti's poem) are significant elements in Jenco's poem.

[53] For a discussion of the erotic elements (and their allegorical significance) in the Dante-Matelda encounter in Eden, see Charles S. Singleton's essay "Matelda" in his volume *Journey to Beatrice: Dante Studies 2* (Cambridge, 1958), pp. 204-221.

[54] In his remarks on the theme of the sea and the desert in Romantic literature, W. H. Auden writes: "The sea and the desert are related to the city as its symbolic opposites. There is a third image, in the case of the sea the happy island and in the case of the desert the oasis or rose-garden, which stands related to both. It is like the city in that it is an enclosed place of safety and like the sea-desert in that it is a solitary or private place from which the general public are excluded and where the writ of the law does not run. The primary idea with which the garden-island image is associated is, therefore, neither justice nor chastity but innocence: it is the earthly paradise where there is no conflict between natural desire and moral duty." *The Enchafèd Flood, or the Romantic Iconography of the Sea* (New York, 1967), p. 20.

[55] "Dolore di Rembrandt," now in *Il deserto e dopo*, p. 301.

[56] Ibid., pp. 301-302.

CHAPTER VI

[1] As far back as 1933, Gianfranco Contini noted: "C'è un mito in Montale, che riesce proprio centrale alla sua poesia: ben più che il mare; ed è l'ora del meriggio. . . . La distruzione meridiana è il segno esterno più indicativo di questa figura che è: sciogliersi della vita."

"Introduzione a *Ossi di seppia*," in *Esercizi di lettura* (Turin, 1974), p. 72, first published in *Rivista Rosminiana*, January-March 1933. No critic of *Ossi di seppia* can overlook the motif. Montale's first volume of verse has been reprinted several times. My quotations from the poems are from the edition printed by Mondadori, *Ossi di seppia 1920-1927*, 8th ed. (Milan, 1961).

[2] For a penetrating study of D'Annunzio's influence on the poetic language of Montale, see Pier Vincenzo Mengaldo's "Da D'Annunzio a Montale: Ricerche sulla formazione e la storia del linguaggio poetico montaliano," in *Quaderni del circolo filologico-linguistico padovano*, 1, *Ricerche sulla lingua poetica contemporanea* (Padua, 1966), pp. 163-259. See also Alberto Frattini, "D'Annunzio e la lirica italiana del Novecento," in *Poeti e critici italiani dell'Otto e del Novecento* (Milan, 1966), pp. 48-51.

[3] *Ossi di seppia*, p. 48.

[4] This sentiment or condition brings to mind the similar mood expressed earlier by Montale's fellow Ligurian, Camillo Sbarbaro, in the poems touched on in note 81 of chapter four. We may note here also that two poems of *Ossi di seppia* make up the section entitled *Poesie per Camillo Sbarbaro*.

[5] We may recall here the two early poems by D'Annunzio where, in an oppressive midday, the Adriatic sea flashes "barbagli terribili di lame" and "deserto, / Triste, metallico bolle il mare."

[6] *Ossi di seppia*, p. 54.

[7] If the word *sonnolenza* were not connected by the poet with *meriggio*, it would be possible to interpret the image as indicating an opposition between the immobility (hence, the indifference) of the statue and the cruelty of midday. But *sonnolenza* clearly refers to midday, so that the image suggests that statue and noontide combine to form a unit creating the picture of a perfect (i.e., divine) stasis of indifference. Nonetheless, it is not irrelevant here to compare the divine indifference of Montale's statue absorbed in the midday torpor with Saba's figure (in "Meriggio") of the old man (or beggar) asleep in the "arsa solitudine" of a torrid noontide and indifferent to the meridian blaze.

[8] *Ossi di seppia*, p. 48.

[9] For Dante's Ulysses and his famous *orazion picciola*, see *Inferno*, XXVI, 112-122.

[10] Silvio Ramat has noted the ambivalence if not the negative quality of the light spoken of in the poem: "Questa luce non sembra affatto un'altra letizia; anche se attenuata, traspare la paura avvertita nei

versi *In limine*, di staccarsi dal danno abituale—qui figurato dal 'canneto'—per andare verso una condizione diversa, forse migliore, ma ignorata." *Montale* (Florence, 1965), p. 40.

[11] *Ossi di seppia*, p. 59.

[12] Compare the words "Inerte, tout brûle dans *l'heure fauve*," in Mallarmé's "L'Après-midi d'un faune," and Ungaretti's references to the same color for midday's corrosive light.

[13] For documentation see Roger Caillois, "Les démons de midi," *Revue de l'histoire des religions*, 115 (1937), pp. 156-159. For a discussion of examples from modern literature see the article by Pierre Somville, "Midi tragique et le complexe de Schlemil," *Cahiers internationaux de symbolisme*, 26 (1974), pp. 83-98.

[14] Thus even the *ombra* of "Non rifugiarti nell'ombra" has more "metaphysical" significance than the shade of the midday forest retreat in the long history of the motif before Montale, although the forest with its shade has always had special (even metaphysical) significance. But in Montale's poem the *ombra* seems almost to represent the concept of illusion. The truth lies exposed in the shadowless glare of the midday sun where things are disintegrating. The concept of the shadow in Montale's poetry is fundamental and most often connected with the theme of midday. A whole section of the volume *Ossi di seppia* bears the title *Meriggi e ombre*, but the motif actually runs throughout the work. However, it is not always easy to determine the precise value to be given to *ombra*. The last stanza of "Meriggiare . . ." suggests that the poet has left what little shade, if any, the garden wall may have offered and now walks in total and cruel midday. One of the poems taken to be most representative of Montale's negativity or sense of not being able to participate directly in a perhaps meaningless world is "Non chiederci la parola che squadri da ogni lato." The last of its three quatrains ends with the lines "Codesto solo oggi possiamo dirti / Ciò che *non* siamo, ciò che *non* vogliamo." The poem's second stanza, sandwiched between two stanzas announcing this negativity (which may of course contain a positive ethical value) seems a parenthetical but significant sigh of nostalgia (or is it disapproval?) for the man who has no self-doubts and moves sure-footedly, not concerned with the shadow the blazing summer sun causes him to cast on a peeling plastered wall:

Ah l'uomo che se ne va sicuro,
Agli altri ed a se stesso amico,
E l'ombra sua non cura che la canicola
Stampa sopra uno scalcinato muro!

Whatever we choose to make of the idea of the *ombra* here (is it a symbol of reality or of the precariousness and insubstantiality of man?), Montale either disapproves of or wonders at the man who can disregard being preoccupied with what for him seems to be a symbol connected with his own doubts about the ontological validity of reality. For at the very least (or at most) the *ombra* is an ambivalent thing. In the poem "Ciò che di me sapeste," the ambiguity of the person (and of being) and the inevitable incommunicability of the self to others (who may also be nothing at bottom but "shadows") are suggested by the poet's declaration of his acceptance of himself as a shadow, though in his willingness to offer his *ombra* to others there seems to be the idea of a positive value connected with it: "Se un'ombra scorgete, non è / Un ombra—ma quella io sono. / Potessi spiccarla da me / Offrirvela in dono."

[15] In the poem "Fuscello teso dal muro," Montale develops the motif of the sundial that scans the "career" of both the sun and man's own brief life by means of the shadow it casts.

[16] In a perhaps remote way, one may be reminded also of the sardonically intoned image from Baudelaire's "Une charogne" where the sun rains down burning rays that have the effect of cooking *à point* the rotting carcass of an animal stretched in an obscene position.

[17] "*Ma* sedendo e mirando, interminati / Spazi *di là da quella*, e sovrumani / Silenzi, e profondissima quiete / Io nel pensier *mi fingo*." From "L'infinito," lines 4-7.

[18] "Questo di sette è il più gradito giorno, / Pien di speme e di gioia: / Diman tristezza e noia / Recheran l'ore, ed al travaglio usato / Ciascuno in suo pensier farà ritorno" (lines 38-42). But see especially the entry of January 20, 1821 in Leopardi's notebooks: *Zibaldone*, pp. 532-535. In *Zibaldone di pensieri*, ed. Francesco Flora (Milan 1937, 1961), I, pp. 414-416. And on March 26, 1820, we find: "Nella speranza o in qualunque altra disposizione dell'animo nostro, il bene lontano è sempre maggiore del presente" (p. 131).

[19] In his study on the echoes of D'Annunzio in Montale, P. V. Mengaldo makes the following observation: "Una prima formulazione della poetica montaliana matura, come necessità di uno sguardo coraggioso e disincantato alla realtà frammentaria e disintegrata, richiede subito, ben entro gli *Ossi*, il rifiuto preliminare e parallelo dell'immersione acritica nella natura come rifugio, o come giustificazione all'atonia ('È ora di lasciare il canneto / stento che pare s'addorma / e di guardare le forme / della vita che si sgretola'). In

questo senso risulta anche evidente, per altro verso, che l'unico aspetto del naturalismo dannunziano che Montale può continuare, seppure sporadicamente, ancora all'altezza delle *Occasioni*, sia appunto l'aspetto 'negativo' della realtà fisica inerte, malata, decomposta: e anche qui secondo un processo già ben visibile nella prima raccolta [*Ossi*...], dove la pienezza vitale della natura trapassa continuamente in sordità, indifferenza e minaccioso disfacimento delle cose, e la *gloria* del mezzogiorno si rovescia subito necessariamente in *arsura* e *squallore*." From "Da D'Annunzio a Montale," *Quaderni del circolo filologico-linguistico padovano*, 1 (Padua, 1966), p. 235.

As for Pascoli's "Gloria," see the discussion in chapter two of this study. It seems likely to me that Pascoli's poem had a direct influence on Montale. So too, perhaps, did Saba's "Meriggio" with its polemical thrust at the invading "glory" of the midday sun's light. Jenco's "Umiltà," on the other hand, was probably influenced by Montale as well as by the other two poets.

[20] Jean-Paul Sartre's thoughts on Leconte de Lisle's "Midi" are particularly relevant to our discussion for they apply to Ungaretti and Montale at least as much as they do to the French poet. It is interesting to see that Sartre speaks of the dark night of nothingness as being seen in the intense yet corrosive light of midday which, as we know, is a major theme and image in Ungaretti and appears in other Italian poets as well: "L'implacable justice de Midi, dévoreur des ombres, c'est la parfaite équivalence des boqueteaux, des champs déserts qu'il consume, l'anéantissement par la lumière des rapports, des valeurs et finalement (mais symboliquement) de toute vie, c'est la découverte du *Non-Sens* non comme je ne sais quelle opacité ténébreuse de l'être mais comme son éblouissant et sublime éclatement, come sa gloire. Absorbé 'dans la flamme implacable du soleil,' le poète lui emprunte sa puissance d'anéantissement, il fait de la lumière corrosive son propre regard: en plein jour, sous les feux de midi, il se rejoint à cette Nuit future, à 'la grande Ombre informe, dans son vide et sa sterilité [...] où git la vanité de ce qui fut le temps et l'espace et le nombre.' Ces catégories trop humaines ne sauraient qualifier l'être véritable qui est éternité: c'est l'homme qui se prétend la mesure de toute chose; mais il est mortel, il est mort et la mesure disparaît avec lui. En s'identifiant avec le Soleil, le poète refuse les catégories cardinales de la pensée et, du même mouvement, la pensée elle-même: il revient vers les cités infimes, pour regarder les gens et leurs agitations avec des yeux solaires, du point de vue de la non-vie, de la non-pensée, du non-savoir et finalement du non-être: s'il con-

serve le 'néant divin qui a trempé son coeur,' il l'utilisera à *déshumaniser* les hommes, à les saisir non tels qu'ils se pensent ou se vivent mais tels qu'ils sont, c'est à dire dans ce Non-Sens originel qu'ils n'ont même pas égratigné de leurs futiles significations." Jean-Paul Sartre, *L'Idiot de la famille: Gustave Flaubert de 1821 à 1857* (Paris, 1972), III, pp. 363-364.

[21] It is interesting to compare Montale's solitary cicada with the image of a late-singing solitary cicada introduced by Carducci in the prose passage we quoted earlier. In the fullness of summer (July) Carducci, we recall, identified himself with the wildly chirring chorus of cicadas, a symbol of nature's fervent life force. Now he evokes the memory of a single cicada who has persisted beyond summer after the first September rains. And again the poet, in the autumn of his life, associates himself with that cicada. Though he does not have any regrets, in the midst of the cool autumn breezes he cannot help thinking back to the vibrant heat of the summer of 1857. And there is clearly the suggestion of something desperate in the reference to the heroic effort that the cicada, as though out of a sense of duty, continues to make in singing. Indeed, the author admits that there is something profoundly sad in the stridulation of the solitary cicada in the surrounding hiss of the chilly winds: "In Toscana e in Romagna le cicale durano a cantare, più sempre rade, è vero, e via via più discordi, fino in settembre; e a me è avvenuto di sentirne qualcuna a punto dopo le prime pioggie settembrine. Come si affaticava, quasi per un senso di dovere, la figlia della Terra a pur cantare! ma come era triste quello stridore di cicala unica tra il ridesto sussurio de' venti freschi e la dolcezza del verde rintenerito! E anch'io sono oramai una cicala di settembre: non rimpiango né richiamo né invidio; soltanto tra le brezze d'autunno ricordo gli ardori del luglio 1857 e le estati della dolce Toscana." *Prose di Giosue Carducci 1859-1903* (Bologna, 1957), p. 946.

[22] *Ossi di seppia*, p. 88.

[23] Let us also recall here the passage from *Il trionfo della morte*, where, on being seized by the sacred horror of a canicular midday, Giorgio Aurispa feels that "in fondo a quel suo vago sgomento si moveva qualche cosa simile all'ansietà di chi sta nell'attesa di un'apparizione repentina e formidabile."

[24] The poem "Non rifugiarti nell'ombra," we have seen, is an appeal to avoid immobility, and in the poem "Scirocco" Montale writes: "oggi sento / La mia immobilità come un tormento." The situation is quite different in other poems, as in "Arremba su la

strinata proda" of which one critic has written: "Dal timore di uno svolgimento nasce il desiderio di mantenere a tutti i costi quell'immobilità sicura come un porto riparato, e qui Montale rischia davvero di far della propria voce un invito all'inerzia, all'assenza, al distacco immobile e abulico." Lucio Lugnani, "Ossi di seppia," in the Montale commemorative issue of *La rassegna della letteratura italiana*, 70 (May-December 1966), nos. 2-3, p. 264. On this same poem Giuliano Manacorda speaks of "una rinuncia ben meditata e sofferta, non vilmente precostituita, ma come punto d'arrivo di una convinzione estrema che al non essere della vita deve corrispondere il non fare, che la tempesta incombe ad ogni istante e che meglio di ogni cosa è l'angusto ma sicuro riparo nel piccolo porto che nasconde e protegge." In *Montale* (Florence, 1969), p. 33. The suggestion that the hour of crisis in this poem is noontide has been made by Alvaro Valentini in his *Lettura di Montale: Ossi di seppia* (Rome, 1971), p. 122: "Penso che la spiegazione di Manacorda possa diventare più evidente se immaginiamo che l'ora a cui Montale allude sia, al solito, l'ora meridiana nella quale il disfacimento della realtà (il vaporare delle cose come essenze) sembra più evidente." For other interesting observations on the theme of immobility, see Manacorda, *Montale*, pp. 37, 39. See also Marco Forti's *Eugenio Montale: La poesia, la prosa di fantasia e d'invenzione* (Milan, 1973), p. 101. No critic can deal with Montale without considering so fundamental a motif in this poet's work as that of the tension or opposition between motion and immobility, between the flow of time and stasis.

[25] On the other hand, the prefatory poem to the volume of *Ossi di seppia* seems to echo Valéry's invitation to throw off immobility and welcome the wind. "In limine" begins, in fact, with the exhortation: "Godi se il vento ch'entra nel pomario / Vi rimena l'ondata della vita." But like all the great archetypal images (e.g., the sun, the sea) that recur over and over in Montale's verse, the wind (forerunner also of storms that may bring either salvation or destruction) has an ambiguous value in the overall context of the volume. Thus in the important poem "Fine dell'infanzia" (from the section *Meriggi e ombre*) the wind that comes to disturb the *finta calma* of the waves is a negative element. The polyvalent character of such archetypal images in Montale's poems can be explained both by the fact that they are all experienced as positive and negative in the actual life of humans, and by the particular situation and mood of any given poem. The parallel of the vital wind of "In limine" with the wind of Valéry's "Le cimetière marin" is noted by A. Valentini who makes

several references to the French poet in connection with Montale. See his *Lettura di Montale: Ossi di seppia*, pp. 26, 34, 58, 60, 88, 90, 129, 158, 178.

[26] Again there comes to mind a passage by Boine that expresses the sentiment of pure ambiguity, of enchanted bewilderment, of suspension (in a midday atmosphere) between being and nonbeing. In the prose lyric "Fuga," we read: "Le paurose bonaccie dell'immobilità, che magico il mondo pare un vano rispecchio di lago: *è, non è?* e il respiro è sospeso." As with the noontides of Nietzsche (in *Human, All Too Human*) and Valéry, here too a wind comes up to dispel the magic (positive or negative?) stasis: "—improvvisa le spazza la frescata levante. . . ."

Bibliography

Bibliographic information for works cited in this study is given in the notes. What follows is a bibliography restricted to works in which the theme of midday is given scholarly attention.

Arbesmann, Rudolph. "The *Daemonium Meridianum* and the Greek and Latin Patristic Exegesis." *Traditio*, 14 (1958), 17-31.
Bollnow, Otto Friedrich. *Das Wesen der Stimmungen*. Frankfurt am Main, Vittorio Klostermann, 1943, pp. 195-212.
―――. "Der Mittag: Ein Beitrag zur Metaphysik der Tageszeiten." In *Unruhe und Geborgenheit im Weltbild neuerer Dichter*. Stuttgart, W. Kohlhammer, 1953, pp. 143-177.
Caillois, Roger. "Les démons de midi." *Revue de l'histoire des religions*, 115 (1937), 142-173 and 116 (1937), 54-83, 143-186.
Gallas, K. R. "A propos du titre Le Démon de Midi." *Neophilologus*, 4 (1919), 371-372.
Gillet, Joseph E. "El mediodía y el demonio meridiano en España." *Nueva Revista de Filologia Hispanica*, 7 (1953), 307-315.
―――. "Further Additions to the Diablo Meridiano." *Hispanic Review*, 23 (1955), 294-295.
Kuhn, Reinhard. *The Demon of Noontide: Ennui in Western Literature*. Princeton, N.J., Princeton University Press, 1976, pp. 42-43.
de Labriolle, P. "Le démon de midi." *Bulletin Du Cange*, 9 (1934), 46-54.
Landersdorfer, S. "Das *daemonium meridianum* (Ps. 91 [90] 6)." *Biblische Zeitschrift*, 18 (1929), 294-300.
Leopardi, Giacomo. "Del meriggio." *Saggio sopra gli errori popolari degli antichi*. In *Le poesie e le prose*, II. Edited by Francesco Flora. Milan, Mondadori, 1953, pp. 280-283.
Meurs, Johannes Van. *Opera omnia*, V. Florence, Tartini and Franchi, 1745, cols. 734-737.
Perella, Nicolas J. *Night and the Sublime in Giacomo Leopardi*. Berkeley and Los Angeles, University of California Press, 1970, pp. 139-151.
Rivers, E. L. "Cassian's *Meridianum Demonium*." *Hispanic Review*, 23 (1955), 293.

Roscher, W. H. "Meridianus daemon." *Ausführliches Lexicon der griechischen und römischen Mythologie*, II, ii. Leipzig, B. G. Teubner, 1894-1897, pp. 2,832-2,835.

Rosenmeyer, Thomas G. *The Green Cabinet: Theocritus and the European Pastoral Lyric*. Berkeley and Los Angeles, University of California Press, 1969, pp. 67, 76, 88-89, 91.

Somville, Pierre. "Midi tragique et le complexe de Schlemil." *Cahiers internationaux de symbolisme*, 26 (1974), 83-98.

Tieghem, Paul Van. *Le Sentiment de la Nature dans le Préromantisme Européen*. Paris, A. G. Nizet, 1960, pp. 61-67.

Verhoeven, Cornelis. *The Philosophy of Wonder*. Translated by Mary Foran. New York, The Macmillan Company, 1972, pp. 44-58.

Worrell, William H. "The Demon of Noonday and Some Related Ideas." *The Journal of the American Oriental Society*, 38 (1918), 160-166.

Index

Absolute, the, midday as image of, 6, 19-20, 27, 32, 60, 131, 147, 154, 160, 184, 260
Acedia (sloth), 10, 11, 35, 36, 269n13, 270n15
Actaeon, 7, 8, 41-45 passim, 51, 80, 191, 238, 281n15
Ambivalence, of midday, vii, viii, 6, 11, 14, 28, 47, 107, 110, 124, 158, 165, 198, 203-204, 221, 246, 259, 260, 262, 263, 271n16, 323n14
Ambrose, Saint, 31, 34
Anguish (Angst), at midday, 103, 122-123, 170, 198-200, 238, 255, 291n41. See also Crisis
Apollo, 6, 17, 278n2, 292n50
Ariosto, 48-50, 57, 88
Assunto, Rosario, 283n24
Auden, W. H., 321n54

Bachelard, Gaston, 4, 15
Barbieri, Guiseppe, 284n40
Baudelaire, Charles, 284n40, 290n28, 324n16
Bertoncini, Giancarlo, 301n16
Bettini, Pompeo, 91
Bilenchi, Romano, 310n82
Boccaccio, Giovanni, 37-41, 42, 43, 44, 50, 53, 56, 62, 72, 231, 232, 264, 280nn9,12,13, 281nn14,15, 285n2
Boine, Giovanni, 155-166, 228, 257, 260, 301nn16,17,18, 302n23, 304n30, 328n26
Bollnow, Otto Friedrich, 271n16, 275n37
Bourget, Paul, 270n15
Brancati, Vitaliano, 14, 312n6

Breeze, and midday stasis, 20, 25, 39, 53, 65, 69, 185, 274n28, 279n7, 281n15, 285n2, 291n41, 328n26
Burke, Edmund, 17, 31, 278n46

Cagnoli, Agostino, 87-89
Caillois, Roger, 8, 268n8, 272n16, 323n13
Callimachus, 7-8, 293n50
Cambon, Glauco, 314n39, 318n42
Camus, Albert, 268n6, 312n6, 317n39
Cardarelli, Vincenzo, 195-199, 247, 248, 309n76
Carducci, Giosue, 98-107, 108, 111, 112, 122, 147, 167, 184, 194, 244, 289n26, 292n42, 294n15, 298n4, 326n21
Carrara, Enrico, 282n20
Cary, Joseph, 319n47
Cassian, John, 10, 11
Cavalcanti, Guido, 46
Cesarotti, Melchiorre, 60-61, 283n29
Chenier, André, 100, 229, 286n3, 319n45
Christian tradition, midday in, 10, 11, 28-32, 278n3, 279nn5,7
Cicada, emblem of midday tension, 10, 13, 14, 37, 38, 49, 56, 62, 88, 89, 101, 102, 103, 110, 111, 115-116, 160, 170, 190-191, 192, 198, 201-202, 227, 228, 242, 253, 255, 273n20, 292n50, 302n23, 318n43, 326n21
Cirillo, Albert R., 276n43
Clark, Kenneth, 219, 316n32
Classical antiquity, midday in, 7-10,

Classical antiquity (*cont.*)
83, 268*nn*7,8, 280*n*8, 292*n*50. *See also* Caillois, Roger; Callimachus; Ovid; Theocritus; Virgil
Claudel, Paul, 5-6, 19
Coleridge, S. T., 4, 5, 29-31, 267*n*4, 273*n*26, 277*n*44
Comi, Girolamo, 80, 181-182
Conti, Angelo, 15-17, 21, 172, 273*nn*24,26
Contini, Gianfranco, 321*n*1
Cope, Jackson I., 276*n*43
Crisis, midday as hour of, 11, 14, 23, 29-31, 49, 124, 144, 157, 158-162, 199, 256, 299*n*11, 302*n*23

Daniel-Rops, Henry, 28
D'Annunzio, Gabriele, 13, 39, 42, 86, 90, 111, 112, 114-144, 145, 146, 147, 149, 150, 166, 168, 169, 170, 172, 183, 185, 186, 193, 194, 196, 208, 211-212, 223, 229, 232, 240, 243, 244, 248, 254, 256, 260, 264, 294*nn*12,13, 296*n*26, 297*nn*27,28, 298*n*4, 299*n*6, 304*n*30, 305*n*37, 316*n*36, 322*nn*2,5, 324*n*19
Dante, 31, 33-37, 44, 47, 48, 110, 111, 150, 235, 236, 245, 248, 264, 276*n*42, 278*nn*2,3, 279*nn*5,6
Darkness: as aspect of midday light, 31, 113, 171, 203-204, 227-228, 278*n*46, 312*n*6; at noon, 28, 29, 278*n*3
Death, midday and, 6, 26, 60, 83-84, 105, 112-113, 159-162, 211, 213, 224-228
De'Giorgi-Bertola, Aurelio, 65-69
Delirium, midday, viii, 49, 121, 123, 142, 147, 169, 174-179, 203, 259, 319*n*47. *See also* Demon
Del Serra, Maura, 299*n*13
Demon, the midday, 6, 8, 10-12, 18, 21, 28, 30, 61, 94-97, 125, 150, 180, 206-208, 213, 223, 238, 269*nn*11,12, 270*n*15, 271*n*16, 290*nn*28,30, 319*nn*46,47
Desert (aridity), as image of midday, 48, 61, 115-116, 117, 154, 168-169, 201, 203-211, 216, 240-242, 309*n*81, 310*n*82, 313*nn*9,11. *See also* Mirage
Destruction, hour of, 38, 61, 94. *See also* Death; Heat
Diana, 7, 8, 9, 42-45 *passim*, 51, 54, 78, 79, 80, 233, 238, 280*n*13
Dickinson, Emily, viii, 147, 298*n*4
Dolfi, Anna, 304*n*36
Durling, Dwight L., 283*n*27

Ecstasy, at midday, 20-22, 23-25, 26, 84, 126, 131, 133, 143, 146-147, 158-159, 170, 182, 196, 201-202, 288*n*18
Eden, nostalgia for, 70-73, 79-80, 214, 231, 235, 236, 314*n*18
Eigeldinger, Marc, 284*n*40
Eliade, Mircea, 22
Eliot, T. S., 13, 199
Encounter, at midday, 123-124, 132, 158, 172, 178, 181, 208, 225
Eroticism, midday, 7-9, 39-46, 50-56, 61-64, 72-73, 78-80, 92, 98, 118-121, 125-126, 186-191, 206, 210-212, 216, 229-239, 280*nn*12,13, 286*n*3, 313*n*9, 321*n*52. *See also* Diana; Faun; Nympholepsy; Pan
Eternity, sense of, 21, 22, 23, 24, 32, 86, 133, 157, 184-186, 275*n*37. *See also* Timelessness

Faun, midday, 39, 42, 43, 54, 80, 90, 119, 122, 167, 186, 191, 236, 281*n*14, 286*n*3, 295*n*19, 297*n*28, 319*n*47
Fontanella, Girolamo, 56
Forti, Marco, 327*n*24
Foscolo, Ugo, 70-73, 79, 80, 93, 100, 199, 209, 228, 264, 285*n*2

Index

Fromentin, Eugène, 204-205, 208
Frugoni, Carlo Innocenzo, 62, 284*n*32
Fullness, at midday, 6, 19, 24, 32, 34, 138, 139, 142, 144, 149, 196, 212, 214, 221, 226, 261

Gifford, Henry, 271*n*15
Glory, and midday sun, 29-32, 34, 35, 47, 84, 92, 98, 110-111, 114-115, 131, 133, 147, 155, 158, 181, 192-194, 247, 254, 288*n*24, 277*n*45, 325*n*19
Goffis, Cesare Federico, 292*n*42
Gombrowicz, Witold, 265
Goncharov, Ivan, 271*n*15
Grande, Adriano, 182-186
Guardini, Romano, 31, 32
Guerrini, Olindo (Stecchetti, Lorenzo), 89, 319*n*45
Guglielminetti, Marziano, 299*n*13

Heat, destructive midday, 29-30, 56-58, 60, 94, 95, 96, 97, 98, 108, 284*n*4, 310*n*82. *See also* Sun, as Gorgon
Heiler, Friedrich, 288*n*18
Hildebert, bishop of Tours, 9
Hindu tradition, midday in, 21, 22, 26
Hohl, Reinhold D., 298*n*1
House, Humphrey, 274*n*26, 277*n*44

Jastrow, M., 269*n*12
Jeffries, Richard, 288*n*16
Jenco, Elpidio, 193-195, 321*n*52
Jerome, Saint, 269*n*11

Kuhn, Reinhard, 270*n*15, 303*n*29

Lanier, Sidney, 18, 20
Lanza, Franco, 305*n*37, 307*n*50
La Rochefoucauld, François, 33, 69, 113
Laski, Marghanita, 20

Leconte de Lisle, Charles, 84-85, 199, 221, 251-252, 288*n*19
Leone de Castris, Arcangelo, 295*n*19
Leopardi, Giacomo, viii, 75-87, 88, 89, 93, 100, 102, 103, 106, 136, 137, 140, 146, 154, 160, 165, 180, 183, 184, 185, 186, 199, 200, 206, 229, 232, 233, 234, 236, 244, 250, 251, 253, 260, 264, 287*nn*11, 12,13,15, 289*n*20, 291*n*41, 292*n*45, 299*n*13, 316*n*36, 319*nn*46,47
Levi, Carlo, 310*n*82
Light, at midday, 11, 12, 13, 15-17, 20, 27, 59, 90-92, 106, 109, 126, 130, 136, 138, 139, 158, 166, 172, 197, 219-220, 246, 247, 277*n*45, 278*n*46
Locus amoenus, 9, 32, 44, 50, 55, 62, 65, 83, 89, 119-120, 286*n*2
Lollo, Renata, 311*n*3, 320*n*48
Lonardi, Gilberto, 319*n*47
Lugnani, Lucio, 327*n*24

Malaguzzi, Daria Banfi, 153, 299*nn*10,11
Mallarmé, Stéphane, 39, 42, 80, 90, 100, 110, 119, 186, 208, 229, 232, 233, 236
Manacorda, Giuliano, 327*n*24
Mann, Thomas, 161
Manning, Elizabeth Wheeler, 283*n*26
Manzoni, Alessandro, 73-75, 199, 286*n*4, 294*n*15
Marinelli, Peter V., 282*n*19
Marino, Giambattista, 55
Mauzi, Robert, 273*n*23
Mazzotti, Artal, 298*n*2
Meditation, hour of, 35, 46-47, 59
Meli, Giovanni, 64-65
Melville, Herman, 277*n*45
Mengaldo, P. V., 322*n*2, 324*n*19
Metastasio, Pietro, 61-62
Mezzacappa, Carmine Anthony, 318*n*43, 319*n*47

Michelangelo, 176, 178
Millelli, Domenico, 90
Milton, John, 29, 285n40
Mirage, hour of, 168, 202, 208-209, 234, 255, 314nn11,16, 319n47. *See also* Oasis
Montale, Eugenio, 84, 117-118, 162, 165, 168, 169, 199, 200, 208, 240-262, 265, 291n41
Morando, Bernardo, 55-56
Moravia, Alberto, 310n82
Moretti, Walter, 310n82
Motion-immobility, paradox of, 14, 15, 26, 107, 165-166, 174, 178, 181, 190, 240, 260-261, 273n23, 308n63

Nash, Ralph, 282n20
Negativity, of existence, 6, 117, 200, 240, 247, 249, 262
Negri, Ada, 190-191
Nietzsche, Friedrich, 22-28, 32, 121, 133, 138, 142, 149, 154, 274n28, 275nn32,35, 285n2, 302n23
Nirvana, 13, 22, 26, 84, 85, 102-103, 244, 260, 271n16, 288n18
Noontide, the great, 22-25, 152, 275nn35,37
Nothingness, 20, 83, 84, 103, 112-113, 124, 126, 157, 160-165, 198, 203, 205-206, 208, 213-219 *passim*, 221, 225, 228, 239, 246, 252, 260, 261, 262, 309n80, 313n9, 315n28
Numinous, sense of the, viii, 8, 10, 11, 58-59, 60, 268n7
Nympholepsy, 7, 41, 43, 53, 72, 79-80, 92-93, 94, 98-100, 144, 228, 230-239, 281n15, 285n2, 287n13, 297n28. *See also* Actaeon; Diana

Oasis, 208, 320n48. *See also Locus amoenus*; Mirage
Olcott, W. T., 269n12

Onofri, Arturo, 160-181, 305n37, 306nn39,41,49, 307n50
Ossian, 60-61, 64, 283n29
Ossola, Carlo, 314n13, 318n43
Otto, Rudolf, 137, 276n39
Ovid, 7-10, 41-45 *passim*, 51, 52, 53, 54, 281nn14,15

Palazzeschi, Aldo, 191
Pamphysism, 141, 142, 296nn25,26
Pan, 7, 10, 12, 25, 54, 83, 100, 121, 123, 127, 129, 130-131, 140, 181, 268nn7,8, 294nn15,16, 295n19
Pantheism, 100, 101-102, 119, 129, 147, 152, 166, 171-172, 174, 184
Pascoli, Giovanni, 107-113, 147, 170, 192, 193, 194, 228, 244, 251, 292nn47,50, 324n19
Pavese, Cesare, 316n36
Peruzzi, Emilio, 287n15
Petrarch, Francesco, 41-47, 51, 53, 59, 80, 97, 238, 264, 281nn14,15, 16,17
Picard, Max, 12
Picchio, Luciana Stegnano, 320n48
Piccione, Leone, 313n9
Pindemonte, Ippolito, 63, 67-69, 81, 87, 284n40
Plato, 106, 280n8
Pope, Alexander, 277n45, 283n31

Ragusa, Olga, 319n47
Rahner, Hugo, 28
Ramat, Silvio, 322n10
Rebay, Luciano, 319n47
Rebora, Clemente, 145-155, 165, 169, 174, 179, 182, 238, 298nn2,3,4
Refuge, at midday, 9, 12, 18, 34, 37-40, 49, 50, 57, 59-60, 62, 65, 66, 99, 105, 108, 110, 162, 169, 192, 231, 244-245, 246
Rembrandt, 237-238
Rimbaud, Arthur, 21, 154, 299n13
Rosenmeyer, Thomas G., 83, 268n7

Index

Rousseau, Jean Jacques, 4, 164-165, 303n29

Saba, Umberto, 192-193, 322n7, 324n19
Saint-Lambert, Jean-François de, 59, 61, 283n28
Salmon, William, 56
Sannazaro, Jacopo, 50-55
Sartre, Jean Paul, 158-159, 325n20
Sbarbaro, Camillo, 309n81, 322n4
Schopenhauer, Arthur, 16, 26
Schuré, Edouard, 171
Scott, J. P., 272n17
Shadows (shade), 9, 16-17, 24, 36, 37, 39, 49, 59, 78, 111, 117, 194, 217, 218, 225, 230, 231, 235, 244, 248, 315n28, 323n14. See also Refuge
Shelley, Percy Bysshe, 83
Silence, 11, 12, 13, 14, 27, 103, 106, 108-110, 128, 130, 132, 133, 136-137, 138-139, 146, 147, 158, 160, 180, 183-184, 189, 198, 201, 228, 230, 296n21, 317n39. See also Stasis
Singleton, Charles S., 278n2, 321n53
Soffici, Ardengo, 317n39
Solar cycle: diurnal, 3, 6, 21, 23-26, 47, 58, 66, 67, 68, 73-75, 87, 138, 153, 194-195, 197, 214, 217, 225, 248, 267n1, 271n15; seasonal, 3, 57, 64, 75, 138, 194-199, 213-215, 225, 266n1
Solitude, hour of, 46, 81-83, 223, 254-255; existential, 212, 255, 313n9
Stasis, midday, 6, 13, 20, 21, 22, 24, 30, 60, 82-83, 84-85, 91, 104, 106, 109, 129, 130, 132-133, 136, 140, 149, 158, 173, 180-181, 188-189, 192, 195, 196, 203, 243, 249, 252, 253, 256, 259, 262, 271n15, 287n15, 288n19, 291n40, 308n63, 322n7

Stecchetti, L. See Guerrini, Olindo
Steiner, Rudolf, 166, 171
Stevens, Wallace, 4, 5, 18, 184, 218
Sun: as Gorgon or hostile force, 6, 29-30, 60, 75, 94-97, 105, 117, 134, 198, 202, 220, 221, 223, 246, 285n40; as libido symbol, 94, 125-126, 134, 211; as negativity or void, 112, 117, 242; as symbol of deity, 31, 33-34, 38, 47, 150, 155, 181, 277n45, 278n46, 288n24; as symbol of glory, 110-111, 114-115, 131, 146, 147, 155, 158, 181, 192-194, 247-248, 249, 254, 277n45, 289n24; as symbol of justice, 34, 35
Susanna and the elders, 9, 237
Swinburne, A. C., 13, 129-131, 142

Theocritus, 7, 23, 37, 93, 268n7
Thomson, James, 3, 58-60, 61, 64, 66, 97, 299n12
Timelessness, at midday, 26, 91, 105-107, 110, 132-133, 189, 197. See also Eternity; Stasis
Tolstoy, Leo, 161
Tommaseo, Niccolò, 289n24
Turner, J.M.W., 219
Tuve, Rosemund, 283n24

Unamuno, 161
Ungaretti, Giuseppe, vii, viii, x, 84, 158, 168, 169, 195, 196, 199, 200, 201-239, 251, 252, 253, 258, 264, 313nn8,9

Valentini, Alvaro, 327nn24,25
Valeri, Diego, 299n13
Valéry, Paul, 19-21, 33, 69, 178, 184, 199, 246, 260, 274n27, 285n2, 309n80, 327n25
Valli, Donato, 305n37
van Gogh, Vincent, 172, 174, 218, 219
Van Tieghem, Paul, 58, 283n24

Vaughan, Henry, 31, 277n45
Verga, Giovanni, 93-97, 117, 289nn26,27, 290nn29,30
Verhoeven, Cornelius, 11, 12, 271n16, 301n20
Villaroel, Giuseppe, 90, 186-190, 319n45
Virgil, 9, 37, 40, 50, 56, 64, 75, 108, 190, 232

Wagner, Richard, 16, 123, 124-126
Warren, Robert Penn, 277n44
Wenzel, Siegfried, 269n13
Wordsworth, William, 4, 291n40

Zaehner, R. C., 296n25
Zanella, Giacomo, 92-93, 289n26
Zanzotto, Andrea, 13, 191, 273n20

Library of Congress Cataloging in Publication Data
Perella, Nicolas James, 1927–
  Midday in Italian literature.

  Bibliography: p.
  Includes index.
  1. Italian literature—History and criticism.
  2. Noon in literature.   I. Title.
  PQ4053.N64P4   850'.9   78-70313
  ISBN 0-691-06389-3